Language and Linguistic Diversity in the US

This highly engaging textbook presents a linguistic view of the history, society, and culture of the United States. It discusses the many languages and forms of language that have been used in the US—including standard and nonstandard forms of English, creoles, Native American languages, and immigrant languages from across the globe—and shows how this distribution and diversity of languages has helped shape and define America as well as an American identity. The volume introduces the basic concepts of sociolinguistics and the politics of language through cohesive, up-to-date, and accessible coverage of such key topics as dialectal development and the role of English as the majority language, controversies concerning language use in society, languages other than English used in the US, and the policies that have directly or indirectly influenced language use.

These topics are presented in such a way that students can examine the inherent diversity of the communicative systems used in the United States as both a form of cultural enrichment and as the basis for sociopolitical conflict. The author team outlines the different viewpoints on contemporary issues surrounding language in the US and contextualizes these issues within linguistic facts, to help students think critically and formulate logical discussions. To provide opportunities for further examination and debate, chapters are organized around key misconceptions or questions ("I don't have an accent" or "Immigrants don't want to learn English"), bringing them to the forefront for readers to address directly.

Language and Linguistic Diversity in the US is a fresh and unique take on a widely taught topic. It is ideal for students from a variety of disciplines or with no prior knowledge of the field, and is a useful text for introductory courses on language in the US, American English, language variation, language ideology, and sociolinguistics.

Susan Tamasi is Senior Lecturer and Director of Undergraduate Studies in the Program in Linguistics, Emory University, Atlanta. She has presented at NWAV, AAAL, Sociolinguistics Symposium, and American Dialect Society. Her areas of research include sociolinguistics, language variation, language attitudes, American English, and health communication.

Lamont Antieau is an independent language consultant who has held positions as Research Associate (University of Wisconsin-Milwaukee), Visiting Instructor (Western Carolina University), and Lecturer (Mississippi State University). He has presented at NWAV, American Dialect Society, Southeastern Conference on Linguistics, and International Association of Forensic Linguists. His areas of research include language variation, dialectology, American English, corpus linguistics, and biomedical informatics.

Language and Linguistic Diversity in the US
An Introduction

Susan Tamasi
Lamont Antieau

Routledge
Taylor & Francis Group

NEW YORK AND LONDON

Visit the Companion Website for this book at www.routledge.com/cw/tamasi

First published 2015
by Routledge
711 Third Avenue, New York, NY 10017

and by Routledge
2 Park Square, Milton Park, Abingdon, Oxon, OX14 4RN

Routledge is an imprint of the Taylor & Francis Group, an informa business

Library of Congress Cataloging-in-Publication Data
Language and linguistic diversity in the US: an introduction/
Susan Tamasi, Emory University; Lamont Antieau,
Independent Scholar.
  pages; cm
  1. Language and languages—Variation—United States.
  2. Language and culture—United States. 3. Multilingualism—
  United States. 4. Sociolinguistics—United States.
  I. Tamasi, Susan. II. Antieau, Lamont David.
  P120.V37L326 2014
  417′.7—dc23
  2014020624

ISBN: 978-0-415-80667-1 (hbk)
ISBN: 978-0-415-80668-8 (pbk)
ISBN: 978-0-203-15496-0 (ebk)

Typeset in Sabon and Helvetica
by Florence Production Ltd, Stoodleigh, Devon, UK

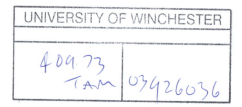

Selected Contents

Contents

Illustrations

Figures

Tables

Boxes

Preface

This book is intended to take the reader on a journey through the American linguistic landscape. It presents the diversity of language in the United States, past and present, and examines the complex connection between language and an American identity. Crucially, it shows that the linguistic diversity apparent in the United States today is directly related to the histories and experiences of the American people.

Throughout this book, we focus on the interaction of language and society, with a particular focus on the processes and outcomes of language variation and change. We discuss the many different social and regional varieties of English spoken in the United States, for example, African American English and Standard American English, as well as several of the immigrant and heritage languages that have played, and continue to play, significant roles in the linguistic identity of the US, such as Spanish, Arabic, German, Hawaiian Creole, Navajo, and American Sign Language. We not only examine the histories and structures of these linguistic systems, but we also investigate the attitudes, perceptions, and ideologies that surround their use. Additionally, we discuss official and unofficial policies, such as those toward immigration, education, and Native American languages, as well as Official English legislation.

A fundamental concept that runs through the entire book is the connection between language and identity. As it applies to the linguistic diversity within the United States, this idea often presents itself as the connection between language and national identity. This book asks readers to think about the roles that language plays in their own lives as well as in the lives of others in the US, including native-born Americans as well as immigrants from a variety of countries, to include those who are native speakers of English, those who have learned English as a second language, and those who do not speak English at all. We also ask readers to consider the role of language in the overall identity of the United States. Furthermore, we tackle several debatable and potentially controversial issues, for example, whether English should be the official language of the United States and whether the US is a multilingual or monolingual nation. While these questions are highlighted in individual chapters, readers are able to draw from the linguistic, social, and historical information presented throughout the book in order to answer these complex questions. We ask readers to look at the evidence objectively and thoroughly before coming to their conclusions on these matters, and to examine any preconceived notions they have concerning these topics as we address them.

The book has several pedagogical features designed to help readers work through and understand the material. In order for the book to be accessible to an audience with little or no training in linguistics, the linguistic concepts that are needed to understand the material are introduced in the beginning chapters and then in individual sections as they are needed. To direct readers through the material in the most useful way, each chapter begins with Guiding Questions, an Overview, and a set of Common Myths about the material covered in each chapter. We recommend that these be the first and last readings of each chapter. Additionally, at the end of each chapter are Discussion and Research Questions that ask readers to think more deeply about these topics, research them further, and apply these topics to their own lives. There is also an online glossary to help with vocabulary items that are being introduced and terms with which some readers may not be familiar; such words and phrases are marked in bold.

Finally, this textbook has an accompanying Companion Website that contains a generous amount of supplementary information and resources. For topics that have accompanying information on the Companion Website, a symbol will appear in the margin of the text to direct students there for more information. For students, the website includes a variety of video, audio, and online sources that explain concepts further and/or push readers to think differently about the presented topics. For instructors, it contains an entire store of pedagogical materials, including syllabi, teaching notes, test questions, and student assignments.

COMPANION
@
WEBSITE

0.0

Acknowledgments

We knew that writing a textbook would be a labor of love that could only be accomplished through the support of a great number of people, and this was reaffirmed throughout every step of the process. Accordingly, we would like to thank the following: All of the anonymous reviewers who gave thoughtful comments and helped shape the structure of this book; the students of Ling 101 at Emory University, without whom this book would never have been conceived; and the Emory College of Arts and Sciences and Program in Linguistics for their support through the Winship Award.

We would also like to thank the following individuals for their feedback and unwavering encouragement: Alyssa Stalsberg-Canelli, Marc Muneal, Jennifer Hughes, MorganAmanda Fritzlen, Betsy Evans, Elizabeth Canon, Allison Burkette, Scott Kiesling, Robert Bailey, Betsy Barry, Clayton Darwin, Jonathan Pearl, Lior Ben-Ami, Marjorie Pak, and Corey Blount. Bill Vicars deserves our enduring gratitude for providing the illustrations for the chapter on American Sign Language, as do Dennis Preston for helping with the maps in Chapter 3 and Dana Gorman for creating maps used in several chapters of the book. Additionally, we are very thankful for our editorial team at Routledge: Darcy Bullock, Mary Altman, Ivy Ip, Elysse Preposi, and Leah Babb-Rosenfeld. They were beyond patient.

Susan would like to give a special thank you to Jamie Martin and Maribeth Coleman for providing daily support and mental reinforcement.

Lamont would like to show his gratitude to Alicia Nott, Heather Yenglin, George Felis, and Brian Swafford for their support and encouragement.

This book is stronger because of each and every one of them. Of course, any weaknesses are purely our own.

Language and Linguistics

GUIDING QUESTIONS

1. What is language?
2. What is linguistics?
3. In what ways do linguists discuss and analyze language structure?
4. Why do languages change over time?
5. How does language vary and why?

OVERVIEW

Laying the foundation for how language will be discussed throughout the book, this chapter defines language and introduces readers to several significant concepts needed for learning about language and discussing linguistic diversity in the United States. After presenting a brief overview of the field of linguistics, we present several key principles that linguists have regarding language structure and use: languages are governed by rules, all languages are created equal, languages change, and languages vary. We discuss how linguistic variation and change, rather than being evidence of linguistic and perhaps even cultural disintegration, are natural processes that are integral aspects of language that enable languages to remain vital and relevant. Finally, we discuss a concept that is fundamental to many of the discussions found throughout this book—that language is an inherent and essential part of human identity.

COMMON MYTHS

> *By definition, a linguist is someone who speaks many languages.*

> *Language change is language decay.*

> *Language variation is dysfunctional.*

> *I don't have an accent.*

> *A linguist is necessarily someone who wants to fix your grammar.*

INTRODUCTION

The main aim of this chapter is to introduce readers to the field of linguistics and the investigation of natural human language. Because we assume that our readers have no prior background in formal linguistic study (even though they have extensive experience as speakers of individual languages and dialects), we use this chapter to present and define several key terms, concepts, and principles that are at the foundation of linguistic study and that underlie many of the topics discussed throughout this book. These concepts will help readers begin to understand what linguistics is, how linguists think, and how languages work. While there is much more to say on each of the issues presented in this chapter, our concern here is to not overload readers with an exhaustive treatment of linguistics, but to give enough information so that they are able to follow—and eventually lead for themselves—discussions of language and linguistic diversity in the United States. We start by defining language.

LANGUAGE

Language is a word that can be used in a variety of ways; for instance, one hears of legal language, the language of love, or the Python programming language. One might even hear the word used in reprimands such as "Watch your language!" As linguists, we use the word to refer to a tool of communication and cognition that humans share, and we aim for a definition that applies to all of the world's natural languages. For our purposes, **language** is defined as *an open, arbitrary, conventional system of sounds used for communication within a linguistic community*. Below, we illustrate how each of the key words of this definition relates to language.

At the core of our definition is that language is a SYSTEM. Language is not random, but rather, both in its production and perception, language is a complex system governed by rules, a truism that we revisit later in this chapter and rely on throughout the book. This system is made up of SOUNDS, which language relies on as its smallest building blocks. This attention to sounds highlights that language is a spoken phenomenon first, and that writing, as a derivative of spoken language, is secondary. Despite its systematicity, language is essentially ARBITRARY in that there is no inherent link between sound and meaning. For instance, the organic compound consisting of two parts hydrogen and one part oxygen is called *eau* in French, *agua* in Spanish, *voda* in Russian, *séui* in Cantonese, and *water* in English. Despite referring to essentially the same matter, these individual words exhibit differences in sound and structure that they would not if the link between sound and meaning were not arbitrary. Rather, if there were a direct correlation between sound and meaning, then all languages would use the same set of sounds for an individual concept. Additionally, any claim that H_2O is inherently more like one word than another, for instance, that it is more *eau*-like than *water*-like, or vice versa, is impossible to justify on objective grounds.

So if the link between sound and meaning is arbitrary, why is it not the case that H_2O is referred to as *water* by some English speakers and as *tree* or *Todd* by others? The reason is that language is CONVENTIONAL; it relies on speakers to agree (often unconsciously) on the relationship between a word and its meaning. The group of speakers that does so is referred to as a LINGUISTIC COMMUNITY, a group of people who interact using a shared set of linguistic forms and social norms governing those forms (Gumperz, 1964). One of the purposes for these linguistic systems is COMMUNICATION, by which we are referring to the interchange of thoughts, opinions, or information among members of linguistic communities via speech. Finally, in part due to the demands of communication in an ever-changing world, but for other reasons as well that we discuss later in the chapter, we recognize that linguistic systems are not static and closed, but rather that they are dynamic and OPEN; that is, they allow speakers to adopt new forms, to avoid forms they consider obsolete, or to use old structures in new ways, for example, by creating or borrowing new words for novel concepts, by varying their pronunciation, or by expanding or limiting their range of meanings.

LINGUISTICS

Linguistics is the scientific study of language, and as such it aims to view language objectively in order to answer a broad range of questions contributing to our general knowledge of human language, including its structure, its use, and its place in society. Linguistic research can be theoretical or empirical, qualitative or quantitative, and the field as a whole is highly interdisciplinary, as can be seen in the variety of subfields that exist, such as structural linguistics, cognitive linguistics, historical linguistics, computational linguistics, and the area that this book concentrates on, sociolinguistics, which investigates the interaction of language and society. The general questions that are most relevant to the current volume include how and why languages change, how and why languages vary in terms of regional and social patterns, and how languages in contact exert influence over each other. More specifically, our investigation in this textbook focuses on how these questions apply to languages that have contributed to the American experience.

One way in which linguists are able to answer these questions and to work with the broad and sometimes abstract nature of language is to break it down into several, more manageable components. At the smallest level of language, linguists study **phonetics**, which relates to the physical characteristics of speech; in this book, we focus on **articulatory phonetics**, which is concerned specifically with how speech sounds are produced. The sound system, or **phonology**, of a language comprises the sounds that are considered distinct in a given language. Linguists working in the area of phonology investigate how sounds are organized in languages and dialects, examining, for instance, how sounds are perceived and classified by speakers. **Morphology** refers to the rules of word formation in language. With respect to morphology, linguists examine not only word-formation processes, such as compounding (e.g., *butter* + *fly* = *butterfly*) and blending (e.g., *smoke* + *fog* = *smog*), but also how words consist of **morphemes**, that is, smaller units that carry meaning, such as roots, suffixes, and prefixes (e.g., the root *fix* + the prefix *pre–* 'before' and the suffix *–es* 'more than one' = *prefixes*). **Syntax** pertains to the rules governing phrase structure, or the order in which words can be combined in a given language for them to convey meaning. For example, in English, most sentences follow the order of Subject-Verb-Object (SVO). **Semantics** refers to meaning and its study, and **pragmatics** is the examination of meaning in context or of the social rules of language. Although these are not the only areas of linguistic structure, these are the basic building blocks used to understand what language is and how it works. Additional information about these areas as well as other aspects of linguistic structure will be discussed below and throughout this textbook.

In their detailed examinations of linguistic systems, researchers, whether looking at a language's phonology, morphology, syntax, etc., focus on individual elements, or **linguistic features**. Such features can be, for example, a grammatical construction (e.g., the formation of past tense); a specific speech sound (e.g., [s] or [t]); or a set of related forms (e.g., vowels). Individuals can also study individual words or sets of words, and, in this regard, the term **lexicon** is used to refer to the vocabulary of a language or, in the case of an individual, to a "mental dictionary." In some investigations, linguists focus primarily on the description of individual features within a language. However, depending on the goals of the research, a linguist can, for example, compare these features to (1) a similar set of features used by speakers of another language; (2) the same set of features used during an earlier period of the same language; or (3) a set of features used by different social groups who speak the same language. Such investigations contribute to our general understanding of human language, of linguistic change, and of the relationship between language and society. Note that this work does not require linguists to speak numerous languages or to translate between them. While some linguists are indeed fluent in several languages, others study only their own native languages, or they study aspects of other languages without necessarily learning to speak them.

Linguists examine linguistic features as they occur in natural spoken language. This is not to say that linguists do not study the written word, but rather that they recognize that writing is derivative of spoken language. In some instances, it is necessary to collect, analyze, and distribute linguistic data in written form; however, doing so poses a problem because various languages rely on different writing systems, or **orthographies**, and these are often fraught with irregularities or, as with the writing systems of Chinese or Japanese, are not reflective of speech sounds at all. For instance, regarding English, it has often been noted that one can spell the word *fish* as *ghoti*, by stringing together the sounds represented by the letters <gh> in *laugh*, the letter <o> in *women*, and the letters <ti> in *nation*. An extreme example, to be sure, but few people have dared to argue that English is entirely consistent in its spelling, given the status of *rode*, *road*, and *rowed* as **homophones**, 'words with different meanings that sound the same,' or given the number of distinct sounds represented by the letters <ough> in written representations of *rough*, *trough*, *though*, *through*, and *drought*.

Because of such irregularities, and because work in linguistics, particularly research in phonetics and phonology, requires an accurate representation of the spoken sounds of the language, researchers developed a single, unified system in which there is a consistent one-to-one relation between symbol and sound for most, if not all, of the speech sounds in all of the world's languages. This system, known as the **International Phonetic Alphabet**, or **IPA**, is an invaluable tool for all linguists. Further information about the IPA as well as a list and description of its symbols that are used in this book are presented in Box 1.1.

1.1

BOX 1.1 **The Sounds and Symbols of American English**

1.2

Here we provide the phonetic charts for the vowels and consonants of American English so that readers have easy access to the phonetic symbols that are used (sparingly) throughout this book. Due to the limitations of space, we cannot give the full set of symbols for all of the world's languages or explain in detail all of the terminology associated with those symbols that are provided; however, the Companion Website has links to several online sources, as well as references for good introductory linguistics textbooks, where one can learn more about phonetics and phonology. We recommend that readers new to linguistics take a few minutes to watch the video tutorials that are listed.

TABLE 1.1 The vowels of American English in IPA

Height and tension		Backness								
		Front				Central		Back		
High	Tense	i								u
	Lax		ɪ						ʊ	
Mid	Tense		e			ə				o
	Lax			ɛ		ʌ		ɔ		
Low	Tense									
	Lax				æ		a			

Note: Rounded vowels appear in bold.

[i] *beet, pizza, tea*

[ɪ] *bit, pick, women*

[e] *bait, crepe, may*

[ɛ] *bet, leper, flex*

[æ] *bat, half, frack*

[ə] *above, sofa, Lisa*

[ʌ] *but, the, among*

[a] *botch, crop, spa*

[u] *boot, loop, grew*

[ʊ] *book, put, good*

[o] *boat, note, grow, beau*

[ɔ] *bought, caught, song, law*

Diphthongs:

[aɪ] *bide, thigh, sky*

[aʊ] *bout, couch, how*

[ɔɪ] *Boyd, noise, toy*

Online tutorial for vowels: http://marjoriepak.com/IPAVowels.mp4.

BOX 1.1 *(continued)*

TABLE 1.2 The consonants of American English in IPA

Manner of articulation	Place of articulation												
	Bilabial		Labio-dental		Dental		Alveolar		Palatal		Velar		Glottal
Stops	p	b					t	d			k	g	ʔ	
Fricatives			f	v	θ	ð	s	z	ʃ	ʒ				
Affricates									tʃ	ʤ				
Nasals		m						n				ŋ		
Liquids								l, r						
Glides		w								j			h	

Note: Beneath the headings for place of articulation, phones that appear in the left cells are voiceless, and those in the right are voiced.

[θ] *thin, thank, bath*　　　　　　　　　　[tʃ] *chair, chin, church*
[ð] *that, this, bathe*　　　　　　　　　　 [ʤ] *judge, jury, gerbil*
[ʃ] *shoe, shadow, push*　　　　　　　　 [ŋ] *sing, wrong, running*
[ʒ] *genre, measure, beige*　　[j] *you, yellow*　　[ʔ] *uh-oh, uh-huh*

Online tutorial for consonants: http://marjoriepak.com/IPAConsonants.mp4.

KEY PRINCIPLES IN LINGUISTICS

As linguistics is still a relatively young field, there remains much to learn about what language is and how it works. However, there are several key principles that have proven to be essential to work in linguistics and that are germane to the discussions of language structure and use that appear throughout this book. They are:

- Language is governed by rules.
- All languages are created equal.
- Language changes.
- Language varies.

Language is Governed by Rules

One point that cannot be overemphasized in this chapter is that language is governed by rules. These are not the same as the rules that you might have learned in English class prescribing how language should be used; for example, "A sentence should never end with a preposition." Rather, these rules are used to describe what is or isn't possible in language and what types of structures are more or less likely to occur in different languages. In English, for instance, adjectives generally precede nouns; the consonant cluster /str/ is possible at the beginning of words but /smr/ is not; and the suffix –*est* can be used to create superlative forms of adjectives, as in *fastest, lightest, easiest*.

1.3

Linguistic rules are at work despite how chaotic a specific language might seem, especially during one's initial exposure to it. While some types of rules can be found in many languages (e.g., sentences follow subject-object-verb word order), others are found in only a relative few (e.g., object-subject-verb), but each individual language is unique in the total set of rules and features it contains. Moreover, the adherence of language A to a rule that language B does not follow does not make language A any more or less logical than language B is for following a different rule. Other examples of rules include how verbs in a language are marked for tense; whether adjectives in a language precede or follow the nouns they modify; and whether or not nouns in a given language are marked for **grammatical gender** (and if they are, whether there is a two-way distinction between feminine and masculine gender, as in French, or a three-way distinction between feminine, masculine, and neuter, as in German).

We mentioned earlier that linguistic systems are open in that they can admit new forms or allow for modifications of their existing structures. It is important to recognize, though, that such forms are not allowed to operate randomly within the system, but rather, as they are incorporated, they generally adhere to the rules that already exist. For example, when English borrows nouns from other languages, it typically adopts only the singular form of the word; instead of also borrowing the plural form of the word, English instead imposes its own pluralization rule on its singular form. So despite that the borrowings *kayak* (from Inuktitut *qajaik*), *landscape* (from Dutch *lantscap*), and *robot* (from Czech *robot*) are pluralized as *qajait, landschappen*, and *roboty* in their respective languages, in English they are pluralized as *kayaks, landscapes*, and *robots*. These plural forms are based on the most common rule of pluralization in English, which simply adds the morpheme -s to singular nouns, as in *book → books, cat → cats, snack → snacks*. Now consider *strollic*, a **nonce word** (a word made up for an occasion, such as introducing a linguistic concept). If *strollic* were a noun denoting an item sitting on your desk, and your friend put another one on your desk, what would you have on your desk? Your answer illustrates one of the ways in which language is governed by rules. The kinds of rules that underlie grammatical structure, and your unconscious knowledge of many of them, will be covered in greater detail in Chapter 2.

All Languages are Created Equal

All languages are equal in that they all are complex, rule-governed systems that offer their speakers the resources to meet their linguistic demands in a highly diverse and continuously changing world. All languages are able to adapt to new situations; these means of adapting are covered in detail below in our discussion of language change and variation. Most importantly, no languages are primitive; rather, all languages are structurally complex. This applies to each of the 7,000+ languages in the world today, regardless of the number of speakers who use the language, whether it sounds "pleasant" to speakers of other languages, whether it has a written form, or whether it is spoken in an industrialized nation.

1.4

To say that languages are created equal is not, of course, to say that they are the same. The languages of the world are a diverse lot, at every level of linguistic structure. At the level of phonology, for instance, some languages work with small sets of distinct sounds. For example, Pirahã, a language spoken in the Amazon rainforest of Brazil, has only 13 distinct sounds; however, it supplements these sounds with a variety of tones, akin to many Asian languages, including Chinese and Vietnamese. Tones are also utilized by many African languages, and some of these languages also use phonetic clicks. (Please see the Companion Website for an example of Xhosa, a language that uses both tones and clicks.)

1.5

To say that all languages are created equal is not to say that they do all things equally. English, for instance, has been particularly adept at borrowing vocabulary from other languages, which, among other characteristics, has resulted in the language compiling an enormous lexicon that consists of, according to some estimates, around one million words. Despite this large vocabulary, however, there are still some lexical and semantic distinctions that are made with greater efficiency in languages other than English. Some Native American languages, for instance, have sophisticated kinship terminologies in which different terms are used to refer to the sister of the speaker's parents depending on whether she is the sister of the speaker's mother or the speaker's father. In most, if not all, varieties of English, however, speakers have only the word *aunt* to refer to their parents' sisters, and thus they must rely either on context or additional language to specify whose sister is being referred to in conversation. When we look at the world's languages objectively, we often discover that they include features that it might seem useful for a language to have, yet we find no comparable feature in our own language or others with which we are familiar. Despite such shortcomings, languages continue to perform the tasks that speakers set out for them to do.

1.6

Overall, when we look at linguistic systems holistically, we recognize that all languages and varieties of languages are created equally. They are each made up of linguistic structures that are complex and rule-governed and that allow their speakers to talk about almost any topic they desire—or allow them to create new forms to fill in grammatical or semantic gaps. As we will see throughout many of the discussions in this book, however, even though linguists know all languages are equal, the wider public does not always see or treat all language systems as socially equal.

Language Changes

All languages change through the course of their lifetimes, and these changes constitute natural processes that occur in all languages, and at every linguistic level. Despite forces that attempt to combat linguistic change, such as stylebooks and language authorities (as we discuss in detail in the next chapter), language change marches on. Even Esperanto, an artificial language created in part to overcome language change, has changed naturally since its inception (Gledhill, 2000). From a linguistic viewpoint, change is inevitable, and linguists do not believe that language change is decay, nor that such change is even undesirable; rather, linguists know that change is a sign of a healthy language attending to the needs of its users in a continuously changing world.

As an exercise in how pervasive language change can be, consider the following text from about 1,000 years ago:

> Fæder ure þu þe eart on heofonum eardast; Si þin nama gehalgod to becume þin rice gewurþe θin willa on eorθan swa swa on heofonum, urne gedæghwamlicam hlaf syle us todæg and forgyf us ure gyltas swa swa we forgyfaθ urum gyltendum and ne gelæd þu us on costnunge ac alys us of yfele soþlice. (11th century; as presented in Krapp & Dobbie, 1936)

To most modern-day English speakers, this could very well be a foreign language, and, in fact, some colleges offer courses in it as such; however, this passage is actually an example of Old English, or **Anglo Saxon**, the earliest form of the English language. The language of the same text in today's Modern English is perhaps more familiar to readers:

> Our Father in heaven, hallowed be your name, your kingdom come, your will be done, on earth as in heaven. Give us today our daily bread. Forgive us our sins as we forgive those who sin against us. Save us from the time of trial and deliver us from evil. Amen. (1988; English Language Liturgical Commission)

There appear to be many more differences than similarities between these two versions of the "Lord's Prayer," and the changes that occurred between the Anglo Saxon version and the modern-day version of the prayer pertain to every level of the language: phonology (*nama* [nama] → *name* [nem]); morphology (*forgyfaθ* → *forgiveth* → *forgive*); syntax (*Fæder ure* → *our father*); and semantics (*syle* → *sell* → *give*). Even the spelling conventions of English changed during the time between the two versions, as illustrated by the sounds represented by Old English scribes as <þ> and <θ> that have since been replaced by <th> (although in IPA, they are represented as /ð/ and /θ/).

As this example illustrates, not only do languages change, but these changes can be so great as to render earlier versions of a language unrecognizable over time.

So how has English managed to change so radically that some native speakers cannot recognize, let alone totally comprehend or casually articulate, earlier incarnations of it? There are many reasons for linguistic change, and classifying these reasons by whether they are (1) internal, linguistic factors, or (2) external, social factors can be useful in understanding this process. Two common examples of **internal factors** that result in language change are ease of articulation and analogy. With respect to ease of articulation, speakers replace difficult sounds or sound clusters with sounds or sound clusters that are easier to articulate. For instance, many languages avoid clusters of two or more consecutive consonants because of the difficulties they pose for speakers, and they do so by providing speakers with several strategies for making these clusters more manageable, including (1) the elimination of one or more of the sounds in the cluster, and (2) the insertion of one or more vowels between the consonants. The English word *knee* serves as an example of the first strategy, as historically the /k/ was pronounced, whereas today the word is one of several spelled with an initial letter <k> that is "silent" (others include *knight*, *know*, and *knife*). In the passage from Old English above, the word *hlaf* appears in approximately the middle of the passage. As in the case of *knee*, the initial consonant cluster of *hlaf* also proved to be vulnerable to the process of deletion in an effort to ease articulation, as /hl/ became /l/ when the initial /h/ was lost, and the word took one step closer to its current articulation as *loaf*. Of course, all languages have a tendency to simplify certain aspects of their grammar, including phonology, but that does not mean that all languages recognize the same processes or sounds as being difficult or that they rank these difficulties in the same way.

Internal changes also occur by analogy, that is, by changing a linguistic pattern of one or more items to follow patterns of similar items in the language. In abstract terms, this means that the patterning of A and B is used as a model for finding a new counterpart to C (Campbell, 1998). To illustrate, above you were asked to use your implicit knowledge of English to provide the plural for the nonce word *strollic*. For the sake of argument, let's assume that you used the most common pluralization rule of English to produce *strollics* by adding a final -s to the root word. Now, let's say that some speaker came to believe that the word *strollic* holds less in common with nouns such as *cat* and *tulip* and more with a noun such as *deer*, which is pluralized without a change in form, and decided to pluralize *strollic* in the same manner as *deer* by analogy. If that speaker were the only one to adopt the new plural form, then there would be little effect on the language as a whole; however, if a large enough number of speakers accepted this outcome, then *strollic* would not only serve as both the singular and plural form of the word, but it would also serve as an excellent example of the concept of linguistic change by analogy.

If this scenario seems unlikely, consider a change by analogy that is currently underway in American English—the manner in which the present-tense verb form *dive* is conjugated for past tense. At an earlier point in the word's history, the past-tense form that was most commonly used was *dived* (Campbell, 1998, p. 104). However, based on structural similarities that the word had with such verbs as *drive*, *ride* and *strive*, which rely on vowel alteration to produce the respective past-tense forms *drove*, *rode* and *strove*, *dove* was introduced as the past-tense form of *dive* by analogy. In some circles of American English, *dove* has since become the preferred form, as suggested by the distribution of *dived/dove* in the Google Books Ngram Viewer presented in Figure 1.1.

1.7

FIGURE 1.1 Use of *dived* and *dove* with personal pronouns in books written in American English, 1800–2008.

Source: https://books.google.com/ngrams/.

An interesting aspect of the change from *dived* to *dove* is that the change affects a form that was already produced in the most common manner of creating past tense (i.e., adding -ed to a verb), replacing it with a form produced in an irregular and (by today's standards) less common manner (i.e., a word-internal alteration). Change by analogy typically involves regularization; however, cases such as *dived/dove* show that language change has more than one route that it can take at any given time. Additionally, this example illustrates that language change can be a very slow process; as the research shows: even a relatively simple change such as *dived → dove* can take several centuries from start to finish.

Another internal factor in language change is **reanalysis**, whereby a form of one structure is misinterpreted as being of a different structure due to ambiguity. One example of how this phenomenon can lead to change is provided by the history of the word *apron* in English. Originally borrowed from Old French around AD 1300, *napron* was a word that referred to an item to be worn to protect one's clothing while working. Once borrowed into the English linguistic system, the rules of English were applied to the word, two of which are: (1) a noun can be preceded by an indefinite article; and

(2) the indefinite article *a* precedes nouns beginning with a consonant, while *an* precedes those beginning with a vowel. While speakers who were familiar with the French noun adhered to these rules in forming the noun phrase *a napron*, those who were unfamiliar with the word misanalyzed the phrase as *an apron*, and, over time, the noun itself became recognized as *apron*. More recent cases of reanalysis at work include *Rio Grande river*; *ATM machine*; *lariat rope*; and *could've* written as *could of*. Rather than changes such as these being indicators of language decay or lack of intelligence among the people who use them, they are the product of natural linguistic processes and may one day, as with *apron* and *knee*, be the preferred forms in the English language.

In addition to these internal factors, there are also **external factors**, that is, social, historical, and/or political events that lead to linguistic change. One type of external factor that plays an important role throughout this book is **language contact**, that is, contact between speakers of different linguistic systems. One example of language contact that had a significant impact on the English language was the period of Norman French rule over England that began with the Norman Invasion in AD 1066. Although this influence was felt throughout the language, it was most apparent in changes to the lexicon, where the French language provided words for new concepts that the French rulers were introducing, such as *parliament*. There were also cases in which French and English words were in competition, with the French word eventually becoming the preferred term; for example, the English words *burhsittend* and *ceasterware* lost out to the French word *citizen*. In some cases, French contributed a word for a concept that English already had a term for, and instead of the English term being lost, one of the two words would shift in meaning. When French words shifted in meaning, they often took a meaning that was more positive or higher in value than the English word, reflecting the social division at the time between the French speakers, who had political and economic power, and the English speakers, who were relegated to the level of peasants. For example, English borrowed the French word *maison* 'house,' even though the word *house* already existed in English. Thus, over time, the borrowed French term came to be used for a special kind of house, that is, a *mansion*. Furthermore, Old English used the same name for animals whether they were in the barnyard or on the plate, but during Norman rule, English borrowed French words to differentiate between the two, retaining, for instance, *pig* and *sheep* as the names of the animals and borrowing French *porc* and *mutton* for these animals when they're served as a meal.

Although it is often the lexicons of languages that are impacted the most by contact with other languages, other linguistic structures are influenced as well. For instance, while French has had a great impact on the English lexicon, it has also had an influence on English phonology and syntax. With regard to the former, Old English did not recognize /v/ as a distinct sound; however, with its extensive borrowing of French words that began with initial /v/, such as *veal*, *venison*, and *very*, English also adopted /v/ rather than modifying these words to fit the sound system already in place in English. English also borrowed the sound /ʒ/ from French via such words as *azure*, *beige*, and *rouge*.

Of course, as noted above, French is not the only language English has borrowed from, and another example of phonological change through language contact is the incorporation of the consonant cluster [sk] from Scandinavian languages in approximately the 10th century AD in words such as *sky, skirt, scare,* and *Scandinavian.*

While linguists know that all languages will change and that these changes will occur at every level of linguistic structure, we are not able to predict the exact trajectory of language change. For example, we know that the morphological system of English has changed, quite dramatically in fact, since the time of Anglo Saxon, and we know that over the next millennia there will be more changes, potentially just as dramatic, but we do not know which aspects of English morphology will be altered. For example, because English most commonly pluralizes nouns through the addition of the morpheme -s, perhaps all other ways of forming the plural will be discarded. Or the -s morpheme might itself become obsolete, and thus plurality might be formed syntactically instead of morphologically. Again, we do not know what direction language change will take, but we do know that not only is it inevitable, but also, until a language no longer has any speakers, it will change continuously.

Although language change is inevitable and constant, these changes are not always uniform. Language change affects different groups of speakers at different times: While a specific change has reached completion in some groups, for others, the change is ongoing, and for still others, the change never occurs. Furthermore, even within a linguistic community that has undergone a specific linguistic change, there may be subgroups of speakers for whom the change does not happen or for whom the newer (or older) form is used in only certain linguistic contexts. When language change differs, among different groups of people, in different places, or at different times, the outcome of this change is language variation. (See discussion below.)

Regardless of why it occurs or whether it happens through external or internal factors, change is an important part of language growth and development, and every language, past or present, has undergone change at every level of its structure. Such changes are not only structurally necessary and inevitable, but they also allow for languages to meet the communicative needs of their speakers. In later chapters we continue the discussion of language change as it pertains to contemporary and historical changes in the linguistic systems in the United States.

Language Varies

Besides language change, another phenomenon that exists in all languages is linguistic variation, which is a general term for the systematic differences exhibited in a language by groups of speakers and individuals. And, like change, variation occurs at every level of linguistic structure. For instance, different groups of speakers often use lexical variants that refer essentially to the same object: some groups of speakers use the word *pop* as a generic term for a sugary, carbonated beverage, while others use *soda,* others use *coke,*

BOX 1.2 Language Family Trees

As shown above, English has changed so dramatically since its inception that its earliest forms are not even recognizable to contemporary speakers of English. We also noted above that language change can occur along different paths, among different groups of speakers. So what happens when these various groups of speakers use linguistic systems that become undeniably dissimilar? In some cases, linguistic varieties diverge so much that they actually become their own independent languages. For example, varieties of Latin, over a period of hundreds of years and over a space of hundreds of miles, became the languages that we now know today as French, Italian, Spanish, Portuguese, Rumanian, and Catalan.

Languages created through language change are structurally and historically related to one another, and in order to talk about these types of linguistic relationships, linguists use the analogy of the family tree. Presented in Figure 1.2 is the family tree for the Germanic language family, of which English is a member.

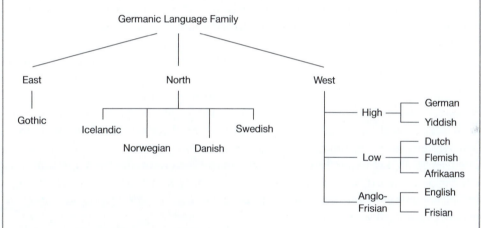

FIGURE 1.2 Germanic language family tree.

According to this tree, all the languages that appear at the end of branches were derived from a single Germanic ancestor. Over time, three main branches of the Germanic language evolved: the East, the North and the West. The East developed into Gothic; the North into Icelandic, Norwegian, Danish, and Swedish; and the West into the High branch, which developed into German and Yiddish, the Low branch, which developed into Dutch, Flemish, and Afrikaans, and the Anglo-Frisian branch, which developed into Frisian and English. In this book, we spend a great deal of time on English, but, in terms of this tree, we also look at German, Yiddish, and Dutch. Of course, we also discuss several other languages, including Spanish and Arabic, which are members of other language families.

and still others use *soda pop*, *soft drink*, *dope*, or *tonic*. This example serves as another lesson of the arbitrariness of language that we discussed earlier: there is nothing about this substance that is inherently pop, soda, or coke. Moreover, this example shows that there isn't one variant that is correct and all of the others wrong; language change does not lead to better or worse forms of language. Rather, these variations in language are simply remnants of language change. Similarly, speakers do not use particular variants because they have good or bad language; rather, a term is used by a set of speakers because it is the form most familiar to them and/or is the form used in the speech community with which they identify. In some instances, speakers might choose to use a variant simply because they prefer it.

Although the lexicon of English provides many excellent examples of language variation, all levels of linguistic structure reveal variation at work. In terms of English phonology, there are hundreds of systematic variants that are quite well known, including *route* as [raʊt] or [rut]; *roof* as [ruf] or [rʊf]; and *coyote* with two syllables ['kaɪot] or three [kaɪ'oti]. At the level of syntax, some speakers of American English might ask "Do you want to come with?" or "Would you like to go with?" whereas, for others, *with* in these constructions must be followed by an object: "Do you want to come with us?" or "Would you like to go with me?" Variation can and does exist at all linguistic levels.

1.8

As stated above, a variant might be used by an individual because it is the form that is used within the community (or communities) with whom he/she identifies or is the variation that is most common where the speaker lives. Language is shared by sets of speakers in linguistic communities, and as a group adopts a form and continues to use it regularly, if not exclusively, the variant may become associated with that particular group. For example, the word *y'all* is often associated with speakers in the American South. In fact, in the United States, one of the most salient, and certainly one of the most discussed, ways that language is associated with a group of speakers is by region. For instance, the two-syllable pronunciation of *coyote* mentioned earlier is generally associated with speakers in the western United States. The preference for the lexical variants *pop*, *soda*, and *coke* mentioned above is also influenced by region, as illustrated in the map presented at the Pop vs. Soda Page, www.popvssoda.com/.

1.9

The knowledge that some language variation is based on region is not new, as illustrated by the following historical example. According to both the Hebrew Bible and the Book of Judges, after winning a battle against Ephraim, soldiers from Gilead recognized that Ephraimites were fleeing the battlegrounds by disguising themselves as Gileadites. The Gileadites began to stop people who were leaving the area but lacked a way to determine who was who merely by appearance. Eventually, they devised a test based on a linguistic difference that had been observed previously between the two groups, namely, that in the pronunciation of the Hebrew word *shibboleth* 'grain,' the Gileadites used an initial [s] (as in the initial consonant of English *sigh*), whereas the Ephraimites used [ʃ] (as in English *shy*). The Gileadites then asked each of the individuals leaving the battlefield a question that would elicit *shibboleth*: those who began the word with [s] were released, and those who used [ʃ] were killed on the spot. This story might not only represent the first case of linguistic profiling, but also gives us the word **shibboleth,** which refers to a linguistic feature that can be used to distinguish members of specific social groups. Shibboleths can exist at any level of linguistic structure and can be associated with any social group. Some of those associated with regional dialects in American English will be discussed in Chapter 5.

During the course of this book, we will investigate several languages that are used in the United States, including English, Spanish, French, Gullah, and Yiddish, which can all be considered "linguistic varieties." But we are also concerned with varieties within these languages—varieties that are associated with a particular group of speakers and that have related, yet different, linguistic structures. The term used to refer to this type of linguistic variety is **dialect**. We define *dialect* as: a variety of language associated with a specific region or social group. The use of the word *dialect* in this way differs from the way that it is used sometimes by nonlinguists, where it is often used pejoratively or as a way to refer to something that only other speakers use. From a linguistic perspective, however, dialects are a natural outcome of language variation; as Rickford says, "All languages, if they have enough speakers, have dialects—regional or social varieties that develop when people are separated by geographic or social barriers" (1999, p. 320). As such, there are, for example, national dialects, such as American English and British English; regional varieties, such as Southern American English and Upper Midwest English; and ethnic varieties, such as Chicano English and Jewish English. Dialects are distinguished from one another by (sometimes relatively minor) variations in the lexicon, phonology, morphology, and syntax.

All languages change, and because all languages change, languages vary; because all languages vary, all languages have multiple dialects. In fact, there is no singular, pure form of a language—to speak a language is to speak a variety of that language. As such, it is important to recognize that dialects are natural forms of language, and just as all languages are equal, all dialects are equal in their linguistic complexity. Remember, the differences between dialects are regular variations within a rule-governed system, not the product of language decay. Even more important is the recognition that all speakers of a language speak a dialect. For example, the authors of this textbook speak English, but more precisely, they speak a dialect of English known as American English. Finally, not only do all speakers use a dialect of a language, but many actually speak more than one, each indexing the speaker's identity related to a particular region, ethnicity, age, or other social characteristics.

Like the word *dialect*, the term **accent** is sometimes used by nonlinguists pejoratively, often with respect to non-native speakers, as in "She has such a thick accent that it's hard to understand her." For linguists, however, accent is a neutral term referring to both the way in which speakers of a particular variety pronounce words and the rules that govern these pronunciations (i.e., the phonology). Every language is spoken in many different accents, and each individual speaker has an accent that is determined by the dialect of the language that he/she speaks. In other words, as long as an individual is using a variety of language that follows a set of phonological rules—that is, any language or dialect—the individual has an accent. Moreover, as with dialects, accents are representative of the speaker's social characteristics, such as age, gender, socioeconomic status, education, region, and ethnicity.

Every speaker also has an **idiolect**, an individual variety of language that incorporates all of the linguistic varieties—languages and dialects—that the person knows and uses. Idiolects are based on the native language, acquisition of other languages, personal characteristics and identities, and even physical characteristics, such as the speed with which the vocal cords vibrate. Idiolects are influenced by speakers that one interacts with; as such, the places in which speakers have lived, the people with whom they have been associated, and how strong their ties have been to these places and groups have an important bearing on a speaker's idiolect. But, at the end of the day, an idiolect is something uniquely one's own.

While speakers make use of different linguistic features based on the social groups they belong to, they can also vary their language stylistically, meaning that all speakers have access to both formal and informal forms that are a part of the language or dialect. Speakers, often unconsciously, choose the level of style and the features that reflect that style based on the context or the perceived communicative needs of the situation. The types of language that speakers use, for instance, in the company of close friends vs. grandparents, with siblings vs. colleagues, and at a ball game vs. at a business meeting, all differ not only because of the different topics that might be discussed in each setting but also because of perceived differences in formality and appropriateness. In fact, if people were to behave linguistically in every situation they encounter in the exact same way, it would suggest they did not understand the social rules of language use.

Here again, differences can be observed at every level of the linguistic structure. With respect to the lexicon, there are certain circles where speakers might feel comfortable using slang or taboo language and others where they would not; one might feel free to use a shibboleth such as *ain't* with some people and not with others; and in some situations, the words *ubiquitous* and *shibboleth* might seem appropriate, while in other situations they might not. In terms of pronunciation, a speaker might be sure to articulate *all right* as two syllables in some situations; in others, a one-syllable pronunciation of the word might suffice. And finally, in some contexts it might be beneficial to articulate clearly, as well as use an address term, in the formal greeting, "How are you doing, Sir?" whereas, in other situations, it might be better just to say, "How you doing?" and, in still others, anything more than "What up?," "Hey!," or "Yo!" would raise suspicion. Here, we reiterate the importance of variation to living languages; without it, languages would cease to function as they do, as they would lack both the creative power that variation gives to its speakers and the ability that speakers have to project their identities through language.

BOX 1.3 **Taboo or Not Taboo**

Taboo language, that is, language that is banned from discussion in certain social situations, often results in lexical variation, as speakers discuss the banned topics by adopting **euphemisms**—words or phrases that replace other words that are considered offensive or as having unpleasant associations. Topics that are often considered taboo and are thus also fertile soil for euphemistic language include death, money, religion, sex, body parts, and bodily functions. During the 16th and 17th centuries, leaders of the Puritan movement—a religious movement with strong ties to Colonial America, as will be discussed in Chapter 4—sought to eradicate the influence of the Catholic Church from their own practice of Christianity, going so far as to replace the word *saint* with the word *sir* to create such designations as *Sir Peter* and *Sir Mary*; some even tried to replace *Christmas* with *Christ-tide* in an effort to avoid any reference to Catholic mass (Mencken, 1921).

Another example of social change leading to language change originated during the reign of Queen Victoria (1837–1901), when England adopted a code of strict moral standards and, consequently, speakers of the English language created euphemisms for anything remotely related to sex and body parts, including *male cow* for *bull*, *bosom* for *breast*, *hose* for *stockings*, and *retire* for *to go to bed*; additionally, in some company, *legs* could only be referred to as *limbs* (Mencken, 1921). Although the reasons for these words to be used this way might seem trivial today, the fact that many are still in use or have been replaced with other euphemisms show the profound effect that taboo can have on language use.

1.10

LANGUAGE IS A REFLECTION OF IDENTITY

An essential concept that runs through most, if not all, of the topics that will be covered in this book is that, for its speakers, language is an inherent and integral part of human identity. Languages and dialects are intimately connected to, and are a reflection of, the people who use them. First, linguistic systems evolve to meet the needs of their speakers; if a word or a structure or even a more precise meaning is needed for communication, then the language will change accordingly. If this need applies to only a particular community of speakers, then the change will happen only within that group. Thus, even the structure of language—its grammar and its lexicon—are reflections of the people who communicate with them.

Language also reflects identity in that linguistic variation is a meaningful and significant symbol of group membership. Speakers acquire the linguistic systems of the group (or groups) around them, for example, who they live with, who they work with, and who they socialize with, particularly those groups with whom they want to be identified. At the same time, as the members of a group continue to use sets of linguistic features, those forms become inherently linked to the group itself and become readily identified as such by those both inside and outside of the community. Thus, when speakers use particular dialects or accents, they actually present themselves as members of those communities. Furthermore, because of this association and the recognition of it, individuals are able to actively index group membership through speech.

We must also recognize that speakers have not one, but many identities that may be reflected in their speech. For instance, Americans speak a national variety of the language that can be distinguished from that of speakers of British English or Australian English, and at the individual level speech may reflect education, gender, socioeconomic status, age, and region, among others. For example, one might identify as male, Midwestern, middle-aged, heterosexual, white, and Jewish, and it is possible that the languages, dialects, and even individual linguistic features that he uses would reflect one or more of these identities. According to their communicative needs, speakers may (consciously or subconsciously) switch between linguistic systems and the identities they represent.

CONCLUSION

In this chapter, we have introduced readers to the subject of this book by presenting a brief overview of language and linguistics. As part of this introduction, we have provided the definition of language that we will adhere to throughout the book, and we have touched upon a number of concepts that are key to understanding language, including the systematicity of language structure and the universal processes of variation and change. We also discussed the connection between language and identity and the idea that language is intimately and inherently connected to its speakers. Each of these basic concepts is necessary for understanding the discussions in this textbook about language structure, language use, and linguistic diversity within the United States.

The definition given at the beginning of this chapter presented language as a rule-governed structure used within a linguistic community. In much of the remainder of this book, we will question what it means for one to be a part of a linguistic community, and we will examine what it means for a community to be unified through language. In our discussions of linguistic communities in the United States, we will focus much of our attention on English, including the development and use of the many English dialects that are spoken in the United States, but we will also examine other languages, such as Spanish, Arabic, and Yiddish, that not only are spoken in the US, but that have helped define the linguistic community that is the United States.

DISCUSSION AND RESEARCH QUESTIONS

1. In this chapter, we mentioned that some estimates set the number of English words at about a million. What might the difficulties be in pinning down the number of words in any language? Use what you've learned about the levels of language structure and the key principles of linguistics to formulate your answer.
2. Has your idiolect, that is, the speech that you use as an individual, changed over the course of the past several years? What changes has it undergone? Why do you think these changes have taken place?
3. Make a list of words that you have heard pronounced in two or more ways. Try writing your answers using the phonetic alphabet. Next, compare your list to others in your class. Are there some words that appear in several lists and others that are unique? If so, how do you account for this distribution? What reasons can you give, if any, for some of these variant pronunciations?
4. *Rio Grande river*; *ATM machine*; *lariat rope*; and *could of* (as a written representation of *could have*) are all cases of reanalysis at work. For each, indicate whether you are familiar with the example and, if so, explain how it exemplifies reanalysis. Are you familiar with other variants you hear that might be cases of reanalysis? State what they are and how they exemplify reanalysis.
5. The pronunciation of some US place names is also prone to variation, particularly those place names with origins in languages other than English, including *Colorado*, *Illinois*, *Missouri*, *Nevada*, *Oregon*, *New Orleans*, and *Spokane*, and sometimes this variation is used to show who is a member of the community and who isn't. Have you heard different pronunciations of these names? What are the different variants you've heard? Do you know whether these differences could be linked to insider/outsider status? If so, who uses which variant? Do you know any other place names that show variation and are used by locals in the same way?
6. Write out a list of terms that describe your identity, such as your ethnicity, age group, gender, sexual orientation, socioeconomic status, religion, level of education, and the region where you grew up and/or currently live. Next, consider your own linguistic identity. How does your speech align with these aspects of your identity? Are there any parts of your identity that are not in some way reflected in your speech?

Grammar, Standardization, and Language Authorities

GUIDING QUESTIONS

1. What is grammar?

2. What is the difference between descriptive and prescriptive grammar?

3. What does it mean to judge language as grammatical or ungrammatical?

4. Who are the authorities on language?

5. What is a standard dialect and how is it developed?

OVERVIEW

In this chapter, we present and define the concept of grammar from both a prescriptive and descriptive point of view. We examine the difference between declaring language as correct or incorrect and judging utterances as grammatical or ungrammatical. We also introduce the concept of language authorities and identify the people and institutions that have been granted—or have claimed—authority in language, such as dictionary writers and grammar mavens. Finally, we discuss the power and prestige given to standard forms of language and explain both how and why some languages become standardized. Along with Chapter 1, this chapter provides background information about language and linguistics for readers who are new to the field.

COMMON MYTHS

A word isn't a word unless it's in the dictionary.

Grammar pertains only to punctuation and the use of proper forms.

Good grammar is attained through diction classes and diagramming sentences.

The standard form is the only correct form of language.

INTRODUCTION

What is the first thing that comes to your mind when you hear (or see) the word **grammar**?

Ask any group of people this question, and you are bound to get a wide range of responses. Some mention the endless hours spent diagramming sentences in grade school. Others refer to drills that they were given to eliminate passive voice or run-on sentences. Still others recall getting school essays returned to them dripping with red ink and covered with notes about comma splices and verb tenses. Before the first author of this book studied linguistics, this question conjured visions of her "scary sixth grade English teacher. And commas—awful, awful commas." While these images hold negative connotations for some, for others the term *grammar* has more positive associations. Of course, the people who have these associations are often very proud of the hard work they did to correct all of those red marks—or they never received them in the first place.

Not only do people have specific associations concerning grammar, but many are inclined to express their opinions about language quite openly. Such comments appear regularly and frequently in both private conversations and public discourse. For example, online discussions are filled with remarks like the following: "*Irregardless* is not a word"; "Why can't people understand the difference between *they're*, *their*, and *there*?"; and "Your poor spelling is literally killing me." There are even t-shirts emblazoned with such statements as, "Good grammar is sexy." In some cases, these comments actually endorse particular reactions to specific points of grammar:

> For any true stickler, you see, the sight of the plural word "Book's" with an apostrophe in it will trigger a ghastly private emotional process similar to the stages of bereavement, though greatly accelerated. First there is shock. Within seconds, shock gives way to disbelief, disbelief to pain, and pain to anger. Finally (and this is where the analogy breaks down), anger gives way to a righteous urge to perpetrate an act of criminal damage with the aid of a permanent marker. (Truss, 2003, p. 1)

While the intensity and severity of these reactions to grammar vary greatly, a quick analysis of these comments reveals that they generally pattern around a few key ideas: (1) there are rules to language use; (2) these rules should be followed; and (3) some people are quite emphatic about ideas 1 and 2.

Before we delve further into public and private comments about grammar and correctness in speech (a topic that we discuss below and expand on in Chapter 3), we must first discuss what grammar is. Crucially, we must recognize that there are actually two different, sometimes competing, definitions that people reference when talking about grammar—a distinction that few people even know exists. In both cases, *grammar* refers to the rules of language, but the scope and focus of each definition are very different. **Prescriptive grammar** promotes rules of language that dictate a formal, standard usage and is the more common of the two definitions, while the other, **descriptive grammar**, depicts the rules of naturally occurring speech and is the approach taken by linguists. The specific definition that one uses not only determines the types of rules that are included within the construct of grammar, but also affects how one views and defines language itself. As we move through this discussion, we ask you to consider language and its rules from these two different perspectives and to question your own beliefs about grammar.

PRESCRIPTIVE GRAMMAR AND DECLARATIONS OF CORRECTNESS

When people talk about grammar, they frequently refer to the rules of proper speech and writing that they were taught in school, including "Don't use double negatives"; "Avoid passive voice"; and "Separate complete thoughts with semicolons instead of commas." These types of rules, referred to as prescriptive grammar, are generally focused on formal, written language. These are the rules that are *prescribed*—set down, ordered, imposed—by those who write grammar books and style guides, including such works as Strunk and White's *The Elements of Style*. Often based on older forms of English or even on the structure of other languages, these are also the rules that promote a nonvarying, nonchanging, standardized form of speech. In fact, those who look at grammar from a prescriptive view regularly believe that any type of linguistic change or variation is decay.

2.1

One well-known prescriptive grammar rule states that speakers should not split infinitives; thus, according to this rule, speakers should use "to go boldly" instead of "to boldly go." This rule, like other prescriptive rules, centers around the promotion of stylized, formal language, and those who follow it (or those who endorse others to follow it) claim that doing so will help to streamline one's words and make one's prose more elegant. For example, according to Strunk and White (2000), the split infinitive "should be avoided unless the writer wishes to place unusual stress on the adverb" (p. 58). While prescriptive grammar focuses on elegance of style, it does not generally concern itself with the history of, or the logic behind, the formation of the rule itself. Therefore, when prescriptive rules are analyzed, they are often recognized as arbitrary and even sometimes unnecessary.

For example, the split infinitive rule, which was not included in most grammar books until the 19th century, is based on the rules of Latin, a language idealized by early grammarians as logical, pure, and superior to English. However, Latin has a grammatical structure different from English. While English constructs its infinitive with two words (*to* + verb) and thus creates the possibility of a split infinitive, the Latin infinitive is a single word (e.g., *ambulare* = "to walk") that does not allow for an intervening modifier. In other words, it is impossible to split an infinitive in Latin even though it is possible to do so in English. Moreover, the English language is not derived from Latin, and the two languages are only remotely structurally related. Thus, there is no linguistic reason why the English infinitive should resemble or follow the same morphological pattern as the Latin infinitive. We, therefore, see that the rule to not split infinitives is founded on a linguistic analogy rather than on the structure of English.

Some scholars claim that the split infinitive rule was created as a reaction to newer forms of language since the infinitive in Old English was, like Latin, a single word (Shay, 2008). (Remember, prescriptive views of language often promote the idea that language change is decay and, thus, that older forms are better.) Nonetheless, the two-word infinitive has been in use in English since at least the 13th century. For example, in the poem *Cursor Mundi*, written in approximately AD 1300, we find:

Blessid be þou lord off henyn . . . Synfull men
For **to** þus **lede** in paradice
'Blessed are you, heavenly lord, to thus lead sinful men in paradise'
(Cursor Mundi Ld MS 18443, as cited in
van Gelderen, 2006, p. 129)

We must therefore wonder where the line should be drawn between "newer" versus "older" forms in language. Furthermore, we should ask whether it is appropriate to base a grammar rule on a form that does not exist in the current structure of English. We should also consider how—or if—adhering to this rule improves clarity or communication between speakers. Is there a semantic difference between someone who "needs to leave quietly" and someone who "needs to quietly leave"?

The case of the split infinitive highlights that prescriptive grammar is often more focused on style—what someone "ought" to use in "proper" speech—rather than on the structures of the language that underlie naturally occurring speech. In fact, when defining *grammar* from a prescriptive view, many mistakenly believe that stylized language and permissible structures are actually the same. As we show below, they are not. Thus, prescriptive rules are often created as external prohibitions rather than internal descriptions of language. The example of the split infinitive also shows that the rules of prescriptive grammar tend to be followed and endorsed even when there is no natural basis for them. As stated in *Merriam-Webster's Dictionary of English Usage*:

> The commentators recognize that there is nothing grammatically wrong with the split infinitive, but they are loath to abandon a subject that is so dear to the public at large . . . To repeat, the objection to the split infinitive has never had a rational basis.
>
> (1994, p. 868)

Additionally, in his own discussion of the split infinitive rule, journalist and self-proclaimed "moderate prescriptivist" John McIntyre refers to the construction as a "baseless prohibition." He says: "It just will not die. It has been shot down, demolished, exploded and buried at a crossroads with a stake through its heart. It should be as dead as Marley, but it *keeps coming back*" (2008; emphasis in the original).

While some prescriptive rules are based on the structures of other languages, some others arise from ideas that are not even linguistic. One example of this type of rule is, "Don't use double negatives." In his influential text *A Short Introduction to English Grammar* (1762), grammarian Robert Lowth argues that language should follow the same logic as mathematics, which holds that two negatives equal a positive, and, based on this premise, he claims that it is stylistically improper to use double negatives in English. However, throughout the history of English, speakers and writers have not only regularly used double negatives, but they have even strung together triple and quadruple negatives. To this point, Mencken says: "Like most other examples of 'bad grammar' encountered in American [English] the compound negative is of great antiquity and was once quite respectable. The student of Anglo-Saxon encounters it constantly" (1921, pp. 311–312). He then gives an example of a compound negative from Chaucer's *The Knight's Tale*, written at the end of the 14th century:

> He **nevere** yet **no** vileynye **ne** sayde
> In al his lyf unto **no** maner wight.

2.2

Thus, English clearly allows and accepts these constructions. But prescriptive rules die hard, and Lowth's stylistic choice still appears as prescriptive law even after 250 years.

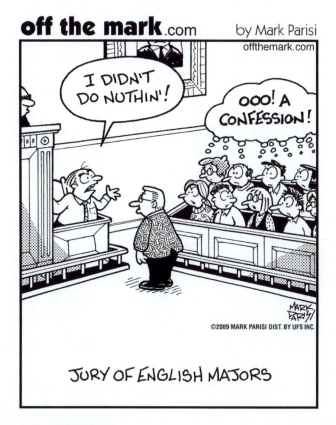

FIGURE 2.1 "Jury of English Majors."

Source: Off the Mark, May 19, 2009.

Finally, are we to believe that only Modern English must follow the rules of logic and mathematics, while other linguistic systems, both historical and contemporary, do not? Other languages, in fact, do use double negatives quite regularly, such as standard French:

Je ne sais pas.	*Je ne sais jamais.*
I not know not	I not know never
'I don't know'	'I never know'

If we recognize that avoiding double negatives, split infinitives, or other naturally occurring constructions that prescriptivists condemn is neither a linguistic nor even a logical necessity, then why do we continue to follow them as absolute and immutable laws of English?

Of the two definitions of *grammar*, the prescriptive takes a much more narrow approach to language and what is allowable in it. This view regards language as both invariant and immutable; it endorses only the structures that are a part of a written standard and mandates these as the only usable forms. To prescriptive grammarians, double negatives or split infinitives are not seen as stylistic choices; rather, they are considered linguistic vagaries that must be extinguished from written and spoken forms of language. Consequently, through the promotion and prescription of these rules, any language use that deviates from this ideal is deemed wrong, and, by extension, those who use these "deviant" forms are often considered aberrant as well. Through a prescriptive lens, language and its speakers are automatically marked as correct or incorrect.

DESCRIPTIVE GRAMMAR AND GRAMMATICALITY JUDGMENTS

In contrast to a prescriptive approach, descriptive grammar refers to the underlying structure of a language as it is used naturally by native speakers. Descriptive grammarians do not concern themselves with prescribing stylized ways of using language or declaring speakers "correct" or "incorrect," but instead are interested in describing the principal structures of natural linguistic systems. Through scientific linguistic investigation (as discussed in Chapter 1), researchers analyze speech for systematic patterns to define the rules—that is, the grammar—of a language. Furthermore, the rules of descriptive grammar take into account all forms of naturally occurring speech, not just the standard forms that prescriptive grammar acknowledges.

Descriptive linguists infer rules from the language that people actually use and record the grammar accordingly. By observing the use of English by native speakers, a descriptive linguist would conclude, for example, that nouns are systematically preceded rather than followed by adjectives, such as in the phrase *white cow*. Because this structure is found to be a regular pattern of the language, "adjectives precede the nouns they modify" would thus be considered a descriptive grammar rule in English. Additionally, in conversational English, one regularly hears English sentences that begin with *and* or *but* or that end in prepositions, and modifiers have been known to boldly split infinitives in both spoken and written English. These structures occur regularly, even without any apparent breakdown in communication, and thus they are a part of the descriptive grammar of the language.

Descriptive grammar may also include rules about structures absent in naturally occurring speech. For example, whereas in French and Spanish nouns are categorized as masculine or feminine, in English they are not. Therefore, a descriptive rule in English is "nouns are not marked for grammatical gender." Compare this descriptive rule with the prescriptive, "speakers should not use double negatives." The former describes permissible structures, while the latter proscribes a particular stylistic preference.

BOX 2.1 Descriptive Grammar: Aspiration in English Consonants

Experiment:

> Hold a sheet of paper in one hand loosely in front of your mouth and pronounce the word *pit* naturally. In most cases, this utterance will cause the paper to move. Now, try pronouncing it in a way that prevents the paper from moving, and notice how this changes the quality of the sound.

Most native speakers of American English adhere to a phonological rule that, at the beginning of a word, /p/, as in *pit*, is aspirated—meaning that a breath of air is released when the /p/ is pronounced—while the /b/, as in *bit*, is not. This **aspiration** is conditional, though; it is present in certain phonetic contexts in which /p/ is produced but absent in others. For instance, /p/ aspiration is absent in the words *spare*, *staple*, *rapper*, and *tips*. This rule is also not found in all languages or even all dialects of English worldwide. However, native speakers of American English use this rule daily, despite the unlikelihood that anyone ever taught it to them directly. Instead, as is the case for most grammar rules, native speakers simply acquire this rule by hearing other speakers use it. In fact, most speakers do not even realize that the rule exists.

There are thousands of descriptive grammar rules pertaining to every aspect of linguistic structure—from pronunciation and word formation to the structure of phrases and sentences—which speakers use unconsciously in the production of natural speech. Over time, these rules can change and, as such, variations of these rules may appear in different places or among different sets of speakers, as we discussed in Chapter 1. Therefore, descriptions of the grammar of a language at different points in time and/or in different places show that distinctive, complementary sets of rules can and do exist within one language. For example, in standard British English, the speech sound /r/ is not pronounced fully after a vowel, as in the word *park*; similarly, there are areas within the United States, such as parts of Charleston, New York, and Boston, that share this same rule (think: "pahk the cah in Hahvahd yahd"). In most varieties of American English, however, /r/ is clearly articulated in this linguistic context. Thus, we find two complementary grammatical rules for the pronunciation of /r/ in English; certain dialects of English have the rule "/r/ is articulated after vowels," while in other dialects "/r/ is not articulated fully after vowels."

2.3

Descriptive linguists embrace the view that speakers are inherently experts in their native language(s). With little or no conscious thought, a native speaker creates unique and novel utterances that require complex and precise physiological movements to produce contrasting speech sounds (phonemes) which he/she then joins together in meaningful ways (words) and places into complex grammatical structures (phrases and sentences). With the exception of relatively infrequent slips of the tongue, native speakers produce speech that follows the inherent rules of their linguistic system, even when they are not consciously aware of them. When people produce speech that adheres to the rules of a particular language or dialect, we say they are following the grammar of that linguistic system. If an utterance follows these rules, it is **grammatical**; if it does not follow these rules, the utterance is **ungrammatical**. As such, descriptive linguists concern themselves with determining which structures in a language are grammatical and which are ungrammatical, rather than focusing on the aesthetic judgments of prescriptive grammar. In other words, descriptive linguists are interested in what native speakers do say, as opposed to prescriptivists, who are interested in dictating what speakers should or should not say.

Consider the following utterances:

1. Peter went to the store.
2. *Store the Peter to went.

As a native speaker of English instinctively knows, example 1 is a well-formed, and thus grammatical, English sentence, whereas example 2 is ungrammatical and would not be produced by a fluent speaker. In example 2, the words themselves are well formed, that is, they are structurally appropriate and have meaning in English—unlike, for example, *sklrmng*—but the sentence violates the rules of English syntax that govern how phrases and sentences are constructed. (Note: an asterisk that precedes an example is used in linguistics to indicate phrases or sentences that are ungrammatical, and a question mark that precedes an example is used to signify those that are questionably grammatical.)

Now, examine this (famous) example:

3. Colorless green ideas sleep furiously.

While this sentence lacks semantic coherence, its syntactic form complies with the structure of English. Therefore, we consider it a well-formed sentence; that is, it is grammatical. And, as the following example shows, fluent speakers are often able to be creative with the words they choose while still observing grammatical rules:

The Jabberwock, with eyes of flame,
Came whiffling through the tulgey wood,
And burbled as it came!

(Carroll, 1871)

Next, analyze these three examples. Are they grammatical or ungrammatical?

4. And Peter went to the store.
5. I ain't got none.
6. Where is the library at?

For the sentence(s) you marked as ungrammatical, why are they so? Moreover, what makes the other sentence(s) grammatical? Consider how you make these distinctions. Do you form **grammaticality judgments** based on empirical data? In other words, are your judgments based on how people actually talk, or are they based on how you (or someone else) thinks they should talk?

According to the underlying grammar of American English, sentences 4 through 6 are perfectly grammatical. They fit within the structure of the language, are produced naturally and fluently, and are the kinds of sentences heard every day. Initially, you might have been inclined to label these sentences ungrammatical because they are not examples of "proper" or "formal" speech; from a prescriptive viewpoint, they might be considered incorrect and, thus, first appear ungrammatical. However, from the perspective of descriptive linguistics, in which grammaticality judgments simply identify whether the form fits within the structure of naturally occurring speech, these sentences are grammatical. Of course, you may choose to avoid these forms in your own speech, but that is a matter of personal preference rather than an issue of permissible linguistic structures.

Next, consider:

7. ?She visited daily when he was in hospital.

While most speakers of American English would classify this sentence as ungrammatical because, for them, the word *hospital* requires a preceding article (*the*), speakers of British English use this sentence structure naturally and, therefore, would consider it grammatical. As with the example of **post-vocalic** /r/ above, such linguistic variation shows that a single language, such as English, can have different grammatical rules for its individual dialects. It is important to note that variations in grammatical structure are not incorrect versions of a primary, correct rule; rather, they are each separate, complementary, complex structures. In other words, it is not the case that American English is correct and British English is incorrect, or vice versa; they are both grammatical systems.

Even though native speakers are already experts in language, they often overlook their own expertise because they subscribe to a prescriptive view of language and grammar. In fact, most speakers do not even recognize that another approach to language, namely, the descriptive view, exists. This is primarily because the prescriptive view is the only view promoted by most educational systems. Subsequently, when only the prescriptive perspective is presented, false information about the structure and function of language—such as "Change is decay," "Variation in language is just bad speech," or "*Ain't* is not a word"—flourishes. Even the spell checker in the word processing program used to write this chapter marked *ain't* as incorrect.

For those readers who argue that upholding a standard, prescribed form is the same as judging grammaticality, we ask you to compare example 2 to examples 6 and 9:

2. *Store the Peter to went.
6. Where is the library at?
9. He needs to quickly leave.

While one might consider there to be better, more appropriate constructions than those in examples 6 and 9 for, say, a formal essay, one must objectively acknowledge that, unlike example 2, these are still naturally occurring examples of spoken English sentences and, as such, are grammatical by descriptive standards. A prescriptive approach would most likely lead one to classify these sentences as "bad speech." But again, examples 6 and 9 are descriptively grammatical, regardless of whether or not their structures also convey formality or social prestige.

Unlike descriptive grammar rules, which preside over every single conversation and encompass all acts of speech, whether formal or informal, standard or nonstandard, the rules of prescriptive grammar are generally those that are found in standard grammar books or writing style guides. These prescriptive rules do not allow for variation or change in language, and they treat language as if it is a static system with fixed, invariable rules. For instance, someone who takes a prescriptive view of language may loudly decree that an utterance is not correct English if it contains a split infinitive or that speakers will not be understood if they fail to distinctly articulate the different vowels in the words *Mary*, *marry*, and *merry*. In contrast, descriptive linguists will agree that it is permissible in English to not split an infinitive and to pronounce *Mary*, *marry*, and *merry* in three different ways, just as they will note that it is also grammatical in English to split an infinitive or to pronounce *Mary*, *marry*, and *merry* with two different vowels (or even pronounce them exactly the same way). Although descriptive linguists may argue against the sole authority of a prescriptive point of view, they fully recognize the rules of prescriptive grammar as a subset of a larger linguistic system. Conversely, those who take a strict prescriptive view not only denounce the possibility of any other grammatical form, they may even go so far as to completely deny the entire validity of descriptive grammar itself.

2.4

LANGUAGE AUTHORITIES

Of the two approaches to grammar, the prescriptive view is generally the most dominant, or, at least, it is the one that most people have been exposed to, especially as it is the only view of grammar employed by the American educational system.

Consequently, most speakers are unaware or unaccepting of their personal expertise in language. When speakers deny or are systematically denied their inherent expert status, they leave decisions about grammar rules and "good" language usage in the hands of others and designate only certain sources as language authorities; they give away their linguistic power and authority. They believe that language is something that needs to be actively learned and practiced, and that only those with specialized knowledge are able to possess linguistic prestige and authority. As stated by Curzan and Adams in their book, *How English Works* (2006):

> Most speakers assume that there are centers of authority for the English language, but they rarely step back to analyze this assumption critically. Who makes decisions about what is "standard"? Throughout our schooling, we have been sent to dictionaries, grammar books, and style guides in order to learn "the rules" for the written language, but who are the people empowered to write these books? Why do they assume authority over English, and why do we cede authority to them?
>
> (p. 34)

The term **language maven** is often applied to those who are given widespread language authority, including "copy-editors, dictionary usage panelists, style manual and handbook writers, English teachers, essayists, columnists, and pundits" (Pinker, 1994, p. 385). Devoting their careers to the presentation and promotion of standard grammar, these so-called language mavens are among the most publicly vocal about language; they are also the least flexible in their approach to traditional grammar. From their positions of influence, they are able to endorse and promote the prescriptive view, which is then accepted as the only way of looking at language. As speakers come to see prescriptive grammar as the only valid form, those who espouse this view maintain their status as language authorities.

While the term *language maven* can be used to refer to anyone who takes a prescriptive view of language, it is most often reserved for those who exalt standard grammar and decry and denounce other forms. It applies to those who, by claiming authority and expertise in language, feel a need, or even a duty, to prescribe to others the "correct" form of language. Well-known language mavens include William Safire, who wrote the "On Language" column for *The New York Times* from 1973 to 2009; Lynne Truss, author of *Eats, Shoots & Leaves: The Zero Tolerance Approach to Punctuation*; and accountant-turned-grammarian Nevile Gwynne, writer of *Gwynne's Grammar*. Similar to a physician who prescribes medicine to promote better health, language mavens doctor the grammar of others in order to promote "better" use of language. However, language is not health, and nonstandard linguistic structures, such as double negatives or split infinitives, are useful methods of emphasizing a point, not symptoms of systemic breakdown. Thus, it is important to understand that language mavens are considered authorities in language not because they are wholly (and solely)

2.5

correct, but because they uphold the status quo as promoters of this particular view. (To view responses by descriptive linguists to claims made by highly prescriptive language mavens, please see the Companion Website.)

2.6   Not all who are given widespread authority in linguistic matters take a prescriptive view of language. One of the most notable, informative, and utilized sources of linguistic information is the dictionary, and most **lexicographers**, that is, those who write dictionaries, believe their job is to objectively describe rather than subjectively prescribe the language they observe.

Contemporary lexicographers follow language change, and when they observe a new word gaining regular usage or an older word taking on a new, commonly used meaning, they edit their texts to include that word or description. Even Samuel Johnson, the man noted for developing the precursor to all contemporary dictionaries and promoting prestige forms of highly stylized language, realized in the writing of his *Dictionary of the English Language* (1755) that a prescriptive view of language is misleading, and he acknowledged that language change is natural and inevitable. In the Preface to his dictionary, Johnson (1755) states:

> When we see men grow old and die at a certain time one after another, from century to century, we laugh at the elixir that promises to prolong life to a thousand years; and with equal justice may the lexicographer be derided, who being able to produce no example of a nation that has preserved their words and phrases from mutability, shall imagine that his dictionary can embalm his language, and secure it from corruption and decay, that it is in his power to change sublunary nature, or clear the world at once from folly, vanity, and affectation.

2.7   Even though lexicographers aim to describe rather than prescribe language, they cannot control how the public views their work. People tend to regard dictionaries as the ultimate source of correct language. In fact, we often talk about "THE" dictionary as if there were only one, akin to a religious text. Of course, more than one dictionary exists, and there is even more than one accepted idea of what types of information a dictionary should include. Some dictionaries incorporate the history, or **etymology**, of each word while others include example sentences. Some even contain pictures. Additionally, rival publishing houses produce competing dictionaries, and individual publishers produce different types of dictionaries, including comprehensive, collegiate, and children's editions, intended for a range of audiences. (Please see the Companion Website for a detailed discussion of the most comprehensive dictionary of the English language, *The Oxford English Dictionary*.)

2.8   The rise in the authority assigned to dictionaries has led to the common misunderstanding that a word is not a "real" word if it cannot be found in a dictionary. However, lexicographers do not sit around all day thinking up new words so people can increase the size of their vocabulary. Lexicographers are reporters, not creators, of language; they simply report and describe what they see and hear. That said, while their mission is to describe language objectively, lexicographers necessarily make subjective decisions. They must decide when a word is common enough to be regarded as a permanent fixture in the lexicon, what definition(s) to include in the word's entry, and which spellings and pronunciations to acknowledge and which to disregard.

For example, it would be impossible to include every existing pronunciation of every word; therefore, lexicographers often choose to present only those pronunciations that their research indicates are the most common or standard. (In some cases, they do include one or two common variations when, for instance, there are different standard British and American pronunciations.) Furthermore, the publication of dictionaries takes time, and lexical change often happens much more quickly than dictionaries can be revised. As most dictionaries include entries for only the words and meanings that are in common usage, lexicographers must wait until they have proof of the consistent usage of a new word or a new meaning before altering the texts. *The Oxford English Dictionary* will often wait ten years before adding a new entry, and even in their online version, they release a list of new words only four times a year.

2.9
2.10

Finally, there are also limits to the authority given to those who create dictionaries. As indicated in the quote given above from *Merriam-Webster's Dictionary of English Usage*, even if editors are not supportive of a prescriptive rule, such as the split infinitive, they may continue to include it in their publications because the public—and language mavens, in particular—demand it. Moreover, many of these authorities recognize their own limitations as experts, as can be seen in comments in the language surveys completed by members of the usage panel for *The American Heritage Dictionary*. For example, author and literary critic Malcolm Cowley notes, "[t]here is always the danger that we, the so-called authorities, should become too damned pedantic," and writer Isaac Asimov warns that "[m]y opinions are strong, but not necessarily authoritative. Please realize that" (Steinway, 2014). Additionally, statements from lexicographers and usage panelists also reveal that language experts are not unanimous in their proscriptions about usage. For example, as reported in *The American Heritage Dictionary of the English Language*, 5th edition (2011), the usage panel voted both *dove* and *dived* as acceptable past-tense forms of *dive*, with approval ratings of 92% and 72%, respectively. Therefore, authority over a homogeneous, invariant language is given to those who recognize that language is neither homogeneous nor invariant.

2.11

Even when they must make choices, lexicographers are attempting to provide a factual record of the language, not a statement about correctness of its usage. However, when people see one form highlighted in a dictionary, they interpret it as the one "correct" form and subsequently infer that any other form is incorrect. Furthermore, many who read and reference dictionaries take these decisions to be comprehensive and inalterable standards. In other words, even though lexicographers take a descriptive approach to language, their work is often read as prescriptive.

BOX 2.2 Urban Dictionary: Crowd-sourcing Authority in Language

Given that so much authority is placed into the hands of lexicographers, what happens when just anyone is allowed to write a dictionary? Does it change who has the authority to tell speakers what is appropriate to say? Does it reveal the fact that it is the speakers of a language who truly have the ability to create and change language, and that lexicographers only have the authority to report these changes?

One example of a **crowd-sourced dictionary** is Urban Dictionary (urbandictionary.com), where anyone with an Internet connection is able to create or revise an entry. The submission process is quick and anonymous, and Urban Dictionary specifically requires its authors to identify themselves only by pseudonyms. The submission page prompts authors to submit the correct spelling of the word they are entering, its definition, and an example sentence. As such, authors are required to make specific decisions about proper or authentic forms of language. In other words, in the creation of dictionary entries, these self-appointed authors both record and standardize the language used around them and, as such, their work parallels that of professional dictionary writers. But should they be called lexicographers?

Readers go to Urban Dictionary either to look up words they do not know the definition of or to find new words they have not heard of before. By doing so, readers recognize the dictionary as a valid reference for language, and they give the dictionary and its authors at least a type of authority. Unlike standard dictionaries that have an editing staff and a panel of usage experts, the authenticity of entries in Urban Dictionary is crowd-sourced to the general public, just as the entries themselves are. Specifically, readers vote thumbs up or down on whether they approve of the definition provided. This process not only gives feedback on particular entries, but it also grants authority to the users by providing a quantitative measure of the acceptability or popularity of a given word. The obvious question this dictionary begs though is should it be afforded the same prestige or authority as other, formal dictionaries? And, if not, what type of authority is it entitled to?

2.12

2.13

Even though linguists recognize native speakers as de facto experts in their grammars, the public dismisses this view and gives authority to only a select group of people and institutions. It is generally these proclaimed authorities—such as language mavens, the educational system, dictionaries, and grammar books—that promote prescriptive grammar and a homogeneous, standardized language. Thus, with the backing of such authority and prestige, prescriptivism is the primary view that is promoted and, subsequently, taken as fact. It is a cyclical process, and it is one with a very long history. While we are not able to fully explicate how a prescriptive view of language became the dominant view in the public discourse, in the next section, we discuss how a standard dialect of language forms and, to some degree, how it gains prominence.

STANDARDIZATION AND A STANDARD LANGUAGE IDEOLOGY

Whereas language mavens and their followers concern themselves primarily with prescriptive grammar and the promotion of a standardized form of language, we must recognize that the creation of a standard dialect is not a natural part of language. This creation is, instead, a socially conditioned, overt process. In fact, the vast majority of the world's approximately 7,000 languages have not gone through **standardization**. Thus, if the development of a standardized dialect—the process of which we discuss below—is not a natural part of language, then why are people so focused on the idea that the standard is the only valid form of language, and why is it granted such prestige? Does the creation of a standard form automatically mark other linguistic varieties as substandard? Moreover, why would anyone want to standardize language in the first place?

There are actually several reasons why a community would want to standardize its linguistic system; even descriptive linguists (especially those writing textbooks or reading essays written by their students) see a need for shared rules for formal and/or written language. First, standardization eases communication, especially among speakers of very different dialects. While language change and variation are interesting, dynamic, and natural parts of language, one outcome of language change is the possible creation of dialects that are different enough from one another that speakers may encounter some difficulty understanding particular words, pronunciations, or grammatical structures of dialects that are not their own. Any American high school student who struggles reading Shakespeare can attest to this. One, however, does not have to travel back four hundred years to find varieties that are difficult for speakers of other dialects to understand. For instance, have you ever needed subtitles to understand a contemporary speaker of English in a movie or television show, or have you ever seen a film or show that assumed that you would need access to subtitles?

2.14

It is easy to fathom that if all speakers of a language were to speak exactly the same way, from place to place as well as across time, then communication would be easier. However, just as we recognize that complete homogeneity in any language is helpful for communication, we must also recognize (as we discussed in Chapter 1 and explain further below) that an invariable, unchanging language simply does not and cannot exist.

Second, a standardized language has the power to unify its speakers. As users of the same linguistic system, speakers of the standard are connected, and any social or political group that the language is associated with is further unified. Historically, the view that linguistic unity equals political unity is often broached within broader discussions of regionalism or nationalism. Standard language can even be a symbol of national pride. (For a recent example, see the Companion Website for a discussion of arguments about Americanisms infecting British English.) Overall, the potential for unifying the masses is very powerful, and national unity through a standard linguistic form is an intriguing, yet highly complex issue. As applied to the United States, this issue will arise several times throughout this textbook, and the description of a standard American English—what it is, where it comes from, and what it stands for—is a complex discussion we continue in Chapter 8.

2.15

There is, however, a downside to the process of linguistic standardization. While speakers of a standard dialect are unified through a shared system, those who are not speakers of the standard dialect are automatically tagged as outsiders, and the benefits afforded to the former group are denied to the latter. In other words, the people who speak (or grow up speaking) the standard are automatically given entrée into the system, but others have to actively learn a new linguistic system in order to access the same rights and respect. (Contrary to popular belief, learning a new linguistic system—even a dialect of the same language—is no easy task. It requires focus, energy, time, and hard work to accomplish and, even then, learning a new dialect may not be wholly achievable (see Lippi-Green, 2012).) Historically, those given the authority to select the standardized form choose a linguistic system close to their own speech. Thus, the trajectory of language and power is cyclical: those with social and/or political power possess the authority to create a standard form, and when they use their own speech as the standard, they automatically renew their own prestige.

Another negative outcome of standardization is that all of the linguistic systems not selected as the standard are subsequently marked as nonstandard or even substandard. Dialects that are equal in terms of their linguistic structure become unequal socially, pedagogically, and, oftentimes, politically. These nonstandard dialects are thus set within a hierarchy where the standard reigns supreme. In other words, dialects are placed in competition with one another, but it is an inherently unfair competition since the standard form not only possesses societal prestige but also the weight of those social, political, and educational support structures behind it. Furthermore, owing to the hierarchical structure that standardization creates, the standard form is elevated and thus presented as the only valid form of the language. The standard form consequently becomes synonymous with the language itself, which, in turn, promotes the idea of one English (or one French or one Russian). For example, when you study a foreign language in school, is it presented to you as just one possible dialect of a larger linguistic system (e.g., Parisian French, Castilian Spanish, or Beijing Mandarin) or as the totality of the language itself (i.e., just French, Spanish, or Chinese)?

This outcome of standardization leads us back to our original discussion of language and grammar being prescribed as right or wrong, correct or incorrect, as opposed to being described as grammatical or ungrammatical. Through standardization, the prescribed rules become accepted as correct, while everything else becomes perceived as wrong. In fact, the educational system frames its curricula around the standard and teaches students that no other forms are permissible. While other varieties could be presented as different instead of deficient, they are instead ignored and overlooked as valid linguistic options. Furthermore, because the educational system tests students' knowledge of the standard, the speech of the children when they enter the school system already marks them for success or failure. The promotion of one standard linguistic form, therefore, actually requires many individuals to make a choice: either abandon (or, at the very least, displace oneself from) the home dialect in favor of the standard in order to succeed in the educational system or eschew assimilation and risk educational, and possibly even professional, failure.

The view of a standard variety as the only correct form of a language along with the social consequences that stem from this view can be explained as a part of a **standard language ideology**. As defined by Lippi-Green (2012), standard language ideology is:

> a bias toward an abstracted, idealized, homogenous spoken language which is imposed and maintained by dominant bloc institutions and which names as its model the written language, but which is drawn primarily from the spoken language of the upper middle class. (p. 67)

This ideology is both persistent and widespread. It promotes the primacy of prescriptive grammar, demands that native speakers give up their own authority in language, and ignores descriptive findings of how language works. However, when one begins to question the linguistic and social assumptions behind standard language or to directly compare prescriptive with descriptive grammar, one must conclude that the concept of a standard language, and thus a prescriptive view, is only a social ideal, and not a linguistic fact. In order to better understand this logical conclusion, we must examine the steps required for the development of a standard variety of a language.

The Process of Standardization

In order for a language to be standardized, it must go through a multi-stage process, which, as described by Haugen (1972), is actualized through four main steps. Two of these steps—selection and codification—are associated with the language's form, while the others—elaboration and acceptance—have more to do with its social function. Therefore, standardization works not only to cement the grammatical system of the language but also to dictate how it operates and how it is perceived in day-to-day interactions. The primary aim in creating a standard is to "fix" the language and, in this context, the dual meaning of *fix* is quite telling. First, *fix* refers to setting the language, making it something that will neither change nor vary, that is, "it is set in stone." Second, the use of *fix* promotes the view that any linguistic variation is an indication that the language is broken and thus needs to be repaired.

The first step of the standardization process is the **selection** of the form. Because this is an external process, any linguistic form can technically become the one chosen. Moreover, as all varieties are linguistically equal, there is no single form intrinsically better suited for the job. However, standardization is, after all, a social process, and thus the form that is declared the standard usually comes from the dialect already spoken by, or associated with, those in power. In the case of French, the dialect of the elite in Paris was chosen, as it was the speech of government and high society at the time of standardization. While it is often only one specific dialect that is chosen to become the standard, there are times in which authorities may "build" and "blend" the standard from different parts of related dialects—a pronunciation from here, a phrase structure from there. This process more closely resembles standardization in England, where a strong London base mixed with a handful of features from other eastern dialects to produce a British standard. Today, this British standard accent is known as RP, or **Received Pronunciation**.

Next in the process of standardization is **codification**. This step focuses on producing minimal variation in form. A true standard dialect will have one unwavering form for every aspect of the language: one pronunciation and one spelling for every word, one structure for every grammatical form. Once the linguistic forms are selected, they are presented as the only viable forms available, or as the only forms that are "correct." For example, if we decided to standardize American English, we could declare that the first syllable in the word *envelope* would always rhyme with *pen* and never with *on*, and that people would only write *thru* instead of *through* and *color* instead of *colour*. To understand the arbitrariness of these decisions, we must recognize that we could have just as easily chosen any of the other given options, since the decision of which forms to standardize is based on stylistic preferences, not on the grammaticality or so-called "superiority" of a form. Through both selection and codification, the goal of standardization is two-fold: first, to promote the supremacy of one form, and, second, to remove all other variations as possible choices.

While codification aims for minimal variation in form, **elaboration** aims for maximal variation in function (Haugen, 1972). Once the standard is selected and codified, its usage must then be expanded into multiple areas of society. Its use might begin in one arena, such as government, and then pass to another, such as education.

Over time, its use might be extended to other areas, such as law, literature, and religion, and even, perhaps, to everyday usage in written and spoken forms. This leads to the last stage of the standardization process: **acceptance**. In order for a standard to survive and thrive, community members must actually acknowledge the form's prestige and choose to use it (even subconsciously), at least within the proper or appropriate domains. Of course, the social norms that arise from acceptance of the standard variety prove fascinating. As we discuss in greater detail below, those who fully accept the standard are allowed entrée into the whole of the community, while those who do not are excluded.

Whereas the process of standardization is theoretically straightforward, its implementation is more complex. Language change is normal and natural, and no matter how hard society tries, as long as a language has native speakers, it will continue to change and vary. Due to the inevitability of language change, the creation of new forms, and the emergence of new words, speakers must always actively maintain the standard form. Through the sub-process of acceptance, the standard must go through continual renewal. The reality remains, however, that there will never exist a community in which every person uses the standard form in every utterance. Therefore, if a linguistic standard is never fully realized, we must recognize it for what it is—an abstract form or a linguistic ideal—rather than a homogeneous way of speaking. Or, as described another way, standard language is only a social ideology, not a linguistic fact.

CONCLUSION

We have examined how different definitions of grammar lead to contrasting views toward language and its speakers. On the one hand, those who take a prescriptive view find correctness and prestige in formal language use that follows the rules of traditional grammar. Most language mavens tout this view, and it is the one most commonly referenced in the public discourse. On the other hand, those who take a descriptive view—linguists, most contemporary lexicographers, and students taking courses on language and linguistic diversity in the United States—strive to describe the rules underlying language as it is used day-to-day by fluent, native speakers. The main concern of descriptivists is whether an utterance fits into the phonological, morphological, and syntactic structure of the language, not whether a type of speech is correct according to the rules of an abstract and arbitrary standard. Linguists recognize that grammatical forms are acquired through natural language acquisition (internally), not by rote memorization of punctuation rules (externally). In other words, descriptivists concern themselves with the grammaticality of language.

In this chapter, we have also shown that a dialect becomes the standard out of sociopolitical happenstance rather than linguistic superiority and that many of the rules of prescriptive grammar come from outdated or misunderstood ideas about language.

Thus, language should not lend itself to moral judgments of its forms or the speakers who use them. A variety is neither "right" nor "wrong"; its speakers cannot be classified as "correct" or "incorrect." Rather, a linguistic system may be grammatical or ungrammatical. Moreover, while authority over a standard form is generally bestowed upon a select group of so-called language experts, it is actually the everyday speakers of the language who are in control of the natural processes of language variation and change. Thus, when viewed through a descriptive rather than prescriptive lens, grammar is no longer seen as a negative construct overseen by language mavens and scary sixth grade English teachers, but instead, is recognized as the natural, systematic structure of everyday language. When it comes to discussions of grammar, however, the first author of this text still contends that commas will always be perfectly awful.

DISCUSSION AND RESEARCH QUESTIONS

1. Where do discussions of language and grammar occur in the public discourse? What types of sources are found and who is the intended audience?

2. Find a blog or editorial that discusses language and its usage. Does the author present a prescriptive or descriptive view of language? If there are comments, what views do the readers hold about language? Do the views expressed in the commentary conflict or agree with one another and/or the author?

3. Look up the definition of one or two words in three different dictionaries, for example a comprehensive dictionary such as *The Oxford English Dictionary*, a collegiate dictionary, and a compact dictionary. You may even choose to examine a crowd-sourced dictionary. Analyze the types of information included in all three sources as well as those omitted in one or more. What do these similarities and differences reveal about the organization of dictionaries and the goals of lexicography?

4. In an early section of this chapter, we asked, "If we recognize that avoiding double negatives, split infinitives, or other naturally occurring constructions that prescriptivists condemn is neither a linguistic nor even a logical necessity, then why do we continue to follow them as absolute and immutable laws of English?" How would you answer this question?

5. Discuss whether those who write crowd-sourced dictionaries should be given the title of "lexicographer." Similarly, explain whether crowd-sourced dictionaries should be given the same authority in language as other dictionaries. Are there sets of vocabulary for which a crowd-sourced dictionary, such as Urban Dictionary, would have even more credibility or authority than more established dictionaries, such as *The Oxford English Dictionary*?

Language Attitudes

GUIDING QUESTIONS

1. What are language attitudes?

2. What are the methods for studying language attitudes?

3. What perceptions and stereotypes are commonly attached to language variation?

4. Where do people think dialects exist in the United States?

OVERVIEW

This chapter discusses common stereotypes and perceptions of standard and nonstandard dialects in the United States. It also presents the connections that speakers regularly make between language and nonlinguistic traits, such as politeness and trustworthiness. Finally, it examines the link between language attitudes and linguistic discrimination. We encourage readers to question the validity of these attitudes, examine their origins, and consider why they are perpetuated. We also ask readers to recognize and evaluate their own linguistic attitudes.

COMMON MYTHS

> *Southern speech is uneducated, New York speech is rude, and Midwestern speech is unaccented.*

> *Perceptions of standard and nonstandard dialects are always based on linguistic fact.*

> *Nonstandard dialects carry no linguistic value or social prestige, even for their own speakers.*

INTRODUCTION

People have strong opinions about language. These opinions—such as whether someone has a strong accent, whether it is wrong to end a sentence with a preposition, or whether the dictionary is the final word on all things linguistic—are often supported by prescriptive or descriptive views of language. Personal linguistic experiences, perceptions of one's own idiolect, and interactions with other speakers also inform (or bias) these opinions. While personally held, these opinions are not always kept to oneself. Instead, they are broadcast openly and emphatically through a range of channels and to a variety of audiences—in editorials, letters to the editor, blog posts, classroom lectures, and day-to-day conversations with friends, colleagues, and family. Note that everyone, not just language mavens or the authors of linguistic textbooks, has the opportunity—and the right—to express their views of language and, once we take notice, we quickly realize that opinions about language are regular visitors to ordinary, daily discourse.

In certain instances, these opinions about language can be categorized as part of the **complaint tradition,** that is, those discussions (or monologues) in which people disparage language as it shifts and changes (e.g., "Those kids today and their constant use of *like*!"). However, in many such instances, these statements simply serve as evidence of speakers' observations of the language used around them. For example, have you ever made a remark about someone's speech (e.g., "She had such a strong accent!") or guessed a speaker's hometown (e.g., "Is that a Texas drawl I hear?")? Have you made

3.1

3.2

assumptions about what people are like after only hearing their voices? Did they sound uneducated, trustworthy, or uptight to you? Did you draw a picture in your mind of what they might look like, even with respect to such details as attractiveness, height, or ethnicity? If so, you are not alone. Not only do such reactions occur, they abound.

In this chapter, we explore these types of linguistic perceptions, and we examine the opinions and attitudes that they reveal about both the speakers who utter them and the language itself. Just as everyone speaks a dialect and everyone has an accent, everyone holds perceptions of and attitudes toward both the speech and the speakers around them. As noted within our discussions of the universality of linguistic variation (Chapter 1) and competing definitions of grammar (Chapter 2), things are not always what they seem when language is involved. Thus, it is important to recognize not only the origin and basis of these opinions and attitudes, but also how they shape the ways we think about and use language. Furthermore, as we will show throughout the remaining chapters of this book, understanding the attitudes that people hold with regard to language is crucial to understanding both the development of and the reactions to language and linguistic diversity in the United States.

LANGUAGE ATTITUDES

The term **language attitudes** refers collectively to the perceptions, attitudes, and stereotypes associated with language use, linguistic structure, and, oftentimes, with speakers themselves. These attitudes can range from positive to negative, and they can be applied widely: to social groups of varying sizes (e.g., Midwesterners, African Americans, SoCal Surfers), to entire linguistic varieties (e.g., American English or Southern American English), to individual speakers (actual or imagined), or even to independent linguistic features (e.g., lexical or phonological). Additionally, language attitudes can be triggered by anything from long stretches of discourse to individual words or pronunciations. In some instances, in fact, there may be no linguistic input given at all, but instead, the perception is based merely on the expectations of what we think a person should or shouldn't sound like. Finally, there are many ways in which these attitudes affect our daily interactions; whether consciously or unconsciously, we often use our linguistic perceptions and language attitudes to try to ascertain a speaker's character and background and to determine whether we want to interact with him or her.

3.3

BOX 3.1 **Thinking about Language Attitudes**

To illustrate how naturally language attitudes arise, here is a short thought experiment:

> You're out for a stroll when you overhear a man say to his companions, "Y'all, wait for me." You do not know this person, and in fact, you don't even see him. But there is this word he has just used: *Y'all*.

What ideas, attitudes, perceptions, or stereotypes come to mind as a result of this word being used? You might make the connection that *y'all* is commonly used in the Southern United States and, in your experience, is rarely used in other locations. So, you infer that this speaker is most likely from the South. Here, a presumed connection between language and place gives you an idea about who this speaker might be. Other attitudes and perceptions about this speaker might extend from your association with speech and place. You might form opinions about the speaker's character or, perhaps, draw from a stock of stereotypes about the South or about Southern English and its speakers. If you ever lived in the South or had a personal connection with Southerners, you might feel solidarity, sentimentality, or quite possibly even contempt. On the other hand, if you never spent time in the South or with its residents, you might view this speaker with indifference, curiosity, or trepidation. You might also realize that you find Southern speech aesthetically pleasing or that you use speech to draw conclusions about a speaker's intelligence. Whatever your response, it is important to recognize that it was only a single linguistic cue that indexed perceptions of place, personal experiences, and specific social characteristics, both real and imagined. Moreover, these judgments were most likely made instantaneously and subconsciously.

Now, try this same thought experiment by substituting *y'all* with another variant of the second-person plural, such as *you guys* or *yinz*, and see how your responses and perceptions differ.

SOCIAL PSYCHOLOGY AND LANGUAGE ATTITUDE RESEARCH

The last 50 years have seen the development of different lines of research that focus on the elicitation and examination of language attitudes. Researchers in this interdisciplinary field are interested primarily in the attitudes and perceptions of laypersons (including self-proclaimed "language experts") rather than those of individuals trained in descriptive linguistics. Various theoretical and methodological approaches contribute to the scientific understanding of lay opinions of language and, across disciplines, researchers have found that there are significant patterns and shared norms that are associated with language attitudes.

The systematic study of language attitudes was born from research in social psychology with the work of Lambert and his colleagues in the 1960s. Lambert's interest in language attitudes was first piqued when he overheard a conversation that was rife with attitudes concerning the use of French versus English in Quebec. Here he retells his story:

> My attention was suddenly drawn to the conversation in front wherein one lady said something like: "If I couldn't speak English I certainly wouldn't shout about it," referring to the French conversation going on behind them. Her friend replied: "Oh, well, you can't expect much else from them." Then one of the ladies mentioned that she was bothered when French people laughed among themselves in her presence because she felt they might be making fun of her. This was followed by a nasty interchange of pejorative stereotypes about French Canadians, the whole discussion prompted, it seemed, by what struck me as a humorous conversation of the two attractive, middle class French Canadian women seated behind them. The English ladies couldn't understand the French conversation, nor did they look back to see what the people they seemed to know so much about even looked like.
>
> (Lambert, 1967, pp. 92–93)

This brief encounter led Lambert to develop a research paradigm to investigate language attitudes, specifically focusing on the connection between the choice of language spoken and individual social traits assigned to the speakers. In his study, Lambert and his colleagues asked a group of informants, or "judges," to listen to recordings of different speakers reading translations of the same passage, of which half the recordings were in French, and half in English (Lambert, 1967). The informants were then asked to evaluate each speaker on 18 different personality characteristics that Lambert grouped into three distinct categories: competence (e.g., intelligent, ambitious, self-confident); personal integrity (e.g., dependable, kind, sincere); and social attractiveness (e.g., sociable, affectionate, likeable). Before the task, judges were "reminded of the common tendency to attempt to gauge the personalities of unfamiliar speakers heard over the phone or radio" (Lambert, 1967, p. 93).

The methodological twist of this exercise was that while the judges believed they were listening to and evaluating different speakers, they were actually hearing a set of bilingual speakers, each reading the passage twice, once in French and once in English. Lambert's hypothesis was that if the two readings of a single speaker were judged differently, and the only factor that differed between the readings was the language spoken, then the differences in the evaluations were really a reflection of the attitudes toward the languages themselves, not of the speakers. Significantly, this **"matched-guise" test** did reveal notable differences in how the two languages were evaluated. Specifically, Lambert found that informants generally rated the French voices negatively and overall held more positive attitudes toward the English guises (1967). For example, speakers were judged as better looking, more intelligent, kinder, more dependable, and even taller when they read in English than when they read in French. Notably, the same attitudes existed regardless of whether the judges identified themselves as being primarily English or French speaking.

Lambert's study led to a large body of research that not only fine-tuned the matched-guise technique but also revealed a conclusive pattern: people do commonly connect social traits to language when speakers use different languages or even different varieties of the same language (see Tucker & Lambert, 1969; d'Anglejan & Tucker, 1973; Carranza & Ryan, 1975; Kramarae, 1982; Gardner & Clément, 1990; Carter, Lynch, & Neal, 2013). Given that we all form evaluations about speakers through linguistic cues, this finding was somewhat expected; however, we must recognize the significance of such research in proving how widespread and normalized these supposedly personal responses to language actually are. In other words, this research demonstrates that these are not simply an individual's personal tastes about what he/she likes or dislikes about language—we all find certain voices aesthetically pleasing or annoying—but instead, these are deep-seated, culturally bound attitudes that greatly affect how we perceive languages and their speakers.

3.4

This line of research also revealed that these connections and associations between language and social characteristics tend to pattern in specific ways. Whereas Lambert originally grouped his social characteristics into three major categories, further research pared these down to two: **status** and **solidarity**. Overall, this research has shown that speakers who use standard language varieties considered to be prestigious throughout the community are rated higher for traits related to status, such as intelligence, ambition, and confidence. Speakers of nonstandard dialects, while rated low for issues of status, are commonly given high ratings for traits associated with solidarity, such as dependability, sociability, and trustworthiness.

While we regularly connect social traits to language use, we must recognize that the connections themselves are arbitrary. Just as there is no one-to-one correlation between a word and its meaning, there is no set correlation between a linguistic feature and a personal trait. For example, how would the lack of articulation of the /r/ in *park*, or the use of second-person plural *yinz*, naturally attach to a concept such as determination or dependability? Or, since all language varieties are equivalent in their systematic linguistic complexity, how could speakers of one variety necessarily be "more ambitious" or "more affectionate" than speakers of another? Moreover, these connections between language and social traits are not absolute: a specific linguistic pattern might be thought of positively within one community yet negatively in another.

For example, dropping post-vocalic /r/ is considered a prestige form in England but is a stigmatized form in New York City. Thus, the attitudes, perceptions, and stereotypes that we apply to language are features of a social system that is separate from, albeit closely linked to, linguistic structure.

FOLK LINGUISTICS AND PERCEPTUAL DIALECTOLOGY

Parallel to the research conducted in social psychology, a second line of language attitude studies developed within the field of sociolinguistics. Researchers such as Labov and Preston began to investigate whether non-expert opinions about language could provide insight into the intersections between language and society as well as into the study of language variation and change. Named **folk linguistics** due to its focus on non-expert perceptions of language, this research turned its attention to **metalinguistic** knowledge, that is, talk about talk. By utilizing different methodologies for data collection, such as those described below, investigators in folk linguistics gained access to attitudes and perceptions concerning a wide variety of linguistic issues: regional and social dialects, first and second language acquisition, language and education, and even descriptive linguistics (see Niedzielski & Preston, 2000).

For example, by asking where "ordinary speaker[s] believe language differences exist geographically," Preston focused his work in folk linguistics on attitudes toward regional variation (1989, p. 2). Called **perceptual dialectology** due to its connection to traditional work in dialect geography, this line of research investigates where people perceive dialect boundaries to be, as well as which linguistic and social traits they associate with salient regions. Borrowing the concept of "**mental maps**" from work in cultural geography (see Gould & White, 1986), Preston found that people carry culturally influenced, personal images of geographic space and that these mental images are compounded from "current stereotypes, some factual data, awareness of ethnic differences and the ways other people talk" (Cassidy, as cited in Preston, 1989, p. ix). Thus, Preston found that eliciting and analyzing mental maps, from individuals as well as from communities of speakers, exposes the stereotypes, perceptions, and other ideas that work together to form language attitudes about regional speech.

Draw-a-Map Technique

To elicit the attitudes and mental maps that people have regarding dialectal variation, Preston created a set of tasks for respondents to perform. For the first task, respondents were given an unlabeled line map of the target area (e.g., the United States) and were instructed to draw dialect boundaries "around areas where they believe regional speech zones exist" (Preston, 1989, p. xxxiv). Additionally, participants were instructed to label

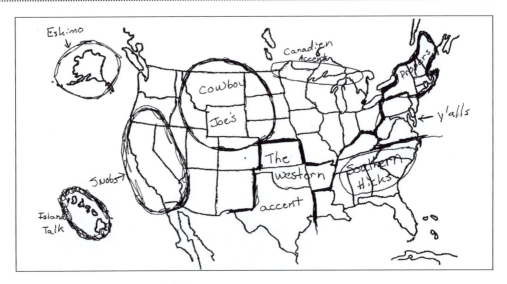

FIGURE 3.1 Southeastern Michigan hand-drawn map.

Source: Courtesy of Dennis R. Preston.

each region with the name they would normally use to describe or refer to it. Preston then examined these hand-drawn maps for individual respondent attitudes as well as for patterns in responses across the sample population. Examples of individual respondent maps are shown in Figures 3.1 and 3.2.

Figure 3.1 shows how a Michigan respondent perceived nine distinct dialect regions, which he labeled with terms such as "Propers" for the Northeast, "Southern Hicks" for the Deep South, and "Cowboy Joes" for the Great Plains states. Note that several parts of the map were not incorporated into any specific dialect area. Also, while the Michigan respondent did reference geographic or regional divisions—using "Western," "Southern," and "Canadian"—he included other items that inform his mental maps. For example, linguistic information is represented with the inclusion of the words *y'alls* and *accent*, social characteristics with *snobs*, *hicks*, *Cowboy Joes*, and ethnicity with the term *Eskimo*. The term *Propers* could be considered a social trait, if referencing social status, or a pseudo-linguistic trait, if referencing a prescriptive view of correct language. As for the areas of the map left blank, they also offer significant insight into the places where the respondent believed that unremarkable, "normal" speech was used or where he simply had no knowledge or opinion. (We would argue for the former, since Michigan, where the respondent lived, is included in this unmarked area.)

In the second map (Figure 3.2), we are offered another view of American English, this time from a Southern respondent. Even more than the one- or two-word labels given by the Michigander, the longer comments provided by this South Carolinian respondent

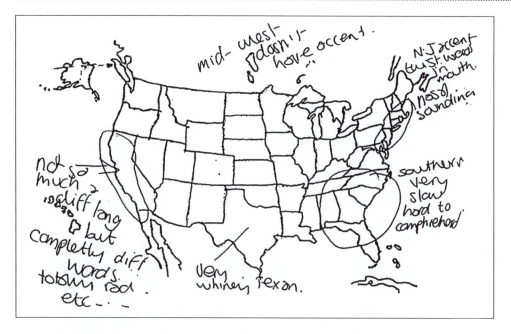

FIGURE 3.2 South Carolina hand-drawn map.

Source: Courtesy of Dennis R. Preston.

clearly show a defined set of personal attitudes. The respondent claimed that Southerners are "very slow" and "hard to comprehend," that Texans are "very whiney," and that New Jersey speakers are "nasal sounding" and "twist words in [their] mouth[s]." In her perceptions of California, she noted that while there were no major grammatical differences ("not so much a diff[erent] lang[uage]"), she perceived variation in the lexicon ("totally rad"), and as evidenced by her map, these "completely diff words" were all she needed to separate that state from the rest of the country. Furthermore, similar to the Michigan respondent, the South Carolinian left a section of the country unmarked and, for her, the majority of the US fits into this normal, unknown, or unremarkable speech area.

Even in the absence of hand-drawn lines, the South Carolinian's comments provide insight into where she believed additional regional boundaries exist. For example, even though she did not isolate a Midwestern area on the map, she did distinguish it from the rest of the country with the label "doesn't have accent." In light of these observations, especially with respect to her comments regarding her own speech region, we should question whether her responses reveal perceptions and attitudes that the respondent personally observed, or if they reflected larger, widely held stereotypes about language in the United States of which she was aware. Could she really not understand the speech of her fellow Southerners? Or, more likely, was she told, or had she inferred

3.5

from comments by others, that Southern speech is: (1) different from the rest of the country, and (2) hard for people to understand?

Ultimately, Preston's research illustrates that even though respondents' mental maps reveal views of linguistic variation to be highly individualized, there are common patterns in perceptions of where different dialects exist in the United States. A composite map of the dialect regions created by the responses of 147 informants from Michigan is shown in Figure 3.3. Notably, the South was consistently the most salient dialect region for respondents, with 94% of them drawing some sort of linguistic South. This finding was not only true for these Michigan respondents but has been replicated several times over in research in the area of perceptual dialectology (see Hartley, 1999; Tamasi, 2000). A Northern dialect area—in this case, the area where the respondents actually lived—appeared as the second most common region, with 61% agreement among respondents. A Northeast and a Southwest dialect region were also commonly recognized.

In addition to the agreement that respondents had with each other, Preston found that, even though they weren't being tested for accuracy, their perceived dialect areas generally coincided with the boundaries of regional dialects that have been shown to exist in the United States. (Empirical research on regional variation in American English is discussed in detail in Chapter 5.) He also discovered that informants were surprisingly correct in identifying speaker location, when such questioning was included in the methodology.

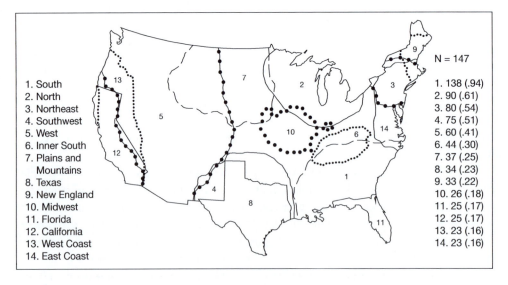

FIGURE 3.3 Perceived American dialect regions from Michigan respondents.

Source: Courtesy of Dennis R. Preston.

Overall, perceptual dialectology has developed into a highly productive area of research within the last 30 years. As such, the theories and methods that Preston originally created have been modified, expanded, and subsequently used to study attitudes in several locations in the United States, including Michigan, Indiana, New York, Hawaii, Oregon, Georgia, New Jersey, and Washington state (Preston, 1989; Hartley, 1999; Lance, 1999; Niedzielski & Preston, 2000; Tamasi, 2000; Evans, 2012), and in countries throughout the world, such as Brazil, Japan, Turkey, Korea, Hungary, and Germany (Preston, 1985; Dailey-O'Cain, 1999; Demirci & Kleiner, 1999; Long, 1999; Kontra, 2002; Long & Yim, 2002; Kennetz, 2008).

3.6

3.7

Pile Sort Method

Tamasi (2003) manipulated Preston's methodology to further investigate perceptual dialect regions and, more specifically, the roles that geography and regionality play in language attitudes. Most notably, she removed the map from Preston's Draw-a-Map task. Rather than marking dialect areas on a map, respondents sorted a deck of 50 cards, each bearing the name of a US state, into piles according to where they believed people speak similarly versus differently from one another. Because the respondents were not manipulating a map directly, as in Preston's studies, their answers were not limited by the geographic orientation of the states. They were, however, restricted in that respondents had to follow state boundaries in the creation of their dialect regions, as this **pile sort method** did not allow for individual states to be subdivided.

Figure 3.4 is a geographical representation of the six dialect areas created by one of Tamasi's Georgia respondents. (In this map, each individual pattern or shade represents one of the piles that the respondent created; the patterns themselves are not meaningful.) The most apparent and significant characteristic of this map is that none of the respondents' dialect groups form geographically bound regions. In fact, even the South—which Preston, Tamasi, and other researchers have shown to be the most salient dialect region—is not geographically bound.

As other respondent maps yielded similar results (see Figure 3.5, as well as the Companion Website, for additional maps), Tamasi's study showed that folk perceptions of American dialects are not geographically cohesive. In other words, she found that geographic location was not the core means for grouping dialect areas, a finding that could not be revealed through traditional Prestonian mapping techniques. As such, when compared with previous perceptual studies, this pile sort methodology presents a unique picture of American speech.

3.8

To some, it might appear that the findings of perceptual dialectology are affected by respondents not having a sound grasp of US geography. This is not a far-fetched assumption, as a National Geographic study found that only half of 18- to 24-year-old Americans were able to locate New York and Mississippi on a map (Roach, 2006).

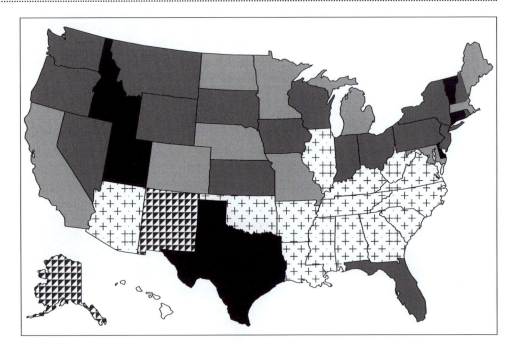

FIGURE 3.4 Six perceptual dialect regions from a Georgia respondent.

Source: Tamasi (2003).

However, as part of the methodology of Tamasi's study, respondents did have access to a labeled map of the United States that they could reference while creating their dialect piles. Respondents were also asked to think aloud while sorting cards, and their comments, which were audio recorded and later analyzed, indicate that they knew very well where the individual states were. Significantly, the respondents associated language with space or place without issue; not only did they complete the pile sort task with ease, but most also directly stated that arranging the piles was easy (and, for some, even fun). These incongruous dialect regions, therefore, are not simply a result of insufficient geographic knowledge or a lack of association between language and place. Instead, these perceived regions are products of multiple layers of geographic, social, and linguistic information that join together to inform respondents' mental maps and overall perceptions of language.

The respondent map presented in Figure 3.5 further illustrates the aforementioned finding—that multiple layers of information are bound together in folk perceptions of language. It also exemplifies one of the core and paradoxical findings of perceptual dialectology: Even though linguistic attitudes regularly reflect shared patterns and common evaluations, they also show that views are highly individualized. In this map from a New Jersey respondent, we observe more regional grouping than in the map

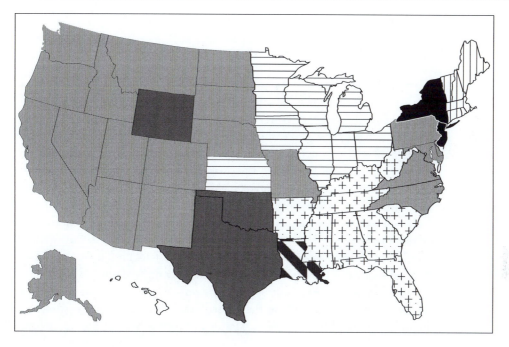

FIGURE 3.5 Eight perceptual dialect regions from a New Jersey respondent.

Source: Tamasi (2003).

from the Georgia respondent; in fact, it shows more geographic cohesion overall than most of the maps generated in the study (Tamasi, 2003). Furthermore, this New Jersey informant's responses provide an eye-opening glimpse into the various types of information that shape our views of American speech. Here, Texas, Oklahoma, and Wyoming (marked in dark gray) are placed together as an independent dialect region, indicating that the varieties of speech in these states are perceived to be similar to one another as well as distinctly different than those found in the rest of the country. When asked why he placed these together, the New Jersey respondent nonchalantly announced, "Because that's where the cowboys live."

While the responses of one individual may seem odd or even humorous, it is exactly this type of information—whether it be stereotype, personal experience, geographic knowledge, or even actual linguistic knowledge—that converges to form our views of language and the attitudes we hold toward linguistic variation. One common finding that further illustrates this point is that respondents regularly place Florida in the same dialect group as New York. When questioned about this choice, respondents stated that it is "common knowledge" that New Yorkers move to Florida when they retire and, as a result, the two places must share the same linguistic characteristics (Tamasi, 2003).

"Correct" and "Pleasant" Speech

In light of the findings from early research in social psychology, research in folk linguistics has also examined the social characteristics that non-experts associate with regional linguistic variation. These data not only allow for a better understanding of the different layers of information that affect non-expert views, but also help clarify the findings of respondents' mental maps.

3.9

Focusing on the issues of status and solidarity that had been found to be salient for attitudinal research in social psychology, Preston (1989) asked participants to rate each of the 50 states, plus New York City and Washington, DC, on a scale of one to ten (1 = least, 10 = most) for "correct" and "pleasant" speech. Here, "correct" was a surrogate for status traits, while "pleasant" stood for solidarity. Note that, in this task, Preston did not ask respondents to evaluate specific voices, as had been done in matched-guise tests; rather, he elicited these social traits as they related to informants' linguistic mental maps. Figure 3.6 is a composite map of Michigan speaker attitudes toward "correct" speech, and Figure 3.7 is a Southern view of "pleasant" speech.

3.10

This seemingly simple ratings task yielded several informative and intriguing findings about perceived "correctness" in the United States. First, the South, which is the most commonly perceived dialect region, stands out particularly as an area where

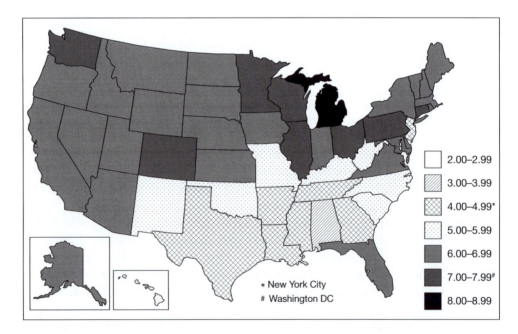

FIGURE 3.6 Michigan correctness ratings, on a scale of 1 (lowest) to 10 (highest).

Source: Courtesy of Dennis R. Preston.

"correct" speech does not exist. As shown in Figure 3.6, the Michigan respondents not only gave the South low ratings, they actually rated the Southeast lower than any other area of the country. Second, although it is more difficult to see on the map, the Michiganders also evaluated New Jersey and New York City, two other areas that are often stereotyped and stigmatized, as places of incorrect speech. Third, while disapproving of speech in the South, New York City, and New Jersey, the Michiganders were very secure with the speech in their own state. Not only did they rate the North and the Midwest higher than the rest of the US, they also rated the speech of Michigan, and only that of Michigan, highest of all.

3.11

Since speakers in Michigan claimed their own state to have the most correct speech in the US, one might assume that it is one's familiarity with a location that figures most prominently in the assessment of "correct" speech. However, while the home of the respondent has been shown to make a significant difference in respondent mental maps, research from the Southern point of view shows that the hypothesis that local speech is perceived as the most correct does not always hold (Preston, 1999; Tamasi, 2000, 2003). Instead, it has been found that negative stereotypes of stigmatized speech clearly run wide and deep, and speakers of these stigmatized dialects not only recognize that these stereotypes exist, they also appear to accept them as truth. For example, the Southern respondents in Preston (1997) rated the South lower in terms of correctness than they did much of the rest of the country, although they did not give themselves the lowest ratings possible. One such example is shown in Figure 3.2 above, in which the South Carolina informant characterizes Southern speech as hard to understand. In this respect, the findings of perceptual dialectology reinforce those of language attitude studies in social psychology in which language varieties that are considered linguistically standard or socially prestigious are regularly associated with high evaluations of status traits, while varieties that are nonstandard or stigmatized are given low evaluations for status, even by those who speak them.

However, when we examine the ratings of "pleasant" speech, we find an alternate, yet complementary, view of language. While nonstandard dialects are evaluated negatively for issues of status, they are given high ratings for issues of solidarity. Figure 3.7 represents the ratings of "pleasant" speech from a group of Southern informants at a university in Alabama (respondents were from Alabama, Georgia, and South Carolina). Here, we find a view of American dialects that is almost completely the opposite of that presented in the Michigan map of "correct" speech. And here, it is the South that is marked as pleasant, and the farther a state is from the South, the more negatively it is evaluated. Furthermore, these Southern informants marked the most "pleasant" speech in the United States as that which is found right at home, an assessment that parallels the Michigan respondents' own correctness score. In other words, while Southern respondents are willing to accept the view that their speech is substandard in terms of correctness, they continue to hold very positive views of the

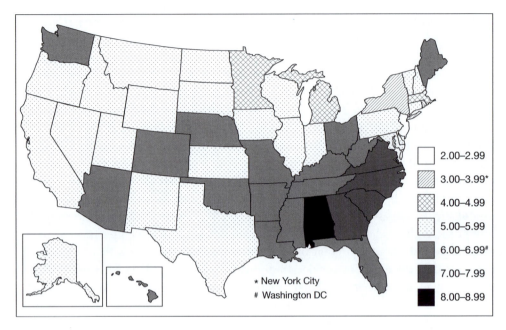

FIGURE 3.7 Southern pleasantness ratings, on a scale of 1 (lowest) to 10 (highest).

Source: Courtesy of Dennis R. Preston.

social aspects of their speech. One Georgia respondent even commented: "We may not be correct, but we sure are nice."

Therefore, the Southern informants' responses reveal a range of perceptions that people have of linguistic variation and standard versus nonstandard dialects, and they also provide insight as to why obviously stigmatized linguistic systems continue to be used. Remember, nonstandard dialects are still grammatical forms of language, and their use has nothing to do with whether a speaker is aware of the "correct" way to speak. Instead, nonstandard dialects are used—and furthermore, even thrive—because they reflect a sense of solidarity among their speakers. Language unifies us, and these dialects reflect a sense of community as well as a shared history among their speakers. Even though speakers of stigmatized dialects recognize that their speech is considered non- or even substandard—and such views are regularly reinforced by the media and the larger society—speakers continue to use these linguistic systems specifically because they sound pleasant, friendly, and trustworthy to them. For such speakers, these linguistic systems not only comprise but also represent traits of solidarity. For many, such as the respondent whose map is shown in Figure 3.8, this sense of community is often the crucial factor in informing linguistic perceptions. Solidarity clearly trumps status in this case.

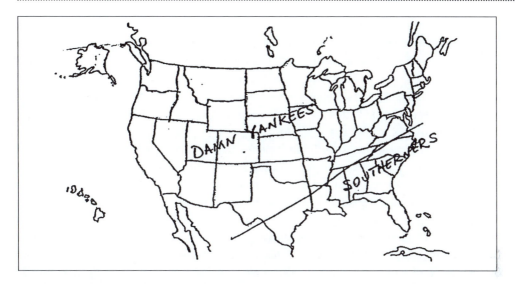

FIGURE 3.8 Another South Carolina hand-drawn map.

Source: Courtesy of Dennis R. Preston.

ADDITIONAL INSIGHTS FROM FOLK LINGUISTICS

Whereas in the matched-guise tests linguistic input (i.e., speech) was the primary means of determining outcome, studies in folk linguistics show that language attitudes can be elicited even in the absence of linguistic cues. Therefore, in examining these findings, we must recognize that while these are attitudes toward *language*, they are frequently not connected to actual linguistic data. People not only hold perceptions of language when there are no immediate linguistic cues to trigger such attitudes, they also carry specific, detailed attitudes toward speech they have never heard. For example, one of the respondents in Tamasi (2003) said that while she had never met nor heard anyone from Hawaii, she was positive that the speech there must be pleasant but not very correct. Thus, we might recognize that while some perceptions are based on personal knowledge of the speech of an area, others are regularly based on stereotype or anecdote alone. Furthermore, even if an attitude is based on a particular linguistic feature—a certain word or pronunciation, for example—the specific feature may not actually exist in the speech of the area where it is believed to be used.

The reality of studying language attitudes, however, is that the accuracy of the respondents' knowledge of linguistic features does not affect the significance of their perceptions. Even if one's perceptions are not based on actual dialectal features, he/she continues to carry the same perceptions, nonetheless. For example, did the New Jersey respondent who created the map in Figure 3.5 have personal experience with cowboys, or did he associate a particular linguistic feature with cowboy speech? Is it even true that cowboys live in these locations? If the answer to any of these questions is no, it doesn't matter: his attitudes still exist. Furthermore, does the potential disconnect between linguistic accuracy and respondent perceptions make studying these attitudes invalid? Emphatically, our answer is "No." These attitudes are not uninformative but instead are proven to be highly complex and individualized, and are therefore worthy of further study.

Additionally, in order to fully understand the influence of language attitudes in social interactions, it is crucial to recognize that many of the linguistic perceptions that we observe are not necessarily direct assessments of language itself. This is especially true of those that are negative. Instead, these linguistic perceptions are actually indicative of the attitudes toward the *speakers* of these linguistic varieties. As all dialects are linguistically equal and structurally complex, a particular linguistic system cannot be incorrect, uneducated, or unpleasant. Thus, the dialect assumes the stigma or prejudice that its speakers evoke. For example, the word *y'all*, the pronunciation of *pen* as [pɪn], or even Southern American English as a whole may be considered to be "bad English," not because of the development or structure of the linguistic system, but because of the lack of wider prestige for its speakers. Where this type of social, cultural, or political stigma originated is a long, complex historical discussion that we haven't the time to go into here. But just think for a moment: If the South had won the Civil War, would Southern speech still be viewed as ignorant and backward and Northern speech as socially and politically prestigious? Or, would that view be reversed?

Therefore, we must stress that while certain perceptions of speech promote highly negative views of language and its speakers, having judgments about or attitudes toward language is not problematic in and of itself. Having linguistic perceptions is perfectly natural: We all carry personal likes and dislikes about language, and we all associate social and regional information with particular types of speech. That said, it is crucial to recognize that many of these views stem from stereotypes or misconceptions about language, such as a standard language ideology, and are thus linguistically unfounded or insupportable. Subsequently, we must maintain awareness of the ways in which people act toward one another based on these attitudes. These linguistic perceptions may lead not just to negative judgments of individuals or groups of people, but as we discuss below, they can even lead to real cases of prejudice and discrimination.

Finally, in focusing on characteristics of status and solidarity, we find that linguistic perceptions reveal views toward other linguistic varieties as well as views of one's own speech community. As in the case of the Michigan respondents who agree that they speak the most correct English, some folks have high levels of **linguistic security**. Others, such as the Southerners in Preston's study, have accepted the view forced on them that their speech is incorrect, thus revealing signs of **linguistic insecurity**. Sadly, these attitudes toward dialects—particularly toward nonstandard varieties—flourish. Some speakers become so linguistically insecure, they even actively try to abandon their own speech patterns. In fact, accent reduction courses have exceptionally high enrollments in geographic areas with stigmatized speech.

There is one other crucial point that we must make about language attitude research. As this chapter focuses primarily on the findings from studies on perceptions of regional dialects, we must acknowledge that language attitudes exist for all types of linguistic variation, including those varieties associated with ethnicity, gender, sexual orientation, age, education, or socioeconomic status. Moreover, we restricted our discussion to that of the perceptions of English in the United States and, thus, excluded other languages used in the United States as well as the use of English elsewhere. Please see the Companion Website for a discussion of attitudinal studies that investigate these other issues.

3.12

3.13

LANGUAGE PREJUDICE AND LINGUISTIC DISCRIMINATION

Most attitudes toward language are simply benign observations, for example whether one finds the local speech to be pleasant or believes that Floridians sound like New Yorkers. However, there are some perceptions of language and linguistic diversity that are used as foundations for acts of **language prejudice** and **linguistic discrimination**. Examples of such acts include the removal of an individual from his job for having "too strong" an accent or, if because of his use of nonstandard speech, a candidate was never considered suitable for the job in the first place. As with race, sex, age, disability, or sexuality, the use of speech as the basis for prejudging someone can be highly problematic. However, the problem lies not in the fact that language attitudes exist, but in that many language attitudes, particularly those that are based on misunderstandings of language, are used to justify such prejudices. Furthermore, because attitudes toward language are generally a reflection of attitudes toward the speakers themselves, negative stereotypes of nonstandard language are often used as veils for other types of social discrimination. As Lippi-Green (2004) states: "Accent serves as the first point of gatekeeping because we are forbidden by law and social custom, and perhaps by a prevailing sense of what is morally and ethically right, from using race, ethnicity, homeland, or economics more directly" (p. 296).

Limitations of space allow for little coverage of language discrimination here; therefore, we refer interested readers to Rosina Lippi-Green's (2012) book *English with an Accent: Language, Ideology, and Discrimination in the United States*, as well as to our own Companion Website, for more information and a detailed discussion.

3.16

3.14

3.15

BOX 3.2 Housing Discrimination and Linguistic Profiling

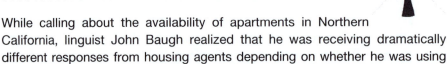

While calling about the availability of apartments in Northern California, linguist John Baugh realized that he was receiving dramatically different responses from housing agents depending on whether he was using features of African American English or Standard American English in his speech. Suspecting that he was being racially profiled based on his speech, Baugh developed a systematic way to study the connection between language and racial discrimination. Using a variation of the matched-guise test, Baugh called to inquire about available apartments and, in different calls to the same agent, alternated between Standard American English, African American English, and Chicano English, each of which is a natural part of his idiolect. (To hear Baugh describe the study and his methodology, including examples of his different guises, please visit the Companion Website.) In short, Baugh and his colleagues found that his use of Standard American English received more returned calls than either African American English or Chicano English. The researchers concluded that people were using linguistic cues to make judgments about the speaker's ethnicity, which they then used to determine whether they were willing to rent the speaker an apartment, a practice that is discriminatory and illegal (Purnell, Idsardi, & Baugh, 1999).

In a second study, Baugh and his colleagues created an experiment to test whether one could accurately assess ethnicity based on linguistic cues alone. Not only did they determine that their respondents could accurately identify the ethnicity of speakers in the study, they also found that the respondents could do so based solely on the first syllable of the word *hello* (Purnell et al., 1999). Therefore, their work in linguistic perceptions and **linguistic profiling** provides scientific evidence of the connection between language use and judgments of ethnicity, findings that can be used to inform cases of discrimination.

CONCLUSION

In this chapter, we examined what language attitudes are, how they are studied, and how they affect daily interactions. Additionally, we introduced a complex picture of how lay people (nonlinguists) view the language around them. Everyone makes personal judgments about speech, and it is perfectly understandable to find some voices or even some dialects more aesthetically pleasing than others. However, one must recognize that these opinions are simply that—opinions. Furthermore, it is crucial to acknowledge that even when shared by a larger community, many of these views are based on misinformation and, thus, are not factual statements about language. Therefore, one must not only acknowledge the perceptions and attitudes he/she personally holds, but also understand their origins (and possible consequences).

Often, linguistic attitudes are connected to a standard language ideology that promotes a singular view of language. As we discussed in Chapter 2, if one approaches language as a standardized, invariant structure, it would follow that all other, nonstandard forms are perceived as incorrect. However, we know that language naturally changes and varies. Thus, these attitudes are based on a prescriptive view of language rather than on the language itself. This is a crucial distinction to make, as there are significant, real-world consequences to the negative attitudes that proceed from this line of thought. For example, Lippi-Green concludes that because of negative attitudes based on a standard language ideology, whole groups of people become convinced that they "do not fully or adequately possess an appropriate human language" (2004, p. 296). Thus, an important goal of language attitude research is to show speakers that their voices are valid, no matter what dialects they speak or how others may perceive them.

The first three chapters of this book were designed to encourage readers to begin to think about language from different perspectives and to provide the tools needed for the critical examination of both language and the discussions surrounding it. In these chapters, we asked readers to reflect on their own ideas, views, and perceptions about language and to question their own linguistic beliefs. Following the presentation of this background information, the following chapters focus on discussions of actual language use in the United States, including the history and structure of regional and social dialects. We ask you, the reader, to think about the information provided in these first chapters as you work through the issues presented throughout the remainder of the book.

DISCUSSION AND RESEARCH QUESTIONS

1. Look back at the hand-drawn maps presented in this chapter and discuss each in terms of the respondent's linguistic security or insecurity.
2. Find an example of language attitudes in the popular media and analyze it based on the concepts presented in this chapter. Do the attitudes presented refer to regional variation or to social characteristics connected to language (or both)? Does your example reference a particular linguistic feature or features directly? Does it perpetuate a particular stereotype?

3.17

3.   Watch the clip of Ali G that is posted on the Companion Website and write an analysis of its portrayal of language attitudes, prescriptive and descriptive views of language, and/or a standard language ideology. (You should make sure to research who Ali G and Andy Rooney are before you begin your analysis.)

4.   Conduct your own study in perceptual dialectology. Using a map of the United States (downloadable from the Companion Website), or a smaller geographic area such as a single region or even an individual state, ask five to ten respondents to mark where people speak differently as well as where people speak "correctly" and "pleasantly." Make sure to have respondents note where they were raised as well as where they currently reside. Do their responses pattern with the findings presented in this chapter? Do these responses resemble your own linguistic perceptions?

3.18

Colonial American English

GUIDING QUESTIONS

1. How did the English that the early American colonists spoke differ from that spoken in the United States today?

2. How and why did British and American English diverge?

3. What roles did languages other than English, such as Spanish, French, Dutch, and various African languages, play in the formation of American English?

4. How did the development of American English parallel the creation of an American identity?

OVERVIEW

In this chapter, we examine the social and linguistic events in Great Britain and in North America that led to the emergence of American English as a colonial and, later, national variety. The separation of the English language on both sides of the Atlantic—physically, and then politically—played an important role in the divergence of American English from British English. However, this separation was only one of several factors contributing to the differentiation of the two varieties. Other factors included speakers from different parts of England being brought together in the New World; contact between colonists and speakers of the Native American languages that had existed in North America for thousands of years; and contact between English colonists and colonists from other European countries who arrived on the continent during the same period. Under these conditions and over time, American English emerged as a new variety modified to meet the linguistic needs of the New World, while at the same time distinguishing itself from British English and becoming an important symbol of American identity.

COMMON MYTHS

English was the first European language to have a continuous presence in North America.

The early British colonists all spoke the same type of English.

American English is simply a defective variety of British English.

Spelling differences between British and American English always indicate differences in pronunciation between the two.

INTRODUCTION

In the first few chapters of this book, our aim was to provide readers with a foundation in linguistics for understanding the discussions and debates that are presented in subsequent chapters. As such, we discussed language structure and use in general terms, while also examining how forces of standardization and language attitudes play a role not only in the way that speakers view language, but also in how they use it. In the next several chapters, we turn our attention to American English and its diversity in terms of regional, social, and ethnic variation. We begin in this chapter by focusing on the emergence of American English during a 200-year span that began with the advent of English colonization in North America and ended with the United States winning its independence from England, at which point American English rose in stature from a colonial variety of English to a national variety.

As some of the changes that impacted American English had been set in motion long before the American colonies were established, we begin by highlighting important events in the history of the English language leading up to and including the Age of Discovery. Then, we discuss the earliest British settlers and the first great waves of migration from the British Isles to the colonies, since the earliest continuous populations in a place wield a disproportionate influence on its subsequent makeup. We also address the presence of other languages in North America at the time of colonization and the linguistic effects they had on American English, particularly with respect to the lexicon. Finally, we address how American English diverged from British English and present some of the reasons for this divergence. In this chapter, we focus primarily on the past, whereas in the following chapters we examine variation in contemporary American English.

THE FOUNDATIONS OF COLONIAL AMERICAN ENGLISH

To understand the beginnings of American English, it is important to know the origins of the speakers who participated in its formation. More than 95% of those who settled in the original colonies were immigrants from Great Britain (Fisher, 2001, p. 59); thus, our primary focus is on early British settlers, their backgrounds and, to the extent that they are recoverable, the varieties of English they spoke before arriving in North America. In addition to describing the state of English at the time of colonization, we discuss changes that had been in progress in the language long before the first ships of English colonists set sail for the Americas. The continuation of these changes along different trajectories in the British Isles and in the American colonies played an important role in the divergence of British and American English.

At the time that the first English colonists were setting their course for the New World in the late 16th century, the English language had existed for about 1,000 years, the product of West Germanic-speaking Angles, Saxons, Frisians, and Jutes who sailed from present-day Denmark and Germany to invade present-day England beginning in AD 449.

4.1

As the invaders settled into communities in their adopted homeland and interacted with one another in various ways, their different dialects eventually developed into the English language. However, the language at this stage was very different from today's English; in addition to the version of the "Lord's Prayer" presented in Chapter 1, this selection from *Beowulf* also illustrates just how different it was:

> Hwæt! We Gardena in geardagum,
> þeodcyninga, þrym gefrunon,
> hu ða æþelingas ellen fremedon.
> Oft Scyld Scefing sceaþena þreatum,
> monegum mægþum, meodosetla ofteah,

egsode eorlas. Syððan ærest wearð
feasceaft funden, he þæs frofre gebad,
weox under wolcnum, weorðmyndum þah,
oðþæt him æghwylc þara ymbsittendra
ofer hronrade hyran scolde,
gomban gyldan. þæt wæs god cyning!
ðæm eafera wæs æfter cenned,
geong in geardum, þone god sende
folce to frofre; fyrenðearfe ongeat
þe hie ær drugon aldorlease
lange hwile. Him þæs liffrea,
wuldres wealdend, woroldare forgeaf;
Beowulf wæs breme (blæd wide sprang),
Scyldes eafera Scedelandum in.

4.2

Written at some point between the 8th and 11th centuries, *Beowulf* is an example of English that is commonly referred to as Old English, or Anglo-Saxon. The time span that marks the historical period that Old English was used in and the names and dates of other periods in the history of the English language appear in Table 4.1.

It is important to note that these periods are generalizations that help us to conceptualize, analyze, and discuss the language in historical terms. It should also be noted that the dates that are provided are not based purely on linguistic changes, as language change of any magnitude rarely happens in the abrupt way suggested by these dates; rather, these dates are often based on social events that are acknowledged to have had some bearing on language change. For example, the beginning of the Old English (OE) period is marked by the year that the Germanic invaders arrived in the British Isles, and its end is marked by the Norman Conquest. Both of these events were to have a significant bearing on the language to come.

With respect to its linguistic nature, Old English was, like the West Germanic dialects it descended from, highly **inflectional**; that is, its grammar required the use of morphemes called **affixes** (prefixes and suffixes) to indicate the grammatical roles that

TABLE 4.1 Periods in the history of the English
language

Period	Dates
Old English	AD 449–1100
Middle English	1100–1450
Early Modern English	1450–1700
Modern English	1700–present

TABLE 4.2 Declension of *dæg* 'day' in Old English

Case (Grammatical role)	Singular	Plural
Nominative (Subject)	*dæg*	*dagas*
Accusative (Direct Object)	*dæg*	*dagas*
Genitive (Possessive)	*dæges*	*daga*
Dative (Indirect Object)	*dæge*	*dagum*

Source: Adapted from Quirk & Wrenn (1957, p. 21).

words played in sentences. For instance, as shown in Table 4.2, the noun *dæg* 'day' was inflected depending on **case**, that is, the grammatical function of the word in a given sentence, and on whether the word was being used to denote singularity or plurality. In addition, OE marked grammatical gender (masculine, feminine, neuter) by inflecting nouns, and it also had a complex verb system.

From practically its very beginning, English has borrowed freely from a variety of languages, with particular languages having greater influence at different stages of its history. For example, during the OE period words were borrowed extensively from the Scandinavian languages of the Vikings who regularly invaded England at the time; these borrowings included *sister*, *skirt*, *sky*, and *window*. During the Middle English period, it was French that became the main source of borrowing by the English, as it was the language of power after the conquest of England by the Norman French in 1066. Thus, English speakers began borrowing French words to replace OE words and also adopted new lexical items for new concepts introduced by the French. Borrowing from French during this period was especially prevalent with respect to words relating to the law and government, and included the adoption of such words as *council*, *evidence*, *parliament*, and *tax*.

In addition to rampant borrowing from the French, several other important changes occurred in the transition from OE to Middle English (ME) at the levels of morphology and syntax. First, the use of inflectional endings to indicate case and gender were lost, partially due to phonological mergers in the unstressed syllables in word endings that made it difficult to hear subtle differences between them. Second, and related to the first, the language changed from being one that relied on case marking to indicate the grammatical roles of nouns in sentences to being one that relied on word order to indicate these roles (Curzan & Adams, 2006, p. 457).

4.3

As the ME period progressed, the linguistic varieties that began to emerge throughout England during the OE period developed into the regional dialects of Northern, Midlands (East and West), East Anglian, Kentish, and Southern (Curzan & Adams, 2006, p. 452), as represented in Figure 4.1. Of these, the Northern dialect was the most greatly influenced by the Scandinavian languages, particularly in terms of Scandinavian loanwords and the reduction of inflectional endings. At one time spoken

FIGURE 4.1 Major regional dialects of Middle English.

throughout southeastern England, including London, the Kentish dialect was very similar to OE in terms of syntax and morphology, but it had an innovative phonology. Its geographical range gradually diminished due to the expansion of the East Midlands dialect, especially after Kentish was replaced as the dialect of prestige in London by East Midlands. The Southern dialect was influenced least by the Scandinavian languages. Considered intermediate between the Northern dialect and the Southern and Kentish dialects, the Midlands dialect region comprised important differences between the East and West Midlands varieties. Most importantly, the Scandinavian languages exerted a much greater influence on East Midlands than West Midlands, and once adopted in London, East Midlands emerged as the British standard. Finally, East Anglian was the dialect spoken in the easternmost area of Britain and includes the counties of Norfolk, Suffolk, and Cambridgeshire; this dialect plays an important role in the story of American English because of the great number of East Anglians who migrated to the American colonies.

While ME dialects presented lexical and syntactic differences from one another, their major differences were phonological in nature. For instance, the pronunciation of words with /a:/ in OE was retained in northern England during the ME period but over time became /o/ in southern England, resulting in, for example, the articulation of *home* as [ha:m] in the North and [hom] in the South. Dialects also varied in their patterns of voicing for certain classes of words: speakers of Kentish voiced word-initial fricatives to produce, for instance, *vixen* 'female fox'; speakers of West Midlands devoiced past-tense endings in contrast to other ME dialects so that while an illness was *cured* in East Midlands, it was *icuret* in West Midlands (Curzan & Adams, 2006, p. 452). Dialectal differences also extended to the pronunciation of individual morphemes; for instance, in regional variation in verb endings used to show agreement with nouns based on number, *-s* was the verb ending used with third-person singular and plural nouns in the North (*It keeps*); *-th* in the South (*It keepeth*); and *-th* and *-en* for the singular and plural, respectively, in the Midlands (*It keepeth, they keepen*). (Works of literature representing the major ME regional dialects still exist today; see the Companion Website for examples.)

4.4

The Early Modern English period (*c.*1450–1700) corresponds roughly to the Age of Discovery, a period in which European powers began to explore the globe in search of new resources and alternative trade routes to existing markets. In 1497, John Cabot, an Italian seaman hired by the English to find a western route to the Indies, discovered a route to Newfoundland instead; his failure to reach the Indies led the English to abandon world exploration and focus on domestic issues, while other European powers continued to sail to the New World. It was not until the reign of Queen Elizabeth (1558–1603) that the English turned their serious attention back to North America once again; "[t]he change in English attitude toward colonization was the result of many factors: increasing nationalism, commercial expansion, international rivalries, religious changes as a result of the Protestant Reformation, and the intellectual renaissance" (Barck & Lefler, 1958, p. 22). Thus, the English set sail for the New World to establish colonies on several islands in the Atlantic Ocean and Caribbean Sea, as well as at several locations on the Atlantic coast of North America, as illustrated in Figure 4.2.

During the Early Modern English period, the lexicon of English expanded through exposure to languages throughout the world. Sometimes this exposure was secondhand, as English speakers adopted Native American words for foods produced in the Americas from Spanish before the English had ever set foot in the New World themselves. Such words included *avocado, chocolate, maize, potato,* and *tomato* (Bright, 1976, p. 217). The English playwright William Shakespeare (*c.*1564 to 1616) had knowledge of some of these words, as evidenced by their appearance in his writings. Many of the first English colonists in America were contemporaries of Shakespeare and would have been familiar with, if not speakers of, the same varieties of English used by him and the characters of his plays.

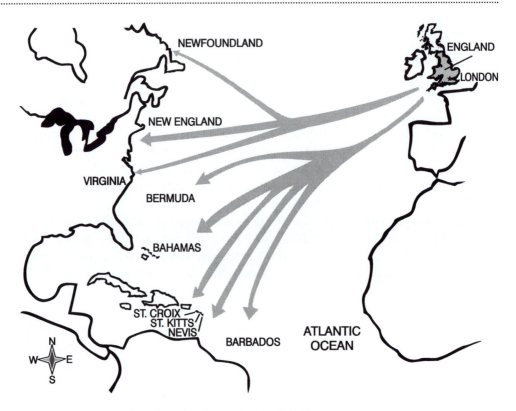

FIGURE 4.2 Routes of English migration to the New World.

Source: Courtesy of Dana Gorman.

Some of the variation that would later be exhibited in Colonial English was based on linguistic changes taking place in Great Britain at the time of the colonists' departure for the New World. One of these changes was the replacement of the old third-person singular indicative ending with the new, as in *taketh → takes*. As Fisher and Bornstein (1984, p. 261) point out, speakers and groups of speakers do not change from one of these forms to another overnight; rather, there is an alternation between both forms for a period of time. The following passage, written by Virginia colonist John Smith and published as *Generall Historie of Virginia, New England and the Summer Isles* (1624), shows consistent and conservative usage in regard to this change, as he only uses the older form:

About his person ordinarily *attendeth* a guard of 40 or 50 of the tallest men his Country *doth* afford. Every night vpon the foure quarters of his house are foure Sentinels, each from other a flight shoot, and at every halfe houre one from the Corps du guard *doth* hollow, shaking his lips with his finger betweene them; vnto whom every Sentinell *doth* answer round from his stand: if any faile, they presently send forth an officer that *beateth* him extremely.

(Reprinted in Fisher & Bornstein, 1984, pp. 30, 285–286;
emphasis ours)

Alternatively, the following passage from a personal letter written by the New England leader John Winthrop in 1630 or 1631 does show variation in his choice of these forms, using the *-th* ending in the word *hath* 'has' and the *-s* for all other third-person singular indicative verbs, as shown below.

Now (my good wife) let us [join] in praysinge [our] mercifull God, that (howsoever he *hath* afflicted us, both generally & particularly mine owne family in his stroke upon my sonne Henry) yet myself & the rest of [our] children & family are safe & in health, & that he *upholds* [our] hearts that we fainte not in all [our] troubles, but can yet waite for a good issue. And howsoever our fare be but coarse in respect of what we formerly had, (pease, puddings & fish, being [our] ordinary diet, yet he *makes* it sweet & whole-some to us, that I may truly say I desire no better: Besides in this, that he *beginnes* [with] us thus in affliction, it is the greater argument to us of his love, & of the goodnesse of the work [which] we are about; for Sathan *bends* his forces against us, & *stirres* up his instrument to all kinde of mischief, so that I think heere are some persons who never shewed so much wickednesse in England as they have doone heere.

(Reprinted in Fisher & Bornstein, 1984, pp. 284–285;
emphasis ours)

In time, use of the *-th* ending was nearly lost altogether, surviving primarily in works of literature, legal documents, and religious texts, rather than as a morpheme used in everyday speech.

Another important change to English occurring during American colonization was the **Great Vowel Shift**. This was a change that originated during the late Middle English period (in the 14th or 15th century) and involved the raising of long vowels from their historical positions to those of the next highest vowel; so that, for instance, the vowel sound of the word *room*, which was spelled with two vowels to show vowel length, shifted from [ro:m] to [ru:m]. Exceptions to the general trends of the shift included that the highest vowels became diphthongs, [ɛ:] was raised to [e] then to [i] in many cases, and [a:] was fronted to [æ] then raised to [e]. Examples are provided in Table 4.3.

As the Great Vowel Shift moved toward completion in the 17th and 18th centuries, English vowels were in a highly variable state; for instance, the shift was in its final stages in southern England, while the shift was only in its early stages in other areas of the British Isles (Montgomery, 2001, p. 142). Thus, since the people who migrated to the American colonies were from British communities at different stages in the shift, there were numerous vowel patterns employed by the colonists, and alternating forms were sometimes used even in the same colonies.

4.5

TABLE 4.3 Examples of words that underwent the Great Vowel Shift

Shift	Word	Pre-shift pronunciation	Post-shift pronunciation
[u:] → [aʊ]	house	[hus]	[haʊs]
[o:] → [u]	boot	[bot]	[but]
[ɔ:] → [o]	boat	[bɔt]	[bot]
[a:] → [æ] → [e]	make	[mak]	[mek]
[e:] → [i]	feet	[fet]	[fit]
[ɛ:] → [e] → [i]	beak	[bɛk]	[bik]
[i:] → [aɪ]	ride	[rid]	[raɪd]

4.6

Another change that English was undergoing at the time of American colonization affected its pronoun system, specifically the second-person pronouns. In Old English, the second-person pronoun *thou* and its variant forms (*thee, thy, thine*) were used to reference a singular person, while *you* and its variant forms (*ye, your, yours*) were used to address more than one person, with *thou* and *ye* being used as subjects and *thee* and *you* as objects (Crystal, 2004, p. 307). During the late 13th century, speakers began using *you* in place of *thou* in some social contexts, reflecting a similar phenomenon in other languages, such as French and German, in which the plural form is used to show formality or politeness. Additionally, *you* and *ye* became interchangeable in the subject position and, at some point in the 16th century, *you* became the standard second-person pronoun for both the subject and object position. By the mid-17th century, *thou* had disappeared from Standard English, remaining only in some regional varieties. Additionally, Quakers, disapproving of how social distance had been created by the use of singular *you*, began to use *thou* forms with everyone, believing that this better reflected the egalitarian discourse that Christ and his disciples would have had (Crystal, 2004, p. 310). Although its use was rapidly waning, *thou* was still in use at the beginning of English colonization in the Americas and sometimes surfaced in the early writings of colonists (see, for example, the writing of Roger Williams in Box 4.2 on page 78). Indeed, the form was still making its way into print in 1800; however, as illustrated in Figure 4.3, it has been in a steady state of decline in American books since the 1820s and is virtually non-existent in literature today.

The expansion of *you* at the expense of *thou, thee,* and *ye* represented a serious simplification of the earlier second-person pronoun system. However, it also meant the loss of a useful distinction between the singular and plural second-person pronoun that English speakers have been trying to regain ever since, as reflected in the adoption of such regional forms as *you all, you'uns, yinz, y'all,* and *you guys,* an issue we will return to in the next chapter.

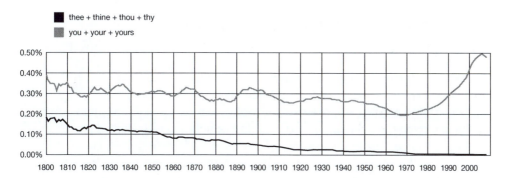

FIGURE 4.3 Distribution of *thou* and *you* in American books, 1800–2008.

Source: https://books.google.com/ngrams/.

The language spoken by English settlers bound for the Americas, therefore, had several significant differences from the English of today. Variation in the vowel system, in word endings, and in the second-person pronoun paradigm represented only some of the many changes that the language was undergoing at the time. The direction these changes would take in the colonies is an important part of the story of American English.

ENGLISH SETTLEMENT OF THE AMERICAN COLONIES

In his "Doctrine of First Effective Settlement," Zelinsky (1973) argues:

> Whenever an empty territory undergoes settlement or an earlier population is dislodged by invaders, the specific characteristics of the first group able to effect a viable, self-perpetuating society are of crucial significance for the later social and cultural geography of the area, no matter how tiny the initial band of settlers may have been . . . Thus, in terms of lasting impact, the activities of a few hundred, or even a few score, initial colonizers can mean much more for the cultural geography of a place than the contributions of tens of thousands of new immigrants a few generations later.
>
> (pp. 13–14)

The disproportionate effects that these earliest populations can have on later populations of a settlement make it important to document such groups to better understand later developments. In the case of American English, this means that a study of the earliest English settlements along the Atlantic seaboard allows for a better understanding of Colonial American English as a whole, but also sheds light on contemporary regional language use that we will explore in the next few chapters.

BOX 4.1 **The Lost Colony of Roanoke**

In 1584, Sir Walter Raleigh, under pressure from Queen Elizabeth to colonize North America, sent an expedition to Roanoke Island, an island off the coast of present-day North Carolina. Raleigh had hopes that building a colony on Roanoke would provide a port through which gold and other natural resources could be extracted from the New World and transported to England. At the same time, he believed the island could provide an ideal base of operations for conducting raids on Spanish ships carrying gold from the New World back to Spain.

After sending several voyages to Roanoke, the English finally colonized the island in 1587 when 150 men and women were transplanted there under the leadership of John White. However, the colonists—fearful of hostile relations with local Native American tribes—implored White to return to England to attain greater support for the colony. White finally relented and, in late 1587, left for England, leaving behind about 115 people, including Virginia Dare, the first child born in the Americas to English parents. Due to a series of mishaps, White did not return to Roanoke until the summer of 1590, and when he finally did return, he found that none of the colonists remained. Their disappearance remains a mystery that has given rise to several possible explanations concerning their fate and a nickname for Roanoke: "The Lost Colony."

As illustrated by the example of Roanoke (Box 4.1), it took several attempts before the English could establish an enduring colony in the present-day United States, and it wasn't until the early 17th century that they were able to do so. Migration to the colonies can be viewed in terms of four great waves (following Fischer, 1989):

1. the Puritans to New England (1629–1641);
2. the Cavaliers and their servants to Virginia (1642–1675);
3. the Quakers and others to Pennsylvania (1675–1725);
4. the Scots-Irish to Appalachia (1717–1775).

The English that emerged in the colonies was largely a product of those who entered the New World during these great waves of migration. Although Fischer identifies the colonists who traveled to New England as the first major wave of immigration, we begin our description of British settlement with the colonization of Virginia, as it was here that the English established their earliest permanent settlement in North America at Jamestown.

Virginia

In 1607, a group comprising more than 100 passengers assembled by the Virginia Company of London landed on a site near the Chesapeake Bay and began to develop the colony of Jamestown, Virginia. Toward this end, they built an Anglican church, created a government, and cultivated tobacco as a cash crop. Although Jamestown itself would fall into decay by the late 1600s as settlers made their way to more suitable land up the James River, the settlement marks the beginning of a continuous population of English speakers in what is now the United States. Therefore, 1607 is often acknowledged as the birth year of American English (Algeo, 2001, p. 4), despite that it ultimately took years for it to become a cohesive linguistic variety in its own right.

4.7

4.8

The major wave of migration to Virginia occurred from 1642 to 1675. Although these settlers came from every county in England, most were from the south and west of England, as well as the suburbs of London (Fischer, 1989, pp. 236–237). The settlers of Virginia tended to be from England's upper classes and lower classes; that is, the group included wealthy landowners as well as illiterate farmers and unskilled laborers from rural England (Algeo, 2001, p. 10). Many early Virginians were Cavaliers—Englishmen who had shown loyalty to King Charles I and King Charles II during and after the English Civil War. However, the majority of settlers who migrated during this wave were male indentured servants, that is, men who had signed contracts with landowners to work for a number of years (typically four to seven years) in exchange for transportation to the New World and food, clothing, and shelter for the duration of their servitude. In addition to this wave of migration, there were deportations of inmates—primarily offenders found guilty of such petty crimes as vagrancy—from London's Bridewell Prison and Hospital to Virginia from 1607 to the 1640s (Wright, 2001, p. 236). In 1619, Jamestown became one of the earliest sites for slave trading in the American colonies, and the resulting blend of upper- and lower-class British usage, as well as the language use of the slave population, became the basis of Southern American English (Algeo, 2001, p. 10).

4.9

New England

Whereas the Virginia settlers were a group of adventurers, landless men, and indentured servants seeking social and economic opportunity in the New World, the early migrations to New England were largely composed of entire families from the middle classes of England searching for a place to live freely according to the tenets of their religion. Many of these Puritan Separatists (or "Pilgrims," as their leader, William Bradford, called them) had left England in 1608 upon threat of religious persecution and had eventually settled in Leiden, Holland. However, after several years, many from the group became fearful that their children were becoming too Dutch. Thus, several dozen members of the Leiden congregation and additional passengers from London boarded the Mayflower and set out across the Atlantic Ocean bound for North

---

BOX 4.2 Roger Williams

There were rather strict rules of conduct in the Massachusetts Bay Colony, and those who refused to conform to the norms of the colony were prone to censure and, in extreme cases, banishment. One early resident of the colony who created controversy was Roger Williams, a theologian whose arguments for the strict separation of church and state, as well as for fair trade practices with Native Americans, put him at odds with leaders of the colony. On the brink of being banished from the Massachusetts Bay Colony, Williams left and subsequently founded "Providence Plantations" in present-day Rhode Island in 1636. There, Williams wrote a description of the Narragansett language that he called *A Key into the Language of America* (1643), which was the first description of a Native American language to be published in English. In its pages, Williams challenged the beliefs of many colonists concerning differences between themselves and Native Americans:

> Boast not proud English, of thy birth and blood
> Thy brother Indian is by birth as good.
> Of one blood God made him, and thee, and all.
> As wise, as fair, as strong, as personal.
> By nature, wraith's his portion, thine, no more
> Till grace his soul and thine in Christ restore.
> Make sure thy second birth, else thou shalt see
> Heaven ope to Indians wild, but shut to thee.

Williams was perhaps the first English writer to question explicitly the popular idea of the day that Europeans were superior to Native Americans.

America, landing at Plymouth on December 11, 1620. Settlement of New England began in earnest in 1630, with the arrival of Governor John Winthrop (whose written correspondence with his wife was presented above) and about 1,000 other Puritans with a charter granted by King Charles recognizing the Massachusetts Bay Company. The colony experienced heavy migration over the course of the next decade, giving rise to the cities of Boston and Salem. Among the New World colonies, the settlement of the Massachusetts Bay Colony was the most strongly motivated by religious freedom and expression, and the leaders of the colony challenged their residents to set a positive example for other cultures to follow, or, in the words of Winthrop, to be viewed "as a Citty upon a Hill" (as quoted in Boorstin, 1958, p. 3).

4.10

Although the early settlers of New England hailed from communities scattered throughout England, approximately 60% came from an eastern region of England that in 1643 was called the Eastern Association; in particular, the settlers came from the counties of Suffolk and Norfolk, the major counties of East Anglia, as well as Essex (Fischer, 1989, p. 33). Mainly consisting of craftsmen and their families, the group was generally motivated to migrate for political as well as religious reasons, although some individuals did migrate for purely economic reasons. Colonists in this group tended to be urban and literate, and their respect for education is evidenced by their creation of Harvard College in 1636. While Massachusetts has always been the cultural center of the New England region, settlement in outlying areas, such as the present-day states of Rhode Island and New Hampshire, occurred early in colonial history and helped establish the speech of East Anglia throughout the New England region.

4.11

Pennsylvania

Another wave of settlement began with the arrival of Quakers from the North Midlands and Wales in the Delaware Valley in 1675 and gained steam in 1681, when the Quaker William Penn received a charter from King Charles II to establish a colony in the New World and name it Pennsylvania. Although Quaker immigrants came to Pennsylvania from communities throughout England, they mainly came from the North Midlands (Algeo, 2001, p. 12). Pennsylvania, particularly southeastern Pennsylvania, appealed to other religious groups, too, including Lutherans, German Reformed, Amish, Mennonites, and Moravians. Other early Pennsylvania settlers were transplants from the German Rhineland and German-speaking Switzerland, French Huguenots who sought to escape war and religious persecution by transplanting primarily to south-eastern Pennsylvania, and the Scots-Irish, who will be discussed in greater detail below. Most of the early immigrants to Pennsylvania were farmers, but the group also consisted of artisans and shopkeepers.

4.12

Appalachia

The fourth wave comprised the Scots-Irish: commoners from northern England, northern Ireland, and Scotland who entered America at several points along the Atlantic seaboard and moved inland, finally settling in the Appalachian Mountains. Beginning in earnest in 1717 and lasting until 1775, this was the longest and largest of the great waves of immigration from the British Isles; it also lacked the political and religious motivations of earlier migrations (Algeo, 2001, p. 13). As Montgomery (2001) reports:

> In America the great majority of Scotch-Irish landed in Delaware or Pennsylvania and soon headed to frontier areas, reaching the interior of Virginia in the 1730s and the Carolinas in the 1750s. They and their descendants settled and were culturally

dominant in much of the interior or Upper South—the Carolinas, Georgia, Tennessee, and Kentucky—within two generations.

(p. 91)

4.13

Many of the cultural characteristics that the Scots-Irish brought to America with them were used to shape the culture of Appalachia, including their language. Fischer (1989), for instance, points out similarities between the speech of the American "backcountry," of which Appalachia is part, and the borderlands of the British Isles that include northern England and Scotland.

Although these were the four largest waves of migration to the American colonies during the formative years, they were hardly the only ones. For instance, in 1634 Maryland was established as a haven for Roman Catholics from Britain, despite that Protestants outnumbered Catholic settlers in the area from the beginning (Algeo, 2001, p. 9). Additionally, numerous English who were unaffiliated with any of the major waves migrated to the American colonies during the years between 1760 and 1775, many of them young, indentured males (Algeo, 2001, p. 14).

Thus, we see that by the time of the French and Indian Wars (1754–1763) a broad cross-section of the population of the British Isles had transplanted to the Atlantic seaboard of North America. These included people from all counties of England, as well as Scotland and Ireland. But it also included people from all walks of life, including wealthy landowners, indentured servants, farmers, clergyman, teachers, artisans, and even vagrants. People arrived on American shores from the British Isles, some as political refugees, others as adventurers and opportunists, others as outcasts. These differences were reflected in the varieties of English the earliest settlers spoke, and these varieties served as the foundation of Colonial American English.

OTHER LANGUAGES IN THE NEW WORLD

Speakers of English hardly lived in a vacuum in the New World, and early settlers often relied on the resources of speakers of other languages who were established in different parts of the continent before them, particularly Native Americans, but also French, Spanish, and Dutch explorers, traders, and colonists. Even in those cases in which there had been previous contact between speakers of English and speakers of other languages in Europe, the colonies presented a new setting for communication between these groups. In the subsections that follow, we describe languages other than English with a presence in and around the early British colonies in America. We should note that some of these languages will be covered in greater detail in Chapters 10 and 11, so here we concentrate on the influences these languages wielded on the development of Colonial American English.

Early in colonial history, British settlers lived along or near the Atlantic coast near neighboring indigenous tribes, including the Delaware, Massachusett, Powhatan and

Pequot. From these people, the settlers borrowed terminology for fauna (*chipmunk, moose, opossum, raccoon, skunk, terrapin*) and flora (e.g., *hickory, pecan, persimmon, squash, tamarack*) that they had had no knowledge of in the British Isles. Settlers also learned aspects of Native American culture and words that were useful for domestic life, including terms for foods (*hominy, pecan, pone, succotash*), housing (*tepee, wigwam*), cultural artifacts (*moccasin, tomahawk, totem*), and society (*papoose, squaw*), most of which were borrowed from the Algonquian family of languages (Bright, 1976, p. 217). There is no domain in the English lexicon that owes a greater debt to Native American languages, however, than place names, as numerous names for American states, counties, cities, rivers, lakes, and mountain ranges have been borrowed from languages that were spoken in North America long before the arrival of the first European explorers.

Some of the influence that Native Americans wielded extended beyond the simple borrowing of single words and, instead, referred to entire cultural concepts that were new and unfamiliar to the earliest explorers and colonists. For example, because the

---

BOX 4.3 Anglicization

When a language borrows a word from another language, it often changes the pronunciation of the word to agree with its own rules and conventions. This process typically results in such changes as shortening, consonant cluster reduction, vowel deletion, and the replacement of sounds that do not exist in the borrowing language with similar ones that do. In English, such changes are referred to as **Anglicization**. The words *squash* and *raccoon*, for instance, were Anglicized versions of the words *askutasaquash* and *arahkunem*, respectively, which were borrowed from the Algonquian languages. **Folk etymology**, which is a faulty inference by a speaker that an unfamiliar word has a certain meaning based on its superficial similarity to a known word, can also play a role in such changes. Thus, the Cree or Ojibwa word *otchek*, or *odjik*, became *woodchuck* (Pyles, 1971, p. 72), when the two syllables were reanalyzed as familiar English morphemes that could be associated with an animal often sighted near wooded areas. Another is the word *whiskey-jack* 'Canada jay' from the earlier *whiskey-john*, originating from the Cree *wiskitjân* (Bright, 1976, p. 217). Speakers of Halkomelem, a Central Coast Salish language of the Pacific Northwest, used the word *sthəqəy* to refer to a local fish; due to the difficulty English speakers had with comprehending and/or articulating the word, they derived the word *sockeye* from the original word by folk etymology to create the compound *sockeye salmon* (Denning & Leben, 1995, pp. 38–39).

early colonists were themselves subjects of European political systems that were only beginning to emerge from feudalism during the advent of colonialism in North America, they had little experience in making decisions by consensus; however, not only were they exposed to the concept of group meetings when they first met with Native Americans, but they learned the word that the Algonquian people had for such meetings: *caucus* (Weatherford, 1991, p. 197). These meetings were often attended by a holy man called a *powwow*, and because dance was one of the salient activities of these holy men, the colonists began using the word *powwow* for any Native American celebration and eventually applied it to their own celebrations (Weatherford, 1991, p. 203). Later, the meaning of the word was extended to refer to group discussions.

In addition to English colonists, the Spanish, French, and Dutch all established settlements in North America during the Age of Discovery. Of these, the Spanish were the earliest Europeans with a continuous presence in the present-day United States, but they did not have regular contact with the English, since their settlements were to the south and west of the English holdings. Spanish claims included the present-day states of Florida, where St. Augustine was founded in 1565, and present-day New Mexico, where San Juan was established in 1598 (Bills, 1997, p. 154). While the influence of Spanish on the everyday language of Colonial English was limited, Spanish exerted a great influence on the varieties of English that later emerged in the western United States, with some words eventually gaining national currency, including *cockroach*, *lariat*, *lasso*, *ranch*, and *tequila* (Marckwardt, 1958, pp. 41–42). Among the words that English borrowed from Spanish are those that Spanish had previously borrowed from Native American languages. For instance, Spanish borrowed the word *coyotl* from the Nahuatl language, and English in turn borrowed the word from Spanish as *coyote*; similarly, Spanish borrowed the Arawak word *barbacoa* 'wooden frame on posts,' and English borrowed it as *barbecue*.

Like the Native American languages, Spanish was the source of many place names in the United States, including the names of cities, counties, states, rivers, and mountain ranges. Spanish place names are particularly prevalent in areas that the United States acquired from Spain in the 18th and 19th centuries, including Florida, Texas, Colorado, and California. Many of these names have been Anglicized in various ways. In Colorado, for instance, *Rio de Nuestra Senora de los Dolores* and *El Rio de Las Animas Perdidas en Purgatoria* were shortened to their current official names: the *Dolores River* and the *Purgatoire River*, respectively; the latter is typically called the *Purgatory River*, and some locals refer to it as the *Picketwire* (Antieau, 2004). There were also names for geographical features that underwent literal translation from Spanish to English, as in a Colorado mountain that was named *Cuerno Verde* 'green horn' by the Spanish, now officially referred to as *Greenhorn Mountain*. A word created by literal translation in this way is called a **calque**.

Although they arrived after the Spanish, the French not only settled in the New World before the English, they were also the first Europeans to seek religious freedom on the shores of North America, when French Huguenots built Charlesfort on Parris Island in 1562 (Picone, 1997, p. 119). Once the English began colonizing in North America, Huguenots lived in communities scattered throughout the English land claims; however, the French presence was greatest outside the British colonies, particularly to the north, in eastern Canada and Maine, and west of the Appalachians. French words that were borrowed by early English speakers in America and still have a place in American English include *bureau, cache, cent, chowder, depot, dime, gopher, lacrosse, levee, mill, prairie, portage, pumpkin, rapids, rotisserie,* and *shanty* (Marckwardt, 1958, p. 35). As in the case of Spanish, some of the words that English borrowed from French in the colonies were words that French had previously borrowed from Native American languages; for instance, *caribou* originated from an Algonquian language and *bayou* from Choctaw *bayuk* 'stream' (Pyles, 1971, p. 52). French place names can be found throughout the United States, particularly in areas of early French exploration, as well as in sites in which the fur trade flourished, including the Great Lakes region, the Mississippi Valley, Louisiana, and the Rocky Mountains. These were, like place names of Native American and Spanish origin, also subject to Anglicization.

Dutch provides one of the best applications of Zelinsky's "Doctrine of First Effective Settlement" with respect to Colonial America. Despite arriving in the present-day United States later than other European colonial powers, including the English, the Dutch had an important presence on the Atlantic seaboard during the Age of Discovery, mainly in the area of present-day New York. In 1609, the English explorer Henry Hudson, on a quest to find a northwest passage to the Orient under the Dutch flag, traveled inland on the Hudson River to present-day Albany, claiming the entire area for the Dutch and calling it "New Netherland." Bearing the name "New Amsterdam," present-day Manhattan served as the site of a Dutch fur trading settlement beginning in 1625. In 1664, the English took possession of the Dutch holdings, renaming the region New York and the port New York City. Despite this transfer of title and power, the Dutch remained a major influence on the culture of New York, particularly in terms of architecture and people. Although they are not great in number, the Dutch words that have survived in American English are an interesting lot that include *boss, caboose, coleslaw, cookie, cruller, dope, dumb* 'stupid,' *poppycock, Santa Claus, saw buck, sleigh, smearcase, snoop, spook, stoop* 'porch,' and *waffle* (Marckwardt, 1958, p. 48). There are also many place names of Dutch origin in New York, including those ending in *-kill* 'channel,' such as *Catskill, Fishkill,* and *Schuylkill,* but also names that have been translated into English, including *Flatbush, Hell Gate,* and *Sandy Hook* from *Vlacht Bos, Helle Gat,* and *Zandt Hoek,* respectively (Doyle, 1907, p. 30), as well as *Bowery, Bronx,* and *Yonkers.* The word *yankee* is often attributed to the Dutch, but its etymology is unclear, as it is sometimes attributed to Algonquian tribes that met the first English explorers and settlers near the shores of the Atlantic.

The largest group of non-British immigrants in the colonies consisted of Germans, with several settlers arriving in Jamestown in 1608 and larger immigrations arriving in

4.14

Pennsylvania from southwest Germany as early as 1683 (Romaine, 2001, pp. 173–174). The majority of German words adopted by English include terms for food and drink, such as *sauerkraut*, *delicatessen*, *frankfurter*, *noodle*, *pretzel*, and *schnitzel*, but also include terms for social activities, such as *Christmas tree*, *pinochle*, and *turnverein*, as well as such words as *hex*, *nix*, and *ouch* (Marckwardt, 1958, pp. 52–53). Because Germans did not arrive in great numbers until somewhat late in the development of the colonies, there are few place names of German origin in the US, and those that do exist are generally in the Midwest and West, which we will discuss at greater length in Chapters 5 and 11.

The first Africans were transported to the American colonies in 1619 by a Dutch captain who traded 20 slaves in Jamestown for food; by the time Congress finally abolished the slave trade in 1807, an estimated 400,000 Africans had been transported to the United States (Algeo, 2001, p. 15). Although slavery expanded into the Northeast after its introduction in Virginia, the presence of African slaves in the North was never as significant as on the plantations of the Southeast, and it wasn't until the late 19th and early 20th centuries that migration resulted in significant African-American populations in the North (Mufwene, 2001, pp. 313–314). With respect to the lexicon, African words that have earned a place in American English include *banjo*, *hoodoo*, *juke*, *voodoo*, and *zombie*.

By the time of the first US census in 1790—which covered the 13 original states, the districts of Kentucky, Maine, and Vermont, and the Southwest Territory, which was the name for present-day Tennessee—the various migrations by Europeans and the

---

BOX 4.4 African Languages

Analogous to classifying such unrelated languages as German, Hungarian, Basque, and Finnish as "European" based on the continent where they originated, when we use the term "African" in reference to languages, we are referring to the continent where the languages originated and not necessarily to a historical relation between the languages. Africa constitutes a highly diverse and rich linguistic region with approximately 2,000 languages from four large language families in use on the continent (Heine & Nurse, 2000, p. 2). In addition to contributing to varieties of English, African languages have also played an integral part in the creation of creoles throughout the Western Hemisphere, including the language Gullah, or Sea Island Creole, which emerged in the islands off the coast of Georgia and South Carolina. Creole languages spoken in the United States are the focus of Chapter 13.

transportation of African slaves had contributed to a population of nearly four million in the United States (Algeo, 2001, p. 4). After the defeat of the British in the American Revolutionary War and the birth of a new nation, the time had come for Colonial American English to become American English, a national variety of language that would serve the needs of Americans in their everyday lives, including the need for an American identity separate from the British.

4.15

THE EMERGENCE OF AMERICAN ENGLISH

The creation of American English as a variety distinct from what we now call British English required three elements: space, time, and identity. Space in this context refers

---

BOX 4.5 Lexical Expansion in the New World

One of the strategies that speakers use to adapt their language to unfamiliar terrain is to broaden the definitions of terms that already exist in their lexicon to include the new referents they encounter, particularly those bearing a resemblance to or sharing similar functions previously covered by the term. Early American colonists, for example, expanded the semantic range of the English word *corn* 'grain' to include the vegetable the Native Americans called *maize*; eventually, the semantic range of *corn* was narrowed to arrive at its current meaning in American English. Other words applied in similar ways to refer to new entities included *bluff*, *cliff*, *neck*, *bottoms*, *pond*, and *creek* (Boorstin, 1958, p. 276).

Compounding, the joining of two or more independent words as a single word, is the most common word-formation strategy in many languages of the world (Bauer, 1988, pp. 33–34) and has been productive in English since the days of the Angles and the Saxons (Pei, 1967, p. 23). Compounding was particularly productive in the creation of new words for encounters in the New World, as evidenced by the creation and adoption of such compounds in American English as *bullfrog*, *mudhen*, *catbird*, *catfish*, *razorback*, *gartersnake*, and *groundhog*, as well as *backwoods*, *backlog*, *backstreet*, and *backcountry* (Boorstin, 1958, p. 276). It is also not unusual for compounds in American English to combine words from different languages, such as *cornpone* (from English *corn* + Virginia Algonquian *pone* 'bread' = a type of cornbread); *sleigh bells* (from Dutch *slee* 'sled' + English *bells*); and *ranchman* (from Spanish *rancho* + English *man*).

to the thousands of miles of ocean between English speakers in Europe and those in America, which, at that time, made it impossible for speakers on both sides of the Atlantic to converse on a daily basis with each other. For the colonists, this space meant isolation from the British Isles and the varieties of English that were continuing to evolve there. At the same time, the colonists were disproportionally influenced by each other, a relatively small group of speakers with whom they communicated every day. Space also refers to the new and unfamiliar geographical features that the colonists encountered in the New World; accounting for these features linguistically meant reshaping the English language, particularly with respect to the lexicon. Differences between the New World and Old were reflected in the areas of weather, people, topography, and flora and fauna, as well as, secondarily, the occupations and recreational activities made possible by these differences, as was illustrated above. While some of these words and concepts were an integral part of colonial life, many had little or no value for people who remained in the British Isles and, as such, were never adopted by them.

Space alone, however, did not create American English. The Jamestown settlers did not wake up in the New World after their long voyage and begin speaking a variety of English distinct from the variety they had used in England; rather, it took time for a definitely American form of English to develop. Some linguistic changes were set into

---

BOX 4.6 Printing and the Written Word in Colonial America

The presence of advanced technology early in the development of Colonial America may have contributed to the ease of communications between colonies and had a stabilizing influence on the linguistic habits of different groups of speakers. The first printing press in the colonies went into operation in Cambridge, Massachusetts, in 1639, and additional presses were established in Philadelphia and New York in 1685 and 1693, respectively; by the year 1765, there were 43 newspapers operating in the colonies (Blake, 1972, p. 93). Early in the development of the colonies "[t]he printed word ceased to be the property of a literary class and began to belong to the public" (Boorstin, 1958, p. 267), and "[t]he increased interest in reading and writing in the late colonial period is closely related to the fact that the American Revolution has been called 'the most literate war' ever fought" (Barck & Lefler, 1958, p. 414). While the effect that this access to the written word might have had on early American speech is open to debate, at the very least colonists of different dialects were bound together by the written word and their ability to read it (Pei, 1967, p. 74).

motion on one side of the Atlantic and not the other, as in the lexical expansion that was occurring in American English, some of which made little or no impact on British English, while at the same time, linguistic changes were occurring in Britain that had little effect on American English. Some of these changes were the result of contributions from other languages in the New World, including those of the Native Americans, as well as Spanish, French, and Dutch. In this way, the English language was reshaped to meet the needs of the American experience over time.

Just as the United States earned its independence on the battlefields of the Revolutionary War, American English had to earn its status as a unique variety of English. One of the first publications to attempt to devise an exhaustive set of unique American features appeared in 1781, when the Scotsman John Witherspoon, who served from 1768 to 1794 as the president of the College of New Jersey (later renamed Princeton University), presented his collection of "Americanisms"—a term he used to refer to words, sayings, and "grammatical errors" associated with the English of the American colonies (Fisher, 2001, p. 66). Witherspoon's collection was followed by similar works, such as Pickering's *Collection of Words and Phrases Which Have Been Supposed to Be Peculiar to the United States of America* (1816), suggesting that the American experience had indeed carved out its own particular brand of English.

Finally, it wasn't enough for American English to be viewed as separate from British English, it also needed to be recognized as its equal, if not by the British, then at least by its own speakers. Even after the War of 1812, American English was being compared unfavorably to British English, by scholars and pundits on both sides of the Atlantic. For instance, the American linguist and philologist John Pickering (1816) wrote:

> It is true, indeed, that our countrymen may speak and write in a dialect of English, which will be understood in the United States; but if they are ambitious of having their works read by Englishmen, they must write in a language that Englishmen can read with pleasure.

> (p. 2)

British literature, in particular, served as the standard by which all other English literature was measured, leading the British writer and cleric Sydney Smith (1820) to pose the question: "In the four quarters of the globe, who reads an American book?"

However, two developments in the early 19th century raised the status of American English immeasurably. One was the birth of an American literature that, rather than emulating British literature, was to find its own voice, with the work, for example, of Washington Irving, William Cullen Bryant, and Edgar Allan Poe. A second development was the publication of Noah Webster's *American Dictionary of the English Language* (1828), which established rules for the spelling, grammar, and pronunciation of the American variety of the English language. These developments served to command new respect and authority for American English globally and in the estimation of its own speakers.

4.16

In addition to its use of individual features that differentiated it from British English, American English also presented some general characteristics that observers commented on early in its development. The first of these was its relative homogeneity compared to the diversity of English as it was used in England. For instance, Pei (1967, p. 74) contends that "[o]ne trait of American English which was recognized almost as early as the language itself is its fundamental tendency toward unity." Witherspoon (1815) reports:

> The vulgar in America speak much better than the vulgar in Great Britain, for a very obvious reason, viz. that being much more unsettled, and moving frequently from place to place, they are not so liable to local peculiarities, either in accent or phraseology. There is a greater difference in dialect between one county and another in Britain, than there is between one state and another in America.
>
> (p. 269)

In addition to the role that mobility in the colonies might have played in this perceived uniformity of American English, scholars proposed that this uniformity was the product of **colonial leveling,** a tendency of all colonies toward linguistic uniformity. In Colonial America, this process manifested itself in the avoidance of dialectal forms that distinguished speakers as being from a specific English community in the Old World in favor of broader terms that marked the speaker as a member of the New World.

In addition to uniformity, another issue pertaining to American English and other varieties of English with colonial roots is the idea that colonial varieties of a language are more conservative than the parent variety. As an early proponent of this view, Ellis (1869–1889) claimed:

> there is a kind of arrest of development, the language of the emigrants remains for a long time at the stage in which it was at when emigration took place, and alters more slowly than the mother tongue, and in a different direction. Practically the speech of the American English is archaic with respect to that of the British English, and while the Icelandic scarcely differs from the old Norse, the latter has, since the colonization of Iceland, split up on the mainland into two distinct literary tongues, the Danish and the Swedish. Nay, even the Irish English exhibits in many points the peculiarities of the pronunciation of the XVIIth century.
>
> (p. 19)

The notion that colonial varieties preserved forms that had outgrown their usefulness in the parent variety is called **colonial lag** (Marckwardt, 1958). In the United States, this concept has been particularly applicable to the speech of isolated areas, such as Appalachia or North Carolina's Outer Banks, and has resulted in characterizations of language varieties used in these places as "Elizabethan" or "Shakespearean." In describing Appalachian speech, Frost (1899), for instance, contends:

the rude language of the mountains is far less a degradation than a survival. The Saxon pronoun "hit" holds its place almost universally. Strong past tenses, "holp" for helped, "drug" for dragged, and the like, are heard constantly . . . The greeting as we ride up to a cabin is "Howdy, strangers. Light and hitch your beastes." Quite a vocabulary of Chaucer's words which have been dropped by polite lips, but which linger in these solitudes, has been made out by some of our students. "Pack" for carry, "gorm" for muss, "feisty" for full of life, impertinent, are examples.

(p. 313)

That archaisms do exist in American English, particularly in isolated regional dialects, has been well documented.

Recently, however, some scholars have assessed the concept of colonial lag as oversimplified and its role in distinguishing American and British varieties of English as exaggerated (Görlach, 1987; Hundt, 2009). Hundt (2009), in particular, argues that characterizations of American English as presenting signs of colonial lag not only greatly simplify the relation between American and British English but suffer from attempting to understand language change through a linear model; rather, American English was actively changing to meet the myriad needs of the members of its evolving speech community, just as British English was undergoing its own changes. As Fisher (2001, p. 74) points out, earlier scholars such as Krapp (1925) and Kurath (1928) showed that all features of American pronunciation could also be found in the dialects of Britain. Thus, although the frequency with which individual features appear in the two varieties might differ, the inventories of both varieties comprise many of the same elements, and favoring one feature over another could be as much an act of identity as any inclination toward conservatism or progressivism.

BRITISH VERSUS AMERICAN ENGLISH

In 1877, the philologist Henry Sweet predicted that within a century "England, America, and Australia will be speaking mutually unintelligible languages owing to their independent changes of pronunciation" (1877, p. 196). Yet, it still seems that speakers of British, Australian, and American English have only minor difficulties communicating with one another today. Furthermore, even those problems that do occur in speech can be alleviated through negotiation and are not generally seen as a problem in writing.

This is not to say, of course, that there are no linguistic differences between British and American English, nor that such differences are confined to a single aspect of the English grammar, as, in fact, they exist at every level. Differences in pronunciation are perhaps the most apparent; some general distinctions are that speakers of American English tend to pronounce the vowels of unstressed syllables that British speakers often delete, as in the third vowels in the words *inventory* and *military*. In words ending in the letters <ile>, such as *fertile*, *fragile*, and *servile*, British speakers tend to pronounce the second syllables as the diphthong /aɪ/, while speakers of American English generally pronounce them with a reduced vowel or syllabic /l/, so that, for instance, the American pronunciation of *fertile* rhymes with *turtle*. Differences in the pronunciation of individual words also exist; for instance, the initial sound of *schedule* is a single consonant /ʃ/ in British English but is /s/ (followed by /k/) in American English.

There are also grammatical differences between the two varieties. For instance, in British English, it is acceptable to say "I must go to hospital" or "He goes to university," whereas speakers of American English generally use the definite article before *hospital* or *university*. American English and British English also differ in their grammatical treatment of collective nouns: in American English, speakers generally use the singular verb in sentences such as "The government is inefficient," whereas British speakers have the option of treating such nouns as either singular or plural (Butters, 2001, pp. 336–337).

4.17

In addition to differences in pronunciation and grammar, there are also lexical differences between the two varieties. A small sample of these differences is presented in Table 4.4. Such examples are further support for the idea that the link between words and their referents is arbitrary, as discussed earlier in Chapter 1. It is also worthwhile to note that while British and American speakers tend to use one of the two variants in accordance with the national preference, these variants are not group exclusive, for example the word *flat* appears in real estate advertisements in many American cities,

4.18

including Milwaukee, Wisconsin, which is home to many of the *Polish flats* that survive in the US today. Finally, there are differences in the spelling systems of the two varieties, as illustrated in Table 4.5. While some differences in British and American spelling are indicative of pronunciation differences between the two varieties, for example *glycerin/glycerine*, *aluminium/aluminum*, the pairs illustrated in Table 4.5 are not motivated by such differences (Upward, 1997). Furthermore, American English spelling does not merely present minor deviations from British spelling; instead, it is a

4.19

TABLE 4.4 Some lexical differences between British and American English

British	American
flat	apartment
pavement	sidewalk
rubber	eraser
chips	fries
tram	trolley
trolley	shopping cart

TABLE 4.5 Some spelling differences between British and American English

British	American
Americanisation	Americanization
colour	color
catalogue	catalog
programme	program
travelled	traveled
centre	center

system with a history and style of its own (Venezky, 2001, pp. 352, 355). Some differences in the systems were motivated by the desire on behalf of Americans to declare their independence from a British convention, but more often they reflect the efforts of spelling reform that have a long history in the United States.

CONCLUSION

In this chapter, we have examined issues surrounding the development of American English, which began life in North America as a colonial variety and then became a national variety as the colonies gained their independence from Britain and forged ahead as a new country. An important part of the development of any language or variety is the population of speakers that exists at the initial stages; therefore, we have described in some detail who these speakers were and the language that they might have used. Because of the great distance between England and its American colonies, there was relatively little communication between the two places, and thus linguistic changes occurred in both places independent of one another, leading to divergence between the two varieties. Furthermore, despite English being the primary means of communication among and within the American colonies, other languages had a presence in or near the colonies, and these languages also contributed to differences between American and British English, particularly in terms of the lexicon.

The variety of English to emerge in the American colonies was not improper or incorrect; rather, it reflected differences in the social histories of the British American colonies and England. These included differences in the sets of people who used the varieties, the social structures in which they used them, the cultural norms and values of the two peoples, and even in the physical geography of the two places. Finally, divergence of American English from British might also be in part attributed to the projection of a new identity by Americans, eager to declare their independence from the Old World through such linguistic acts of defiance as the coining of "Americanisms," the borrowing of words from Native American languages, and even a spelling system to represent a New World English.

DISCUSSION AND RESEARCH QUESTIONS

1. As discussed in Chapter 1, language reflects the identity and the experiences of its speakers. Discuss what the development of a Colonial American English reveals about the development of a new American identity.
2. Consider the use of the family tree model, as presented in Chapter 1, as a representation of the historical relationship of languages to one another. One way

to look at the division between American and British English is that of American English branching off from British. Is there enough evidence to suggest that these varieties of the same language should actually be considered to be two distinct languages? Why or why not? Are your reasons social or linguistic? State your reasons.

3. As discussed in Box 4.6, printing was an important part of life in Colonial America from almost the very beginning. Brainstorm ways in which printing affected American English and its separation from British English that weren't mentioned in the text box.

5 Regional Variation in American English

GUIDING QUESTIONS

1. What are the regional dialects of English in the United States?

2. Why do regional patterns of speech exist?

3. What linguistic features are associated with different regions of the US?

4. Are regional differences in American English disappearing due to mobility and mass communication?

OVERVIEW

In this chapter, our focus is on regional variation in American English. We first examine some of the reasons for regional variation in language, both in general terms and with particular reference to the American experience. Then, we discuss the major American dialect research projects, in terms of their methods and aims, as well as in terms of how their results proceed from empirical data that have been systematically collected to reveal patterns in regional American English. The results of these projects together provide evidence of four major regional dialects of American English: the North, the South, the Midland, and the West. As part of this chapter, we describe the social histories of these regions and the linguistic features associated with them, particularly at the levels of phonology and the lexicon. We also describe several subregions. Finally, we discuss the current status of American regional dialects, which are persevering in spite of the homogenizing effect that compulsory education, the geographic mobility of Americans, and the influence of the mass media are assumed to have on regional language variation.

COMMON MYTHS

The weather of a particular region has an effect on the linguistic features of the region's inhabitants; for example, Northerners exhibit nasality because of the cold winters they endure, and Southerners have a drawl due to the high temperatures and humidity of the South, which work together to slow down their rates of speech.

Lifelong inhabitants of the American West speak the purest form of American English.

Inhabitants of Appalachia speak a variety of Elizabethan English and therefore talk much like Shakespeare did.

The linguistic feature y'all *is only used in the Southern United States, and all native Southerners use it.*

INTRODUCTION

In the previous chapter, we described American English as a colonial variety that emerged as its speakers reshaped the varieties of English they brought with them from Britain by adopting words from languages they encountered in the New World and using their linguistic creativity to meet the cognitive and communicative demands of the American experience. As part of that discussion, we focused on the cohesion of Colonial American English rather than its diversity in order to draw comparisons between it and British English.

Despite the perceived homogeneity of Colonial American English, regional and social differences in the speech patterns of the colonies did exist, and they began to attract attention as early as the 1740s (Forgue, 1986, p. 512). Such differences would be expected given the variety of social groups that migrated to different parts of North America, as discussed in the previous chapter; however, it wasn't until the United States attained cultural, economic, and political status on its own terms that attention turned from the nation's differences with Britain to its own regional differences. As the country developed and matured during the 19th and 20th centuries, these regional differences continued to gain recognition by linguists and nonlinguists alike.

Regional variation in American English remains an area of interest to academics and the public at large today, as evidenced by its coverage across a broad range of media; for instance, countless books, journals, newspaper articles, websites, and even comedic sketches have been devoted to highlighting differences between regional varieties of American English. Recently, *The New York Times* even reported that its most frequently visited story in 2013 was an interactive feature centering on a dialect quiz (Meyer, 2014). American regional dialects are fascinating, not only for what they say about other Americans but for what they tell us about ourselves and our communities, and they present this information through an aspect of culture that everyone can relate to on some level: language.

5.1

Our focus on language variation in the next few chapters means a return to several concepts that were introduced in Chapter 1, including *dialect* and *shibboleth*. This chapter also builds on our discussions of language standards and attitudes in earlier chapters. As shown in Chapter 3, non-expert views of, and perceptions about, regional speech are common—and are strongly held—but they are also often incorrect or based solely on stereotype. In this chapter, we focus on the facts of regional American English as determined through the efforts of **dialectology**, the systematic study of dialectal variation. Additionally, we examine the factors that play a role in regional dialect formation and, in particular, how these factors played a role in the formation of regional dialects in the US.

FACTORS IN DIALECT FORMATION

According to research, regional variation in American English is the product of some of the same conditions that factored into the divide between American English and British English. These include settlement history, physical geography, contact with other languages, and the influence of cultural centers (McDavid, 1958). In this section, we focus on how these factors promote dialect differences, and we show how specific linguistic features associated with American regional dialects have resulted from these factors.

Settlement History

Just as settlement history was a factor in the linguistic differences of colonies along the eastern seaboard, it also played an important role in the formation of American regional dialects. As Americans expanded the frontier westward, and to a lesser extent northward and southward, they took with them the speech of the cities they originated

5.2

in, such as Boston, New York City, Philadelphia, and Charleston, a trend that continued after the United States gained its independence and well into the 19th century. Early migrations inland often occurred in a due westerly fashion to the extent that geography would allow for unimpeded travel. Construction of the National Road began in Cumberland, Maryland, in 1811, and by the end of the decade the road was being used by thousands of settlers to cross the Allegheny Mountains on their way into the state of Ohio and beyond. North of the National Road, the Erie Canal opened in 1825, providing a waterway for the passage of goods and passengers from the Atlantic Ocean to the Great Lakes region. From the southeastern coastal cities of Charleston and Savannah, migration proceeded into the interiors of South Carolina and Georgia, with subsequent migrations leading into the present-day states of Alabama, Mississippi, Louisiana, Tennessee, and Arkansas. Just as these routes allowed for the inland passage of Americans, they also allowed for immigrants who entered through eastern ports to take their languages into the heartland of the nation as well.

In the mid-19th century, the appeal of homesteading on the Great Plains or striking it rich in the mineral rushes of California, Colorado, and other western territories led many easterners to heed the imperative (commonly attributed to Horace Greeley) to "Go West, young man, go West and grow up with the country." While much of the impetus for migration to the West had economic motivations, some groups ventured west for religious or political freedom. The Church of Christ of Latter-Day Saints, for instance, migrated from Upstate New York to present-day Utah to practice their religion freely, and eventually established communities throughout the West (Meinig, 1965).

The large-scale migrations of the 20th century had very different orientations from the westward migrations of the 19th century. For example, northern industrial cities such as Chicago, Cleveland, Detroit, and Milwaukee received an influx of Southerners during and after both World Wars, as part of a general movement to the Great Lakes region for jobs in manufacturing. Beginning in the 1970s, trends in migration patterns once again began to change, as a decrease in manufacturing in America's "Rust Belt" spurred migrations out of the Northeast and Midwest and into the South and West (Anderton, Barrett, & Bogue, 1997, p. 339). Such large-scale migrations often result in dialect mixture, by allowing native inhabitants of one region to contribute linguistic features to new regions. Conversely, these migrations sometimes produced closely knit communities in which speakers retained much of their culture, including their speech, as observed in the presence of Appalachian English in Ypsilanti, Michigan (Evans, 2004) and in the Wisconsin "cutover" region (Larmouth & Remsing, 1993).

Physical Geography

Theories concerning the effects of physical geography on language variation have resulted in a number of unsupportable claims. As pointed out by McDavid (1958), even some scholars have attempted to link linguistic variation with climate:

the "Southerner" is supposed to speak with a drawl, because the climate is so hot that it makes him lazy, although Bengali, in a far hotter climate, is spoken at an extremely rapid tempo. A professor of pedagogics at the University of Colorado once declared that Minnesotans nasalize their speech because of the damp climate; Eric Partridge [a 20th-century lexicographer] has repeatedly attributed the supposed nasalization of Australian speech to the excessively dry climate. When so many claims, often contradictory and often in complete disagreement with observable fact, are made for the influence of the climate, it is easy to see that the investigator must look elsewhere for the origins of dialect differences. He finds these origins in the relationships among people.

(pp. 482–483)

McDavid (1958, p. 484) notes that physical geography does not have a direct impact on speech but, instead, has indirect effects on speech by influencing such factors as migration patterns and contact between different communities.

The impact that physical geography has on migration and settlement histories was noted above in that Americans selected certain westward routes due to the presence of mountain ranges, which impeded migration, and rivers, which both impeded and facilitated westward progress. Geographical features and/or long distances between communities can also lead to isolation, which can lead to dialectal differences; for example, the isolation of Appalachian communities, as well as those of Tangier Island in Chesapeake Bay and Ocracoke Island in North Carolina, has played its part in producing some of the most distinct dialects in the country. Finally, the way in which speakers codify geographical features in their surroundings can have an impact on regional and local lexicons. The first English speakers in the West, for example, borrowed words such as *arroyo*, *corral*, and *mesa* from Spanish; repurposed *park* and *hole* to mean 'mountain meadow' and 'mountain valley,' respectively; and coined (via compounding) *cottonwood*, *copperhead*, and *bull snake* (Marckwardt, 1958, p. 87) in response to environmental differences between the eastern and western US. While some words acquired in this manner were eventually absorbed into general American English, others remained useful only in the West and became shibboleths of the region.

5.3

Cultural Centers

Cultural centers often exert an influence on smaller communities in the same region. As McDavid and O'Cain (1973) observe: "Cities are not atypical of the geographical areas in which they lie, but are cultural foci from which the urban linguistic consensus —a complex of blended regional characteristics and urban innovations—radiates" (p. 141). Thus, cities such as Boston, Charleston, Chicago, New Orleans, and Los Angeles absorb regional characteristics and then diffuse them throughout metropolitan areas to reinforce regional identity, doing so through media outlets and education but, more importantly, through the interactions of city dwellers and those who come to the city from outlying areas for work and recreation. The kind of language that is emblematic for a region occasionally surfaces at the national level, often via film and television as well as through the success of musical acts or regional sports franchises, where it is open to imitation and, occasionally, ridicule. These include such slogans as *Who Dat?*, *Boston Strong*, or *Mile High Salute*.

Contact with Other Languages

Regional dialects can also be influenced by the presence of other languages. The effect of these languages is especially apparent in the lexicon and is particularly prevalent in

---

BOX 5.1 **Food for Talk**

In addition to place names, the most recognizable linguistic contributions to American English by speakers of non-English languages are perhaps in the names of foods, in terms of both ethnic dishes and the ingredients that go into making them, with some of these becoming regional shibboleths in their own right. For instance, some of the lexical contributions of African languages to Southern American English were *goober* 'peanut,' *gumbo*, *okra*, and *yam*. In Pennsylvania, sizable German and Polish populations contributed the foods *scrapple* and *pierogi*, respectively, and thus the names of these foods were added to the lexicon of the region. The Danish contributed a pastry called the *kringle* to southeastern Wisconsin culture. A pastry filled with meat and vegetables called a *pasty* [pæsti] was introduced by Cornish miners (or *Cousin Jacks*, as they were called) to mining regions in Pennsylvania, the Great Lakes region, and the Upper Midwest. In Michigan's Upper Peninsula, the *pasty* was adopted by the Finnish, who then introduced it to southeastern Michigan and Wisconsin after the mines were closed. In the Southwest, Spanish contributions to both American food culture and the lexicon of American English have included *jerk(y)*, *taco*, *tamale*, and *tortilla*.

Contribution to the lexicon via the introduction of foods to local cultures is an ongoing phenomenon; for instance, Chicago's Humboldt Park neighborhood claims to be the birthplace of a sandwich called the *jibarito*, or at least the site of its introduction to the United States. Since debuting in a Puerto Rican restaurant in the neighborhood in the mid-1990s, the *jibarito* is now offered in Latin American restaurants throughout Chicago as well as in cities throughout the Midwest.

5.5

5.6

place names, which often indicate characteristics of early populations in an area. As mentioned in Chapter 4, every region of the United States has cities, towns, and topographical features that were either named by or named for Native Americans. Spanish and French terms are also pervasive in this respect and can be found in several regions of the US, especially in places where they had an early presence. Although place names are marginal in terms of language structure, variation in the pronunciation of names such as *Des Moines*, *Missouri*, *New Orleans*, and *Saguache* can mark speakers as locals or as outsiders, and are often the subject of social commentary.

5.4

Together, such factors as settlement history, physical geography, cultural centers, and contact with other languages play important roles in regional language variation in general, not only individually but in combination. The linguistic outcomes of factors such as these are discussed later in the chapter. In the next section, we investigate the methods used to reveal language variation associated with region, as that is one of the principle aims of American dialectology.

AMERICAN DIALECT SURVEYS

Scholarly interest in dialectal diversity in the United States culminated in the creation of three major projects during the 20th century: the American Linguistic Atlas Projects, the *Dictionary of American Regional English*, and *The Atlas of North American English*. The general aim of each of the projects from their inception was to replace the impressionistic, subjective, and qualitative view of regional variation held by many individuals (see Chapter 3) with access to findings based on systematic, objective, and quantitative methods for identifying dialects through the investigation of areal distributions of linguistic features using large datasets.

American dialectology was not created in a vacuum, but instead used dialect research that had been conducted in Europe earlier as its model. In particular, American dialectologists saw the work of the French linguist Jules Gilliéron as a model for dialectology in the US. Gilliéron sent a fieldworker on a bicycle to conduct face-to-face linguistic interviews with native residents of communities throughout France, while he remained in the office, plotting the responses on maps as they were received through the mail. Through this approach, Gilliéron succeeded in moving rapidly from planning to publication of the *Atlas linguistique de la France* (Gilliéron & Edmont, 1902–1910). In doing so, Gilliéron's study established the method for doing dialectology throughout Europe, and one that would be emulated, to the extent that it could be, in the United States.

One of several similarities that the three major American projects share with Gilliéron's research is the use of questionnaires designed to elicit select linguistic targets known to exhibit variation in the language, such as the *pop/coke/soda* distinction that we looked at earlier. Another is the selection of native residents of communities to serve

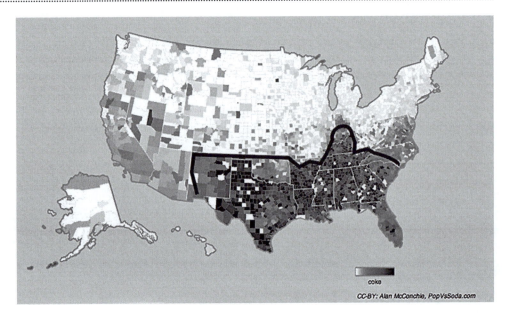

FIGURE 5.1 Isogloss depicting the regional usage of the term *coke*.

Source: Adapted from Alan McConchie, PopVsSoda.com.

as linguistic informants so that the data that are obtained are representative of the local speech of the area. Furthermore, maps are used by all three projects to show where different linguistic features were found in the region of study.

While maps are useful for presenting findings on the areal distribution of linguistic features, they are also used as analytical tools by researchers to discover patterns of usage and reasons for these patterns. To do so, dialectologists identify places on the map where a specific linguistic feature is used and then locate patterns in its distribution by using an **isogloss**, a line drawn on a map demarcating areas in which a particular linguistic feature is used from those where it is not. When several of these isoglosses occur in approximately the same area, the result is an **isogloss bundle**, which can be indicative of dialect boundaries. An example of an isogloss for the word *coke* 'sweet, carbonated beverage' is provided in Figure 5.1.

Examining the distribution of linguistic features in this way raises several issues; perhaps the most important to bear in mind as you read this chapter is that linguistic features are typically **group preferential** rather than **group exclusive** (Smith, 1985). That is, while there may be a tendency for one group to use a feature more than another group (group preferential), it is atypical for a linguistic feature to be confined to use by a single group and not by anyone else (group exclusive), despite how strongly a feature might be linked to a group. As mentioned in Chapter 3, for instance, *y'all* is strongly associated with the American South; however, the South is not the only place in the US (let alone, in the world) where English speakers use *y'all*. While isoglosses, bundles of isoglosses, and the concept of dialect in general can be useful for characterizing regional speech, we must keep in mind that (1) dialectology relies on sampling, using a small number of informants to represent large areas; and (2) no two individuals speak exactly the same way.

American Linguistic Atlas Projects

Planning for a wide-scale linguistic survey of the United States had been discussed as early as 1889, the year the American Dialect Society was established. However, it wasn't until the 1920s that a project took shape under the tutelage of Hans Kurath, who adopted Gilliéron's framework and modified it to meet the demands of linguistic work in North America to initiate the American Linguistic Atlas Projects (ALAP). Kurath (1949) states the aims of the project as follows:

5.7

> to determine the present geographic and social dissemination of individual expression in the Eastern States, to observe the coalescing of word boundaries with a view toward identifying speech areas, and to relate these speech areas and their boundaries to settlement areas, trade areas, and culture areas. This procedure gives us a realistic historical account of a selected body of vocabulary in the oldest part of English-speaking America.
>
> (p. 10)

Due to the nation's size, ALAP research was divided into several components, the first focusing on New England.

Before fieldwork for the project began, Kurath selected communities to include in the investigation and compiled worksheets comprising hundreds of target items from the everyday language of people, regardless of socioeconomic class, level of education, and profession. A small, representative sample of the kinds of questions included in the worksheets is as follows:

1. a. What do you call a room in your house used for entertaining guests?
    b. What is the term used around here for a noisy wedding celebration?
    c. Do you have a name for when the sun is shining while it's raining?
    d. If you wanted to leave a place quickly, what would you say? "Before they find this out, we'd better _____!"

Such questions were designed to elicit vocabulary, pronunciation, and grammatical variants that could indicate regional dialect patterns.

Fieldwork in New England commenced in 1929, with fieldworkers traveling to communities and locating native inhabitants in communities who were willing to submit to the long interview format. Lacking today's technological advances in recording, fieldworkers asked questions of their informants to elicit target items and recorded their responses by writing detailed phonetic transcriptions by hand in field books. When the interviews were finished, the data were taken or sent back to the office, where workers tabulated variants from field records and created maps showing where fieldworkers had observed the use of individual linguistic features. The results of the New England fieldwork appeared as the *Linguistic Atlas of New England* (*LANE*; Kurath, Hanely, Lowman, & Bloch, 1939–1943).

5.8

The New England project was followed by a survey covering all the states on the Atlantic coast, from New York to Florida, as well as the landlocked state of West Virginia; the survey, called the Linguistic Atlas of the Middle and South Atlantic States (LAMSAS), began in 1933. The data from LAMSAS and *LANE* were used to describe Eastern speech in terms of vocabulary (Kurath, 1949), pronunciation (Kurath & McDavid, 1961), and grammar (Atwood, 1953), which provided evidence of regional dialectal patterns.

Data collected for ALAP provided evidence of the North and South as dialect regions; however, Kurath (1949) contends that "[t]he common notion of a linguistic Mason and Dixon's Line separating 'Northern' from 'Southern' speech is simply due to an erroneous inference from an oversimplified version of the political history of the nineteenth century" (p. vi). Instead, the ALAP data from the eastern states indicated a third major dialect that intervened between the North and South, and that Kurath named "the Midland." This region originated in Pennsylvania, with one part of it extending from the vicinity of Philadelphia south through the Shenandoah Valley and into the piedmont of the Carolinas and Georgia, and another extending from Pittsburgh south into the Ohio Valley in Ohio and Kentucky (Kurath, 1949, p. 11). In addition, early ALAP work indicated the existence of 18 subregions in the eastern states. (These regions and subregions are illustrated in the map presented at www.csiss.org/classics/content/17.)

5.9

After coverage of the eastern states, ALAP methods culminated in the *Linguistic Atlas of the Upper Midwest* (Allen, 1973–1976) and the *Linguistic Atlas of the Gulf States* (Pederson, McDaniel, & Adams, 1986–1992). Fieldwork for several projects was completed in the West in the mid-20th century, but the results were never published; furthermore, many areas of the West were never surveyed, a lack that motivated Pederson to create the Linguistic Atlas of the Western States (LAWS) project in the late 1980s (Pederson & Madsen, 1989; Pederson, 1996). The most recent fieldwork for ALAP was conducted in Colorado as part of the LAWS project by this textbook's second author (Antieau, 2006). The transcripts of the Middle Rocky interviews, which are written in machine-readable, standard English orthography, are easily downloadable for use at http://illocutioninc.com/site/products-data.html, and LAWS audio files are available at www.lap.uga.edu/Projects/LAWS/Speakers/. The ALAP website is www.lap.uga.edu/.

5.10

Dictionary of American Regional English

The *Dictionary of American Regional English* (*DARE*; Cassidy & Hall, 1985) was founded by Frederic G. Cassidy at the University of Wisconsin in 1965. The project sought evidence of variation in American English by compiling data from several resources, including written sources as well as face-to-face interviews with speakers in every state of the country. *DARE* fieldworkers relied on the ALAP worksheets but modified and expanded them to emphasize lexical items (Cassidy, 1993, p. 98), with the worksheets eventually comprising 1,847 questions in 41 categories, including this group of related questions:

H26   A round cake of dough, cooked in deep fat, with a hole in the center:

H27   Do you have any joking names for doughnuts (or other word)?

H28   Different shapes or types of doughnuts (or other word)?

H29   A round cake, cooked in deep fat, with jelly inside:

H30   An oblong cake cooked in deep fat:

H32   Names used around here for fancy rolls and pastries: (according to shapes, etc.) (open question).

DARE fieldwork resulted in a collection of 2,777 interviews in 1,002 American communities in all 50 states (Hall, 1997, p. 298); in addition to the interview, over 1,800 informants submitted an audio-recording of their speech that usually included a reading of "Arthur the Rat," a nonsensical story designed to elicit important pronunciation variants in American English. The first volume of *DARE* (covering words beginning with the letters A–C) was published in 1985, the fifth and final volume (SL–Z) was published in 2012, and a digital version was released in late 2013. The URL for the *DARE* website is http://dare.wisc.edu/.

5.11

DARE relied on multiple methods not only for collecting evidence of variation in regional American English but for presenting the results as well. For each variant, *DARE* provides one or more definitions, excerpts from informants and print sources supporting these definitions, and generalizations regarding the regional distribution of the variant. As part of this format, *DARE* uses 37 regional labels, including those established by ALAP, namely, *North*, *South*, and *Midland*, as well as such labels as *Appalachian*, *Pacific Northwest*, *Inland North*, *Inland South*, and *West*; *DARE* also qualifies these labels with the use of such terms as "chiefly" and "especially." For example, the areal distribution of *antigodlin* 'lopsided, askew, aslant, out of line' is noted as being chiefly South, South Midland, and West; the areal distribution of *tag sale* 'a sale of used household items' is noted as being chiefly North, especially southern New England and New York City. Additionally, *DARE* shows the geographic distribution of select lexical variants on a specially designed map of the United States that reflects the population size of states rather than their physical size. (For example, see the *DARE* website for the entry for *blue norther*: http://dare.wisc.edu/?q=node/69.) Through this presentation, *DARE* informs its audience by providing relevant data to provide a general overview of items in terms of their meaning and function in speech, as well as in their regional and social distribution, while also identifying valuable resources for further research on related topics (von Schneidemesser, 1996). According to the *DARE* website, the results of *DARE* fieldwork are used by many professionals for a variety of activities; these include forensic linguists and detectives, who use *DARE* to apprehend criminals, and physicians, who use *DARE* to help understand their patients' use of folk terminology for symptoms.

5.12

TELSUR/*The Atlas of North American English*

In compiling *The Atlas of North American English* (Labov, Ash, & Boberg, 2006), William Labov of the University of Pennsylvania led a research team that conducted telephone surveys (hence TELSUR) to collect linguistic data from 762 speakers who represented all the urbanized areas in the United States, as well as some smaller localities. Using a questionnaire to elicit words containing target vowels, TELSUR interviews focused largely on phonological inventories in North American dialects, and the findings of the project are presented in text, maps, and vowel plots.

5.13

The main objective of TELSUR was to explain contemporary variation and change in American English in terms of **vowel shifts** and **vowel mergers** in the sound systems of American regional dialects. Such sound changes are instantiated when speakers begin to raise or lower a specific vowel in their inventory. As the articulation of the vowel moves to a new position, one of two processes typically occurs: (1) there is a merger in which the two vowels become one, or become so close that any meaningful distinction between them is lost, or (2) the movement of a vowel to a new position forces the vowel already in that position to take a new position, thus starting a chain shift, such as the Great Vowel Shift, as discussed in Chapter 4. TELSUR revealed three contemporary vowel changes that indicate American regional dialect: the Northern Cities Shift, the Southern Shift, and the Low Back merger.

5.14

The **Northern Cities Shift** (NCS) is a phenomenon named for its association with the speech of large northern cities such as Buffalo, Chicago, Cleveland, Detroit, Rochester, and Syracuse. According to the historical evidence, the shift occurred as follows (Labov, 1996):

1. The raising and tensing of /æ/ so that, for instance, the pronunciation of *Ann* by a Northern Cities speaker sounds like *Ian* to speakers of other dialects.
2. The fronting of /a/ to fill the gap left by the shift of /æ/, which results in a word such as *lock* sounding like *lack* to speakers of other varieties.
3. The lowering of /ɔ/ to /a/, so that *stalk* sounds like *stock*.
4. The backing of /ɛ/ to the central vowel /ʌ/.

5. The backing of /ʌ/ to the back vowel /ɔ/.
6. The lowering of /ɪ/ to /ɛ/.

These steps are also illustrated in Figure 5.2, which shows how the NCS proceeded using the frame /b_t/.

5.15

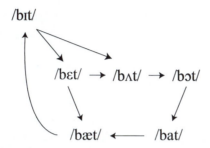

FIGURE 5.2 Northern Cities Shift.

Source: Adapted from Labov et al. (2006).

For TELSUR, the defining characteristic of the South is the **Southern Shift**. The most salient feature of the shift is the articulation of the diphthong /aɪ/ as a long monophthongal /a/ so that, for instance, the word *ride* is pronounced as [ra:d]; monophthongization of /aɪ/ is also sometimes realized in the articulation of words such as *tire* and *fire* as *tar* and *far*. Another aspect of the shift is the apparent reversal of /i/ and /ɪ/ in such words as *feel* and *Phil*, respectively. In addition to the Southern Shift, the phonology of the South is noteworthy for the conditioned merger of /ɛ/ and /ɪ/, by which both sounds are pronounced as /ɪ/ before nasal consonants, a characteristic often referred to as the **pin-pen merger** because both words are pronounced as [pɪn] after the merger.

In the Midland region, TELSUR found evidence of the **Low Back merger**, a phenomenon in which the vowels /a/ and /ɔ/ are both realized as /a/ in the speech of those with the merger. This merger, variantly called the **cot-caught merger** and the **Don-Dawn merger**, was found in the speech of many informants who lived in New England, western Pennsylvania, West Virginia, and Kentucky, as well as the American West. The two vowels remained distinct, however, for (1) most speakers who lived in the state of New York, (2) most speakers who lived along the Atlantic seaboard and through the Southern states into East Texas, and (3) some speakers in the Great Lakes region. (For the distribution of this merger, see Map 1 at www.ling.upenn.edu/phono_atlas/ICSLP4.html.)

The results of dialectology are always a snapshot of the past for several reasons. First, fieldwork, analysis, and distribution of the data take time, and, since language

5.16

BOX 5.2 The Harvard Dialect Survey

Conducted by Bert Vaux and Scott Golder, the Harvard Dialect Survey is a project that was conducted with students at Harvard and online participants, with questions given in multiple-choice format. The survey asked questions aimed at eliciting phonological, lexical, and syntactic variants. This type of elicitation is less than ideal for a dialectological study, particularly with respect to phonological variation, because of inaccuracies that can arise when people self-report such information, as opposed to natural, spoken data in face-to-face interaction; however, the method proved to be successful in eliciting a large amount of data in a fairly short amount of time. Joshua Katz, a Ph.D. student in statistics at North Carolina State University, used the data gathered by the survey to create heat-map visualizations of individual results and, based on these responses, to infer where participants learned to speak American English. These results can be found at http://spark.rstudio.com/jkatz/DialectQuiz/; a link to an article featuring the test was also provided in the introduction above. Vaux is now working on a new survey with Marius L. Jøhndal called *The Cambridge Online Survey of World Englishes*, which can be accessed at www.tekstlab.uio.no/cambridge_survey/.

change is continuous, some aspects of language can change from the onset of a project to its end. Furthermore, there has often been an emphasis in dialectology on collecting the speech of older informants: McDavid (1972, p. 37) contends that the aim of a linguistic atlas is to provide "a body of stable folk evidence, from which one may work backward, comparatively, to set up affiliations of the dialect regions with those in older settled areas and in the British Isles," while Cassidy (1993), with respect to informant selection for *DARE*, reports an "emphasis on older generations who, presumably, would know a wider range of usages, especially those that might be dying out" (p. 96). Despite this preference for older speakers, the results of dialectology are invaluable for the evidence they provide of language variation and change, particularly in the discovery of regional dialect patterns.

The three major American dialect projects all have different aims and findings that are equally useful for those interested in the regional dialects of American English. ALAP offers myriad data in such forms as phonetic transcription and lists of lexical items. Recently, it has moved toward digitizing existing audio recordings and offering them to researchers online. While ALAP's coverage of the Eastern states is comprehensive, its coverage of the West is fragmented. *DARE* is useful for scholars and laypeople alike, as it can be found in university and public libraries, and also has an online presence. The TELSUR findings are accessible via *The Atlas of North American English* (Labov et al., 2006); it offers the most recently collected data among the three projects and covered the entire United States in a relatively short period of time; however, it provides only phonological data. (See more at www.atlas.mouton-content.com/.)

5.17

AMERICAN REGIONAL DIALECTS

In this section, we use data from ALAP, *DARE*, TELSUR, and other sources to describe regional American English. Although there is vigorous debate surrounding these regions, for example where lines should be drawn, which features should be considered emblematic of regional dialects, and even how many regions there are, Figure 5.3 shows the consensus of these projects in terms of major regions.

The culmination of research in regional American English and other sources indicate four major dialect regions of the United States: the South, the North, the Midland, and the West. Although these reflect differences in linguistic structure, as shown by distributions of individual features, these differences are also a reflection of settlement history, geography, cultural centers, and contact with other languages,

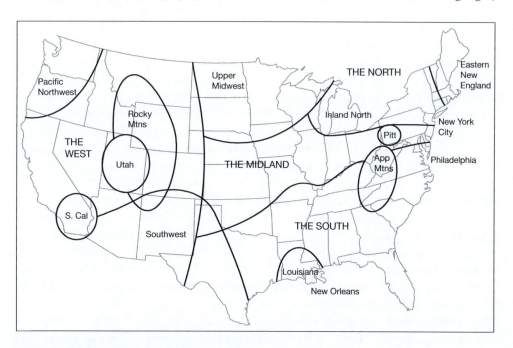

FIGURE 5.3 Map of American regional dialects.

Source: Adapted from Kurath (1949), Carver (1987), and Labov et al. (2006).

as discussed above. We also observe that these are not fully homogeneous speech regions, as reflected in each of the major regions' subregions, some of which we describe in the discussion below.

The South

Covering a large area extending from Virginia in the north to Florida in the south and stretching from the Atlantic coast to Texas, the South consists of a diverse mix of people of English, Scots-Irish, Native American, and African descent. Besides English, other languages with high concentrations of speakers in parts of the South have historically included French in Louisiana, German in Texas, North Carolina, and Louisiana, and Spanish in Florida, Louisiana, and Texas; Spanish continues to proliferate not only in these states but in others in the South as well. The combination of people and languages throughout the region has helped create some of the most distinctive speech patterns in the US. And, despite influxes of Americans from other parts of the country, particularly the North, traditional Southern identity, as measured by linguistic distinctiveness, is alive and well in the New South (Bailey & Tillery, 1996).

According to the ALAP, lexical variants associated with the South have included such words as *light bread* 'bread, loaf bread'; *clabber* 'curdled milk'; *shoals* or *shallows* (a shallow place in a body of water, usually sand and/or gravel); *cur dog* 'mongrel'; *crackling* (crisp skin of an animal eaten as food); *(corn) pone* (cornmeal flatbread); *blue John* 'skim milk'; *polecat* 'skunk'; *lightwood* 'kindling'; *(corn) shucks* 'husks'; *veranda* 'porch'; *tommytoes* 'cherry tomatoes'; *pulley bone* 'wishbone'; and *y'all* as the most common second-person plural pronoun. Distinctive words in current circulation in the South include the use of *coke* as a generic term for a sweet, carbonated beverage; *mash* 'press firmly' as in "mash the button"; and *carry* 'to drive a person somewhere.'

Phonologically, one of the most salient traits of the South is the monophthong-ization of /aɪ/ as /aː/ and the *pin-pen* merger, which is the merger of the vowels /ɪ/ and /ɛ/ preceding nasal consonants. Speakers who participate in this merger tend to use compounds such as *ink pen* and *stick pin* to avoid misunderstandings with others. An analysis of written responses to the *Tennessee Civil War Veterans Questionnaires* (Dyer, Moore, Elliott, & Moxley, 1985) and data from the ALAP suggests that participation in the merger was relatively infrequent in the early 1800s but had been completed by the 1930s (Brown, 1991).

5.18

Grammatical features associated with the South include double modals, such as *might could*, as in "I might could do that"; perfective *done*, as in "He *done* threw a fit"; and the use of *liketa* 'nearly' and *fixing to* 'preparing to' in sentences such as "He *liketa* killed himself falling off the ladder" and "She's *fixing to* drive into town," respectively (Bailey & Tillery, 1996). The personal dative construction that appears in sentences such as "You got *you* a haircut" and "I bought *me* an old house" is often associated with Southern speech (Wolfram & Christian, 1976; Christian, 1991;

Webelhuth & Dannenberg, 2006); however, its use in other parts of the country, including the American West (Antieau, 2012; Launspach, 2012), has been noted recently as well.

5.19

The South comprises several noteworthy subregions, one of which is Appalachia, an area that was largely settled by Scots-Irish immigrants in the 18th century. While Appalachian speech shares many features with general Southern speech, such as the *pin-pen* merger and monophthongization in words such as *tire* and *fire*, it is also characterized by linguistic features marking it as its own variety. These include an intrusive /h/ at the beginning of words such as *it* and *ain't*; the use of *right* as an intensifier, as illustrated by the sentence "It's a *right* hot day"; and a reversal of morphemes in compounds that include *whatever*, *whichever*, and *whoever*, resulting in *everwhat*, *everwhich*, and *everwho* (Montgomery, 1997). The lexicon of Appalachian English also distinguishes the variety from others and includes *chancy* 'doubtful'; *discomfit* 'inconvenience'; *directly* 'later, in a while'; and *sigogglin* 'built poorly, crooked.' Nonlinguists often use the terms "Shakespearean" or "Elizabethan" in association with Appalachian speech due to its use of some vocabulary items that were replaced in other varieties of English long ago, leading some to postulate that those speech communities have a stronger link with earlier times than other communities do. However, Montgomery (1999, p. 70) argues that there is little evidence for this connection and points out that the features used to support it can be found in other areas of the United States and the British Isles as well.

5.20

Louisiana is a subregion in which linguistic diversity abounds, due to several factors, including the history of languages besides English used in the area as part of a French colony, a Spanish colony, an American state in the Deep South, a port city, and a popular attraction for immigrants and tourists alike. Distinctive vocabulary includes *cush-cush* 'mush'; *boudin* 'sausage'; *lagniappe* 'something extra'; and *beignet* 'fried cake,' as well as a local fish called *sacalait* (Pederson, 2001, pp. 278–279). Other lexical distinctions include *neutral ground*, which refers to the grassy strip between the lanes of a highway; *jambalaya*, a dish that originated in the Caribbean Islands; and *gumbo*, a dish that originated in southern Louisiana in the 18th century. The city of New Orleans is particularly well known for its dialectal diversity, including the presence of the **Yat dialect**, the name originating from the common use of the greeting "Where y'at?" among its speakers. Some New Orleans speech shares features with New York City English, to which it is sometimes compared. Louisiana French, Louisiana Creole, Cajun French, and Haitian Creole continue to have a presence in the region and will be discussed in Chapters 11 and 13.

5.21

Just as the culture and history of Texas are unique among American states, its speech is also distinct among varieties of American English. To some degree, Texas, particularly East Texas, is considered an extension of the South and South Midland dialect regions, based on settlement patterns and the variety's inclusion of several features associated with Southern American English, including the use of double

5.22

modals, perfective *done*, and *y'all*. However, there are other ways in which the speech of the state aligns more with the American Southwest, particularly in its frequent use of Spanish terms such as *mesquite*. Other regional terms associated with Texas include *norther* and *blue norther*, which are used to refer to cold winds that enter the state from the North.

The North

The North comprises New England, New York, and northern Pennsylvania on the East Coast and expands westward to include the Great Lakes area and the Upper Midwest states of Iowa, Minnesota, and the Dakotas. This follows early migration and settlement patterns, as the early English stock of New England and New York migrated into the Great Lakes region, first to take advantage of opportunities in homesteading and in the timber and mining industries, and later for factory work. With the decline of the timber industry in the Upper Midwest, opportunities in agriculture in the region attracted New Englanders, as well as German, Irish, Polish, Swedish, Norwegian, Finnish, and Canadian immigrants (Allen, 1973–1976). In the early 20th century, the Great Migration from the Southern states brought African American populations into urban centers such as Chicago and Detroit. Even more recently, large Arabic populations have settled in areas such as Dearborn, Michigan, and smaller populations of Hmong have moved into communities throughout the Great Lakes region and the Upper Midwest. (See Chapter 11 for more on the use of German and Arabic in the United States.)

5.23

Early ALAP work found several lexical items distinguishing the North from other regions, including *pail* 'bucket'; *teeter(board)* 'seesaw'; *whiffletree* (a plow pulled behind an animal); *johnny cake* (cornmeal flatbread); and *darning needle* 'dragonfly.' In terms of phonology, Northern speakers are associated with a pronunciation of *bag* and *egg* with the vowel /e/ as opposed to /ɛ/; *roof* with the lax vowel [ʊ], rather than the tense vowel [u] of *aloof*; *on* with /a/ rather than /ɔ/; and, among older speakers, *creek* as *crick*. *Pop* is the generic word for a sweetened, carbonated beverage throughout the region, excluding the East Coast and southeastern Wisconsin. Although the coastal cities have several variants for the second-person plural pronoun, *you guys* is the most common form used inland.

Several subregions of the North emerge from linguistic data, and in the map we point out four: Eastern New England, New York City, the Inland North, and the Upper Midwest. Kurath (1972) argues for a division between eastern and western New England, with a line running from Long Island Sound to Canada that divides the states of Connecticut, Massachusetts, and Vermont into two. Shibboleths of eastern New England include *cabinet* 'milk shake'; *tonic* 'soft drink'; *grinder* 'submarine sandwich'; *brook* 'creek'; and *bubbler* 'drinking fountain' (a feature shared with Wisconsin). Another salient feature is *wicked* as an intensifier, in a sentence such as "He's *wicked* smart." New England is noted for several phonological characteristics. The first is r-lessness in post-vocalic environments, as in *car* and *card*. This phenomenon is particularly prevalent in eastern New England and is shared with New York City. Another phonological feature is the "New England broad a," speakers of which make a distinction in the vowel sounds of the words *father* and *bother*, with the former incorporating a vowel between the front low lax vowel in *hat* and the low back vowel in *pot* (Metcalf, 2000, p. 66).

Although often considered a part of the Mid-Atlantic region with respect to geography, New York City is generally considered part of the Northern dialect region (Kurath, 1949; Carver, 1987; Labov et al., 2006). Phonologically, the speech of New York City includes "h-dropping" in words such as *huge*, *humor*, and *humid* and the articulation of [g] after [ŋ] in words and phrases such as *singing* and *Long Island*. The pronunciation of the first vowel in the words *all*, *call*, and *coffee* by some speakers in New York City has been the subject of commentary and stereotypes by the media. Additionally, the speech of some New Yorkers exhibits r-lessness, a characteristic that New York City shares with New England.

5.24

Moving westward into the Great Lakes region, the Inland North includes Upstate New York, northern Ohio, Michigan, northern Indiana and Illinois, and eastern Wisconsin. The salient feature of the region is the Northern Cities Shift, as outlined in the TELSUR project above. There are a number of distinctive lexical features in the region, including *belly smacker*, in reference to a stomach-first dive into water, and a popular card game called *euchre* [jukr]. There are also a number of variants for inhabitants of different areas, including reference to residents of Wisconsin, Indiana, and Michigan's Upper Peninsula, respectively, as *cheeseheads*, *hoosiers*, and *yoopers*.

Finally, speakers of the Upper Midwest region are distinctive in their use of monophthongal /o/, a feature with a geographical distribution that stretches from Michigan's Upper Peninsula to the Dakotas. This feature appears prominently, for example, in the third syllable of *Minnesota*, as well as in the final syllable of *Fargo*, a town in North Dakota and the name of a 1996 Coen brothers movie that is set in the community. This feature is commonly attributed to large-scale immigration to the area in the 19th century, which consisted primarily of Scandinavians and Germans.

5.25

The Midland

As depicted by Kurath (1949), the Midland region comprises much of Pennsylvania and part of the Appalachian Mountains. From its eastern edge, the dialect extends from Philadelphia and the Delmarva Peninsula southward through the Shenandoah Valley and into the Carolinas, while from western Pennsylvania, it extends from Pittsburgh into the Ohio Valley. The founding populations of the Midland region consisted of Germans, Dutch, Scottish, and Irish, and the region had less British influence than either the North or South (Pederson, 2001, p. 265).

The ALAP evidence supporting the existence of the Midland region includes such variants as *blinds* 'roller shades'; *coal oil* 'kerosene'; *roasting ear* 'corn on the cob'; *skillet* 'frying pan'; *spouting* and *spouts* 'gutters'; *a little piece* 'a little way'; *to hull beans* 'to shell beans'; the variants *pine, fat-pine, rich-pine, pitch pine* 'kindling'; *snake feeder* 'dragonfly'; *I want off* 'I want to get off'; *you'ns* as a common second-person plural pronoun, and the phrase *a quarter till* for expressing time. Labov et al. (2006) point to the Low Back merger as the defining feature of the Midland region. A number of other linguistic features are characteristic of the region's speech, including intrusive /r/ in post-vocalic contexts, for example in words such as *wash* [warʃ] and *squash* [skwarʃ] (Pederson, 2001, p. 272), as well as positive *anymore*, which is the use of the adverb *anymore* in an affirmative context, for example "In college basketball *anymore*, any team seems to be able to beat any other team on any given night" (Murray, 1993, p. 173).

As in the North and South, the Midland is not homogeneous, and it has a number of subregions. Labov, Ash, and Boberg (1997) note that "each of the Midland cities—Philadelphia, Pittsburgh, Columbus, Cincinnati, Indianapolis, St. Louis, Kansas City—has its own local character." Here, we focus on Philadelphia and Pittsburgh, as they are perhaps as linguistically different as any two Midland cities. Philadelphia contributed the *cheesesteak* to American culture and the word *hoagie* 'submarine sandwich'; it also shares several lexical features with neighboring New Jersey, including *mischief night* 'the night before Halloween' and *bag school* 'to skip school,' and it shares the second-person plural pronoun *youse* with inhabitants of New Jersey, Baltimore, and New York City. From the perspective of phonology, Philadelphia speakers resist the *cot-caught* merger and, like speakers in several other cities on the East Coast, maintain a distinction between *merry, Mary,* and *marry,* which have been merged in inland dialects. Because of their close proximity, Philadelphia speech shares many linguistic features with Baltimore, including a distinct pronunciation of the vowel before /r/ in *very, American,* and *merry,* such that the latter word sounds the same as the name *Murray* in other American dialects. Philadelphia and Baltimore also share the use of a "dark" or vocalized /l/, particularly at the ends of words (as in *middle* [mɪdoʊ]), and the pronunciation of *water* as [wʊdər] is also a shibboleth of the area.

Located in western Pennsylvania, Pittsburgh holds a unique geographical position in that it is considered part of the northeastern United States by some measures and part of Appalachia by others. With respect to the lexicon, Kurath (1949) recognized such words as *carbon oil* 'kerosene,' *cruds* and *cruddled milk* 'cottage cheese,' and *grinnie* 'chipmunk' as distinguishing Pittsburgh from other areas. More recent Pittsburgh shibboleths include *nebby* and *neb-nose* 'nosy,' *gum band* 'rubber band,' *slippy* 'slippery,' *redd up* 'tidy up,' and *The Bhurg* 'Pittsburgh.' Due to their use of *you'uns*, or *yinz*, as a second-person plural pronoun, speakers of Pittsburghese are sometimes pejoratively referred to as *Yinzers*, a label some locals wear with pride (Johnstone, 2011). Phonologically, the speech of Pittsburgh is Midland in that it exhibits the *cot-caught* merger; however, it has several features distinguishing it from all regions. One is its use of a monophthongal vowel in words such as *house* and *out*, as well as in both syllables in the compound *downtown*, so that the words are pronounced as [ha:s], [a:t], and [da:nta:n], respectively (Kurath & McDavid, 1961; Johnstone, Bhasin, & Wittkofski, 2002). The Pittsburgh speech area is also known for *leave/let* reversal (Johnstone et al., 2002), as in "Leave him go to the movies" and "Let the key under the mat." It's also known for its use of the *likes/needs/wants* + past participle construction, as in "The dog likes walked," "The car needs washed," and "The baby wants picked up" (Murray & Simon, 1999, 2002).

5.26

The West

Of the four major dialect regions in the United States, the West was the last to be acquired, explored, and settled by Anglo-Americans. Exploration of the region began with the Lewis and Clark expedition in 1804, a year after the US and France agreed to the Louisiana Purchase. Early settlers of the American West included Americans from the Eastern states and European immigrants; members of both groups ventured into the region for mining or to acquire property in the mid- to late 19th century under the terms of the Homesteading Act of 1862. Relatively large numbers of Asians also arrived in the West during the 19th century, generally to work as laborers in mining camps or in railroading. Additionally, some groups of Americans ventured into the West in search of freedom; these included African Americans who left the South after the Civil War and established several short-lived communities in the West, and Mormons, who originated in Upstate New York. The Southwest, which includes at least part of Texas and southern Colorado, as well as New Mexico, Arizona, and Southern California, has traditionally had large Spanish-speaking populations. Native American populations remain throughout the region, with specific tribes being particularly significant in some areas, such as the Navajo in the Four Corners region, which is where the borders of Arizona, Colorado, New Mexico, and Utah meet.

5.27

    DARE presents several lexical characteristics associated with the West, particularly in the area of ranching, including *canyon*, *civet cat* 'skunk,' *corral*, *mountain lion*, and *catch colt* 'unintended colt,' which has also been metaphorically extended to 'child born out of wedlock' (Carver, 1987, p. 212). TELSUR provides phonological evidence of the Low Back merger of the Midland regions coinciding with fronted [u] to create a distinct phonological pattern in the West (Labov, 1991). Murray (2004) shows that Midland positive *anymore* is prevalent throughout the West. The sharing of features associated with other regions of the US suggests that Western American English is a dialect still in formation, but it also reflects that speakers came from regions in which there had already been much dialect mixture, for example the Great Lakes region (Jackson, 1956).

    There are several subregions of the West worth noting. One is the Pacific Northwest, which is considered one of the most coherent dialect regions of the West (Wolfram &

Schilling-Estes, 1998, p. 112). Several lexical features are associated with the region, including the names *chinook*, *coho*, and *sockeye* for different kinds of salmon, as well as *geoduck*, the name of a local shellfish that is typically pronounced [guidək] (Metcalf, 2000, p. 131). Another word commonly used in the region is *spendy* 'expensive.'

The Southwest is most notable for its heavy borrowing from the Spanish lexicon. Some western shibboleths originating in ranching include two different variants denoting 'a string of horses': *cavvy* and *remuda*. Spanish provided settlers from the Eastern states with ready-made terms for new and unfamiliar topography and wildlife that they encountered, including *arroyo* 'dry creek, wash'; *chaparral* 'thicket'; and *mesa* 'flat-topped mountain.' Other Spanish loanwords include *adobe*, *pueblo*, and *ramada* 'lean-to.' As mentioned in Chapter 4, borrowings from Spanish were often subject to Anglicization, which could be as simple as **clipping**, for example *chaparreras* to *chaps*, or as complicated as the transformation from *calabozo* 'dungeon' to *calaboose* and then to *hoosegow* 'jail.'

The Rocky Mountain region is primarily marked by lexical differences that reflect the physical geography of the region. *Fourteener*, for instance, is a term used to refer to any of the 50-odd mountains in Colorado that rise above 14,000 feet, and *Front Range* is a term denoting the eastern edge of the mountains, where the Rockies meet the Great Plains. The *aspen (tree)* is an important part of Rocky Mountain culture, including its economy, and lexical variants for the tree include *quaker*, *quakie*, *quakie aspen*, and *quaking asp(en)* (Pederson, 2001, p. 285; Antieau, 2006, p. 294). *Camp robber* is the name for a bird called the *Canada jay* in the North, and a *barrow pit*, or *bar pit*, is a 'ditch beside a graded road' (Carver, 1987, pp. 233–234). Additionally, *pika* refers to a small mammal that is indigenous to the Rocky Mountains, which is also called a *cony* (Metcalf, 2000, p. 125).

5.28

Utah English has several linguistic features that distinguish its speech from that of other regions of the West. The first is the **card-cord merger**. Although often stereotyped as a reversal of /ɔr/ and /ar/ by which a phrase such as *born in a barn* is pronounced as *barn in a born*, it is actually a merger of the two sounds into /ar/ (Bowie, 2003). Utah English is also known for its use of **propredicate do**, as in "I slept in but shouldn't have done," which was apparently contributed by the large number of Brits who migrated to the area to practice the Mormon religion, as the feature is considered more grammatical by speakers of British English than by most speakers of American English (Di Paolo, 1993). In addition, the religious orientation of the early Mormon settlers is reflected in the many Utah placenames derived from people, places, and events in the Book of Mormon, for example, *Nephi*, *Lehi*, *Moroni*, *Manti*, and *Bountiful* (Van Cott, 1990, p. xviii).

A number of linguistic features are associated with California English. Phonologically, the region is marked by a recent innovation called the California Shift, which was initiated by the gap in the phonological system created by the Low Back merger. This shift resembles the Southern Shift in some ways (e.g., in the fronting of some

---

BOX 5.3 **Boontling**

• •

Boontling is a variety of English formed in Boonville, an isolated community of farmers, ranchers, and loggers in California's Anderson Valley, during the late 19th century. The origins of the variety are unclear, although the two most popular theories are that it was a jargon formed by laborers or that it developed as a language game played by children that allowed them to talk in front of adults without being understood by them. The variety comprised over a thousand unique words and phrases from several languages, including Irish, Spanish, and the Native American language Pomo. It also named certain behaviors by using the names of townspeople who were associated with that behavior; for example, *Levi* meant 'to telephone,' since Walter Levi was the first of the town's residents to use a telephone. By the 1930s, Boontling had spread throughout the community. Several books and articles were written on Boontling for both academic audiences and the general public in the late 1960s and early 1970s (e.g., Adams, 1971), and the variety even enjoyed a national audience on late-night television. Today, familiarity with Boontling is limited to aging native residents of the valley, and thus the variety is quickly becoming obsolete. But its existence raises some interesting issues concerning differences between language and dialect, the authenticity of created varieties, and the kinds of conditions that have to be in place to maintain a language variety.

5.29

---

sounds) and the Northern Cities Shift in others (e.g., in the shifting of the front vowels, as shown in Figure 5.2 on page 105). Southern California presents several dialectal features associated with it, and the region's status as the home of the American film industry means that many of these features are broadcast to a larger audience than just the immediate region. These include the use of the definite article before the numerical designation of expressways, as heard in a sentence such as "It is best to get on *the 5* to get to L.A." Other examples of Southern California English will appear in Chapter 6.

Alaska and Hawaii

Finally, Alaska and Hawaii are often ignored in discussions of American English, due at least in part to the lack of systematic linguistic study of the language in each of the two states; however, the linguistic diversity that the states present calls for attention here. Both states have been home to many languages, some of which have influenced the local varieties of English. In Alaska, these languages include numerous Native

American languages, Russian, and French. The vocabulary used by English speakers in Alaska, as a result, includes *skookum* 'strong, great,' *mukluk* 'boot,' and *muskeg*, which is a specific kind of swamp. In Hawaii, influential languages include Hawaiian and those of the laborers who have lived and worked on the plantations throughout the years, including Chinese, Japanese, Portuguese, and Tagalog. Hawaii English has borrowed heavily from the Hawaiian language, including such words as *haole* to refer to someone of European ancestry and *hoomolimali* 'flattery, nonsense,' as well as a food called *poi* (Metcalf, 2000, pp. 150–152). We further touch on the overall linguistic diversity of Alaska and Hawaii in Chapters 12 and 13.

THE TENACITY OF AMERICAN REGIONAL DIALECTS

5.30

One often hears the assertion that regional dialects in the United States are disappearing and that this disappearance is likely due to the homogenizing forces of education, the mass media, and the geographic mobility of Americans. For instance, recent newspaper articles have noted that the speech of southern cities such as Raleigh, North Carolina, is changing, leading some to question whether this is evidence that Southern American English is dying (Madison, 2011). Observations lamenting the death of American regional dialects in general, however, are not new; as Kretzschmar (2000, p. 235) reports, when the American Dialect Society was founded in the late 1800s, there was a sense of concern among some members that rural dialects must be surveyed before they disappeared due to the influence of compulsory education and mainstream culture.

Despite these concerns, research indicates that regional diversity in American English is as prevalent as ever. Labov (1991) points to the distinct vowel systems of urban centers that he collected via the TELSUR project, including the Northern Cities Shift, the Southern Shift, and the Low Back merger, as evidence of diversification in American dialects; Labov and Ash (1997) report that "the local accents [of major American cities] are more different from each other than at any time in the past" (p. 509). Hall (2004, p. 93) notes that, despite the often-heard argument that American English is becoming more homogeneous, "the findings in *DARE* demonstrate that there are still thousands of words, phrases, pronunciations, and even grammatical construc-tions that vary from one place to another." With respect to individual dialects, Bailey and Tillery (1996) contend that Southern American English has maintained its distinctiveness despite new large-scale migrations from the North and its stigmatization by speakers of other regional dialects. Furthermore, Johnson (1996, p. 29) shows in a follow-up study of ALAP interviews conducted in the southeastern United States in the 1930s, that interviews in 1990 actually showed a greater amount of lexical diversity than the earlier records. Thus, it would seem that, despite homogenizing forces at work in our daily lives, linguistic diversity in general and regional dialects in particular continue to survive, if not thrive, in the modern United States.

CONCLUSION

In this chapter, we investigated regional variation in American English, a topic that holds interest for a broad spectrum of people for a variety of reasons. With respect to the question of why region has an impact on language use, we pointed to several factors, including settlement history, contact with other languages, and physical geography. While we have concentrated on examples from American English and the history of the United States in order to illustrate these concepts, note that these factors are not unique to regional variation in either English or in the United States.

As part of this chapter, we briefly summarized the major projects used to investigate regional variation in the United States, including ALAP, *DARE*, and TELSUR. The culmination of decades of work by many linguistic researchers, these projects have compiled large bodies of data that are available for use in the investigation of language variation in the United States. We also explained some of the differences in the aims and outcomes of these projects to provide readers with some guidance on which project to consult according to the research questions they are trying to answer. We then used some of the findings from these projects to provide a picture of regional variation in the United States. The data that have been compiled by these projects provide evidence of differences in American dialect regions and subregions, while also illustrating the highly complex nature of regional variation in American English. (For more on the wide range of variation found in ALAP and *DARE* field records, see Johnson, 1996; Kretzschmar & Tamasi, 2003; Hall, 2004; Kretzschmar, 2009, 2010, 2012; Burkette & Antieau, 2012; Antieau & Darwin, 2013.)

Contrary to the belief held by some observers that dialectal diversity is disappearing due to the homogenizing forces of education and mass media, data provided by ALAP, *DARE*, TELSUR, and other projects show that dialect regions are not converging, but may in fact be diverging from one another, particularly with respect to phonology. For example, the TELSUR project provides evidence of three major phonological changes operating in the eastern United States, as well as a fourth change developing on the West Coast as part of an emerging Western dialect.

While it has an important effect on variation, region is, however, only one influence on language use. In the next chapter, we will look at effects that other social factors have on language variation and change.

• •

DISCUSSION AND RESEARCH QUESTIONS

1. Find three words that appear in both LAMSAS (http://us.english.uga.edu/lamsas/browse) and *DARE*. Compare and contrast the findings for these words in both projects. If there are differences, try to account for them using social data that are

available for the two projects, such as region, age, or gender of speaker. For those differences that you cannot account for in this manner, can you think of differences in the methods of the projects' data collections or analyses that might have contributed to differences in the results?

2. Use findings from one or more of the three dialect projects discussed in this chapter to learn more about the language of your local community. Have you heard linguistic evidence that conforms to the results of the survey? How about speakers who differ? What might account for these differences?

3. Analyze your own dialect features in comparison to research on American regional dialects. First, take the dialect quiz found here: www.nytimes.com/interactive/2013/12/20/sunday-review/dialect-quiz-map.html?_r=1&. As you are taking the quiz, keep notes on the geographical distributions of each of your answers, which are shown on the page following each question. Then, discuss some or all of the following questions:

   - Did the composite map or any of the individual question maps actually align with where you have lived?
   - Alternatively, were you placed in an area of the US that you have never spent any time in or have no connection to?
   - How do the questions asked in the survey correspond to the dialect studies or findings about regional dialects presented in this chapter?
   - Which of your own linguistic features most likely contributed to the results of this survey?
   - What did this survey reveal to you about your own idiolect?
   - Do you speak a regional variety of American English?

Social Variation in American English

GUIDING QUESTIONS

1. How does language reflect the social structure of the community in which it is used?

2. Do men and women speak differently?

3. What kinds of linguistic features are associated with adolescence and young adulthood?

4. How does the study of language and society inform our knowledge of language variation and change?

5. How have social media influenced language use?

OVERVIEW

In this chapter, we turn our attention to the subfield of sociolinguistics by first presenting some of the pioneering research in the field and then by discussing variation associated with specific social groups in the United States. As part of this discussion, we examine several social variables that are associated with variation in language use, including ethnicity, age, gender, and sexuality, and we also discuss several key principles of sociolinguistics, such as networks, identity, and age-grading. To close out the chapter, we present innovative lines of research that investigate the connections between language and new channels of communication, including social media and texting.

COMMON MYTHS

> *The language used by some social groups is illogical.*

> *Slang is improper speech with no redeeming social value.*

> *Text messages do not follow the rules of grammar, and social media are ruining language.*

INTRODUCTION

In the preceding chapter, we examined the role of region in dialectal variation in American English. However, if you recall, the definition of *dialect* that we presented in Chapter 1 applied not only to regional groups, but also to social groups as well. Therefore, we turn our attention in this chapter to extralinguistic variables other than region that play a role in language variation, including gender, age, and ethnicity. Just as speakers tend to share linguistic features with other speakers living in the same region, they also tend to share features with speakers in other social groups of which they are—or wish to be—recognized as members, including groups based on socioeconomic class, gender, age, and occupation. Since language use not only varies but also changes, part of the challenge of maintaining membership in such groups is in recognizing linguistic changes as they are occurring, implementing those that appear to have significant value, and, if one has enough power in the group, setting into motion changes when the need for novel features arises.

The aim of this chapter is to investigate how the social characteristics of speakers influence and are influenced by language use, an area of study called **sociolinguistics**. Sociolinguistics has been a subfield of linguistics since the mid-20th century, despite there being earlier interest in the linguistic differences exhibited by specific social groups. Before the subfield was introduced, however, the description of language varieties used by social groups was often based on anecdotal evidence, rather than on data that had been systematically collected. In addition, before sociolinguistics was conceived, much early work in linguistics disregarded the effect of social variables on language use and instead characterized variation in language use as simply random, or what Hubbell (1950) and others referred to as **free variation**.

In one of the first studies to investigate the intersection of language use and society, Fischer (1958) examined the speech of Boston schoolchildren, focusing on the social variables of sex and identity. In doing so, he argued:

> "Free variation" is of course a label, not an explanation. It does not tell us where the variants came from nor why the speakers use them in differing proportions but is rather a way of excluding such questions from the scope of immediate inquiry.
>
> (pp. 47–48)

By making the central focus of inquiry the reasons why certain groups used linguistic features significantly more or less than other groups, sociolinguists aim to discover the effect that social structure has on language, as well as the effect that language structure and use can have on society. Additionally, some sociolinguists are interested in more than a theoretical understanding of language and society, and instead look for ways to implement their findings. For instance, some have used principles from sociolinguistics or data from their own studies to inform good communication practices in fields such as education, law, and medicine.

PIONEERING STUDIES IN SOCIOLINGUISTICS

As mentioned above, Fischer (1958) investigated differences in linguistic features used by Boston schoolchildren to study the intersection of social structure and language use. Specifically, he was interested in the pronunciation of the final syllable in progressive verb forms such as *walking*, *running*, and *playing*, as he had observed two variants in use: [ɪŋ] and [ɪn] (the latter variant is sometimes referred to as "g-dropping" and can be represented in writing by replacing the letter <g> with an apostrophe, as in *readin'* and *writin'*). As part of this investigation, Fischer looked at quantitative differences in the use of these variants according to select social characteristics of the speakers who used them and the contexts in which they were used. The results of the study showed that which variant speakers chose to use was influenced by speech style (there were more instances of [ɪn] in informal interviews than in tests); by gender (girls chose to use [ɪŋ] rather than [ɪn] more than boys did); and by identity ("model boy" used [ɪŋ] more than "typical boy" did). Thus, Fischer showed that linguistic variants could be correlated with styles of speech and social characteristics and, by doing so, set the tone for subsequent studies in sociolinguistics. He also showed that language variation could be used to mark identity, an important finding that would come to have an important place in sociolinguistic research.

Language and Identity in Martha's Vineyard

The intersection of language use and social structure was taken up again in a seminal study conducted by William Labov on the island of Martha's Vineyard (Labov, 1963). Of primary focus in this study was variation in how speakers on the island articulated certain sounds, notably two diphthongs: the front diphthong /aɪ/, often heard in such words as *lie*, *ride*, and *wine*, and a back diphthong /aʊ/ that often appears in such words as *hound*, *mouse*, and *now*. Labov observed that some residents centralized the first vowel of these diphthongs, pronouncing it as the mid central [ə] rather than the low front vowel [a]. Taking social factors into account, he found a relationship between the variants that speakers used and their age, occupation, and location, the latter of which specifically referred to which part of the island that speakers inhabited. The study also revealed that speakers who were year-round inhabitants of the island used the centralized pronunciation at a higher rate than vacationers did, and residents who had moved away from the island to live on the mainland, only to move back, used the centralized vowel at a greater rate than islanders who had never left. Labov concluded from these results that use of the centralized diphthong was a symbol of group membership and, for those speakers who had left the group for any amount of time, it could be manipulated as a means of reasserting their allegiance to the group.

Socioeconomic Class in New York City

Labov followed his research in Martha's Vineyard with *The Social Stratification of English in New York City* (1966/2006), which Chambers (1995, p. 16) calls the "fountainhead" of sociolinguistic research. A sprawling work covering the speech of New York's Lower East Side, the study introduced several components that would become integral parts of sociolinguistics. At the heart of the research was the **linguistic variable**, an abstract linguistic unit manifested in speech by different variants with the same meaning or function. For instance, in Fischer's (1958) study above, the linguistic variable was (ɪŋ)—its status as a variable represented by the use of parentheses—and its two phonetic variants were [ɪŋ] and [ɪn]. In the NYC study, Labov investigated five phonological and two grammatical constructions that were known to show variability in NYC speech and that were suspected of correlating with a particular social variable in New York City, namely, socioeconomic class.

Once the linguistic variables were identified, methods were developed to examine the presence of these variables in several styles of speech for each informant, ranging from highly self-monitored speech to the informant's most casual speech. To do so, the method utilized several tasks that would become key components of sociolinguistic research: a **minimal pair** list, an isolated word list, and a reading passage. Finally, there was also an interview, which, as compared to the other tasks, was intended to draw out the informant's most casual, most unguarded speech. Quantitative differences in variable use in different contexts not only revealed characteristics of New York City speech that had been unsubstantiated, but also shed light on notions that speakers had concerning correctness and the securities or insecurities they had regarding their own speech.

6.1

One component of Labov's NYC study took another approach to investigate the relationship between language use and socioeconomic class, in addition to variation resulting from speech style. Specifically, Labov was interested in the linguistic variable (r) in words such as *park* and *door*, as "r-lessness" in post-vocalic contexts, at one time a sign of prestige in New York City, had become stigmatized by the time of Labov's study. Hypothesizing that the socioeconomic status of speakers played a role in how speakers articulated the variable (r), Labov elicited speech data from employees at three New York department stores that represented different socioeconomic classes. Based on their locations, as well as their prices and advertising, Labov chose the stores S. Klein's, Macy's, and Saks Fifth Avenue to represent the lower class, the middle class, and the upper class, respectively, under the assumption that the speech of the employees at each store would reflect that of their customers. Labov targeted employees' pronunciations of *fourth floor*, a phrase that provided him with two pieces of data on (r) each time it was elicited, and elicited it by asking employees the location of a department, such as men's hats or ladies' shoes, that he already knew to be on the fourth floor of the store. Once the employee responded to his question, Labov, pretending not to hear the answer, asked the employee to repeat the phrase. In using this framework, Labov obtained **casual-style** responses to the first prompt and **careful-style**, or what he called emphatic, responses to the second.

6.2

After the data were collected, Labov observed the behavior of (r) in the responses of his subjects, that is, when [r] appeared post-vocalically and when it did not. The results were as shown in Figure 6.1. The results showed employees at the store with the highest socioeconomic status (Saks) used the highest percentage of [r] in both *fourth* and *floor* in both casual and emphatic speech. Employees at Macy's used [r] at lower rates than those at Saks, but their performance patterned more similarly to the Saks employees than to the S. Klein employees, who had the lowest percentage use of [r] overall. Thus, the results showed that r-lessness was linked to social class, being less common among speakers who attended to customers at the high end of the socio-economic scale and more common among those who attended to consumers at the low end of the scale. The results also suggested the influence that linguistic security/insecurity had on the variable (r) in careful speech at all three stores, particularly in that the production of [r] in *floor* in emphatic speech at Macy's nearly matched the frequency of its production at Saks.

6.3

New York City not only proved to be a worthy testing ground for Labov's methodological approaches, but it also revealed several aspects of society that influenced language variation, in terms of both social structure and the mechanisms underlying variation and change. First, there were quantitative differences in the rates at which

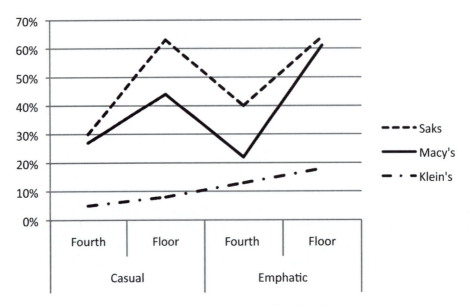

FIGURE 6.1 Percentages of [r] used in *fourth floor* in both styles of speech.

Source: Adapted from Labov (1966/2006, p. 175).

members of different socioeconomic classes selected specific variants, as shown in Figure 6.1. Second, the lower middle class often engaged in **hypercorrection,** which Labov described as:

> the familiar tendency of speakers to overshoot the mark in grammatical usage; in attempting to correct some nonstandard forms, they apply the correction to other forms for which the rules they are using do not apply. Common examples of such hypercorrect forms are *Whom did you say was calling?* and *He is looking for you and I.*
>
> (1966/2006, p. 318)

The tendency among members of the lower middle class to use hypercorrect forms was attributed to linguistic insecurity, due to the effects of prescriptivist grammar and the aspirations of some lower middle-class speakers for upward social mobility (Labov, 1966/2006, p. 318). That is, the lower classes, particularly the middle class, recognized differences in the speech they used and the speech of the social class they wished to join and, resorting to the prescriptive rules that they had knowledge of, over-applied them.

BOX 6.1 **The Observer's Paradox and the Danger of Death**

Early in his investigations, Labov (1970, p. 32) recognized limitations in his data collection due to something he called the **observer's paradox**: while the ultimate goal for linguists in the field was to elicit a person's most natural language, their presence as observers made that naturalness nearly impossible to attain. To overcome this challenge, Labov included a question in his interviews designed to direct informants' focus on the content and emotion of the story rather than on monitoring their speech during the interview. Early on, this was the "**danger-of-death question**," in which interviewers would ask informants: "Were you ever in a situation where you were in serious danger of being killed?" Sociolinguistic studies have since used a variety of other questions to elicit similar types of responses, such as asking respondents to tell about a time they got into trouble for something they did not do. In addition to danger-of-death and related questions, Labov also recognized that the presence of friends and family members at interviews could minimize the effects of the observer's paradox, as conversations between respondents and those close to them commonly incorporate the speech of informants at their most casual.

Social Network Theory

While socioeconomic class has been an important variable in sociolinguistics, researchers have also recognized that membership in social groups within a community could also have an influence on language use. Specifically, social network studies focus on the kinds of social networks that individuals are members of, the strength of ties between members of these networks, and the effects these different networks have on language use. In Figures 6.2 and 6.3, social networks are illustrated in terms of density and multiplexity.

Figure 6.2 represents a **high-density network** in that the members not only all know the central member (Jacob), but they also all know each other. The single line connecting each member to another signifies that the two members have a **uniplex tie**, that is, each member has one and only one relationship with each of the other members. The cast in the spring production of a community play might be represented in this way, or an office in which every worker knows everyone else only as co-workers and not in any other capacity outside of work.

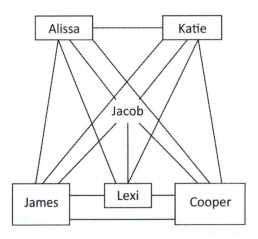

FIGURE 6.2 A high-density network with uniplex ties.

Figure 6.3 shows a **low-density network** in which the central member (Lexi) knows and is known by all of the other network members, who know no one else in the network. Most members have a uniplex tie with Lexi; for example, Max and Lexi might be cousins, or they could be classmates, but, according to this model, they cannot be both. Lexi and Alissa are the only members of this network to have a **multiplex tie**, as represented by the three lines linking them together. Thus, they relate to each other in several different ways; for example, in addition to working together, Lexi and Alissa might also be sisters, take classes together at the local university, or play on the same softball team.

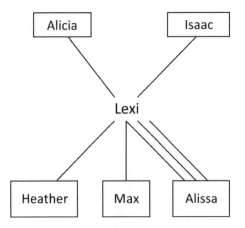

FIGURE 6.3 A low-density network with a multiplex tie.

According to social network theory, a network acts as a "norm-enforcement mechanism" (Milroy, 1980, p. 136) and is instrumental in the maintenance, rejection, or spread of linguistic norms. Closed networks, which are marked by high density and a large number of multiplex ties between group members, promote more uniform language use, as the strongly enforced behavioral norms of the group allow little room for variation. Integration in close-knit networks is vital to the maintenance of nonstandard variants. On the other hand, networks that are more open due to weaker ties between members are less likely to have the authority to demand conformity to a small set of rigid linguistic norms. In a follow-up study, Milroy (1987) found that those members with weak network ties were likely to use variants valued within the network even more often than central members were, possibly using them as a means of integrating themselves more strongly into the network. These peripheral members then introduced the variants they adopted in this network to other networks of which they were a member, and it was their introduction of these variants to core members of the new group that sometimes led to the adoption of the new linguistic features by this group (Milroy & Milroy, 1985, p. 367). Thus, despite the key role played by central members in networks, peripheral members are often important actors in introducing linguistic change to networks.

Several social network studies have been conducted in the United States, including Edwards (1992) on Detroit's East Side; Fridland (2003) in Memphis, Tennessee; and Anderson (2003) in southeastern Michigan, and studies such as these have provided several insights regarding the influence of network membership on language use. The most consistent finding of these studies has been that nonstandard linguistic features are maintained in the speech of those individuals entrenched in closed networks, that is, high-density networks with multiplex relationships. Several studies in the sections below use social network analysis to investigate how language use is affected by social networks, including Eckert's (1989) study on language use among adolescents in metropolitan Detroit and Mann's (2011) study on language variation in a Southern LGBTQ (Lesbian, Gay, Bisexual, Transgender, Queer or Questioning) speech community.

SOCIAL VARIABLES

In this section, we present some of the research that has been done on the language use of several specific social groups. The study of linguistic features as they correlate to social groups raises several issues. First, the link between linguistic features and social groups can be viewed the same as the link between features and regional groups (as discussed in Chapter 5) in that linguistic features are typically group preferential rather than group exclusive (Smith, 1985). In Chapter 5, we reported that while use of the variant *y'all* is strongly linked to the Southern United States, the South is not the only place in the US (let alone, the world) where speakers use *y'all*. Here, we advise readers to expect linguistic variants linked to social variables to behave in a similar way, given the fluidity of social categories, the membership of individual speakers in a variety of sometimes overlapping categories, and the ability for different groups to adopt linguistic variants and to discard them as they see fit.

Although society can be classified in numerous ways, we focus below on several areas that sociolinguists have actively conducted research on, for example age, gender, sexuality, and ethnicity. Due to the limitations of space, we can only briefly summarize some of the research that has been conducted in these areas here; however, we refer readers to the Companion Website, where they can find additional information about a wide variety of sociolinguistic studies.

6.4

Language and Age

Sociolinguists are interested in the intersection of language and age as a key means for exploring linguistic variation and change as well as the connection between language and speaker identity. Simply stated, people of different ages tend to speak differently from one another. For example, older speakers often retain features that they acquired in their youth, but which are no longer being acquired by younger speakers in their communities; younger speakers often choose varieties that align them with their peers over those that are associated with their parents and other authority figures. Socio-linguists who work in this area generally distinguish age-related differences that are socially motivated from those that are caused by physiological changes in the bodies of speakers, such as the ossification of the larynx in elderly speakers and the change in voice, particularly in males, that accompanies puberty. This distinction allows them to focus on the core goals of sociolinguistics: understanding the processes of language variation and change and the connections between language and society.

It is important to note, however, that age is a complex social variable, and the use of the word *age* can be used in several ways: chronological age, which is the number of years since an individual's birth; biological age, which is the stage an individual is at in terms of physical maturation; and social age, which is linked to the reaching of various milestones, such as graduation or marriage (Eckert, 1998). Furthermore, these different ways of viewing age are not mutually exclusive. Some chronological ages serve as milestones, such as birthdays that mark the day an individual can obtain a driver's license, register for selective service, or be served a drink legally. Just as age is a complex variable, its influence on language use can also be difficult to discern. For instance, although many researchers are interested in using age as an indicator of language change, they are challenged in doing so by the phenomenon of **age-grading**, which refers to the use of linguistic forms "correlated with a particular time of life … [and] repeated in successive generations" (Chambers, 1995, p. 188). In the remainder of this section, we focus on a single life stage that is discussed at great length in the sociolinguistic literature: adolescence.

Because adolescence is such an important time for establishing identity and group membership, much of the linguistic research on adolescence has investigated how language is used in these processes. In a study of suburban Detroit high schools in the 1980s, two primary groups were found to operate within the schools: burnouts and jocks (Eckert, 1989). The jock network consisted of those students actively involved in athletics and school activities who had college aspirations and identified with the middle class, whereas the burnout network comprised students who participated in school only minimally, had no intention of attending college, and identified with the working class. The two networks varied linguistically in several respects, particularly in that burnouts selected nonstandard variants, which were popular features in the local dialect, rather than the standard norms that were imposed by the school body. As such, the burnouts were much more likely to participate in the Northern Cities Shift, and this adoption of a local speech norm showed that they belonged to the local community and that their intention was to remain there, while the jocks' use of standard variants served as evidence of their intentions to attend universities and take jobs that extended well beyond their local networks. In addition, Eckert found that burnouts were more likely than jocks to use multiple negation, which was apparently used to show that the speaker was tough and rebellious.

A more general way that adolescents show group membership is through the use of **slang**, that is, highly informal words or phrases, or, as Eble (2004, p. 376) defines it, "deliberate alternative vocabulary that sends social signals." Besides being informal, a key aspect of slang is that it is typically ephemeral, lasting no more than a generation, although occasionally slang from one generation is recycled by a later one. Slang is often used for taboo topics such as sex, drinking, and bodily functions such as vomiting and, in this way, it acts as euphemism or code. It can also be used to add variety or color to everyday language; for example, every generation seems to have its favorite slang terms that are used in place of the high-frequency terms *good* and *bad*. Slang must be constantly updated to remain effective, and while the use of slang in general is a constant, the specific words that are used comprise an ever-changing set of terms. As speakers grow older, they don't necessarily lose the slang they grew up with; however, they have less occasion to use it, and they are less likely to adopt new slang, as they enter the workplace and meet its demands of professional language use. The use of a younger generation's slang by adults can sometimes be used to humorous effect; see the Companion Website.

6.5

6.6

6.7

Adolescents and young adults have also been associated with several innovations that extend beyond the lexicon into the domains of syntax and discourse. For instance, the importance of narration as a genre in adolescent discourse has culminated in several options for dramatizing narratives (Eckert, 2004, p. 367). Among these options is a variety of **quotatives**, markers used to show reported speech or thought, as in the use of *like*, which is illustrated below (Romaine & Lange, 1991, p. 241):

3. Shane's *like*, "She's in Baltimore," and I'm *like*, "No, she's not," and Shane's *like*, "Yes, she is."

In their study, Romaine and Lange (1991, p. 251) found that speakers who used *like* in this way tended to be young and female, and also reported that its use, which had

---

BOX 6.2 Slayer Slang

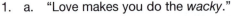

6.8

Television and radio shows, as well as films, often feature interesting uses of language; however, few have garnered as much attention as the language of television's *Buffy the Vampire Slayer* (Whedon, 1997–2003). In particular, the lexicon of the television program, or "slayer slang," was noted, among other things, for its liberal use of particular word-formation processes. For instance, the dialogue of *Buffy* often included words that had been converted from one part of speech to another, for example a noun to a verb, with no change in the form of the word, a word-formation process called **functional shift**. Characters in *Buffy* employed functional shift quite liberally, as illustrated in the use of adjectives as nouns in quotations from the series (from Adams, 1999):

1. a. "Love makes you do the *wacky*."
    b. "Stop with the *crazy*. Go talk to Angel."
    c. "I was making with the *funny*?"

Additionally, characters in *Buffy* often added the suffix *–age* for a variety of functions, as in the following (from Adams, 1999):

2. a. "Sorry I'm late. I had to do some unscheduled *slayage*."
    b. "Hey, speaking of wowpotential, there's Oz over there. What are we thinking, any *sparkage*?"
    c. "It's, like, freeze frame. Willow *kissage*—but I'm not going to kiss you."

6.9

Partially as a response to the amount of attention the language of the show garnered, the creator of *Buffy*, Joss Whedon, wrote and directed an episode called "Hush" that aired during the fourth season of the series. In the episode, the residents of Buffy's town lose their ability to speak, leaving the characters unable to communicate vocally. Thus, the show was able to explore directly the importance of language in the characters' lives.

originated in the early 1980s, was apparently spreading. Currently, this use appears regularly in the speech of both males and females, and its use is even spreading to speakers of various ages, although it is still most commonly associated with adolescents. At the same time, the use of *like* for other functions has increased as well, for example as a **hedge** and a **focus marker** (Buchstaller, 2001; D'Arcy, 2005).

Other forms that have taken on the function of a quotative are *all* and *be all*, as in the following examples (Rickford, Wasow, Zwicky, & Buchstaller, 2007, p. 14):

4. a. He's *all* "Let me see your license; is that your car?"
    b. Our parents would always *be all* "Can't wait till those kids get to bed."

Quotative *all* apparently has its roots in the speech of adolescents, more specifically, adolescents in California in the early 1980s, and by the early 1990s it was the predominant quotative among high school students in the state; however, Tagliamonte (2012) reports that its popularity was apparently short-lived (p. 254), as it was eventually supplanted by other quotatives, old and new, including *like* (Rickford et al., 2007, p. 12).

Language and Gender

If newspaper columns, blogs, talk shows, *The New York Times* bestseller list, comedic sketches, and daily conversations are any indication, there is a great deal of general interest in the linguistic differences of women and men; in linguistics, these differences have been a topic of research for nearly a century. Perhaps the earliest discussion of gender-related differences in language use was presented in a chapter called "The Woman" by the linguist Otto Jespersen (1922). The work of Jespersen and subsequent research along the same lines has been criticized for applying a **deficit approach** to gender-related differences in language use. That is, it assumed the speech of men as the norm, and then, in areas in which the speech of women differed from that of the male model, it assessed women's speech as being deficient in that area, as well as deficient in general.

Fifty years later, in her groundbreaking work on the speech of women, Lakoff (1975) used anecdotal evidence and her own intuitions to study different facets of women's speech, pointing out linguistic features at all levels of the grammar that differentiated the speech of women from that of men. In particular, Lakoff focused on lexical differences, such as a higher use of certain adjectives of approval by women, including *lovely*, *charming*, and *divine*, and a more elaborate color terminology, but she also claimed that grammatical differences, including the use of a greater number of tag questions and "superpolite forms," differentiated the speech of the two sexes.

Despite some of her intuitions on the relationship of women's speech and specific linguistic features being generally supported by subsequent research, Lakoff's (1975) work was the target of various criticisms. In terms of methodology, for instance, scholars were skeptical of the findings because Lakoff had relied on her own observations and intuitions for her conclusions, rather than on systematically collected data. Critics also found fault in Lakoff's interpretation of the linguistic features favored by women as being emblematic of powerlessness (e.g., Holmes, 1990, 1995; Coates, 1993, 1996), and some pointed out that the power of these features varied according to who was using them. For instance, one of the features that Lakoff uses in her characterization of women's speech as powerless, namely, indirectness, is often used by some of the most powerful people in English-speaking society—whether male or female (Tannen, 1990, p. 225).

Several researchers replaced the deficit approach with a **difference approach,** not only in studies on gender, but in investigating other social factors and their influence on language use as well. Tannen (1990), for instance, views males and females as belonging to different subcultures, both of which have been shaped by society to adopt behaviors, including linguistic behaviors, appropriate for their respective cultures. The language that emerges from these socialization processes, according to Tannen (1990), is a **rapport style** for women that is primarily aimed at creating and maintaining relationships and a **report style** for men that is primarily concerned with communicating information and placing themselves within a social hierarchy.

6.10

Several linguistic trends that have been investigated recently have been linked primarily to the speech of women. One of these is **creaky voice,** a low, creaky vibration created by a slow movement of the vocal cords. While creaky voice (also known as **vocal fry**) was historically considered a voice disorder that, if used continually, could damage vocal cords, in recent years researchers have noted its occasional use in speakers with normal voice quality, particularly at the end of utterances (Wolk, Abdelli-Beruh, & Slavin, 2012). Studies of this feature in American English have noted its more frequent use by females, particularly college-aged women (e.g., Gottliebson, Lee, Weinrich, & Sanders, 2007), although more research needs to be done to confirm this finding. Use of the feature has also been noted among Latinos. For instance, Fought (2003) found the feature to be common in the Chicano English of Los Angeles, where it may have been borrowed from the Anglo community. Although Fought found the feature to be used by men and women, it was more common for women in her study, for both Anglo and Latina speakers. Mendoza-Denton (2011) discusses how the feature has been used in the media to project a Chicano gangster persona that has since been adopted by some real-life gang members. Creaky voice appears in varieties of English throughout the world; however, it is associated with different social groups in different places, suggesting that it is being used to project identity. Despite the recent attention creaky voice has garnered, however, it does not appear to be an entirely new phenomenon or one that only affects young people; in one of her studies, Fought (2003) describes its use by a Hispanic woman in her 50s, and Liberman (2011) points to its use by the movie star Mae West in a film from 1933.

6.11

Another relatively recent linguistic trend that has been linked to females is the use of **uptalk,** which features a high rising pattern of intonation in the final syllable or syllables of a statement; in an early article describing this phenomenon, Ching (1982) refers to it as applying "[t]he question intonation in assertions." Now detected in varieties of English around the world, it appears to have spread from the West Coast of the US, where it is associated with the speech of "Valley girls" in Southern California in the 1980s. The function of uptalk in conversation is uncertain: some scholars have argued that it encourages the addressee to participate in the conversation, while others have claimed that it signals to others that the speaker is not yet finished and thus discourages interruption. In a study of contestants on the television game show *Jeopardy*, Linneman (2013) found that uptalk was used more by white, young, female contestants on the show than by male contestants, with males using uptalk more on the show when surrounded by female contestants and in correcting female contestants after they responded incorrectly to a clue. Furthermore, Linneman (2013) also found that the greater success a man had on the show, the less likely he was to use uptalk, and the greater success that a woman had, the more likely she was to use it. However, while this study suggested that uptalk might indicate insecurity on the part of the speaker, other studies have suggested otherwise; for example, McLemore (1991) found that uptalk was used more by sorority sisters with greater seniority and power, and it was used less by newer pledges. Finally, an investigation by Liberman (2005) revealed that President George W. Bush used more uptalk in the speeches he made during the second term of his presidency than in his earlier speeches.

6.12

6.13

In language and gender research, two basic findings have emerged that deserve special merit. One is that women tend to lead linguistic change (Labov, 1990). The discussion of quotative *like* in the previous section as a feature used predominately by young females before becoming more widespread supports this view. The other finding is the tendency for males to use nonstandard linguistic features more than females do, a finding that emerged from the study by Fischer (1958) on the variability of (ing) among schoolchildren that has often been found in gender-based studies since that time (e.g., Trudgill, 1972). Following up on the use of the (ɪŋ), Kiesling (1998) investigates how members of an American college fraternity index working-class cultural models through the variant [ɪn] to present themselves as physically powerful.

Finally, it should be noted that research on language and gender, especially earlier research, has often discussed the categories of male and female as if each were homogeneous (Bucholtz, 2004, p. 417). Newer research has taken diversity among the genders into account (see Mendoza-Denton, 2008; Kiesling, 2009; Lanehart, 2009; Bucholtz, 2011). In particular, studies in this area have become more inclusive, with regard to the experiences of people of color and the LGBT community, rather than attention being focused on gender differences between white, middle-class, heterosexual speakers.

BOX 6.3 Sexist Language

Language change often takes place over long periods of time, with speakers often being unaware that it is happening. The replacement of gendered labels referring to occupation with gender-neutral terms, however, has proceeded relatively quickly and was consciously done to reflect social changes that began in the 1960s. Hence, *steward* and *stewardess* became *flight attendant*, *waiter* and *waitress* became *server*, and *chairman* and *chairwoman* became *chairperson* or, simply, *chair*.

The issue of sexist language has also influenced pronoun usage, especially with regard to the use of the masculine pronoun for both genders, as promoted by Strunk and White, among others:

> The use of he as pronoun for nouns embracing both genders is a simple, practical convention rooted in the beginnings of the English language. *He* has lost all suggestion of maleness in these circumstances . . . It has no pejorative connotations; it is never incorrect.
>
> (1979, p. 60)

Despite Strunk and White's assurances, however, many studies have shown generic *he* to have adverse effects. Martyna (1978) found it to have a cumulative effect on women, in that many of her subjects reported either picturing males when the pronoun was used or not reporting any imagery at all. Through experimentation, Gastil (1990) found that generic *he* in texts created a male bias in readers and, on the basis that the use of generic *he* "interferes with effective communication," suggests that alternative generic pronouns be used (pp. 639–640). Based on the findings of studies such as these, several existing pronouns and pronoun combinations have been used as generics. In addition to using generic *she* or alternating between *he* and *she*, writers have also used *he/she*, *s/he*, *one*, and *they* as generics. However, the use of each of these has presented issues in terms of clarity and formality.

Speakers of English are not the only people concerned with this issue. Recently, the Swedish *National Encyclopedia* admitted *hen* as a gender-neutral third-person pronoun in Swedish (complementing the masculine third-person nominative *han* and the feminine *hon*); however, this did not happen overnight. The word was first introduced by Swedish linguists in the 1960s and was then reintroduced in 1994 by the linguist Hans Karlgren, who suggested that the adoption of such a pronoun would eliminate the problematic use of the Swedish equivalent of *he/she* in writing (Rothschild, 2013). It will be interesting to see whether English and other languages follow the lead of Sweden and one day introduce their own truly gender-free pronouns.

Language and Sexual Orientation

An area of inquiry that has broadened in scope in recent years is the relationship between language use and sexual orientation. Early studies investigating folk beliefs that homosexual women simply thought and behaved like men, while homosexual men thought and behaved like women, found little linguistic evidence to support this position, at least with respect to those qualities that are commonly used to support their similarities, such as pitch (Gaudio, 1994; Zwicky, 1997). Recent research in this area supports the findings of earlier studies that the language use of the LGBT community, as well as its relationship to **heteronormative** speech, is not as easily generalizable as folk beliefs would suggest.

Some researchers in this area have focused on how people observe linguistic features when trying to determine whether speakers are gay or straight. In addition to investigating how accurate people are when linking speech to sexuality, the research also examines the linguistic features people use to make these determinations and whether their attitudes concerning sexual orientation have an effect on their ability to determine an individual's sexuality through their speech. Some studies have found that evaluators listening to speech samples without visual cues can identify the sexual orientation of speakers with some success (e.g., Gaudio, 1994; Pierrehumbert, Bent, Munson, Bradlow, & Bailey, 2004; Munson, McDonald, DeBoe, & White, 2006), while others have found evaluators to be unreliable in their ability to perform this task (Smyth, Jacobs, & Rogers, 2003). Additionally, Gaudio (1994) found that while people in his study were successful at the identification task, there was uncertainty in the linguistic features that they used to make these determinations; Smyth et al. (2003) were also unable to find any clear-cut phonetic cues that were used to identify the sexual orientation of speakers.

In terms of production as opposed to perception, much research on variation in American English among members of the LGBT community has investigated phonetic differences in groups based on sexual orientation. Pierrehumbert et al. (2004) found that the speech of gay men was characterized by articulatory precision that resulted in an expanded vowel space and strong diphthongization. Several studies have been conducted on production of variants of (æ), including one that found gay men produced a "retracted" variant, while heterosexual men produced a variant similar to the tense [æ] of the Northern Cities Shift (Munson et al., 2006); investigators in this study also found that gay men and heterosexual men varied in their production of (s). In a linguistic study of a "diva" persona adopted by a gay man (Podesva, 2004), it was noted that exaggerated stop consonants were a salient feature. Podesva's (2006) ethnographic study of phonetic variation among three gay men investigated the use of style shifting in the LGBT community and ultimately showed that one man's use of one marker of gay speech, namely, pitch raising in declarative utterances, was more frequent in conversational interactions with gay peers than in professional interactions. This finding is in accordance with the observations of some scholars that LGBT speech characteristics are more apparent in group interaction than in one-to-one interaction (Munson & Babel, 2007, pp. 442).

Mann (2011) builds on language attitude research in folk dialectology and social psychology to investigate people's perceptions of American English as it is used by gay males. He also adapts methodologies from social network theory to investigate how the individual attitudes of gay males toward Gay American English (GAE) and their use of it are influenced by their connectedness to several networks. Mann's results show that while speakers of GAE were assessed positively for characteristics associated with status (e.g., intelligence) and solidarity (e.g., friendliness), the results also showed GAE to be associated with "effeminacy," which was negatively evaluated by participants in the study. In light of these findings, Mann (2011) concluded that the use of GAE might hinder a speaker's chances of upward social mobility. Mann's data also show a positive correlation between attitudes toward and/or use of GAE and connectedness to LGBTQ networks and practices. Mann (2012) found that negative attitudes toward the use of GAE decrease the possibility that a speaker will use linguistic features associated with it and is, as a result, less likely to be perceived as gay than men who hold positive attitudes toward the use of GAE.

BOX 6.4 Reclaimed Epithets

A linguistic issue with relevance to the LGBT community is the use of **reclaimed epithets**, which are terms of derision that are redefined, to some extent, as expressions of pride by members of the group they are intended to denigrate (Zwicky, 1997, p. 22). In the LGBT community, *dyke*, *faggot*, and *queer*, for example, have been reclaimed by some individuals and groups, although acceptable uses of these terms are highly dependent on context. As Zwicky (1997, p. 22) says, "The issue for all such lexical items is: For which speakers, in which contexts, and for which purposes has the word been reclaimed?" The LGBT community is not alone in reclaiming epithets, as observed in efforts to reclaim *bitch* and *slut* by feminists (Joreen, 1970; Wurtzel, 1999) as well as the n-word within the African American community.

6.14

Language and Ethnicity

Another social characteristic that has a significant effect on language use is ethnicity. Among ethnic varieties, African American English (which we discuss in Chapter 7) has received the most attention by linguists. Some other English-based ethnic varieties in the United States include American Indian English, Jewish English, and Chicano English. The US has hosted a large number of these varieties, as they have often emerged in areas in which non-English speakers have remained in closely knit networks for any length of time after arriving in the country.

Besides African American English, Chicano English has perhaps the greatest number of speakers among ethnic varieties of English, and as Mexican American communities expand, the number of speakers of Chicano English continues to grow. Chicano English is a dialect of American English that emerged in communities in the American Southwest with large populations of Mexican immigrants living as residents; these groups are often segregated from the larger community and maintain links to Mexico through continued immigration and through cultural practices carried from Mexico. Influenced by the Spanish and the non-native English that their parents spoke, Chicano English was created by the children of Mexican immigrants. It is important to note, however, that Chicano English is not English as a second language but is instead a variety of English that is spoken by fluent English speakers.

Chicano English is considered to have more similarities with English than it does with Spanish; however, its phonology has several features that are associated with Mexican Spanish. For instance, /z/ is often devoiced in Chicano English so that it sounds like /s/ in words like *busy* and *choose*. Additionally, speakers of Chicano English sometimes articulate English /v/ as /b/, for example *very* as *berry*. Many Chicano English speakers also incorporate multiple negation, and speakers of Chicano English in Southern California are reported to have adopted features from local Anglo speakers, a variety that is known colloquially as the "Valley Girl" dialect (Fought, 2001) and was mentioned above.

6.15

BOX 6.5 **Plain English**

There have been several efforts undertaken to make the language of certain professions more readily understood by others. In particular, it is the lexicon that is of most general concern, as many professions have their own specialized terminology, or **jargon**. The fields of medicine and law are particularly well known for the complex vocabulary that they employ, much of which is borrowed from Greek and Latin.

In *The Language of Law*, Mellinkoff (1963) argued for clearer writing in the legal profession, as one of its goals called for the avoidance of Greek and Latin terms, such as *in absentia* 'in absence,' *inter alia* 'among other things,' and *pro bono* 'for the good,' when other terms would do just as well. In the 1970s, a movement advocating the use of Plain English in government communications

6.16

BOX 6.5 *(continued)*

began, ultimately leading to the Plain Writing Act being passed into law in 2010. Linguists have also argued that instructions from the judge to jurors should also be made in English that is simpler to understand (Dumas, 2000; Langford, 2000).

Another area in which there has been demand to make the language of professionals more comprehensible to laypersons is in the field of healthcare, due to the needs of an aging population with greater access to healthcare information than ever before. As in the language of law, there have been concerns in the medical industry that communication between doctors and patients has been hampered by the technical vocabulary that often leaves patients confused rather than informed (West, 1984). In a recent analysis of the linguistic differences in the questions of healthcare providers and healthcare consumers, significant differences were found in word length and pronoun usage (Liu, Antieau, & Yu, 2011). While such differences suggest more work must be done if communication between providers and consumers in healthcare settings is to be improved, the results have already been used to enhance an automated medical question answering system.

Several professional fields are known for their frequent use of abbreviations, initialisms, and **acronyms**, the latter a word-formation process in which the first initial of a set of words is used to create a word, for example *laser*, *scuba*, and *radar*. Two fields in which such processes are used frequently are the medical profession, where, for example, MRI, IV, and NPO, are frequently used, and the armed services, where such terms as MRE, BDU, MOS, as well as *snafu* and *fubar*, can often be heard.

6.17

SOCIAL MEDIA

Even though traditional media have not made us all homogeneous speakers (as discussed in the previous chapter), social media have affected language and have done so in several ways. Several questions arise as to the nature of this type of language change and whether it is a positive or negative change. Because younger people are often early adopters of new technology, research into varieties of language emerging through relatively recent innovations such as instant messaging, Twitter, Facebook, and other social media often focuses on adolescent usage (e.g., Tagliamonte & Denis, 2008; Jones, Schieffelin, & Smith, 2011). In some cases, the relationship between the language used in social media and in speech has been reciprocal, that is, just as spoken forms have had written representations on social media that they haven't enjoyed elsewhere, the written forms used in social media have taken on currency in speech as well, for example, *omg*, *lol*, *idk*, and *jk*. Specific social media have contributed new words to the lexicon, such as *google*, *hashtag*, *retweeted*, and *selfie*, or, more commonly, provided new definitions of words previously in use, such as *twitter* and *tweet*, as well as *friend* and its variants, which include *friended*, *unfriended*, *defriended*, *refriended*, *cold friended*, and *silent friended*. Social media, in particular Facebook, have contributed yet another function of the word *like* to English, as in "I accidentally *liked* that silly selfie of his" or "I *unliked* your status because you and your friends on that thread wouldnt stfu." The main verb of the latter sentence is one example of many using the prefix *un-* to show the reversal of an action in the lexicon of social media, as in *unfollowed*, *untagged*, and *unfavorited* (Zimmer, 2009).

6.18

A common complaint concerning social media, often aimed at young people, is that linguistic competence is being eroded as people grow up using the language of social media and text messaging. People who are irritated by this kind of communication sometimes appeal to linguists for support; however, as you might have guessed by now, linguists do not generally share in this sentiment. Crystal (2008), for instance, points out that the shorthand abbreviations that texting incorporates, and that are often targeted by critics, are not entirely new—let alone devoid of any redeeming value—but, rather, are the same as, or similar to, word-formation processes and orthographic conventions that existed long before social media and cellular technology were even blips on the radar. Such language is an acceptable way of communicating in that speech community and therefore has merit.

6.19

It should also be noted that the varieties of language that are emerging from these technologies cannot be categorized simply as speaking or writing. In an early paper on the language of email communication, Maynor (1994) notes that emails "seem to be attempts to make writing more like speech," and Baron (2000) refers to email "as an emerging language centaur—part speech, part writing" (p. 248). As such, the language of the Internet has gone beyond the contribution of some words and spelling conventions and has morphed into varieties with differences at every level of the grammar. Our approaches to communicating through such channels have even changed the way we use and interpret punctuation.

6.20

BOX 6.6 Representations of Social Variation in American Literature

For many years, American writers have used nonstandard orthography in an effort to show dialectal differences in the speech of their characters and narrators. Mark Twain's representation of African American

BOX 6.6 *(continued)*

English in the speech of Jim in *The Adventures of Huckleberry Finn* (1885) has received a great deal of attention from fans and critics alike; other writers who have incorporated nonstandard orthography to represent ethnicity in their work include William Faulkner, Charles Chesnutt, and Zora Neale Hurston (see Minnick, 2004). The social dialects of New Orleans have been represented in several novels, including *A Confederacy of Dunces* (Toole, 1980), as discussed in Fennell and Bennett (1991).

In *The Catcher in the Rye* (Salinger, 1951), nonstandard orthography and other features are used to show the class differences of its characters, as illustrated in the passage below:

> "All right, chief, let's have it. I gotta get back to work."
>
> "I told you about ten times, I don't owe you a cent. I already gave her the five—"
>
> "Cut the crap, now. Let's have it."
>
> "Why should I give her another five bucks?" I said. My voice was cracking all over the place. "You're trying to chisel me."
>
> Old Maurice unbuttoned his whole uniform coat. All he had on underneath was a phony shirt collar, but no shirt or anything. He had a big fat hairy stomach. "Nobody's tryna chisel nobody," he said. "Let's have it, chief."
>
> "No."
>
> When I said that, he got up from his chair and started walking towards me and all. He looked like he was very, very tired or very, very bored. God, was I scared. I sort of had my arms folded, I remember. It wouldn't have been so bad, I don't think, if I hadn't had just my goddam pajamas on.
>
> "Let's have it, chief." He came right up to where I was standing. That's all he could say. "Let's have it, chief." He was a real moron.
>
> "No."
>
> "Chief, you're gonna force me inna roughin' ya up a little bit. I don't wanna do it, but that's the way it looks," he said. "You owe us five bucks."
>
> "I don't owe you five bucks," I said. "If you rough me up, I'll yell like hell. I'll wake up everybody in the hotel. The police and all." My voice was shaking like a bastard.
>
> "Go ahead. Yell your goddam head off. Fine," old Maurice said. "Want your parents to know you spent the night with a whore? High class kid like you?" He was pretty sharp, in his crumby way. He really was.
>
> "Leave me alone. If you'd said ten, it'd be different. But you distinctly—.
>
> (pp. 133–134)

BOX 6.6 *(continued)*

This example illustrates how nonstandard orthography is used to represent dialect that provides literary characters with voices and, in this specific example, helps to add tension to the conflict by highlighting some of the linguistic differences between the characters.

CONCLUSION

In this chapter, we have introduced readers to the field of sociolinguistics, which is a subfield of linguistics that focuses on the intersection of language and society. The primary focus of sociolinguistics is on language variation and change, and sociolinguists are interested in how linguistic variables correlate with the social characteristics of the speakers who use them for both communication and as identity markers. We devoted a part of this chapter to focusing on single social factors that play important roles in language variation, summarizing some of the research that has been done in these areas. In looking at these groups, however, it is important to remember that human beings are complex creatures who maintain membership of many social groups simultaneously. Even in our professional lives, most of us wear many hats over the course of a lifetime and, sometimes, we wear these hats at the same time.

Besides adding to general knowledge concerning language variation and change, and the social mechanisms underlying these processes, study of the social dimensions of language can be used to meet a variety of needs in society. For instance, obtaining a better understanding of the relationship between different varieties of English and putting this knowledge to work to improve education has long been an aim of sociolinguistics. A great deal more research is needed in this area if we are to meet the needs of students from diverse linguistic backgrounds.

Near the end of the chapter, we looked briefly at the impact that social media have had on language use, not only via the keyboard but also our speech. Contrary to the reactions of some in the general public, linguists are not repelled by the language used in these new media but are interested in the linguistic varieties that are emerging from them, as well as in the benefits to be gained by those who use these varieties. As the influence of these media on our daily lives continues to grow, their effect on language use, and even on how researchers investigate language use, will continue to evolve.

DISCUSSION AND RESEARCH QUESTIONS

1. In his study of Martha's Vineyard, Labov found that speakers used language variation to mark themselves as "islanders," that is, as members of a group that identified themselves as being of the island. Have you noticed any ways in which residents of your community use language to identify themselves as "insiders"? Have you ever observed people from other communities doing the same?

2. Consider the speech of your parents and/or grandparents. What are some ways in which their speech differs from that of yourself or other people your own age? Are there specific linguistic levels where you note differences, for example phonology or syntax? Now consider this: Among the differences you've observed, which would you say are the product of physical aging and which are the result of the eras in which these speakers were raised or entered adolescence or young adulthood? What is the basis for your answer?

3. This exercise allows you to do some research on the effect of the media on language use by investigating (1) lines from television, films, and radio shows; (2) song lyrics; or (3) political slogans. First, brainstorm examples of this kind of language that you are familiar with that you suspect might have currency apart from the source where you heard it. Then, use the *Google Book Ngram Viewer* (http://books. google.com/ngrams/) to find trends in the use of the language you listed. For example, when did the words or phrases begin appearing in the kinds of print matter that the viewer uses as its corpus? Did they appear in print before the source that you are familiar with used it? What is the overall distribution of the feature you are using? Has it started to diminish in use? What do your observations tell you about the effect of such catch phrases? (If you are having trouble thinking of language to use, you could try one of the several lines from the film *Jerry Maguire* that continue to be used in conversation or parodied today: (1) "Show me the money"; (2) "You complete me"; and (3) "You had me at _____." Another option would be to use "to boldly go" from the *Star Trek* opening monologue.) Make sure to use the years 1800 to 2008 as your time range and bear in mind that the program is case-sensitive.

African American English

GUIDING QUESTIONS

1. Is there really such a thing as African American English?

2. Where did African American English come from?

3. What are the features of African American English?

4. Why won't speakers of African American English simply switch to the standard?

OVERVIEW

In this chapter, we present the history and structure of the most stereotyped and stigmatized linguistic system in the United States: African American English. We examine the contemporary grammatical system as well as the historical context in which African American English developed in order for readers to see both its linguistic and sociocultural complexity. We also use this information to show the inherent connections between language and speaker experience and between language and identity. From this perspective, African American English is the linguistic outcome of the experiences of Africans and African Americans in North America. We begin the chapter with a review of some of the early research on African American English, and we end it with an examination of both the stigma and prestige that surround its use.

COMMON MYTHS

> *Ebonics is not a valid form of speech.*

> *All African Americans use AAE.*

> *African American English is just slang.*

INTRODUCTION

Examinations of linguistic variation often focus on the salient features of individual dialects, especially those that differ from a standard form; however, a holistic investigation of any linguistic system must also include the social and historical context in which the system developed. Such investigations show that a language and its speakers are intimately and inextricably connected and that linguistic systems change and grow as a reflection of the experiences of the speech communities that use them. When we take this holistic view, we recognize that every linguistic system has its own social history, every dialect has its own story. While it is beyond the scope and focus of this textbook to tell the stories of each American variety—there are many excellent readings that do present detailed discussions of individual varieties (see Pederson, 1983; Leap, 1993; Boas, 2009; Johnstone, 2013; Wolfram and Reaser, 2014)—here we tell the story of one specific variety: **African American English**.

In the Foreword to *Spoken Soul: The Story of Black English*, Smitherman writes:

> The story of Spoken Soul is not an easy one to tell because it is not *just* about language. To tell the story right, you have to talk about the culture and lived experience of African Americans. You have to talk about a language inextricable from the complex social structure and political history of people of African descent in these United States.
>
> (Rickford & Rickford, 2000, pp. ix–x)

Thus, in this chapter, we show that the development of African American English (AAE) is a direct reflection of the history and experiences of Africans and African Americans in North America. That said, we must not ignore the fact that the history of African

Americans includes experiences, policies, and social injustices that many Americans would like to ignore, such as slavery, racism, and segregation. We must not dismiss these negative points but, instead, should recognize them as events that undeniably shaped the development of AAE.

Particularly because the discussions around AAE are politically and racially sensitive, it is important to note that while there is a close connection between the history of this linguistic system and the history of African Americans, not everyone who identifies as African American speaks AAE, and not everyone who speaks AAE is African American. In other words, AAE is not a group exclusive variety. Furthermore, as is the case with any linguistic system, no individual speaker of AAE uses all of the available features of the dialect, nor does a speaker use the features that he/she has adopted in every possible instance in which they could be used. Therefore, while we discuss African American English in this chapter in broad, generalized terms—including the presentation of AAE as if it were a single, homogeneous form—we do recognize that this linguistic system is regionally and socially variable and that its speakers, as a group, are equally as diverse.

EARLY SOCIOLINGUISTIC RESEARCH ON AAE

There is a significant body of research on African American English, and it is quite possible that there have been more sociolinguistic explorations, descriptions, and examinations of African American English than of any other single linguistic variety in the United States. According to Rickford and Rickford (2000), the earliest discussion of African American English to appear in an academic publication was James A. Harrison's 1884 piece in the journal *Anglia* called "Negro English." In this article, Harrison (1884) attempts to give a "correct re-production" of the pronunciation of the speech of those of African descent living in the American Southeast (p. 232). The article includes ample information of historical and linguistic interest, but any contemporary reader would recognize that Harrison's work is not especially unbiased. The first page states:

> It must be confessed, to the shame of the white population of the South, that they perpetuate many of these pronunciations in common with their Negro dependents; and that, in many places, if one happened to be talking to a native with one's eyes shut, it would be impossible to say whether a Negro or a white person were responding.
>
> (p. 232)

Fortunately, contemporary sociolinguistic studies have taken a more objective approach to analyzing nonstandard linguistic varieties and have since changed the tone for the discussion of African American speech.

Two seminal works on the structure of AAE were published in 1969: Labov's study "The Logic of Nonstandard English" and Wolfram's *A Sociolinguistic Description of Detroit Negro Speech*. This early work on AAE was carried out not only to describe the linguistic structure of a nonstandard English dialect for audiences interested in such academic pursuits, but also as evidence against the discussions of the "verbal deprivation" and poor educational performance of lower-class, inner-city black children that, at that time, were presented by other social science disciplines and were promoted in the public view. Thus, from its early stages, "[o]bservations about African American speech have never been far removed from the politics of race in American society" (Wolfram & Torbert, 2006, p. 226).

Over the last five decades, a body of work, impressive in both academic rigor and sheer number of publications, has been produced, and newer, more focused discussions continue to be published regularly (see Alim & Baugh, 2007, on AAE and educational policy; Lanehart, 2009, for intersections of gender and ethnicity; and Green, 2011, for language acquisition and the complexity of AAE structure). And suffice it to say, even though a plethora of research has been conducted on the topic, culminating in many scholarly publications, there is still much to learn about this linguistic system and its role in both American speech and the African American community. Many questions about AAE have yet to be answered, some can never be answered, and there are even those whose answers are considered to be highly controversial. However, new paths of research are continually being forged and hidden resources are being revealed. Like the linguistic system itself, the study of AAE is always changing.

7.1

A ROSE IS A ROSE

In this textbook, we have chosen to use the term *African American English*, or *AAE*, in reference to this particular linguistic variety, despite that it is not the only name that has been applied to this system, nor is it the only one in current use. Below is a list of alternate names for AAE that have been used in the linguistic literature; the list is not exhaustive:

- African American Vernacular English, or AAVE (AAVE itself can be pronounced in one of three ways: by its initials A-A-V-E; with two syllables [aːveɪ]; or with one syllable [æv]);
- African American Language;
- Black Vernacular English;
- Black English Vernacular;
- Black Language;
- Black Street Speech;
- Black Talk;

- Ebonics;
- Negro English;
- Pan African Communication;
- Spoken Soul.

The names used to describe linguistic varieties are often a reflection of the location, identity, or history of their speakers during their development and/or an indication of their connections to other languages and dialects. For example, the name *American English* used for the general speech of the United States represents not only the location of its use and dialectal development (*American*) but also its sociohistorical and linguistic ties to England and the language that developed there (*English*). In this example, the name also sets up a contrast to other national forms of English, such as British, Canadian, Australian, and Indian.

Many of the names listed above reflect these issues and, due to the inclusion or exclusion of specific terms, different names highlight different concepts. Consciously or not, these names indicate distinctive aspects of AAE's history or structure and, in some instances, they even index divergent research paradigms. For example, AAE has close connections to the American South, but it is not referred to as *Southern American English*, as that term is reserved for another linguistic variety. Instead, ethnic identity and a connection to the history of Africans in America appear to be the most salient factors reflected in these names and, for some of the terms listed above, the name also reflects historical changes in referencing ethnicity in the United States, such as the use of *Black*, *African American*, or *Negro*.

While the term **Ebonics**, meaning 'black sounds,' is commonly used by the American public, it is not a term used regularly by linguists. In fact, as Green (2002) notes, the term was actually coined to "cover the multitude of languages spoken by black people not just in the United States but also those spoken in the Caribbean" (p. 7) and has thus been applied erroneously as a direct synonym of AAE. In this text, we follow the convention established by many linguistic scholars and use the term *Ebonics* exclusively in reference to the controversy surrounding the Oakland school board resolution of 1996. (See our discussion of the Oakland Ebonics Controversy on the Companion Website.)

7.10

Irrespective of the name one chooses to use, here we are referring to a linguistic variety currently spoken in the US that developed out of the history and experiences of Africans and African Americans in North America and is a linguistic system that continues to act as a complex symbol of the African American community, past, present, and future.

HISTORICAL BACKGROUND

The history of a linguistic system is the history of its speakers and, as such, the story of African American English reflects a shared African American experience. This story starts with the first Africans stepping on to the shores of North America; it moves through a turbulent history of racism, segregation, and integration; and it continues through the lives of African Americans today. In other words, the grammar, vocabulary, and discourse style of modern AAE is the linguistic outcome of the settlement, migration, and social experiences of the American descendants of slavery.

As we have already seen in our discussion of Colonial American English and contemporary American regional dialects, differences in language structure and use in the United States can often be traced back to differences in the histories of speakers, including settlement history, migration patterns, and contact with other groups. However, unlike the histories of other groups, many of the details of the African immigrant experience, including the national and linguistic origins for most individuals, have been lost. As Baugh puts it:

> Slave descendants share a unique linguistic history that sets them apart from those whose American ancestors were not enslaved Africans. Whereas typical immigrants to the United States may have come to America in poverty, speaking a language other than English, they usually did so with others who shared a common language and culture. The vast majority of Americans can trace their family ancestry to homelands where the languages of their ancestors are well known. Such is not the case for the typical slave descendant of African origin.
>
> (2006, p. 218)

The history of Africans in North America is generally traced to 1619, when a Dutch captain, in want of food, traded a group of 20 African slaves to the settlers of Jamestown, Virginia. It is unclear whether these Africans were considered to be slaves or indentured servants by the white, British population of Jamestown, but, in either case, their immigration to North America was not by their own choice, nor were they free to live their lives as they pleased. Any question of their possible freedom was answered in 1640 when the Virginia colony instituted lifetime servitude, a law that applied to the African immigrants but not to the whites who worked alongside them (Rickford & Rickford, 2000, p. 135). Additionally, the Slave Code, certified in 1705, established a unified system of laws covering the ownership and treatment of blacks, and the stage was thus set for a long history of Africans and African Americans who were denied access to basic human rights and who were socially and ideologically, if not physically, separated from other American settlers.

This original settlement of Africans in Virginia was followed closely by the continued forced migration of more and more people through the European–African–North American slave trade. Through this triangle trade, millions of Africans, who came from a variety of different countries and spoke perhaps dozens of different languages, were moved from West Africa to areas in the Caribbean, North America, and South America (Figure 7.1). The importation of slaves into the United States was outlawed in 1808,

7.2

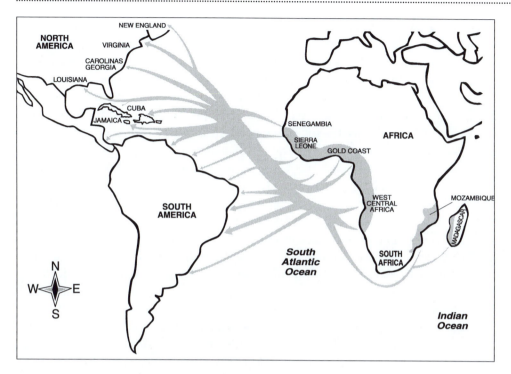

FIGURE 7.1 Map of the transatlantic slave trade.

but, for several decades, ships transporting slaves continued to steer toward American shores, especially to the small and hard-to-police islands off the coast of Georgia and the Carolinas that were exploited by illegal runners and pirates. In fact, there are detailed records of more than 500 slave vessels that were captured between 1808 and 1862 (Justice, 2012); no one knows how many others made it to shore surreptitiously.

Once in North America, steps were taken to ensure that African slaves were psychologically, if not physically, alienated and isolated. Their identities as citizens of specific homelands were stripped; even their names were taken away and replaced with Christianized or Anglicized forms. Moreover, when possible, individuals were placed with others who did not share the same language. This type of linguistic isolation was practiced not only because it was psychologically alienating for those who were not able to communicate with others, but also because the slave owners were taking steps to ensure that their slaves would not be able to work together to plan and execute uprisings. Thus, through these different practices, slaves in North America found themselves to be without an identity; they lost their homes, their countries, their names, and their languages.

At the same time that slaves were denied their own identities, they were also refused equal participation in the larger linguistic community. For one, they were systematically denied access to education, and it was even illegal to teach slaves to read. Therefore, not only were black men and women kept from using their heritage languages in both oral and written forms, they were also denied access to standardized forms of English. These practices kept African Americans from participating in the linguistic majority, and they reinforced the sociopsychological barriers between blacks and whites overall. Thus, linguistically, the stage was set for the development of a linguistic system that could meet the specific needs—for communication as well as for the expression of identity—of an emerging African American community.

Additionally, due to these experiences and practices, African slaves often found themselves in highly multilingual situations, and their daily experiences regularly placed them in contact with speakers of several different linguistic systems. These included various standard and nonstandard English dialects from both America and the British Isles; other European immigrant languages, such as French, German, and Dutch; dozens of West African languages; and, in some cases, Native American languages. Furthermore, those who had spent time in the Caribbean before going on to the North American mainland were also exposed to the linguistic systems found there, including emerging creole languages, such as Jamaican Creole and Haitian Creole. (Creoles are discussed in detail in Chapter 13.) Therefore, African immigrants and their descendants found themselves inhabiting highly complex, multilingual, multidialectal situations. But slaves were not allowed equal access to each of these forms; as mentioned above, steps were taken to ensure they were isolated from both their home languages and standard varieties of English. And because many of these interactions were temporary, as slaves were forcibly moved from place to place, there often was not enough time for these languages to be directly acquired. Therefore, this language contact situation was not one to favor the survival of African heritage languages, nor was it one to support the acquisition of more standard varieties of English; rather, it provided the environment for a new system—AAE—to develop and, ultimately, thrive.

While we know much about the historical context in which AAE developed, its linguistic origins are still contested. Even though we now take for granted the ability to record speech electronically, such technologies were not available throughout most of the history of the United States. Therefore, there are no audio records of the early speech patterns of Africans in North America and, consequently, no precise account of the earliest forms of AAE. Written records of language from this same time period are available, but there is minimal written evidence of the speech of slaves and free black men and women, since legally they were not allowed to read and write. The records that are available were written by whites; as such, they present only an outside perspective and cannot be taken as truly accurate representations of early African American speech. However, informed by the methods of historical linguistics, researchers have been able to hypothesize what early forms of AAE were like and, therefore, what processes converged to form this linguistic system. Additionally, ex-slave narratives from the early 20th century and fieldwork in isolated ex-slave communities have helped to reconstruct the development of AAE.

7.3

While there are many questions about the origin of AAE that are still to be answered, we do know that AAE did develop from the interaction of English dialects and West African languages and that both sets of linguistic systems have contributed, to some degree, to the grammar and lexicon of AAE (which is discussed below). What we do not have, however, is a definitive answer to how much of AAE came from each system. There are several hypotheses concerning the formation of AAE that have been presented in the academic literature, but there is still significant debate as to whether AAE began as a nonstandard dialect of English, similar to Southern American English, or as a creole language, akin to Jamaican Creole. A detailed description and discussion of these hypotheses can be found on the Companion Website.

7.4

The same history that allowed for the development and increased use of AAE also saw the decline of the use of African languages in North America. Even though some ships did continue to arrive in the United States, fewer African immigrants were arriving in the 19th century, and thus the immigration of African languages was also cut off. At the same time, these languages were not being passed through families or communities like other colonial immigrant languages were. Therefore, not only did the use of African languages all but die out in North America, but AAE was also no longer in direct contact with the African languages that had previously added to its structure and lexicon. Even after slavery was abolished by the Thirteenth Amendment in 1865, segregation, racism, and extreme inadequacies in education persisted, serving as at least some of the factors that maintained differences between AAE and other varieties of English. In many ways, therefore, AAE was left on its own to continue to develop on its own trajectory.

As the history of African Americans changed, the use and structure of, and even the need for, AAE also changed. Even though the importation of slaves decreased during the early 19th century, interstate trade increased, and thousands of slaves were moved westward into areas such as Mississippi and Louisiana. As they went, African American English went with them. Additionally, the abolition of slavery opened up the possibility for black men and women to move to new areas, further expanding the range of AAE. For example, during the "Great Migration" (1910–1970), millions of African Americans moved to northern cities in order to leave behind agricultural jobs for new opportunities in the newly expanding industrial sector—as well as to escape overt racism in the South—and AAE was transplanted into cities such as Chicago, Detroit, and New York. As such, over time, AAE found itself in every corner of the country.

Even though speakers of AAE have come into contact with many social and regional dialects of American English as they have settled in different areas of the United States, contemporary AAE does not seem to be incorporating the local linguistic changes that are adopted by the white residents of the areas. For example, speakers of AAE in cities such as Detroit and Chicago are not incorporating the features of the

Northern Cities Shift into their speech. Alternatively, speakers in Atlanta appear to be adopting features of the Southern Shift, but are doing so only as their white urban and suburban neighbors are rejecting the shift (Prichard, 2009). According to Wolfram and Torbert (2006), it appears that, for AAE speakers, social identity is more salient than regional identity in predicting language change. Furthermore, while some recent discussions have recognized regional and social variation within AAE (e.g., Green, 2002; Weldon, 2004; Wolfram, 2007), many maintain that the linguistic system of AAE is relatively consistent across space. As noted by Fought (2006), this homogeneity may simply be a historical effect:

> Because patterns of immigration for [AAE] speakers are relatively more recent than for European-American, we might expect a smaller degree of regional difference in AAE due to settlement history (much as European-American dialects in the West show fewer distinctions than on the East Coast).
>
> (p. 59)

The next generation of study will most likely move from broader views of AAE as a homogeneous system and instead focus more on the investigation of variation and change within AAE.

In this section, we have been able to look back and examine much of the history of AAE. The story continues, and while we do not know what direction it will take, we do know AAE will continue to evolve to meet the needs and reflect the experiences of African Americans in the United States.

THE STRUCTURE OF AFRICAN AMERICAN ENGLISH

In this section, we describe and discuss several lexical and grammatical features that are commonly attributed to or associated with AAE. It is important to recognize that some of these features are shared by other nonstandard English varieties and are thus not exclusive to African American English. For example, the use of multiple negation, such as "I ain't going to give you no hard time" (Tamasi, 2008), is a feature regularly associated with AAE. However, this construction is found in most, if not all, nonstandard dialects of English (and not just American dialects) and, as we discussed in Chapter 2, it has been considered a productive feature of grammatical English for centuries.

The structure of African American English is a complex, rule-governed system, and as Green says, "speakers know more than just a few unique words and phrases when they know AAE" (2002, p. xi). While we are not able to cover the entire linguistic system in this chapter, we are able to present several of the most salient features of AAE at different levels of its structure, including lexical, grammatical, phonological, and discourse features. For those interested in learning more, there are several robust descriptions of the structure of AAE available, including Smitherman (1977), Mufwene, Rickford, Bailey, & Baugh (1998), Rickford and Rickford (2000), and Green (2002). (Also see the list of recommended readings available on the Companion Website.)

7.1

Lexicon

When we discuss the lexical system of African American English, we are referring to words that:

- are used solely, or primarily, by AAE speakers;
- have particular meaning in AAE;
- are used by the broader community but are historically associated with AAE.

Even though many of the lexical features of AAE are not group exclusive, the lexicon has a special salience in terms of social identity. According to Smitherman:

> Basic in Black Talk, then, is the commonality that takes us across boundaries. Regardless of job or social position, most African Americans experience some degree of participation in the life of the COMMUNITY ... This creates in-group crossover lingo that is understood and shared by various social groups within the race.
> (1994, p. 25; emphasis in the original)

Furthermore, as Green (2002) points out, there are many people who are familiar with or use vocabulary attributed to AAE, but who do not use AAE grammar (p. 13). Some lexical items associated with African American English are:

- *ashy* (adj.): dry skin from cold or wind;
- *saditty* (also *seditty* or *sadiddy*) (adj.): snooty; putting on airs;
- *kitchen* (n.): the hair at the nape of the neck, which tends to be the most curly;
- *steady* (adv.): indicates that an action is being done intensely, frequently, and continuously;
- *stay* (v.): to reside in a place;
- *tote* (v.): to carry;
- *mash* (v.): to push in or down, such as to mash a button.

We want to stress that the lexicon of AAE, as with any other nonstandard variety, should not be equated with slang. Of course, AAE does have lexical items that can be considered slang—every linguistic form, even a standard dialect, does—but, as we discussed in Chapter 6, slang is a special type of informal vocabulary, and the term does not generally apply to words associated with regionally or socially based linguistic varieties.

Grammar

The structure of AAE's grammatical system makes it truly distinctive in comparison to other varieties of American English. What are erroneously viewed as bad or incorrect attempts at standard English are actually highly complex structures that bring precision and nuance to language.

Null Copula

The **copula** is any form of the verb "to be," such as *is*, *am*, and *are*. In most varieties of English, simple **stative** sentences are formed with an inflected form of the copula:

> I am late.
> The coffee is cold.
> They are married.

However, in several languages, including Russian (and some West African languages), it is perfectly grammatical for the copula to not appear in indicative sentences in the present tense:

> Кофе холодный.   Кофе был холодный
> coffee cold   coffee was cold
> 'The coffee is cold.'   'The coffee was cold.'

The **null copula** is also a prominent feature of AAE:

> He late.
> The coffee cold.
> They married.

These sentences, despite the copula being absent, provide all of the grammatical and semantic information required to recognize these utterances as syntactically encoding the present tense stative form.

Alternate copula structures in English are not unique to AAE. In fact, in most varieties of American English, the copula can be contracted. Compare the above examples with:

> He's late.
> The coffee's cold.
> They're married.

In fact, the rules that govern the null copula in AAE are generally the same that govern copula contraction in other varieties of English. In the following examples, the use of the copula in the sentence-final phrase *she is* cannot be grammatical in either a contracted or null form:

> That's where she is.
> *That's where she's.
> *That's where she.

However, as is shown, the contraction of the copula in the initial phrase (*that is*) is grammatical.

Absence of Third-person Singular -s

As a historical survey of English shows, the verbal system has never been static or invariable. Most verbal inflections have been lost in English; for example, *singan* 'to sing' has been simplified to *sing*. As Table 7.1 shows, simplifications in the present verbal system are regularly found and appear in standard as well as nonstandard varieties. Therefore, such variations in the verbal system of AAE are neither new nor irregular. In fact, the absence of the third-person singular actually regularizes the verb paradigm and gets rid of a persistent, irregular form.

Aspectual Markers

Aspectual markers are grammatical forms that give additional meaning to the verb and include information such as the progression or completion of the action or whether or

TABLE 7.1 Comparison of English verbal forms

Old English	Middle English	Modern Standard American English	Modern AAE
ic cepe 'I keep'	I kēpe	I keep	I keep
ic helpe 'I help'	I helpe	I help	I help
θu cepest	thou kēpest	You keep	You keep
θu hilpst	thou helpest	You help	You help
he/heo/hit cepeð	he/she/it kēpeth (–es)	He/she/it keeps	He/she/it keep
he/heo/hit hilpð	he/she/it helpeth (–es)	He/she/it helps	He/she/it help
we, ge, hi cepað	we/you/they kēpe(n)(–s)	We/you/they keep	We/you/they keep
we, ge, hi helpað	we/you/they helpe(n) (–es)	We/you/they help	We/you/they help

Source: Old English examples from Pyles and Algeo (1993, p. 160).

not the action performed is habitual. Here, we discuss three aspectual markers that are salient features of AAE: habitual *be*, the use of *been* to reference distant past, and completed action *done*. For more detailed information on these features or the complete aspectual system of AAE, see Green (2002).

Habitual *be*

In AAE, the use of the word *be* (the uninflected form of the copula) incorporates the meaning that the action or state is habitual, that is, something that happens regularly. The linguistic system thus encodes grammatically a distinction between a temporary state (no copula) and the habitual state (*be*) that does not exist in other varieties of English, such as Standard American English (SAE):

AAE	*SAE*
The coffee is cold.	The coffee is cold.
The coffee cold.	The coffee's cold.
The coffee be cold.	The coffee is always/is regularly cold.
John is late to class.	John is late to class.
John late to class.	John's late to class.
John be late to class.	John is always/is regularly late to class.

Therefore, the use of habitual *be* indicates that the AAE verbal system presents a more nuanced meaning than other English forms, and the semantic content is grammatically, as opposed to lexically, transferred. Simply stated, one can use fewer words to get the point across.

Unfortunately, when the form is not recognized, the speaker may be misunderstood, as we see in this example from Smitherman (2006, p. 4):

Teacher:	Where is Mary?
Kesha:	She not here.
Teacher:	(clearly annoyed) She is *never* here!
Kesha:	Yeah, she be here.
Teacher:	Where? You just said she wasn't here.

In this dialogue, the student corrects the teacher's assessment that Mary is regularly absent by stating that "she be here," that is, she is regularly/habitually present, even if she is not here at this moment. The use of the habitual *be* is misconstrued as present tense stative, as if Kesha was contradicting her previous statement by saying that Mary was, in fact, in attendance.

Been

Often written in the literature as *BIN* to highlight the pronunciation and marked stress of the word, *been* in AAE is used as a verbal marker that denotes distant past:

>   A: I saw Sandra the other day. She married?
>   B: She *been* married.

In this example, speaker B is not only answering in the affirmative but is also telling speaker A that Sandra got married a long time ago and is still currently married. Wolfram and Torbert (2006) offer the example "She been known him forever," which, by the inclusion of both *been* and *forever*, gives extra emphasis to the fact that the two people in question have known each other for a very long time (p. 227).

Done

The verbal marker *done* is used in AAE to note that an action has been completed. This is similar to languages such as Russian that have **imperfective** and **perfective** forms for verbs, in which verbs are grammatically encoded with this aspectual information about the completion of the action. In Standard American English, the past tense can be ambiguous in that it does not give information to say whether or not the action is completed; such meaning would have to be inferred or presented through additional phrases. Note the following three answers to the question, "What did he do yesterday?"

>   A1: He read a book.
>   A2: He was reading a book (but did not finish it).
>   A3: He finished reading a book.

In Standard American English, the answer presented in A1 could potentially have the meanings presented in A2 or A3. The use of completed *done*, however, does not allow for this ambiguity. The following sentence specifically states that the action has been completed.

>   He done read the book.

Absence of Plural and Possessive -s

Just as we saw a reduction of inflectional suffixes in the verbal system (see Table 7.1), English has reduced the vast majority of its inflectional endings for nouns as well. In AAE, the grammatical system includes the absence of both plural *-s* and possessive *-s*, as is shown in the following examples:

>   This coke cost me fifty cent.
>   I'll give it to you as soon as we get to my mama house.

Even though the inflectional morpheme *-s* is the most commonly used structure for forming the plural, Standard English (and other varieties) does use other strategies for doing so. For example, as discussed in Chapter 1, English speakers use the suffix *-en* (e.g., *children, oxen*) as well as internal vowel changes (e.g., *mice, feet*). Also used is the absence of any added morpheme or internal change, such as in *sheep, deer,* or *fish*. Therefore, the absence of plural *-s* shown in the example above is not exclusive to AAE. In contrast, as noted by Wolfram (2004), "The absence of possessive -s in sentences like *The dog_ tail was wagging* or *The man_ hat was old* [is] rare among other American English vernaculars" (pp. 124–125), thus showing that AAE retains features that maintain its place as a unique variety.

Phonology

The phonological system of AAE also has several noteworthy, salient features, six of which are presented in Table 7.2. As with other aspects of the grammar of African American English, these phonological forms reveal that many of the features associated with AAE are not exclusive to this linguistic system, but are shared with, or are similar to, structures found in other varieties of English (contemporary and historical) as well as in languages throughout the world. For example, because both systems developed parallel to one another, AAE shares a significant number of features with Southern American English, such as monophthongized [aɪ], which we discussed in the previous chapter as being a significant part of the Southern Shift. As such, investigating these shared features, while allowing researchers to better understand the overall structure of AAE, may also give insight into its linguistic origins.

TABLE 7.2 Examples of phonological features of African American English

Feature	Example
[θ] and [ð]variation	*birthday* as birfday; *brother* as brover
Metathesis in *ask*	*ask* as [æeks]
Front stressing	pO-lice [po'lis], cE-ment [si'mɛnt]
[skr] for [str]	*street* as skreet [skrit]
monophthongized [aɪ]	*time* as tahm [ta:m]
Consonant cluster deletion	cold → col' [kɔl] fifty → fitty [fɪɾi] children → chi'ren [tʃɪɾɪn]

7.5

BOX 7.1 **The Story of *Aks***

Most often associated with African American English in the US, the pronunciation of *ask* as *aks* [æks] has a very long history. Through changes in the word during the Old English period, *ask* has been pronounced as both [æsk] and [æks] for over a millennium. Early writings include *axian* as well as *acsian*, and the "ax" variant appeared as a regular literary form until approximately 1600, when British English adopted *ask* [-sk] as the standard orthography and pronunciation of the word (*The Oxford English Dictionary*). The linguistic process that affected the consonants is known as **metathesis**, which is a natural phonological process in which two speech sounds alternate. In some instances the newer pronunciation becomes standardized and thus the earlier form is dropped from regular use, but in others both pronunciations continue, often as dialectal variants. For example, the word now pronounced as *bird* is a product of metathesis of *brid*. And *prescription* is often metathesized so that we regularly hear both "pre" and "per."

7.6

Discourse Structure

The **discourse** structure of African American English is noted for its sense of verbal play and a strong oral tradition. Among many AAE speakers there exists an appreciation for language that is shown through a sharp linguistic dexterity, and prestige is awarded to those who think quickly and articulate confidently. This linguistic heritage is an enduring tradition, as it was first adopted from West African cultures and then upheld through segregation and the denial of widespread literacy. It can be seen in the speech of preachers and politicians, entertainers and educators, and even in the games children play.

African American preachers are well known for their ability to excite a crowd through their words. As Rickford and Rickford explain:

> With their repertoire of styles and their passion for pageantry and dramatics, black preachers in the traditional black church don't merely deliver sermons. They hold court. When they testify for "King Jesus" in the tradition of the ancestors, the approach is eloquent, compelling, and certain to kick up dust.
>
> (2000, p. 39)

A sermon may be led by one person, but with discourse tools such as **call-and-response** and repetition, it is actually constructed jointly. Martin Luther King, Jr., a preacher

BOX 7.2 **The Dozens**

The linguistic dexterity and verbal play highlighted in the discourse structure of African American English can be used not only in formal situations, such as in church or political speeches as discussed above, but also to index humor and social bonding. Accordingly, many discussions of the discourse structure of AAE acknowledge the hyper-articulate skill necessary for the verbal game called **The Dozens**, also known as Snaps. This back-and-forth battle of words allows speakers to show off their verbal skills and quick-wittedness through ritualized teasing. The best known version of The Dozens follows a particular structure that can be seen in the following examples:

> Yo mamma's so old she was a waitress at the last supper.
> Yo mamma's so poor she waves an ice cube around and calls it air conditioning.
> Yo mamma's so dumb she spent 30 minutes lookin at an orange juice box because it said concentrate.
> Yo mamma's so dirty she made Right Guard turn left.
>
> (from YoMamma.com)

The Dozens has been a part of the African American oral tradition since the time of slavery, and a written record of it goes back at least to 1891 (Smitherman, 1995). According to Smitherman:

> For a people trying to survive under an oppressive racist yoke, the dozens . . . functioned as an outlet for what countless blues people and Jess B. Simple folk called "laughing to keep from crying." It was a form of release for the suppressed rage and frustrations that were the result of being a Black man or woman trapped in White America.
>
> (1995, p. 19)

The game is played by a variety of people, males and females, old and young, and it is usually played among those who know one another so that the teasing is more a form of social bonding than a personal affront. To win, players must show verbal creativity and be spontaneous in their responses; the more exaggerated the comments, the better (Smitherman, 1995, p. 27).

himself, was able to bring this style to a vast public stage. And there are many examples of people, including preachers, politicians, and other public figures, who use these same discourse strategies to electrify and rouse a crowd.

7.7

In a *New York Times* article titled "Obama's English" (September 8, 2012), H. Samy Alim and Geneva Smitherman examine President Barack Obama's use of signifying and "black preacher style." Defining *signifying* as "the use of indirect humor as critique, and a much discussed feature of black speech," the authors give as an example of this discourse style Obama's statement, "My opponent and his running mate are . . . [pause] new [pause] . . . to foreign policy." Through this use of indirect speech, Obama not only claims that his opponents have no real foreign policy experience, but also indicates that he himself does and therefore is the best choice. Additionally, Alim and Smitherman say that a black preacher style is Obama's "strongest mode of linguistic performance." They give as one of many possible examples his use of a "soaring crescendo" at the end his 2012 Democratic National Conference acceptance speech. Visit the Companion Website to view the speech.

7.8

ISSUES OF STIGMA AND PRESTIGE

We started this chapter by stating that AAE is probably the most misunderstood, stigmatized linguistic system in the United States. Having described the history and linguistic structure of the variety, in this section we move forward to examine the stigma attached to AAE from a sociocultural perspective. Additionally, and most importantly, we discuss that even through such stigma, a strong prestige is also found and, for some, AAE continues to positively index a shared experience, culture, and identity.

African American English is stigmatized on multiple levels. First, we recognize that much of the stigma of AAE is based on a standard language ideology: the grammar and vocabulary of AAE are looked down upon as linguistically inferior to a standard American English. For example, even though the verbal system is in some ways more complex than that of Standard American English, its structure is different, and for many this difference is all that is necessary for it to be placed at a lower level in an imagined linguistic hierarchy. Second, as discussed in Chapter 3, the attitudes expressed toward a particular linguistic system tend to actually be a reflection of the attitudes toward its speakers. The views of the group are transferred to its speech and, as such, prejudiced views can be hidden within linguistic perceptions, allowing one to stigmatize, judge, and even discriminate against a group of people all in the name of "good language." Third, in the case of African American English, a history of racism and segregation in the United States also means that there is not only the hidden prejudice that may come with nonstandard speech connected to a particular social group, but there is also a very real and open racism that attaches itself to AAE. In his 1979 *New York Times* article, "If Black English Isn't a Language, Then Tell Me, What Is?," James Baldwin wrote:

7.9

"It is not the black child's language that is in question, it is not his language that is despised: It is his experience."

Part of the stigma surrounding AAE comes from a long history in which African Americans were not given a public voice. Even when black voices appeared to be presented in public contexts, what was given were only stereotypes of black Americans, such as in minstrel shows. In these shows, which were solely for white audiences, black characters were actually played by white actors in blackface, further removing language from its speakers. Additionally, in literature, most early representations of black speech were not written by African Americans but by white authors, a practice that Minnick calls "literary minstrelsy" (2010, p. 187). It has only been recently that African Americans have been able to represent and present their own voices accurately and openly to a wide audience. As media, such as film, television, music, and even social media, expand to allow for these authentic and personal representations, the perceptions of black language use begin to change as well. But as Fought explains, there is a catch: African American characters can sound black "but not too black," otherwise they will not be accepted (2006, p. 67).

Centuries of misinformation and stereotyped portrayals of African Americans and African American speech have left their mark on many in the United States, even to the extent that there is an expectation that African Americans do not—or cannot—speak "accurately" or "appropriately." Even at the end of the Civil Rights era, psychologists and other researchers were still discussing an "inherent" cognitive defect in black children (Labov, 1972). In their 1951 article, "The Relationship of the Speech of American Negroes to the Speech of Whites," McDavid and McDavid argue against previous work that denied a cultural or historical explanation for linguistic differences. They report that "as late as 1949 the author of a widely syndicated 'popular science' newspaper quiz explained that the Negro cannot pronounce a post vocalic /-r/ in such words as car, beard, or bird because his lips are too thick" (p. 4).

While these types of explanations are no longer posited by serious researchers, the notion of the inarticulate black man is still maintained in the public sphere. In fact, descriptions of public figures as "articulate" are regularly applied to African Americans. In this context, the term *articulate* refers not to linguistic dexterity or precision, as it would to a white speaker, but to the use of "correct" standard varieties versus "incorrect" AAE. The use of *articulate* in this way highlights and perpetuates the "racist stereotype of African Americans as ignorant, incompetent, or incomprehensible" (Subtirelu, 2014) and, therefore, upholds the idea that any standard, eloquent, or even coherent speech by an African American counters expectations. And this appraisal is given regardless of who the person is; Alim and Smitherman remark that in the 2008 presidential campaign both "President George W. Bush and Joseph R. Biden Jr. . . . called Mr. Obama 'articulate'" (2012).

Negative attitudes toward African American English and prejudice toward its speakers are quite common in the United States, and innumerable examples of such prejudices can be found in a variety of contexts. In Chapter 3, we discussed the work that John Baugh and colleagues have done on linguistic profiling and how the stigma attached to nonstandard dialects can lead to housing discrimination. Issues pertaining to employment have also been noted, and the authors of this textbook have personally heard more than one story of resumés being tossed in the trash when job applicants used *aks* instead of *ask* in interviews. Furthermore, the backlash over AAE and the American educational system that was seen through the Oakland Ebonics controversy in 1996 and the Ann Arbor Black English case in 1979 revealed not only that a significant stigma was attached to AAE but also that this perception was unrelentingly held by much of the wider American community. (For a detailed discussion of the Ann Arbor case and the Oakland Ebonics controversy see the Companion Website.) Finally, the media continue to be places for the perpetuation of linguistic stigma, and Lippi-Green's 1997 study of the use of language in Disney animated films shows that AAE has historically been used for animal, rather than human, characters and has been used primarily for comic relief; examples include the crows in *Dumbo*, the orangutan King Louie in *The Jungle Book*, and Shenzi the Hyena in *The Lion King* (Lippi-Green, 2012).

7.10

There is no doubt that African American English has, and continues to be, stigmatized in the United States. We have seen that the development of AAE has reflected the history of Africans and African Americans in North America, and it appears that the stigma and prejudice placed on the black community is transferred to this linguistic system as well. In her book *English with an Accent: Language, Ideology, and Discrimination in the United States*, Lippi-Green concludes:

> The real trouble with Black English is not the verbal aspect system which distinguishes it from other varieties of U.S. English, or the rhetorical strategies which draw such a vivid contrast, it is simply this: AAVE is tangible and irrefutable evidence that there is a distinct, healthy, functioning African American culture which is not white, and which does not want to be white . . . The real problem with AAVE is a general unwillingness to accept the speakers of that language and the social choices they have made as viable and functional.

> (2012, p. 209)

Due to the prevalence and depth of this prejudice, it is often asked: If African American English is so highly stigmatized, then why does it persist? The short answer is that, regardless of this stigma, for many, AAE carries significant social prestige.

To answer the question of the persistence of a nonstandard linguistic system through public prejudice and institutionalized stigma, it is important to understand the connection between language, identity, and community. In the case of African American English, a linguistic system was created for and among a group of displaced men and women who were simply trying to survive. The fact that AAE exists is a testament to the perseverance and determination of Africans and African Americans to survive the horrors of slavery and to thrive amidst continued segregation and racism. As AAE allowed slaves to communicate with one another and bond together as a group of varied people who found themselves in the same situation, contemporary AAE continues to index this shared history and acts as both a means for and reflection of group solidarity. In other words, AAE continues to be spoken because it represents a cultural solidarity and shared identity, and thus it maintains prestige.

In order to diminish the stigma and promote the prestige of AAE, linguists are taking steps to bring factual information about this and other nonstandard linguistic systems to a wider audience. The knowledge that AAE is the product of a shared history and culture and is a unique linguistic system, not a defective version of English, can be quite empowering, and it allows many to find positive associations with their language and personal linguistic identities. Information about nonstandard linguistic systems can be incorporated into classrooms at any level of study, K-12, or even in higher education (see Reaser, 2010; Charity Hudley & Mallinson, 2011). This information is used to promote positive attitudes about language and, in some cases, it can also be used to

---

BOX 7.3 A Linguistic Remedy for Racial Prejudice?

In his Foreword to Lisa Green's *Language and the African American Child*, Tom Roeper explains that, in order to fight linguistic prejudice, all children should learn AAE, just as children in Canada learn French. He says:

> It has been my belief for a quarter century that understanding AAE is part of what it should mean to be an American citizen . . . In America, 20 million people, found in every state, speak varieties of AAE. It is often at the advanced edge of the direction of the mainstream dialect. For instance, mainstream English has lost most of its inflections—we no longer say "thou singest," and it is only a matter of time before the last inflection on the third person disappears (he runs → he run), but this step has already been taken in AAE . . . In addition, popular songs and TV incorporate many expressions of AAE . . . Therefore, I think all American citizens should be taught the contrasts and differences between dialects and I believe that a one- or two-month high school course could accomplish this very well.
>
> (Green, 2011, p. xiv)

What do you think about this controversial proposal?

help young students learn to read and/or transition to Standard American English. Even just having teachers who recognize that their students speak a linguistic system that is structurally complex allows students to find prestige in their own language use and educational successes.

Despite such steps being taken, discussions surrounding the stigma and prestige associated with AAE are quite contentious, and these debates elicit a wide range of emotions and opinions, including arguments for its universal acceptance or total eradication. Within the black community, these debates are particularly sensitive, as individuals must often come to terms with feelings of both stigma and prestige. With this conflict in mind, Rickford and Rickford ask their readers to:

> Be conscious of our love-hate relationship with Spoken Soul. The next time a brother or sister starts speaking in deep vernacular during a city council meeting and you feel yourself stinging with embarrassment, try to remember the social conditioning and the historical circumstances behind that private shame. We don't promise that you'll overcome your shame, only that you may begin to understand it and, one hopes, reverse it. By the same token, the next time you find yourself submerged in and surrounded by Spoken Soul, acknowledge it silently. Adore it. Taste it as if for the first time. Try to imagine the same scene, the same ethos and ambiance, without it.
>
> (2000, p. 229)

CONCLUSION

In this chapter, we have presented the unique story of a particular linguistic system found in the United States, which we have referred to as African American English. As with the other languages and dialects that found their way to North America (some of which were discussed in previous chapters, and others that will be discussed throughout the remaining chapters of this book), AAE has its own history that is linked to the immigration and settlement of particular sets of speakers and to the experiences and situations they and their ancestors found themselves in after their arrival.

Even though the linguistic origins of AAE are still unclear, there is no doubt that this system developed out of the history of Africans and African Americans in North America. As noted by Kelley and Lewis:

> Out of the crucible of their suffering was forged a new people—no longer simply Twi, Yoruba, Ashanti, or Kumba. In the Americas, they first became Africans and then African Americans. This process of people making is central to a complete understanding of African-American history.
>
> (2005, p. viii)

This "process of people making" is also the process of language making. In North America, these people were no longer allowed to be speakers of Twi, Yoruba, Akan, or Kumba. Instead, a new linguistic system developed to meet the communicative needs of the people and to represent this new cultural identity.

Over the last four centuries, AAE has developed into a linguistic system that is highly complex and rule-governed. While some of its features are shared with other dialects and languages, as a whole, the system and use of AAE are unique. Of course, it is this uniqueness that, when seen as difference instead of diversity, has led some to perceive AAE as incorrect English, bad language, and/or as problematic for its speakers. However, we have seen that even in the face of heightened, widespread stigma, the prestige of AAE as a symbol of group solidarity prevails.

DISCUSSION AND RESEARCH QUESTIONS

1. Some researchers have discussed a form of "standard" AAE. What would the features of Standard AAE be, and where and by whom would it be spoken?

2. There is an ongoing debate on whether AAE originated as a dialect of English or as a separate creole language. First, research both sides of the debate. (See the Companion Website for suggested readings and additional resources.) Second, discuss why each answer could be linguistically important and/or socially meaningful for contemporary AAE and its speakers.

7.4

3. View the subtitled version of "In Da Club" by 50 Cent. First, note any lexical or grammatical features of African American English that you hear. Second, compare these features with those presented in the Standard English "translation." Finally, discuss what this video says socially and linguistically about the differences between standard and nonstandard forms of language.

7.11

4. Use the information presented in this chapter as a guide to research the structure and history of another variety of American English.

Standard American English

GUIDING QUESTIONS

1. Is there a general American English?

2. Where is Standard American English spoken, and who speaks it?

3. Where did the concept of a generalized speech in the United States originate?

4. Who has the authority to dictate what Standard American English is?

OVERVIEW

In this chapter, we present, as well as question, the idea of a general American English. We examine the development of a standard dialect in the United States and discuss the features that are associated with it. We also question who has authority over language in the United States and introduce the connection between a standard dialect and an American identity. Additionally, we use this chapter to synthesize and further examine many of the concepts that have already been presented in this textbook, such as regional and social dialects, standardization, and language and identity.

COMMON MYTHS

> *I speak Standard American English.*

> *Standard American English is correct English.*

> *General American English is accentless.*

INTRODUCTION

The following exchange was published in the nationally syndicated newspaper column "Ask Marilyn" (2004):

> Q: People who live in certain areas of the Midwest seem to have little or no regional accent when they speak. But isn't this an accent in itself? How did they get to be considered neutral?
>
> A: The English language has developed standards in pronunciation just as it has in spelling. These pronunciations are recorded in dictionaries and do a great service to us all. They help to keep us from fragmenting into dialects that cannot be understood by other Americans. Of the regions in the U.S., Midwesterners pronounce words closest to the dictionary standard, so these people actually have the least accent. When slightly modified, this kind of speech has no accent at all.
>
> The reason accents cause problems is that most have a negative connotation. By disregarding the dictionary pronunciation and using a regional one instead, a person with an accent—especially a strong one—may be perceived as pretentious, uneducated or even dull-witted, depending on the accent. When in doubt, speak like a Midwesterner.
>
> (vos Savant, 2004)

This public exchange about language is a significant example of the complexity that underlies discussions of linguistic variation and standards in American English. While Marilyn vos Savant brings up some interesting points and should be praised for highlighting the fact that views of language use are often issues of perception, her answer centers around a popular, prescriptive view of language and the construct of a standard language ideology. Because her answer is not rooted in descriptive evidence, not only does she misconstrue some of the facts, but she also misses several larger issues about language in the US. What the exchange does clearly show, however, is that a supposedly simple question about accent quickly and automatically elicits the concepts of language variation and change, standardization, language authorities, language attitudes, and regional variation. Crucially, it shows that these concepts are interconnected. Furthermore, it also shows that misunderstandings about language are readily presented as linguistic fact within a public forum. The last line of the answer, "When in doubt, speak like a Midwesterner," is loaded with linguistic misinformation and social judgments, issues that necessitate a more thorough discussion than is offered in vos Savant's answer.

From this, we should recognize that for any discussion of Standard American English (SAE) to be thorough, it must take into account valid and factual information about the nature of language, and it must transcend a prescriptive view and a standard language ideology. American standardization is a complex issue that must be examined in its own right and from multiple angles. While we have already mentioned a standard American English several times throughout this book, we recognize that a more complete discussion—one that includes historical, linguistic, structural, and social information—is needed. Therefore, the purpose of this chapter is to discuss and debate the concept of a standard American English in detail, while also showing how this range of linguistic concepts—some theoretical, and some applied—are all interconnected. The current discussion also shows how Standard American English fits into a larger picture of American speech, particularly how SAE interacts linguistically and socially with other American dialects. Finally, this chapter reinforces many of the concepts introduced in previous chapters.

This chapter is separated into five sections: "Standard Languages," a historical presentation of the outcome of the standardization process in Europe; "American Standardization," which explores the reasons behind and the development (or lack thereof) of an official standard linguistic system in the US; "What is Standard American English?," which is a structural analysis of the dialect; "American Authorities," which investigates some of the different groups who have claimed ownership of SAE; and a "Conclusion" that circles back to the question presented to Marilyn that appears above. In sum, this chapter examines the interrelated historical, structural, and social contexts of Standard American English.

STANDARD LANGUAGES

As we concluded in Chapter 2, the creation of a fully standardized linguistic system is not linguistically feasible. A nation can subject its language to the process of selection and codification and, by doing so, determine a particular set of linguistic features and

TABLE 8.1 The four sub-processes of standardization

Form	Function
• Codification	• Elaboration
• Selection	• Acceptance

rules to be the standard or prestige form (see Table 8.1). However, attaining full elaboration, such that a codified form is extended to all social contexts and used consistently by all speakers, is more of a socially constructed ideal than a linguistic reality. Moreover, even when there is a standard form, other nonstandard varieties remain; people continue to connect their identities to a socially or regionally local way of speaking. We thus recognize that a completely standardized, homogeneous, and uniform language used as the sole system of communication within a nation is an abstract ideal and not a linguistic reality. That said, nations do create and promote standard dialects that are used within particular contexts, such as in broadcasting, journalism, and the educational system.

8.1

8.2

We need only to look to Europe to see a tradition of national linguistic standardization. Every member of the European Union (EU) has a body that oversees national language issues, and all of these bodies are unified under one group: the European Federation of National Institutions for Language. While each EU nation has at least one governmental body that oversees national language issues, not all of these institutions handle standardization specifically. France, Spain, and Italy serve as prime examples of countries that have explicitly standardized their own languages and that have each created a **language academy**, that is, a linguistic arm of the government developed to oversee, maintain, and promote the standard form (see Table 8.2). The reasons and timing for standardization in each country are highly complex and individualized; however, linguistic norms often coincide with the development and promotion of a particular national identity. As Fisher states, "Cultures are universally identified with languages, and this has been especially true since the emergence of nation states in the Renaissance" (2001, p. 59). For example, while an Italian writing system began to be standardized as early as the 1300s, the spoken form was not directly targeted

TABLE 8.2 Examples of European language academies

Country	Year founded	Name	Website
Italy	1580s	Accademia della Crusca	www.accademiadellacrusca.it
France	1635	Académie française	www.academie-francaise.fr
Spain	1713	Real Academia Española	www.rae.es

for standardization until the unification of Italy (from independent principalities) in the 19th century.

These different bodies maintain the standard of their respective languages through time and through inevitable linguistic change. The Académie française, for instance, was created in 1635 to "maintain the language in a fixed state of order and purity" (Adamson, 2007, p. 5) and to "give to the unity of the kingdom forged by political power, a language and style which would symbolise and cement that unity" (Fumaroli, quoted in Adamson, 2007, p. 5). Today, the Académie française, specifically its *Commission générale de terminologie et de néologie* ('General Commission on Terminology and Neologisms'), is tasked with the creation of new French-based words to replace those borrowed from other languages or, as Adamson puts it, "to defend the vocabulary of French against invasion from English words" (2007, p. 54). The French Academy, like other language academies, not only passively maintains the standard but also actively legislates which linguistic changes are acceptable (Curzan & Adams, 2006, p. 34). (To highlight the level of authority that the Académie française has, its 40 members are referred to as *les Immortels* 'the Immortals.') Even as strict as it is in its oversight of the French standard, however, the Académie française does not police the speech of individuals in regular, day-to-day communication, and thus linguistic variation endures.

8.3

8.4

England also has a standardized form, Received Pronunciation (RP, which we introduced in Chapter 2), and a body that oversees language issues, the British Council. The primary task of the British Council is to oversee the teaching of English, through which it promotes the use of standard forms in language education. The council even has its own grammar app (www.britishcouncil.org/english). By examining standard language in the UK, we recognize that large and powerful institutions are given the authority to promote linguistic standards, even if they do not officially or formally seek it. For instance, RP is often referred to as "the BBC standard," despite the British Broadcasting Corporation denying that it has ever served as an authority in the standardization process:

> Although the BBC does not, and never did, impose pronunciations of its own on English words, the myth of BBC English dies hard. It owed its birth no doubt to the era before the Second World War, when all announcers … spoke … Received Pronunciation.
>
> (Miss G.M. Miller, cited in Catherine Sangster,
> *Received Pronunciation and BBC English*, n.d.
> www.bbc.co.uk/voices/yourvoice/rpandbbc.shtml)

Of course, the significance of the BBC's acceptance of RP must not be overlooked; it has functioned as a crucial part of the elaboration of this standard pronunciation. Just as books and newspapers were for centuries able to present to the whole of Britain a written grammatical and lexical standard, the BBC, through radio and then television, has been able to promote to the masses a standardized accent. That said, even with the promotion of the linguistic standard coming from a variety of institutions (the government, education, media), it is estimated that only 3% of all British English speakers actually use RP (Hughes & Trudgill, as cited in Fisher, 2001, p. 71).

Thus, we see that some nations do choose to develop and manage standard linguistic systems, often in order to make an overt connection between language and nationality. It is necessary to recognize, however, that even with the force of the government, the educational system, and other institutions and authorities behind the promotion of the standard, language variation continues to exist and no country is linguistically homogeneous. In the following section we discuss the history of and ideology behind the standardization of American English.

AMERICAN STANDARDIZATION

As is the case with nearly all things linguistic, the issue of a unified standard dialect in the United States is complicated. While there are regular public and academic references to Standard American English (otherwise referred to as General American English, Broadcast English, Proper English, or English of the Wider Community), no such singular, standardized linguistic system has ever been created. An official language academy does not exist in the United States, nor has one ever existed. However, there are standard forms (pronunciations, grammatical constructions, lexical items) that have emerged and that traditionally are presented through formal channels such as journalism, literature, broadcasting, and education. There is a common discourse based on the myth of a prescribed linguistic standard that promotes ideas of correct and incorrect language use and a standard language ideology.

As discussed in Chapter 2, there are several valid reasons why a nation would want to standardize its language. For one, there is the sense of national unity that a shared linguistic system can symbolize and promote; as Fisher states, order in language is commonly associated with order in society (2001, p. 61). For another, ease of communication between all citizens of a nation is a positive, pragmatic goal, especially when its citizens are spread out across a large geographical space and/or are socially isolated from one another.

Although the United States has no official standard, this does not mean that one has never been considered. In fact, some very influential people in American history have argued heatedly for the development of a standard language, including Thomas Jefferson, Benjamin Franklin, and James Madison (Cmiel, 1980, as cited in Minnick, 2010, p. 174). Moreover, language was obviously on the minds of the Founding Fathers, as the First Amendment of the Constitution includes a short yet highly significant reference to speech: "Congress shall make no law . . . abridging the freedom of speech." However, language has not been otherwise legislated at the federal level in the US. (Official language legislation is discussed in Chapter 15.)

One of the most vocal proponents for an official, standard language was John Adams. In a letter to Congress written in 1780, Adams expresses his view that both a unified language and eloquence of speech are crucial components for a nation to be strong. Throughout his letter, Adams gives additional reasons for standardizing English as well as for creating an American language academy:

> I would therefore submit to the consideration of congress the expediency and policy of erecting by their authority a society under the name of "the American Academy for refining, improving, and ascertaining the English Language." The authority of congress is necessary to give such a society reputation, influence, and authority through all the States and with other nations . . . The constitutions of all the States in the Union are so democratical that eloquence will become the instrument for recommending men to their fellow-citizens, and the principal means of advancement through the various ranks and offices of society.
>
> (www.languagepolicy.net/archives/Adams.htm)

8.5

Here, Adams discusses "refining" and "improving" the English language, thus showing that he viewed language as an entity with the potential to go astray as well as to be improved. Additionally, while he specifically does not state that other dialects should be eradicated, he does indicate that people were, and would continue to be, judged by the language they use. It is clear, therefore, that Adams believed that the individuals who would have a voice in influencing the new republic would need to speak a particular way, a way that was decidedly and uniformly American. Additionally, by noting that the US Congress had the power to declare and enforce language standards, beyond what any other body could do, Adams acknowledges the role of authority in the process of standardization. (Of course, as this letter directly addresses Congress, this statement could just be a way of flattering his audience so that they would carry out his wishes, but we won't judge motive here.) Therefore, even within this short excerpt, Adams presents the interconnected roles of authority, prescriptivism, nationalism, and language attitudes in the process of standardization.

Interestingly, Adams also argues that the standardization of English in America would not only strengthen the nation at home but that doing so would also promote the United States as a global power. In a second letter to Congress, written shortly after the one presented above (both in 1780), he states: "An academy instituted by the authority of Congress for correcting, improving, and fixing the English language would strike all the world with admiration and Great Britain with envy" (www.pbs.org/speak/seatosea/officialamerican/johnadams/). In other words, Adams wanted the United States to be the first nation to fully standardize English, an act that would simultaneously embarrass England and validate the United States as a powerful nation. Adams further remarks that while some Englishmen had taken steps toward codifying the language, the British government had fallen short in their linguistic duty:

> Most of the nations of Europe have thought it necessary to establish by public authority institutions for fixing and improving their proper languages. I need not mention the academies in France, Spain, and Italy, their learned labors, nor their great success. But it is very remarkable, that although many learned and ingenious men in England have from age to age projected similar institutions for correcting and improving the English tongue, yet the government have never found time to interpose in any manner; so that to this day there is no grammar or dictionary extant of the English language which has the least public authority, and it is only very lately that a tolerable dictionary has been published even by a private person, and there is not yet a passable grammar enterprised by any individual. [Ed. note: Adams was probably referring to Johnson's dictionary, which had been published just 25 years earlier.]
>
> (www.pbs.org/speak/seatosea/officialamerican/johnadams/)

Although Adams argued rigorously for an American language academy, one never materialized. It appears that Congress had other things to think about in the 1780s, such as the fight for American independence and the creation of a new nation.

One point to note is that Adams could have argued for the standardization of "The American Language" instead of the standardization of "English." The terms *Americanism* and *American English* were already being used by the end of the 18th century (Fisher, 2001, p. 61), so such terminology would not have been unfounded. While his use of "The American Language" would have highlighted a new language for a new nation and emphasized a new sociopolitical identity, by using "English" Adams stresses the language's historical origin and shows that claiming linguistic authority is essentially the same as usurping control from the motherland.

Another proponent for standardization was Noah Webster, who claimed that the use of a uniform language would influence individual feelings of nationalism and argued that people holding on to "their respective peculiarities of speaking ... may imperceptibly corrupt the national language" (Webster, 1789, p. 19). Therefore, like Adams, Webster's arguments were based on prescriptive views of language in addition to a connection between language and patriotism. This second motivation appears to have not emerged until later in Webster's career, but it quickly became the fundamental reason behind his promotion of a standard (Fisher, 2001, p. 62). According to Minnick, Webster believed that "the fledgling nation could not function as a unified whole without a standard version of American English to be spoken by all, and thus that a failure to standardize the language would have political consequences" (Minnick, 2010, p. 174). Furthermore, unlike Adams' focus on the creation of a centralized language academy, Webster's core argument claimed that a common educational system and "uniformity in the use of books" were crucial for "preserv[ing] the purity of the American tongue" (Webster, 1789, as cited in Minnick, 2010, p. 173).

Of all of his writings on language, Webster's two most influential works were *A Grammatical Institute of the English Language* (1783), retitled as *The Elementary*

Spelling Book and known commonly as the "Blue Back Speller," and the *American Dictionary of the English Language* (1828). With these publications, Webster quickly became *the* authority on language in the United States, and the rules that he proposed in his books became the prescriptive rules followed by students and adults alike. In fact, one could argue that these two publications are still among the most influential authorities on American English.

The Preface to the 1908 version of *The Elementary Spelling Book* (see Figure 8.1) states that the focus of the book is "to retain the old mode of Dr. Webster as best calculated to teach *young* scholars the true pronunciation of words" (p. 5; emphasis in original). Although not the word that the publishers felt the need to emphasize with italics, note the use of *true*. The supposition that there is one "true" form in language leads to the logical conclusion that all other varieties are "false," which is the message conveyed to those who followed Webster's text. It is also notable that the first line on the cover says, "The National Standard," and that the publishers even end the line with a definitive period, thus claiming premier authority over an American language. That said, as this spelling book was the main introduction to formal, written English for millions of American children—during the 1850s, it was selling a million copies a year (Crystal, 1995, p. 80)—it is not hard to recognize why the American populace might readily believe in a singular, correct use of language.

FIGURE 8.1 Webster's *The Elementary Spelling Book* (1908).

However, even if Webster's spellings, definitions, and grammatical forms were taken as the standard, his rules were by no means exempt from change or revision. For example, the 1908 edition of *The Elementary Spelling Book* directly states that it is "an improvement on the American Spelling Book" and notes that it has taken out "those words which have become obsolete" and replaced them with "living words" (p. 7). Furthermore, not all of Webster's prescriptions caught on. Several of the spellings that Webster presented, such as *wimmen* for *women*, *tung* for *tongue*, and *ake* for *ache*, were never accepted by the public (Merriam-Webster Online, n.d.). Nevertheless, many of his reforms were preserved: How many Americans today recognize the word *gaol*, a commonly used synonym for *prison*?

A standard variety was also supported by the rise of a new American literature. As American authors, such as Twain and Whitman, created a style that differed from traditional British literature and presented life in a growing and developing United States, they also used the words, spellings, and grammar that Webster and his colleagues promoted. Thus, as these texts were consumed by the literate population, they served as models of good grammar and good usage.

8.6

Therefore, even if no official language academy was created to develop an American Standard English, we see a tradition of authoritative grammar books and dictionaries as well as a national literature that promote a unified linguistic system. As we have seen, one main reason for standardizing the language, especially in the early years of the nation, was to distinguish American from British English; another was to give the US the ability to claim authority over not just any language but that of its oppressors. Of course, underlying each of these motives is also a notable sense of prescriptivism: Not only were early Americans to speak differently and patriotically, they were also expected to speak eloquently!

To summarize, while there may not be an officially codified variety, the United States has a long history of standardized linguistic forms that are presented in dictionaries and grammar books and are taught in schools and modeled in formal writing. (The role of the educational system in promoting both a linguistic standard and a standard ideology will be addressed below.) As such, one could argue that this is where an American Standard developed—not in a governmental academy, but in the texts that were distributed and used throughout the nation. Furthermore, even if there has not been a governing body to oversee their content, the belief in the message of these texts—in terms of both the "correctness" of the standards they present and the linguistic authority they have been given—is pervasive. As such, there is a strongly held perception that a standard English, that is, a singular, correct form of spoken and written language, does in fact exist in the United States.

WHAT IS STANDARD AMERICAN ENGLISH?

While we can argue that there is no one singular standardized dialect in the United States, we do recognize that there are forms—words, pronunciations, and grammatical patterns—that are generally considered to be standard within and across the US. These are the forms that are marked as "correct." They are also the structures by which other features are judged to be nonstandard. Additionally, these are the forms that are presented when comparing a homogeneous American English to other national varieties, such as British English, Australian English, or Indian English. As such, the connection of standard language to both nationalism and prescriptivism, which was significant to Webster and Adams, continues to endure.

That said, if there is a specific set of linguistic features that are considered to be standard, then we should be able to describe what these structures are. So, what does standard American English sound like? Consider the following:

1. Spend a few minutes writing out what you think Standard American English is: What linguistic features does it consist of? Where is it spoken? Who do you hear using it? What region of the country or social group does it come from?
2. Discuss the features that you listed with your classmates. Compare lists and note which of your answers are shared by the group and which are given by only one person. Try to determine why your responses are different and what these similarities and differences reveal about a standard or general American English.

It may or may not surprise you that there is no one correct answer to these questions concerning the linguistic standards of American English. Because no official standard has been created in the United States, instead of saying that we have one specific dialect called Standard American English, it might be more accurate to argue that there exists a set of linguistic features that are considered a part of a generalized American variety. As such, recognition of people as speakers of the standard has less to do with their acquisition of a singular dialect than their usage of particular lexical, phonological, and grammatical features that are associated with a broader, generalized American identity and speech.

As evidenced by the numerous comments about grammatical usage and "the way kids speak today" that appear in public and private interactions, people are very protective of their ideas of what is right and wrong in language (as we saw in Chapter 2). But it is important to remember that standard varieties are perceived as standard only by societal convention, not by any natural linguistic hierarchy. Therefore, what individuals perceive as standard is shaped by their local experiences (linguistic and educational) as well as by the information they are presented with through the wider community. For example, those who pronounce *caught* and *cot* or *pen* and *pin* the same way might not realize that theirs are not considered to be the standard pronunciations

---

BOX 8.1 **Some Linguistic Features of American English**

Of the features in Table 8.3, which ones do you agree are a part of a standard American English? Which are unquestionably nonstandard to you? Did any of these forms appear in the list you made earlier?

TABLE 8.3 Some linguistic features of American English

Post-vocalic [r]	*Sneaked* or *snuck*	*Hella* or *wicked* for 'very'
Northern Cities Shift	Double negatives	Quotative *like*
Cot and *caught* sound the same	Needs + V-ed, as in *needs washed*	*Coke, soda,* or *pop*
Route rhymes with *root* or *out*	Monopthongized [aɪ], *tire* sounds like *tar*	*Caramel* with 2 syllables or 3
Metathesis of *ask*	Southern Vowel Shift	*Through* or *thru*
Trilled [r]	*Milk* as [mɛlk]	*Color* or *colour*
Merger of *pin* and *pen*	*Ain't*	*Gonna*
Monophthongized [o:]	*Lol*	*Groovy*

---

in other areas of the country, and the same can also be said for those who do distinguish between them. Even different grammar texts differ in the prescriptive rules that they present. For example, some American texts used to teach students to preserve the distinction in pronouncing *witch* and *which* with two different initial sounds, but this distinction is generally no longer included; additionally, some contemporary texts teach against splitting the infinitive while others do not mention the rule at all. As such, not everyone is exposed to the exact same set of prescriptive rules and linguistic norms and, therefore, not everyone in the US views the standard as comprising the exact same features.

While the set of features that make up Standard American English is debatable, we do not mean to say that the decision of which forms are standard is solely the opinion of the individual. There are many forms that are regularly and consistently considered standard by the general population. Keep in mind that the definition of a standard entails that it is an agreed-upon norm, even if that agreement is unconscious. Furthermore, a standard is a linguistic form that has been granted social prestige, and it is expected that speakers will recognize this status. In fact, in our discussions of nonstandard dialects in previous chapters, we have, by default, used an assumed implicit knowledge of particular standard features in discussions of nonstandard structures.

In linguistic terms, Standard American English is best discussed as a set of unmarked (versus marked) features, and like the classification of "standard," markedness itself is a subjective categorization. Therefore, the construct of SAE can be broken down into features that are associated with a societally imposed norm. Of course, listing the features that are unmarked, by nature of their being unmarked or "unnoticed," is not always easy. In fact, when talking about SAE most people, including linguists, find it easier to discuss what standard English isn't (marked features), rather than what it is (unmarked). For example, one might more readily assess the use of *ain't* or a double negative as being nonstandard than identifying the use of *am not* or a singular negative as standard.

While standard dialects (like all dialects according to our definition) are varieties of speech associated with particular regional or social groups—for example, in France, there is the Parisian standard, and in England, RP developed primarily from the speech of London—an American standard works somewhat differently. In the United States, standard forms tend to be those that are not easily associated with any particular regional or social group, at least not one outside of a generalized, "average" America. Instead, within the United States, a general American English is the speech of a perceived majority—white, middle class, heterosexual, and educated—as well as non-regional, that is, the speaker could be from any part of the country.

In terms of regionality, many do claim that SAE is the speech found in the Midwest, as Marilyn did in her answer presented in the introduction to this chapter. However, when such statements are analyzed further, one finds that this region is perceived as the standard particularly because the Midwest is associated with a common "Middle America" as well as an unmarked American speech. Similar comments about the West Coast are also heard. One reason behind this perception is that while the East Coast has been host to different varieties of English since the Colonial period, especially cities such as New York, Boston, and Charleston, the Midwest and the West include linguistic forms that are the product of dialect mixing and dialect leveling, as was discussed in Chapters 4 and 5. (See the section on Broadcast English below for additional reasons for SAE being associated with the Midwest.) However, when presented with linguistic changes, such as the Northern Cities Shift, that are currently taking place in the Midwest, those who argue that SAE is based in this region confirm that such heavily marked speech could not be standard. Furthermore, because it is not associated with a particular region, Standard American English is oftentimes described as being "accentless," by which accents are misunderstood as only belonging to strongly marked, and often stigmatized, regional speech, such as in the South.

Of course, even if SAE is associated with a generic, normative population, descriptions of the standard generally do not directly specify a connection to a white, middle-class, heterosexual group. (Did you use any of these terms in your description?) Rather, as described above, discussions, including those by so-called language mavens, more likely focus on what SAE is not. (However, the connection between a standard, "correct" way of speaking and education does regularly surface in these discussions.) Thus, SAE is defined by what it isn't, and its speakers are described only in contrast to those who have been determined (by stereotype) to not speak it. As conceived, perceived, and idealized by the wider community, SAE is not associated with African Americans or other ethnic minorities (or at least it is not connected to ethnolects); it is not from the South or New York City (areas with marked, stigmatized speech); it does not include a "foreign" accent (it must be distinctly American); it is not the speech of the uneducated working class or a privately educated, hyper-articulate upper class (see Preston, 1996; Lippi-Green, 2012). Therefore, what we find is that Standard American English is the language of an assimilated American citizenry.

As such, the language becomes a symbol of an assimilation into a larger, unified American culture. Those who speak the standard are seen as "truly American," shedding all linguistic traces of an affiliation with a minority or foreign group or culture. Alternatively, those who continue to speak another dialect are perceived as going against the American grain or of having some other cultural allegiance. Of course, this is precisely why Adams argued for a standard language: linguistic order is supposed to lead to and reflect social order. An acceptance of the standard form shows an implicit, perhaps unconscious, acceptance of the social majority. Therefore, even if the US does not have a singular codified dialect that is overseen by an official academy, we can see that the concept of a standard ideology and a connection between standard language and national identity continue to persist.

AMERICAN AUTHORITIES: EDUCATION, TELEVISION, AND THE MYTH OF AN ACCENT-FREE AMERICA

As discussed above, the first public discussions of an American standard emerged during the early days of the United States, when it was argued that a unified language would symbolize, or perhaps create, a unified nation and that grammatical order would reflect social order. However, unlike European nations that looked toward a wealthy elite for models of the standard, the US took more of a democratic approach to choosing the language that it promoted. For example, Webster included pronunciations that were used by the common, yet educated, man, not those of the socially privileged, as had been the tradition in British lexicography. Furthermore, American publishers were open about the choices they made concerning standard forms; they recognized that multiple variants were competing and thus that changes in new editions were necessary. *The Elementary Spelling Book* states:

> In orthography there are some classes of words in which usage is not uniform. No two English writers agree on this subject; and what is worse, no lexicographer is consistent with himself. In this book, as in Dr. Webster's dictionaries, that mode of

spelling has been adopted which is the most simple and best authorized. The Editor has followed the rules that are held to be legitimate, and has rendered uniform all classes of words falling within them. If established rules and analogies will not control the practice of writers, there is no authority by which uniformity can be produced ... The modifications in this revision are not of a character to embarrass those teachers who use the previous editions in the same class. (1908, pp. 6–7)

However, even a democratic approach to standardization is still standardization, and any process of giving prestige to one form of language over others is inherently problematic.

By using texts such as the "Blue Back Speller" that both model and prescribe the standard form, the educational system has played probably the most important role in perpetuating not just the standard form but also the ideology behind a standard American English. *English for You and Me*, a grammar and style guide for fourth graders that was published in the 1940s, serves as a perfect example of the educational system promoting the idea of a singular, standard English. The book's introduction sets up the idea of "good" language, which is presented in contrast to "bad" language, that is, any other way of speaking or writing:

Has anyone ever said to you, "That is a bad habit" or "That is a good habit"? ... Do you always say *going, playing, coming*? Or do you say *goin', playin', comin'*? The first way is a good habit of speaking; the second way is a bad habit.

(Johnson, Hooper, Goodykoontz, & Dearborn, 1942, p. 5)

Additionally, throughout this grammar book are sections titled "Using Words Correctly," in which the authors give examples of appropriate uses and admonitions for bad linguistic behavior. In one example of their direct prescriptive approach, Johnson et al. write, "Notice how [the speaker in the text] used *threw* and *thrown* ... There is no such word as *throwed*" (1942, p. 89). Additionally, in the section "Using the Lips in Speaking," the book says, "Some persons are very hard to understand, because they have lazy lips. Do you use your lips when you speak?" (Johnson et al., 1942, p. 37).

Of course, as mentioned previously, these texts, while serving as linguistic models, are not static relics of an immutable linguistic system. The forms and features of language that are considered to be standard have undergone continuous revision. One needs only to compare grammar books or literary works from different points over the last 200 years to observe such changes. Even the seemingly immutable Strunk and White's *The Elements of Style* has gone through at least four editions and has revised several rules, such as their advice on the use of masculine pronouns. Furthermore, because there is no singular body for linguistic oversight, even a synchronic analysis of contemporary textbooks will show variation in standard grammar rules.

The educational system—and its personified form, the strict schoolmarm—is not the only recognized model for linguistic standards in the United States. In discussions of the standard, newscasters and journalists are often included. In fact, Standard American English is often referred to as the "Broadcast Standard." In the 1940s, at a time when radio was the prime medium and television was following closely on its heels, the National Broadcasting Company (NBC) presented a set of standard pronunciations that its newscasters and other on-air talent were to use. Just as the spread of literacy and compulsory education allowed for access to written standards, the spread of radio and television gave the average American access to a spoken standard. And, more importantly, they were given access to pronunciations that they might not be exposed to in their local community. For their pronunciations, NBC looked not toward New York or Washington, DC, but to the Midwest for a model of the standard.

8.7

It is important to note that while contemporary newscasters do model a standard American English, different regional broadcasts, like grammar books, present variation in speech. Local news reports quite regularly incorporate pronunciations and lexical items that are associated with the local community. (PBS's *Do You Speak American* provides links to radio broadcasts from around the country: www.pbs.org/speak/sea tosea/americanvarieties/radio/.) Therefore, these broadcasts not only model language that carries prestige, but broadcasters also sprinkle in features that are used by or are familiar to all types of speakers. Generally, these local features are those that are perceived as unmarked—or at the very least not stigmatized—within the local community. As such, it might be more accurate to say that the United States has not one standard dialect but a set of regional standards.

8.8

In the early days of American radio and film, the standard pronunciation portrayed in the media was more internationally based and, compared to American speech today, sounded more British. In the PBS series *Do You Speak American*, sociolinguist William Labov talks about changes in linguistic prestige in America. He says that International English, which was modeled on RP, was the first prestige form in the United States. This accent, while respected across the country, was really only spoken in cities that had historic ties to England, such as Boston, New York, Savannah, Charleston, and Richmond. Labov names Franklin Delano Roosevelt, whose speech reflected his background as an upper-class New Yorker, as a prime example of this standard. (Katharine Hepburn, who was from Connecticut, is another good example.) Therefore, while this "International English" was seen across the country as a prestigious way of speaking, it was generally not the same speech that was modeled by teachers and presented to students in different regions. However, as Labov states, after World War II, the standards of pronunciation "flipped," and a general American standard became the more prestigious form.

8.9

8.10

8.11

Another vehicle for the presentation and promotion of a standard American English is through accent reduction courses. These courses are found across the country and market themselves primarily to those whose native language is not American English. However, accent reduction courses are especially prevalent in areas of the United States where the local speech is stigmatized, such as in the South and in New York City. They promote the view that there is one accent that is socially prestigious and that other American accents are, at best, not acceptable for many professions and, at worst, are completely incorrect.

Such courses focus on the phonological features of Standard American English, generally omitting morphological and syntactic information. They work from lists of specific pronunciations; however, there is no single standardized system that they all draw their information from and, therefore, different courses present different features for "correct" American English. Furthermore, they often promote the idea of an accentless America, that people can lessen or completely eradicate the accent they already have, hence the name accent *reduction*. Only some instructors explain that what the student is really learning is a new set of linguistic features and that what he/she is actually doing is learning to shift from one accent to another.

The "SpeakUp! Accent Elimination Program" is an audio course with accompanying text that is intended to be used by individuals who want to lose their nonstandard accents. The program walks the listener through a set of exercises that model standard pronunciations while also referencing specific regional variants that are considered to be incorrect. Unlike many accent reduction courses, this program does define a Standard American English accent in the supplementary text:

> [the accent] used by national broadcasters, public speakers, and members of most television show families. It draws no attention to itself; it seems to be the absence of an accent. Because it does not reveal the speaker's origin, the Standard American English accent is *nonregional*.
>
> (Chwat, 1994, p. 10)

The author of the program also extends this discussion by giving background information on his view of SAE:

> Developed and popularized largely by Hollywood and Madison Avenue, Standard American English is a well-known and highly recognizable pattern of speech. The accent is Northern American in style because the Northern states have dominated the communications industry since the Civil War.
>
> During the last half-century, the Standard American English accent—a unique pattern of vowels and consonants—has become the standard for "educated" and "nonregional" speech. Television, radio, and the movies have taught this accent to every pair of ears in America.
>
> (Chwat, 1994, p. 10)

It is not surprising that Chwat focuses on the influence of media on developing and disseminating SAE more than the educational system since he is a dialect coach who has worked in television, film, and theater. However, his discussion of regionality is notable. He says throughout the program that SAE appears to be nonregional, but he also says that the accent is "Northern in style," thereby either contradicting himself or conflating Northern with accentless speech. Moreover, he claims that SAE somehow "draws no attention to itself," yet, in the next breath says that it is "well-known and highly recognizable." Therefore, even when we do find direct descriptions of what SAE is supposed to be, the descriptions are often vague, ambiguous, or even contradictory.

As we have seen through this section, standard forms of American English have been presented through various outlets, particularly education and broadcasting; however, there is no unified set of linguistic features that has been marked as standard. Instead, regional standards have been promoted in different locations across the country. Furthermore, even those varieties that had once been deemed as socially prestigious—International English and Midwestern English—have undergone changes. As long as language authorities continue to claim that there is a correct, accentless Standard American English and promote its use and dominance, responses like Marilyn's above will continue to persist and will continue to disseminate false information about American English.

CONCLUSION

The discussion of a standard American English is not a simple one, even though many public conversations, including Marilyn's answer in the introduction, may make it appear that way. Because the concept of a standard American English must take into account both the abstract and the applied, there are several seemingly contradictory points that arise:

- We can describe the forms and history of standard dialects, but a nonvarying, homogeneous linguistic standard is only an abstract ideal.
- Certain features of American English have emerged as standard, but a singular dialect of Standard American English has never been fully codified or elaborated.
- Even though many Americans will claim that they know what Standard American English is (and often that they are speakers of it), they are not able to describe its features. At best, SAE can be described by what it is not.
- While a homogeneous, national standard is perceived in the United States, it may be more accurate to say that regional standards exist.
- The standard forms that have been (implicitly) agreed upon have changed: from a transatlantic dialect found primarily in New England to a generalized Midwestern accent, through the NBC standard to a nonregional, "accentless" form.

Analyzed through the points given above and viewed through the history of standardization and language development within the US, we must conclude that a singular standard American English is only a myth.

DISCUSSION AND RESEARCH QUESTIONS

1. The first myth listed at the beginning of the chapter is "I speak Standard American English." Explain why this is a myth. Alternately, discuss the ways in which this statement could be considered true.

2. Go back to the "Ask Marilyn" exchange given in the introduction to this chapter and analyze her response in terms of language attitudes, a standard language ideology, and regional dialects.

3. Go to the website of one (or more) of the language academies listed in Table 8.2 and research the information given about the structure and development of the standard form. What would the website for a US language academy say?

4. In our discussions, we have said that standardization is an impossibility; however, one could argue that it is more accurate to say that a fully standardized language is more of an improbability than an impossibility. Present a context (social, linguistic, political) in which a fully standardized language could exist.

5. Record five minutes of your own speech. You may choose to record yourself in both formal and informal contexts. Compare your own pronunciations to those found in the NBC broadcast guidelines: http://archive.org/details/nbchandbookof pro00bend.

6. Can stigmatized dialects have standard forms or features? Explain why or why not.

Multilingual America

GUIDING QUESTIONS

1. How many languages are spoken in the United States, and how many people speak languages other than English?

2. What are factors leading to the maintenance of languages other than English in the US, and what are reasons for shifting to English?

3. What is the connection between language use and immigration policy?

4. How does multilingualism add to or detract from an American identity?

OVERVIEW

In this chapter, we ask the question: Is the United States a multilingual nation? First, we problematize the issue by defining the concept of a multilingual nation both quantitatively, that is, by the number of languages spoken and the number of people who speak them, and ideologically, that is, whether the use or presence of multiple languages is a core part of a national identity. By examining figures from the US Census and other sources, we show that there are, indeed, significant numbers of languages spoken in the US as well as a large number of speakers of these languages. We also show that while there are contemporary changes to the number of speakers of individual languages—some are increasing while others are decreasing—the presence of multiple languages and their speakers has been a permanent fixture throughout US history. We also discuss the connection between immigration and multilingualism and examine the patterns of language maintenance versus the shift to monolingual English. Finally, we ask readers to think about the role that language—and languages—play in the development of an American identity.

COMMON MYTHS

> There is only a handful of languages currently spoken in the United States.

> Throughout US history, speakers of languages other than English have been consistently viewed as un-American.

> In the United States, only immigrants and tourists speak languages other than English.

> Unlike earlier generations of immigrants, those who have recently arrived in the United States are not learning English.

INTRODUCTION

In the first half of this book, we focused specifically on the use of English in the United States, examining its history in North America, its variation along both regional and social dimensions, and the attitudes and perceptions that people have regarding that variation. However, English was not the first language to be used on North American shores, nor was it even the first language used by European settlers in North America. And while it is incontrovertible that English has surfaced as the dominant language in the United States, we must recognize the important roles that a multitude of languages— individually as well as collectively—have played in defining an American linguistic heritage. As such, in the remaining chapters, we expand the discussion of language and linguistic diversity by examining the many languages other than English spoken in the US, past and present, and by analyzing the connection between language and an American identity. In this chapter, we begin by focusing on the issue of American multilingualism.

We approach the concept of a multilingual America from two perspectives. First, we define **multilingualism** simply as the presence and use of more than one language in any given area; in the case of American multilingualism, for example, English, Spanish, and Arabic are all languages that have a presence in the United States. By this definition, the word can also be used to describe the linguistic capacity of an individual who speaks more than one language. For example, if Donald speaks Spanish, French, and English, Donald is multilingual. Second, we extend our definition so that the term *multilingual* also represents a linguistic identity. In this case, we view an entity (whether it be a nation, local community, family, or one person) as multilingual not merely because of its use of more than one language but, instead, due to the existence of these multiple languages as a defining part of who or what it is. In this second approach, as applied to the United States, it is not necessary that all or even most of the population is able to speak more than one language, but rather that the presence of multiple languages (contemporarily or historically) plays a crucial part in defining an American identity. While the first meaning presents multilingualism as a quantitative problem, the second indicates that it is an abstract, ideological construct.

A MELTING POT OR SALAD BOWL?

Whether there is a connection between language (or culture) and national identity is a commonly asked question that generates a great deal of discussion. In Chapter 8, we saw how the promotion of a standard dialect was readily connected to definitions of nationalism and even patriotism, particularly through the rhetoric of Webster and Adams. While the focus of these influential Americans was not on languages other than English, their words exemplify similar discussions and debates about language and cultural diversity, debates that not only existed in the early history of the United States but that still have relevance today.

Within these discussions of linguistic and cultural diversity in America, the use of metaphor has been a common stylistic convention, one that often reveals public and private views about diversity and immigration. In use since the 18th century, the most well known of these is the **melting pot** metaphor. In this metaphor, a wide variety of immigrants, who bring with them a diverse set of languages and cultures, combine together into one unified whole. Within the melting pot—which originally referenced a crucible or a smelting pot—individual elements lose their original form as they dissolve into a whole that is greater than its parts. As such, this metaphor highlights cultural and linguistic assimilation: the melting pot blends everyone together into a singular, homogeneous, American identity. *E pluribus unum*: out of many, one. Or, as explained by de Crevecoeur in his 1782 essay, "What is an American?": "Here individuals of all nations are melted into a new race of men, whose labours and posterity will one day cause great changes in the world" (p. 55).

While an interesting and attractive metaphor, not everyone has agreed that the melting pot and its homogeneous contents adequately represent either the reality of American assimilation or the notion that total assimilation is the best goal. Therefore, a second metaphor has been posited, that of the salad bowl. Similar to the melting pot, the salad bowl is a combination of a variety of ingredients brought together to make a singular dish. However, instead of the final product being completely uniform, the salad maintains some of its variety. That is, the lettuce is still recognizable as lettuce and the tomato is still tomato, but the parts combine in such a way as to make something new, and again the final creation is considered to be more than the sum of its parts.

Thus, the questions we must ask in this chapter are: What do we mean—and what should we mean—by "multilingual America"? What is the linguistic diversity that exists in the United States, and how does it fit into a broader view of American identity? Do immigrants bring languages that eventually melt away in favor of English? Or do languages complement one another, adding flavor and spice to the concept that is America? Would it be more beneficial for multilingual America to retain the identity of its components as the salad does, or is the assimilation of the melting pot more desirable? The aim of this chapter is to address questions like these. Thus, we begin by answering two questions that are central to the issue: (1) How many languages are spoken in the United States? and (2) How many people speak them?

HOW MULTI IS A MULTILINGUAL AMERICA?

The US Census Bureau began collecting data on language use in 1890 and, with the exception of the 1950 Census, it has asked about language use in every decennial survey through 2000. Since 2000, these data have been collected through the US Census Bureau's American Community Survey (ACS) instead of through the decennial survey itself. There are many reasons for compiling an accurate count of the languages spoken in the United States, and the reasons change depending on the needs and interests of the country at the time of data collection. In general, information about languages other than English helps policy makers understand where services, such as bilingual ballots, **English as a Second language (ESL)** instruction, and medical and legal translation, are needed, and thus where they should distribute appropriate resources. These numbers also give detailed information about contemporary and historical trends in linguistic and cultural assimilation as well as information supplemental to other data on American immigration. Furthermore, because all of these data are made public (at www.census. gov), many individuals, groups, and organizations can use this information for their own purposes, for example independent organizations lobbying to make English the official language of the United States or sociolinguists writing about the US as a multilingual nation.

9.3

The American Community Survey collects language data for every individual in a household above the age of five. The survey asks: "Does this person speak a language other than English at home?" and "What is this language?" According to the ACS, there are approximately 325 languages, other than English, spoken in the United States; of these languages, 14 are spoken by more than 500,000 people (US Census Bureau, 2010–2013). The most commonly used languages are shown in Table 9.1.

BOX 9.1 Language Questions Used in Decennial Censuses

Examine how the changes in wording affect the responses given.
What would be the purpose of revising the questions? How would the findings—
and their applications—be affected?

2000: *(Collected for all ages; retained for persons 5 years old and over)*
- Does this person speak a language other than English at home?
- What is this language? How well does this person speak English (very well, well, not well, not at all)?

1990: *(For persons 5 years old and over)*
- Does this person speak a language other than English at home?
- What is this language? How well does this person speak English (very well, well, not well, not at all)?

1980: *(For persons 3 years old and over; tabulated for 5 years old and over)*
- Does this person speak a language other than English at home?
- What is this language? How well does this person speak English (very well, well, not well, not at all)?

1970: *(No age for question; tabulations limited)*
- What language, other than English, was spoken in this person's home when he was a child?

  (Spanish, French, German, Other [specify], _____

  None—English only)

1960: *(For foreign-born persons)*
- What language was spoken in his home before he came to the United States?

1950: *(Not asked)*

1940: *(For persons of all ages; asked under the category of "Mother Tongue [or Native Language]")*
- Language spoken at home in earliest childhood.

BOX 9.1 *(continued)*

1930: *(For foreign-born persons; asked under the category of "Mother Tongue [or Native Language] of Foreign Born")*

- Language spoken in home before coming to the United States.

1920: *(For foreign-born persons)*

- Place of birth and mother tongue of person and each parent. Whether able to speak English.

1910: *(Mother tongue was collected for all foreign-born persons, to be written in with place of birth; also collected for foreign-born parents. Specific instructions on correct languages to write in and a list of appropriate European languages were provided to the enumerator. Similar instructions may have carried over to 1920.)*

- Whether able to speak English; or, if not, give language spoken.

1900: *(For all persons 10 years old and over)*

- "Can speak English" was asked after the two questions "Can read" and "Can write."

1890: *(For all persons 10 years old and over)*

- "Able to speak English. If not, the language or dialect spoken" was asked after the questions "Able to Read" and "Able to Write."

1790–1880: *(No evidence of language questions or English ability questions)*

(From "Historical Language Questions," www.census.gov/hhes/socdemo/language/about/historical.html.)

9.4

While 325 languages is a truly significant number, many linguists believe that the actual number of languages spoken in the United States is much higher. For example, the Endangered Language Alliance (n.d.), an organization that documents living and endangered languages through urban fieldwork, posits that over 700 languages are spoken in New York City alone. Additionally, all of the responses in the ACS are coded as one of approximately 381 pre-defined languages or language groups; therefore, what may be counted as two or even three different languages in one study may be considered one language by the Census Bureau, thus potentially underrepresenting the total number of languages in the US. For example, even though Urdu and Hindi are currently coded as two separate languages, before the year 2000 they were categorized as one.

9.5

TABLE 9.1 Languages other than English spoken by at least 500,000 people in the United States

Language	Number of speakers
1. Spanish	37,579,787
2. Chinese	2,882,497
3. Tagalog	1,594,413
4. Vietnamese	1,419,539
5. French	1,301,443
6. Korean	1,141,277
7. German	1,083,637
8. Arabic	951,699
9. Russian	905,843
10. French Creole	753,990
11. Italian	723,632
12. Portuguese	673,566
13. Hindi	648,983
14. Polish	607,531

Source: From the American Community Survey for 2011 (US Census Bureau, 2010–2013).

Furthermore, because the data are self-reported, the number of speakers of a particular language could be underreported, as those who are bilingual or multilingual may choose to report only their most dominant language (such as English) instead of every language they speak. Additionally, those who speak other languages outside of the home, for example those who use other languages at work or school but not at home with their families, might not report these languages due to the wording of the survey question. Moreover, people who feel marginalized due to their use of a minority language may not wish to disclose this information publicly. Despite such issues, Census records provide the best data for this kind of analysis, and any serious investigation of the distributions of languages in the United States must take these findings into consideration.

9.6

In answering the question of the United States as a multilingual nation from a quantitative perspective, we must examine not only the number of languages spoken but also the number of people who speak them. The ACS reports that the total number of people above the age of five living in the United States is 291,524,091. Of this population, 20.8%, or over 60 million people, reported speaking a language other than English at home (see Table 9.2). Thus, while a notable number of people speak

TABLE 9.2 Numbers of speakers of English only and all other languages, 1990, 2000, and 2011

Language spoken at home	1990	2000	% change	2011	% change
English only	198,600,798	215,423,557	+ 8.5	230,947,071	+ 7.2
All other languages	31,844,979	46,951,595	+ 47.4	60,577,020	+ 29.0

Source: Adapted from the American Community Survey for 2011 (US Census Bureau, 2010–2013).

languages other than English, the vast majority of the population—approximately 80%—reported speaking English only (US Census Bureau, 2006–2008). Furthermore, continuing a trend that has held throughout most of US history, the use of languages other than English has steadily increased over the last 20 years. The numbers presented in Table 9.2 represent not only an increase in speakers of non-English languages, but, because of the overall growth in the total population of the United States, an increase in the number of people who speak only English as well. The increase in total population has occurred at a much slower rate than has the number of speakers of non-English languages, which has almost doubled in fewer than 20 years.

It is important to recognize that while a significant portion of the population reports speaking a non-English language, most of the individual languages in the United States are spoken by only a relatively small number of people. There are 14 languages with over 500,000 speakers and an additional 27 with over 100,000 speakers, which leaves approximately 284 languages (87.4%) that are each spoken by fewer than 100,000 people. For example, of the 325 languages noted here, 134 are indigenous Native American languages, but only one of these languages, Navajo, has over 100,000 speakers. In fact, the Native American languages Yuchi and Serrano have the fewest reported speakers of all languages listed in the 2006–2008 ACS data, with only four and five speakers, respectively. Furthermore, even though half a million speakers appears to be a large number of people, it is still less than 0.2% of the total American population.

It is also important to note that while 60 million reflects the number of people who use non-English languages, it says nothing in itself about whether or not each person also speaks English. However, it is not uncommon to see this number incorrectly interpreted as the number of people in the US who do not speak English. And because of this misinterpretation, this statistic is also used to express alarm that immigrants are not learning English. Therefore, in order to better assess and understand the number of people who do not speak English versus those who speak English as well as another language, the Census and ACS began including the question, "How well does this person speak English?," to which respondents have a choice of four answers: "Very well," "Well," "Not well," or "Not at all." Table 9.3 shows the distribution of answers from the 2007 and 2011 American Community Surveys. Looking at the current numbers,

TABLE 9.3 Self-reported ability in English, 2007 and 2011: percentages of speakers of languages other than English

	2007 (%)	2011 (%)
Spoke English "Very well"	55.9	58.2
Spoke English "Well"	19.8	19.4
Spoke English "Not well"	16.3	15.4
Spoke English "Not at all"	8.1	7.0

Source: Adapted from the American Community Survey for 2010 and 2013 (US Census Bureau, 2010–2013).

we find that the vast majority of those speaking other languages—77.6%—speak English well or very well. This number is even up from 75.7%, reported in 2007. Most notably, only 7% of the respondents who spoke other languages, or approximately 1.5% of the total American population above the age of five, report not speaking English at all, and this is down from 8.1% in 2007. Therefore, we see a growing trend in both the acquisition of English and multilingualism in the United States.

Not only is it incorrect to assume that the use of a language other than English implies a lack of knowledge of English, it is also problematic to assume that people who speak other languages are not native to the United States. According to the 2010 Census, 12.9% of the American population was foreign born (see Table 9.4). Looking at this percentage in comparison to the statistics on language use, it is clear that there are more people speaking languages other than English (60 million) than those who were born outside of the United States (40 million). Therefore, while it is true that many non-English language speakers are foreign born, the use of non-English languages is not—and should not be inferred as—a clear indication of immigration or citizenship status. Additionally, it should not be assumed that everyone who is born outside of the US speaks a language other than English; in fact, over 15% of the foreign-born population reported speaking only English at home (US Census Bureau, 2012: *The Foreign-Born Population in the United States: 2010*).

To summarize, according to Census reports, there are 325 non-English languages used at home by approximately 60 million speakers in the United States. Therefore, with regard to the number of languages spoken and the number of people who speak them, the United States, without reservation, conforms to our notion of a multilingual country. However, only 14 of these languages (15, if English is included) are used by more than 500,000 people, showing that the vast majority of languages in the US are used by small minorities of the population. Moreover, approximately 80% of the population report speaking English only, and over 77% of those who do use other languages also speak English well or very well. Thus, despite the presence of many languages, English is by far the dominant language of the United States.

TABLE 9.4 Foreign-born population and region of birth

	Population (rounded)	Percentage of total population
Native population	269,394,000	87.1
Foreign-born population	39,956,000	12.9
Region of birth of foreign born	**Population**	**Percentage of foreign born**
Africa	1,607,000	4.0
Asia	11,284,000	28.2
Europe	4,817,000	12.1
Latin America & the Caribbean	21,224,000	53.1
Mexico	11,711,000	29.3
Other Central America	3,053,000	7.6
South America	2,730,000	6.8
Caribbean	3,731,000	9.3
North America	807,000	2.0
Oceania	217,000	0.5

Source: Adapted from US Census Bureau (2012), www.census.gov/prod/2012pubs/acs-19.pdf.

LANGUAGE SHIFT AND LANGUAGE MAINTENANCE

Now that the standing of the United States as a multilingual nation has been established, we turn our attention to the investigation of the factors that influence the continued use or disuse of a language in the US. The term **language shift** refers to the transition from the familial language to the dominant, majority language. In the United States, language shift is usually a swift and total assimilation to English, and it regularly occurs within two to three generations. This two- to three-generational shift has remained relatively constant throughout US history, and thus examples of this trend can be seen in many, if not most, American families if one goes back far enough. For example, the first author of this book had grandparents who arrived in the United States speaking Italian and knowing little (if any) English (see Figure 9.1). Their children were raised speaking both languages, but English became the more dominant language for the children as they progressed through the public school system. By the third generation, the grandchildren, including the author, were raised solely as English speakers without any regular exposure to the familial language.

There are many motivating factors that lead to language shift, and many immigrants to the United States are very eager for themselves and their families to shift primarily,

FIGURE 9.1 Carolina Rosso Tamasi and Michel Tamasi, April 20, 1925, in Pettoranello di Molise, Italy, before moving to Princeton, New Jersey, in 1926.

9.7

if not exclusively, to English. Economic factors play a strong role, and the vast majority of immigrants recognize that economic prosperity is much more attainable in the US if one is proficient in English. Additionally, issues of cultural assimilation and national unity are influences that are significant and meaningful, and they relate to both the melting pot and salad bowl metaphors. As Potowski (2010) notes, this shift happens "all over the USA and is likely due to urbanization, universal education, mass communication, and greater regional integration into the national economy" (p. 4).

The two- to three-generational shift to English is a pattern that has held throughout most of US history; however, because of the recent increase in speakers of non-English languages overall, it may appear that this pattern no longer applies to contemporary immigration or to language groups that claim a large number of speakers. Because of the continuous, substantial immigration of Spanish speakers, newer populations may mask the fact that earlier generations have already shifted to English. Although it may appear that immigrants are not learning English or are learning English slower than their predecessors, investigations have shown repeatedly that regardless of the language or location, speakers of non-English languages in the United States continue to shift to English within two to three generations. Research by Veltman actually found that "younger people today are more likely to adopt English than their older peers were when they were young" (as cited in Potowski, 2010, p. 4). Of course, it is true that the exact timing of this shift may fluctuate slightly among individual households and within close-knit communities, and there are a few communities for which this pattern does not specifically hold, such as the Old Order Amish, who have spoken Pennsylvania German for many generations. However, these are infrequent exceptions that apply to only a very small part of the population.

Even though the general pattern is a shift to monolingual English within three generations, the process of English acquisition does not automatically mean that one must abandon his or her heritage language; many individuals and families are choosing sustained bilingualism in their home language and English over monolingualism in either language. The term **language maintenance** refers either to the continued use of a minority language by an individual or group or to the support of such use. Most commonly in the United States, languages other than English are maintained through the efforts of parents and grandparents to pass the family's ancestral language on to younger generations. However, this is just one of many possible avenues for supporting the maintenance of non-English languages in the United States. Particularly in locations where the language is spoken by a significant percentage of the population, community-based policies or programs can be implemented to support the use of a specific language. For example, community educational programs not only expose children to other speakers of the heritage language, but also instruct them in formal and literary registers (see Box 9.2). Furthermore, programs or policies that highlight an essential demand for languages other than English, such as medical or legal translation, are also particularly effective.

Advances in communication and travel are also areas that can support language maintenance. While an immigrant in the 18th century could not easily or consistently keep in close contact with friends and family in the homeland, the cell phones, text messaging, email, and social media of today make it easier for people to communicate with others around the world, sometimes instantaneously. For example, grandparents and their grandchildren are able to chat easily (and cheaply) across the globe through video conferencing programs such as Skype. Similarly, traditional media, such as newspapers, television, movies, and magazines, are also available throughout the United States in a variety of languages, such as Arabic, Yiddish, Korean, and Hmong. Furthermore, for many people, relatively easy and affordable travel back to the country of origin is possible. Thus, families in the United States do not have to be completely isolated from their ancestral languages as they once might have been. Under these conditions, individuals are given more and varied opportunities to access and practice

> ## BOX 9.2 Community-based Language Programs
>
> One of the most influential means of language maintenance is through community-based heritage language programs. These privately run schools are "often created out of a community's desire to pass on their language and culture from one generation to the next in order to maintain connections within families and communities" (Kelleher, 2010). There are hundreds of such programs across the United States, primarily in areas with large populations of non-English language speakers or in areas with sustained immigrant populations. The majority of these programs teach Chinese, French, Hebrew, Italian, Japanese, Korean, Polish, Portuguese, Spanish, Ukrainian, and Yiddish (Kelleher, 2010); however, dozens of other languages have also been offered. The Alliance for the Advancement of Heritage Languages hosts a searchable catalog of community-based as well as school-based heritage language programs: www.cal.org/CALWebDB/Heritage/Default.aspx.

9.8

these languages, which, in turn, create greater incentives for families to pass down the language to younger generations.

One social factor that significantly impacts maintenance of non-English languages is the continued immigration of new populations that use those languages. The influx of new speakers energizes the linguistic landscape and provides newer and greater opportunities for sharing cultural and linguistic traditions. Additionally, language maintenance might symbolize unity and stability for families that find themselves in new living situations in which they might otherwise be culturally marginalized or even stigmatized. If their ancestral language is the same as that of others in the community, its shared use could be welcoming and comforting as a family settles into its new home. Furthermore, while individual immigrant families may choose to no longer maintain their language within their households, the language may continue to be maintained outside of the home through the actions of local communities that provide resources, such as translation and social services, to help new immigrants acclimate to their new home and culture.

While the concepts may seem incongruous, language shift and language maintenance are not necessarily mutually exclusive. Even when the general model of language shift in the United States is toward monolingual English, learning English and even using it as one's primary language does not always necessitate home language loss. As Census figures have shown, people who speak more than one language are not uncommon in the United States, even if the stereotype, as illustrated by the following joke, suggests otherwise:

Q: What do you call someone who speaks two languages?
A: Bilingual.
Q: What do you call someone who speaks one language?
A: American.

9.9

Decisions about language shift and maintenance—whether adopting English monolingualism, maintaining a non-English language, or even choosing not to use English at all—are highly personal, and every individual and family has their own reasons for their choices. However, there are factors at the state and federal level—large-scale programs, policies, and attitudes—that affect decisions about language shift and maintenance in the United States. Reasons that are specific to individual languages or language groups are discussed in the next few chapters; Official English legislation is discussed in Chapter 15.

A NATION OF IMMIGRANTS, A NATION OF LANGUAGES

As the saying goes, the United States is a nation of immigrants, and only a small percentage of the population can claim otherwise. Even if one's family was on the Mayflower or was part of the original settlements of Jamestown, St. Augustine, or New Amsterdam, he/she is still a relative newcomer to these lands. Furthermore, immigrants to the United States have come—and continue to come—from all corners of the globe. And as they come, they bring their languages with them.

History shows there has never been a time when the American population was not growing due to immigration. Of course, the pattern of growth has changed, slowing down and speeding up during different periods, and these fluctuations have been influenced by both official immigration policy and beliefs about cultural diversity and national identity. Table 9.5 paints a historical picture of American immigration, presenting figures for the total population versus foreign-born population from every Census since 1850. Focusing first on the contemporary period, we notice that the United States is currently in a fast-growing upward trend, a trend that began in the 1970s. For example, the number of individuals who were foreign born doubled between 1990 and 2010. However, even with this notable growth, the current percentage of those foreign born (12.9) is lower than it was during much of American history. For example, the foreign-born population held consistently between 13% and 15% between 1860 and 1920, the greatest period of American immigration. Alternately, the slow but steady drop in immigration that begins in the 1920s reflects a period of American isolation

TABLE 9.5 Total population and population of foreign born, 1850–2010

Year	Total population	Foreign born	Percentage of total population
2010	309,350,000*	39,956,000*	12.9
2000	281,421,906	31,107,889	11.1
1990	248,709,873	19,767,316	7.9
1980	226,545,805	14,079,906	6.2
1970	203,210,158	9,619,302	4.7
1960	179,325,671	9,738,091	5.4
1950	150,216,110	10,347,395	6.9
1940	131,669,275	11,594,896	8.8
1930	122,775,046	14,204,149	11.6
1920	105,710,620	13,920,692	13.2
1910	91,972,266	13,515,886	14.7
1900	75,994,575	10,341,276	13.6
1890	62,622,250	9,249,547	14.8
1880	50,155,788	6,679,943	13.3
1870	38,558,371	5,567,229	14.4
1860	31,443,321**	4,138,697**	13.2
1850	23,191,876**	2,244,602**	9.7

Sources: Gibson and Lennon (1999); US Census Bureau (2012).

Notes: *Rounded, as reported. **The slave population was coded as native born.

9.11

that stems from World War I and the Great Depression, as well as from negative reactions to what was perceived as encroaching cultural and linguistic diversity.

During the wave of heavy immigration into the United States during the late 19th and early 20th centuries, the vast majority of American immigrants were from Western Europe. While people did arrive in the US from other regions of the world, government actions, such as the Chinese Exclusion Act of 1882, targeted and decreased the number of immigrants from other areas. Therefore, not only was European immigration high in and of itself, but because a smaller number of people from other areas were allowed to enter, settlers from countries such as Great Britain, Germany, Ireland, and Italy dominated the immigrant landscape.

Even with high population numbers—or perhaps due to these high numbers—groups of immigrants from a variety of countries have been looked down upon and even discriminated against in the United States. At different times in US history, based on the view that they would not (or could not) assimilate, groups as varied as Irish

---

BOX 9.3 Ellis Island

Located in the Upper New York Bay, Ellis Island was the largest and most active immigration station in the United States, and between 1892 and 1924, 12 million people were received there. The first person to go through Ellis Island was a 15-year-old Irish girl named Annie Moore; she and her two brothers reached the United States on January 2, 1892. The station processed 1,004,756 people in 1907 alone, and it reached its peak on April 17 of that same year when 11,747 immigrants went through in one day.

Due to the dramatic changes implemented by the 1924 Immigration Act (see below), the immigration boom of the late 19th and early 20th centuries ended, and the traffic through Ellis Island halted. After 1924, "[t]he main function of Ellis Island changed from that of an immigrant processing station, to a center of the assembly, detention, and deportation of aliens who had entered the US illegally or had violated the terms of admittance" ("Ellis Island Timeline," www.ellisisland. org/genealogy/ellis_island_timeline.asp). The station shut its doors in 1954; however, in 1965 it was taken under the wing of the National Park Service, and in 1976 it opened for visitors.

For more information about the Ellis Island Immigration Station or Immigration Museum or to search for your own family's immigration records, go to: www. ellisisland.org/.

9.10

Catholics, Italians, Chinese, Japanese, and Filipinos were considered second-class citizens. Over time, as more established groups appeared to assimilate, the animosity that had been aimed toward them shifted to newer immigrant communities. And as immigration rates climbed higher and higher in the early 1900s, American ideology turned further and further toward cultural and linguistic assimilation as well as American isolationism, especially during World War I and the subsequent increase in anxiety toward anything "foreign."

9.12

Thus, after 1920, further steps were taken to ensure a decrease in immigration overall, particularly with the passage of the Immigration Act of 1924, which created quotas based on national origin (see Box 9.4). Because this quota system set limits for each country based on the population already present in the United States, Western European immigration continued to be supported over all other nationalities, even if there were fewer European arrivals to the United States than there had been in previous years. In terms of multilingualism, as immigration was affected by changing policies and attitudes, so too were the languages that arrived. European languages were favored and continued to dominate the linguistic landscape, as they had for most of American history. As Wiley points out:

> we should remember that English too has been a major language of immigration, supported by immigration policies that between 1923 and 1965 were particularly favorable to the UK, Canada, and Western European countries. Thus, immigration helps to explain the dominance of English as well as the presence of non-English languages.

(2010, p. 257)

BOX 9.4 The 1924 Immigration Act and US Isolationism

The Immigration Act of 1924, also known as the Johnson-Reed Act, took significant steps toward decreasing the number of immigrants allowed in the United States. Implemented during a time of isolationism following World War I, when fears of national security were still high, the 1924 Act tightened the restrictions on immigration that were already in place and reduced the annual quota of immigrants to approximately 164,000 per year, thus marking the end of mass immigration to the United States (www.ellisisland.org).

The quota system allowed entry to only 2% of the total number of people of each nationality in the US based on figures from the 1890 Census. Unlike previous quota systems that "had been based on the number of people born outside of the United States . . . [t]he new law traced the origins of the whole of the American population, including natural-born citizens" (http://history.state.gov/milestones/1921–1936/immigration-act). For those who were native born, the government commissioned an analysis of last names as an indicator of national heritage; however, the Anglicization of "foreign" names and changes in spelling rendered this information inadequate.

As stated by the US Department of State, Office of the Historian: "In all of its parts, the most basic purpose of the 1924 Immigration Act was to preserve the ideal of American homogeneity" (http://history.state.gov/milestones/1921–1936/immigration-act). These changes in policy, while decreasing immigration overall, highly favored immigration from the British Isles and other Western European countries. Previous policies, such as the "Asiatic Barred Zone" and the Chinese Exclusion Act, had already eliminated most immigration from Asia; however, the 1924 Act continued this trajectory by not allowing entry to anyone

---

BOX 9.4 *(continued)*

who could not apply for citizenship, which included any person of Asian lineage. The 1924 Act was revised by Congress in 1952.

In linguistic terms, the 1924 Immigration Act led to a sharp decrease in the number of speakers of non-English languages, due primarily to a decline in new immigrant populations and secondarily to a subsequent lack of language maintenance. Furthermore, there was a decline in the reporting of non-English language use due, first, to actual language shift and, second, to the negative attitudes toward immigrants and non-English languages that were commonly held.

The dominance of Western European immigration and the subsequent prominence of European languages began to change in the 1950s as the passage of the Refugee Relief Act and the dissolution of both the quota system and the "Asiatic Barred Zone" set the stage not only for increases in numbers of immigrants but also for significant changes in the places from which these immigrants could arrive. While change in policy was the primary reason for increased immigration, a renewed interest in cultural diversity stemming from the Civil Rights movement of the 1960s also led to a more open attitude toward immigration and non-English language use than had been seen for several decades. For example, those who had not previously identified as speakers of non-English languages began to take pride in multilingualism and multiculturalism, and thus began identifying themselves as non-English language users to the Census in higher numbers.

Current numbers (see Table 9.6) show that Western European languages, while still spoken by large portions of the population, are no longer the only prominent languages in the United States; the top-ranked languages come from all corners of the world. Moreover, we see that there is a decrease in the number of speakers of most Western European languages, such as French, German, and Italian, while there is an increase in the number of speakers of several other global languages, including Arabic, Chinese, and Tagalog. (Note that while the table shows a drop in the population of Hindi speakers between 1990 and 2000, this decrease is due to Hindi speakers and Urdu speakers being counted together previous to 2000.)

To summarize, we recognize that changes in immigration policy have led to increases in non-English language use and that the continued influx of immigrants from around the world leads to sustained linguistic diversity. Languages that had been among the most prominent languages spoken in the United States 100 years ago have begun to be eclipsed by the languages of newer immigrant populations. Furthermore, these changes in language use can be explained not only by contemporary immigration

TABLE 9.6 Top non-English languages used in the United States, 1990, 2000, and 2011

Language	2011	+/−	2000	+/−	1990
1. Spanish	37,579,787	+	28,101,052	+	17,339,172
2. Chinese	2,882,497	+	2,022,143	+	1,249,213
3. Tagalog	1,594,413	+	1,224,241	+	843,251
4. Vietnamese	1,419,539	+	1,009,627	+	507,069
5. French*	1,301,443	−	1,643,838	−	1,702,176
6. Korean	1,141,277	+	894,063	+	626,478
7. German	1,083,637	−	1,382,613	−	1,547,099
8. Arabic	951,699	+	614,582	+	355,150
9. Russian	905,843	+	706,242	+	241,798
10. French Creole	753,990	+	453,368	+	187,658
11. Italian	723,632	−	1,008,370	−	1,308,648
12. Portuguese	673,566	+	564,630	+	429,860
13. Hindi	648,983	+	317,057	(−)	331,484**
14. Polish	607,531	−	667,414	−	723,483

Sources: From Ryan (2013) and Shin and Bruno (2003).

Notes: *Includes speakers of Cajun and Patois, as defined by the US Census. **Includes speakers of Urdu.

patterns, but also by the prevailing two- to three-generational shift to English. For example, fewer French speakers are entering the US today, while at the same time younger generations of Americans with French ancestry have shifted fully to English monolingualism; thus, we see a decrease in the number of people reporting that they speak French at home (although French continues to be one of the top languages taught as a second language in schools). Finally, for those languages that are currently seeing increases in the number of speakers, the increase is mostly due to new immigrant populations who are either already bilingual or who are beginning to learn English, and not because there is an increased population unwilling to learn English.

AMERICAN MULTILINGUALISM

Now that we have examined multilingualism as we first defined it, that is, as the use of more than one language in an area, we turn to the second meaning: multilingualism as a part of national identity. According to this view, multilingualism is not about the number of languages spoken by individuals or by the country as a whole, but instead

BOX 9.5 Angel Island

While many people are aware of Ellis Island and the role it has played in American immigration, fewer know about the United States' second major immigration station, Angel Island. Located in the San Francisco Bay, Angel Island was the point of disembarkation for nearly one million immigrants between 1910 and 1940. Although the majority of those coming through Angel Island were from China and Japan, the station processed visitors from over 80 different countries. However, unlike many of those who went through Ellis Island, the immigrants at Angel Island did not receive a hospitable welcome:

> On arrival at San Francisco, passengers would be separated by nationality. Europeans or travelers holding first or second class tickets would have their papers processed on board the ship and [would be] allowed to disembark. Asians and other immigrants, including Russians, Mexicans, and others, as well as those who needed to be quarantined for health reasons, would be ferried to Angel Island for processing.
>
> (http://aiisf.org/education/station-history)

In fact, the station was originally set up as a detention center that was "designed to control the flow of Chinese into the country, since they were officially not welcomed with the passage of the Chinese Exclusion Act of 1882" (http://angelisland.org/history/united-states-immigration-station-usis/). While most immigrants were processed through Ellis Island in three to seven hours, the average time at Angel Island was two to three weeks—and many were kept for months—while they underwent intense interrogations and physical examinations. After its closure as an immigration point in 1940, Angel Island was used as a processing station for Japanese and German prisoners of war during World War II.

The Angel Island Immigration Station Foundation (AIISF) was developed to preserve and restore the station, after a California park ranger in 1970 discovered Chinese poetry that had been carved in the walls of the barracks. In 1997 Angel Island was declared a National Historic Landmark by the National Park Service. For more information on Angel Island, see www.aiisf.org/ and www.aiisf.org/education/station-history/restoration.

9.13

pertains to the citizenry's commonly held beliefs about language, including whether language is an inherent part of a national identity. So we must again ask: Is the United States a multilingual nation? As the issues involved in answering this question are subjective and complex, there is no single correct answer, and so we invite readers to think through the issues presented here (as well as draw from their own experiences) to answer this question on their own.

The metaphors of the melting pot and the salad bowl that were discussed at the beginning of the chapter are a reflection of the ideological debate regarding cultural and linguistic diversity as an integral part of the American experience. The salad bowl metaphor tells of a nation that embraces multilingualism, while the melting pot, by supporting a completely unified nation, inherently rejects multilingualism. In deciding which metaphor best applies to the United States, and thus helping to answer the question of national multilingualism, one must not only investigate which metaphor applies to the contemporary situation, but also consider which metaphor ideally fits. Currently, immigrant families are learning English within the two- to three-generational pattern, which indicates a leaning toward the melting pot, but many individuals and families are also maintaining their home languages even after they learn English, which indicates the applicability of the salad bowl. Approximately 20% of the US population reports speaking a language other than English at home, and a growing number of native English-speaking Americans have some proficiency with a non-English language. Are these trends a reflection of a shared positive attitude toward multilingualism or are they simply a reflection of an increase in the immigrant population alongside an increase in those learning a second language due to educational and economic necessity? Again, which metaphor is ideologically valued?

When determining whether multilingualism is a part of a national identity, one must also examine the official and unofficial policies and attitudes toward both majority and minority languages, as well as the types of support or encouragement the country does or does not give. Reflecting on these policies, one should ask:

- Does the United States support the use of non-English languages by its citizens?
- Does the US support the preservation of indigenous languages?
- Does the US support the maintenance of immigrant languages?
- Does the US support multilingualism as something that is socially, culturally, and nationally valuable?
- Does the US support English as the dominant language?
- Should the US support these ideas?

The remaining chapters of this book discuss many of these policies in depth. We hope that readers will use this information not only to answer these particular questions but also to answer the larger question of whether the United States is a multilingual nation.

CONCLUSION

As we have seen, there are numerous languages spoken in the United States, and a strong and growing percentage of the population reports speaking a language other than English at home. However, we have also seen that, regardless of language or community, the majority of families in the US continue to shift to English monolingualism within three generations. And the patterns and policies toward immigration directly affect the maintenance of non-English languages in the United States. Thus, while satisfying the quantitative requirements of multilingualism, there is still an ideological debate as to whether the United States is truly a multilingual nation.

Furthermore, there is no one-to-one correlation between speaking a language other than English and immigration status. It is true currently in the US that "[o]ver-whelmingly, speakers of languages other than English are immigrants themselves or the children of immigrants" (Fishman, 2004, p. 116). However, this immediate connection between language and immigration does overlook—and in many cases dismisses—those who are speakers of languages that are indigenous to North America as well as those who have made personal choices to learn non-English languages. Importantly, such oversight has real consequences: for the maintenance and status of the languages themselves, for the status of their speakers as "real" members of an American community, and for the policies that are put in place regarding language and language use. These are issues that will be discussed throughout the remainder of this book.

DISCUSSION AND RESEARCH QUESTIONS

1. While the American Community Survey asks about level of English use, it does not define what is meant by: "speaks English very well, well, not well, or not at all." What do you think these distinctions mean? How could differences in interpretation affect the survey responses? What are the applications of this information, and how do these differences affect them?
2. Create a metaphor for linguistic and/or cultural diversity in the United States to replace the melting pot and salad bowl metaphors. Explain in detail not only the description of the metaphor but also why it is a more appropriate fit.
3. Pair up with two or three of your classmates and discuss the reasons why you or members of your family have learned a second language. Then, brainstorm together to create a list of other possible reasons why people choose to study a new language. Finally, discuss how and why the motivation for learning—and continuing to speak—a language could affect the overall maintenance of that language.

4. Both "Language Questions Used in Decennial Censuses" (in Box 9.1) and Michael Erard's (2012) article, "Are We Really Monolingual?" (linked through the Companion Website) list alternate questions for surveying information about language use in a population. Discuss how the wording of these questions could affect the answers that respondents provide.

9.9

5. Think back to the discussion of regional dialects in American English as discussed in Chapter 5. How does your knowledge of this variation factor into your assessment of the United States as a multilingual nation? In your answer, take into account the influence that contact with other languages has had on regional dialects.

10 Spanish as a Heritage Language

GUIDING QUESTIONS

1. What is a heritage language?

2. How has Spanish adhered to models of language shift and maintenance in the United States?

3. What accounts for the apparent maintenance of Spanish in the US?

OVERVIEW

Our focus in this chapter is on the use of Spanish in the United States. Among European languages, Spanish had the earliest continuous presence in the present-day US, and its lengthy history in Florida, Texas, and the Southwest has left an indelible mark on these areas as well as the entire nation. We explore the social context of Spanish speakers in the United States, past and present, including the reasons that Spanish speakers have for immigrating to the US, the primary areas they have settled in, and the varieties of Spanish that they use. We also address the continued use or disuse of Spanish by speakers within local communities in terms of language maintenance and language shift.

COMMON MYTHS

> *Spanish did not have a prominent presence in the United States until relatively recently.*

> *Granting Spanish speakers access to government services in the US, for example by printing Spanish versions of forms, began only recently.*

> *Recent Spanish-speaking immigrants have resisted learning English, which accounts for the large numbers of Spanish speakers in the US today.*

INTRODUCTION

In the previous chapter, we examined the overall distribution of languages spoken in the United States using data from the US Census and other sources. These data showed that many languages besides English are used throughout the country, and some of these languages have relatively large numbers of speakers. In the next few chapters of the book, we focus on these **heritage languages**, which are nondominant languages spoken by groups that are sometimes referred to as "linguistic minorities" (Valdés, 2005, p. 411). Because the languages that are used in their home and neighborhood differ from that of their government institutions and local schools, speakers of heritage languages face many challenges, including the inability to access legal, medical, and educational services in their native tongues. Despite receiving little or no recognition from institutions, however, these languages are vital to the lives of their speakers, creating unity and serving as markers of identity in the communities in which they are used. Over the course of the next few chapters, we examine heritage languages that originated in other parts of the world, particularly Europe and Asia, as well as languages that are primarily associated with the US, including Native American languages, American pidgins and creoles, and American Sign Language.

We begin the investigation of heritage languages by looking at the second most commonly used language in the United States today: Spanish. Although there are substantially fewer native speakers of Spanish in the US than there are monolingual

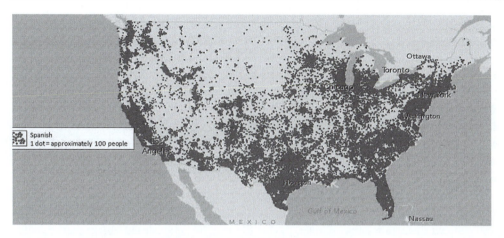

FIGURE 10.1 A map of the distribution of Spanish speakers in the US.

Source: 2011 Language Mapper tool, US Census Bureau.

speakers of English, over half of all heritage speakers in the US speak Spanish, with the number of Spanish speakers being more than 10 times greater than the number of speakers of the third most commonly spoken language in the nation, which is Chinese. While Spanish was at one time associated with only a handful of regions in the US, its use has spread to every region of the country in recent years, and there are now approximately 37.5 million Spanish speakers in the United States, a number that has more than doubled since 1990. The areal distribution of Spanish speakers in the US is shown in Figure 10.1.

A HISTORY OF SPANISH IN THE UNITED STATES

Of the European explorers who reached North America during the Age of Discovery, the Spanish arrived first, and early Spanish exploration of the present-day United States centered on three areas: (1) the Southeast; (2) Texas, the southern Rocky Mountain region, and the Great Plains; and (3) California. Exploration of the Southeast began in 1513, when the first governor of Puerto Rico, Ponce de León, arrived on the coast of Florida during his quest for the fountain of youth. This marked the first recorded presence of the Spanish on what would eventually be US soil. Over the course of the next 50 years, subsequent exploration of the region was conducted by the Spanish not only in Florida, but also in Georgia, the Carolinas, and Virginia. The Spanish established their first permanent settlement near the site of St. Augustine, Florida, in 1565.

Spanish exploration and subsequent settlement west of the Mississippi River began in 1536, when sailors from Spain washed past Florida in a storm and landed near present-day Galveston, Texas. From 1540 to 1542, Francisco Vázquez de Coronado led an expedition in search of the Seven Cities of the Cibolo from Mexico through present-day Arizona, New Mexico, Texas, Oklahoma, and Kansas. Two early Spanish settlements were established near present-day Santa Fe, New Mexico, and El Paso, Texas, in 1598 and 1659, respectively, and in the late 1600s, Father Eusebio Francisco Kino established several missions in Pimería Alta, or "Upper Pima Country," in what is now northern Sonora, Mexico, and southern Arizona. About 250 years after the settlement of Santa Fe, Hispanic settlers from the Taos Valley of New Mexico followed the Rio Culebra into the San Luis Valley, establishing San Luis de la Culebra (later shortened to San Luis) in 1851, making it the oldest town in Colorado.

In the same year that Coronado's expedition was completed, Juan Rodríguez Cabrillo, a Portuguese-born explorer under the flag of Spain, sailed into San Diego Bay and claimed the area for the Spanish, paving the way for Spanish settlement on the coast of California. In 1602, Sebastian Vizcaino was sent by the Spanish government to retrace Cabrillo's voyages; his ship arrived in San Diego Bay late that year, before continuing north to Monterey. Over the next 150 years, the Spanish government sent galleons periodically to explore the California coastline. In 1769, the Governor of Las Californias, Gaspar de Portolá, ventured up the California coast from Baja California with Fray Juniper Serra to establish missions in San Diego and Monterey, and Serra continued on as part of an expedition that eventually found its way north to San Francisco. These explorations and settlements created a network of Spanish-speaking communities throughout the New World and left a legacy of Spanish culture in these regions that exists to the present day.

10.1

Over the course of the 19th century, the United States took possession of all three of these Spanish holdings incrementally. Spain surrendered Florida to the US under the terms of the Adams–Onís Treaty in 1819; Texas gained its independence from Mexico in 1836 and then entered the Union as a state in 1845; and the Southwest was acquired when Mexico ceded California, New Mexico, Arizona, Utah, and Nevada, as well as parts of Colorado and Wyoming, under the terms of the Treaty of Guadalupe in 1848. In addition, Puerto Rico and, for a short time, Cuba were surrendered to the US in 1898 as a provision in the Treaty of Paris at the end of the Spanish–American War. Thus, the first great influxes of Spanish-speaking people into the US were the result of annexations rather than voluntary immigration, as regions and communities in which the dominant language had been Spanish for hundreds of years became part of the United States.

While the 19th-century annexations provided the first great increases in the number of Spanish speakers in the US, mass emigrations from Latin American countries increased the number of Spanish speakers not only in Florida, Texas, and the southwestern United States, but throughout the country beginning in the early 1900s. Hispanic culture in the Southwest was fortified by two major waves of immigration from Mexico—one at the onset of the Mexican Revolution in 1910, and the other soon after

World War II—as well as considerable immigration from Central and South America (Silva-Corvalán, 2004, p. 208). In reaction to the Cuban Revolution in 1959, the number of Cubans seeking asylum in the US, particularly in southern Florida, swelled in 1960, and the number rose again in 1980 due to an economic downturn on the island. In 1994, an agreement was forged between the US and Cuba allowing for 20,000 Cubans to obtain American visas each year. Since the mid-20th century, political unrest and economic uncertainty throughout Latin America have resulted in large numbers of Spanish-speaking immigrants in the United States. Table 10.1 shows the foreign-born population in the US from areas where Spanish is the dominant language, as classified by region and nation.

10.2

TABLE 10.1 US population born in Spanish-speaking countries and regions

Place of birth	1990	2000
Spain	**76,415**	**82,858**
Latin America	**8,407,837**	**16,086,974**
Caribbean	*1,938,348*	*2,953,066*
Cuba	736,971	872,716
Dominican Republic	347,858	687,677
Central America	*5,431,992*	*11,203,637*
Mexico	4,298,014	9,177,487
Costa Rica	43,530	71,870
El Salvador	465,433	817,336
Guatemala	225,739	480,665
Honduras	108,923	282,852
Nicaragua	168,659	220,335
Panama	85,737	105,177
South America	*1,037,497*	*1,930,271*
Argentina	92,563	125,218
Bolivia	31,303	53,278
Chile	55,681	80,804
Colombia	286,124	509,872
Ecuador	143,314	298,626
Paraguay	6,057	11,980
Peru	144,199	278,186
Uruguay	20,766	25,038
Venezuela	42,119	107,031

Source: Adapted from Gibson and Jung (2006, p. 28).

As the table shows, there was growth in the US population born in all Spanish-speaking regions and countries between the years 1990 and 2000. The US population born in Central America more than doubled during that time, and it nearly doubled for both Latin America and South America. Populations born in the countries of Mexico, Guatemala, Honduras, Ecuador, Paraguay, and Venezuela all more than doubled. The population born in Spain, however, grew by only 7%. (It should be noted that the numbers of those born in Puerto Rico are not included in this table because the US Census does not classify them as foreign-born.) These large increases in immigration from Latin American countries to the United States support the maintenance and growth of post-colonial varieties of Spanish in the US.

Historically, there has been a tendency for specific regions of the US to attract Spanish speakers from specific regions and countries. For instance, immigrants from Mexico, Central America, and South America historically tended to settle in the American Southwest, but later tended to settle in the Midwest, and only recently have begun to settle throughout the country. While Cubans have often settled in South Florida, particularly Miami (earning one Miami neighborhood the name "Little Havana"), they have also settled in New Jersey, particularly in Jersey City and Union City. The Northeast, in general, has historically attracted Caribbean immigrants. As citizens of an American territory, Puerto Ricans have had the right to enter the United States freely since the turn of the 20th century, which has enabled them to establish close-knit communities in New York City. In the 1960s, the US government eased travel restrictions for Dominicans that allowed them to obtain US visas during a civil war in the Dominican Republic. Due to political repression and economic hardship in the Caribbean country, Dominicans have continued to move to the US, with many settling in New York City. Recently, the growth of the Dominican population in the city began to outpace even that of the Puerto Ricans (Zentella, 2004). Colombians and Ecuadorians have also settled in the city in large numbers.

While the number of Spanish speakers in the United States has greatly increased, the linguistic rights that were previously granted to Spanish speakers, particularly in areas that were annexed by the US, have eroded over time. In 1849, California's first state constitution explicitly granted a variety of rights to Spanish speakers, including the translation of public documents and legislative proceedings, as addressed in Article XI, Section 21:

> All laws, decrees, regulations, and provisions emanating from any of the three supreme powers of this State, which from their nature require publication, shall be published in English and Spanish.

10.3

The large number of Anglo-Americans who arrived during the California Gold Rush, however, led legislators to reconsider this clause and, ultimately, English was made the sole language of California's official proceedings with the rewriting of the state constitution in 1879.

Another case in which Spanish has been marginalized in an area where it once dominated is symbolized by the case of New Mexico. At the time of New Mexico's admission into the Union as a state in 1912, Spanish had been used in the area for more than 300 years and had served as the dominant language of the area for most of that time. In recognition of this, the state's first constitution required that its laws be published in both English and Spanish for at least 20 years after gaining statehood (in Article XX, Section 12). Upon reaching the end of this period, New Mexico extended this provision for another 20-odd years; however, it allocated no funding for this service (Nichols, 1989, pp. 42–43).

During the 20th century, Spanish speakers began unifying in an effort to consolidate political power and to create an outlet for voicing their concerns on a number of social issues that they faced in the United States, including language rights. Reclaiming an epithet that had been used to insult the children of Mexican migrants at an earlier time in American history, Mexican Americans organized the "Chicano Movement," which gained momentum in the aftermath of World War II, and then banded together with other minority groups in the larger civil rights movement of the 1960s. The 20th century also saw the creation of two broad categories based on ethnicity: (1) *Hispanic*, a term used to refer to persons of Spanish-speaking origin or ancestry, including those from Spain and Latin America, and excluding those from Brazil, where the dominant language is Portuguese; and (2) *Latino*, a term used to refer to anyone of Latin American origin or ancestry, including Brazilians but excluding people from Spain. Changes in immigration patterns from different parts of the Spanish-speaking world or in the settlement patterns of these groups once they are in the US have also resulted in the creation of new ethnic groups. In some American cities, for instance, new classifications based on mixed Hispanic ancestry have emerged, including "MexiRicans" (Potowski, 2008; Potowski & Carreira, 2010).

10.4

By uniting politically, such groups have had an influence on American law and politics, since at least the mid-20th century, with some cases having serious linguistic consequences. *Mendez v. Westminster et al.* (1947) successfully challenged the constitutionality of segregating children of "Mexican and Latin descent" from other public school students. *Madrigal v. Quilligan* (1975) resulted in the adoption of bilingual consent forms for some medical procedures, after it was discovered that Hispanic women who did not understand English well had been sterilized without proper consent. Efforts to encourage these groups to participate in the American political process have met with some success, as evidenced by the role of Latinos in the 2012 American presidential election, when a large majority of Hispanic and Latino voters supported President Obama's bid for re-election (Pew Research Center, 2012). The growing influence of the Hispanic population has not gone unnoticed by the major American political parties, which have had to reframe some of their policies, particularly their immigration platforms, in an effort to appeal to this significant bloc of voters.

SPANISH MEDIA AND EDUCATION

The Spanish language has had a media presence in the United States since the publication of the Spanish newspaper *El Misisipi* in New Orleans in 1808. Although its first issue comprised a mere four pages and the paper was only in circulation for two years, *El Misisipi* ushered in a long tradition of Spanish language newspapers in the US that offered an important service to readers by delivering timely news from their native countries that could not have reached them through other channels (Maynard, 2008). In 2006, there were 38 daily and 384 weekly American newspapers written in Spanish, in addition to 254 local and 162 national magazines (Whisler, 2007). In 2007, the number of Spanish daily newspapers experienced its first decline, along with a general decline in print media; however, rather than folding completely, some of these operations converted from daily publication to weekly (Whisler, 2008).

Spanish also had an early presence in radio broadcasting in the United States, first in local markets and then at the national level. In 1932, Rodolfo Hayes began airing Spanish programs on an American radio station in Los Angeles, California, and by 1941 stations featuring Spanish programming had appeared in Arizona, Florida, New York, and Texas, in addition to California (Albarran & Hutton, 2009). Since the 1980s, Spanish radio has flourished in the United States, not only in major media markets such as Los Angeles and New York, but throughout the country.

The first Spanish language television station went on the air in San Antonio, Texas, in 1955, and since then several Spanish-speaking networks have been created (Silva-Corvalán, 2004). These stations have continued to proliferate and have played greater roles in informing and entertaining Spanish-speaking Americans in the age of cable. Recently, the Spanish language television network Univision hosted presidential forums leading up to the 2012 election. After the 2013 State of the Union address, Senator Marco Rubio delivered the televised Republican response in Spanish as well as in English. Spanish has also been used to some extent on English-medium, American television shows; for instance, in the 1970s the children's program *Sesame Street* began to incorporate a segment highlighting Spanish words during each episode. The expansion of Spanish into these domains is a reflection of the growing importance of Spanish in the US in general.

10.5

As a course of study offered to American students, Spanish has been among the top-ranked foreign languages in the country at every level of education since World War II. During that time, Spanish has had the highest enrollment among foreign languages in grades 9 through 12; there was a 52% increase in the number of students enrolled in Spanish in these grades from 1976 to 1990, and a 55% increase from 1990 to 2000 (National Center for Education Statistics, 2012). Among American universities since 1990, Spanish has ranked highest in the number of graduates earning a degree in a foreign language at the levels of bachelor's, master's and doctorate, and the gap between Spanish and other languages in this regard is widening (National Center for

Education Statistics, 2012). Due in part to the success of Spanish as a foreign language offered in schools, the language is reportedly used in the homes of about 2.8 million non-Hispanics every day (Gonzalez-Barrera & Lopez, 2013).

The history of bilingual Spanish–English programs in American schools has been complicated, and the success of these programs has depended greatly on their location. One place where **bilingual education** has flourished is Miami, Florida: a program that was created at one Miami elementary school in 1963 remains in operation and serves as a model program today. Passage of the 1968 Bilingual Education Act resulted in additional bilingual programs in Miami-Dade schools, as well as in schools throughout the country. While Spanish was not the only language targeted by this Act, the proposal received much support from the Hispanic community, and bilingual Spanish–English programs benefited greatly from enactment of the legislation.

10.6

Bilingual education has not fared well in the state of California. As in Miami, the 1968 Bilingual Act resulted in bilingual programs being established in several of the state's metropolitan areas; however, in 1998 Californians voted for the passage of Proposition 227, which imposed severe restrictions on bilingual education in the state. According to Article 2 of the proposition:

> all children in California public schools shall be taught English by being taught in English. In particular, this shall require that all children be placed in English language classrooms. Children who are English learners shall be educated through **sheltered English immersion** during a temporary transition period not normally intended to exceed one year. Local schools shall be permitted to place in the same class-room English learners of different ages but whose degree of English proficiency is similar. Local schools shall be encouraged to mix together in the same classroom English learners from different native-language groups but with the same degree of English fluency. Once English learners have acquired a good working knowledge of English, they shall be transferred to English language mainstream classrooms.

Recently, this issue has surfaced again. In 2014, California State Sen. Ricardo Lara proposed legislation designed to repeal the prohibitions on multilingual education that were put into place through Proposition 227.

10.7

VARIATION IN THE SPANISH OF THE UNITED STATES

Discussions of Spanish in the United States often take a monolithic view of the language. However, just as English morphed into new varieties when its speakers left the British Isles and settled in the American colonies, so too did new varieties of Spanish in the Spanish colonies of the New World. Such varieties emerged for some of the same reasons that American English did: linguistic drift from the parent variety of the language, adaptation to the new environment, and contact with indigenous languages in the Americas. Furthermore, because at first relatively few Spanish speakers covered a great expanse of land in the New World that included most of South America, Central America, and part of North America, in addition to the Caribbean Islands, many of these varieties were isolated from one another and had contact with sometimes very different Native American languages. Consequently, these varieties adapted differently to the New World and adopted different linguistic characteristics over time (see, for instance, Lipski, 2008).

One Spanish variety that is noteworthy in this regard is **New Mexican Spanish**, a dialect of Spanish spoken in New Mexico and southern Colorado that developed due to geographical and political isolation from other Spanish-speaking communities beginning in the 16th century. The dialect still retains some Spanish words that were current at the time of the new dialect's formation and that have since lost favor in other varieties of Spanish, leading some to romanticize a strong link between New Mexican Spanish and Spain; however, as Bills and Vigil point out:

> The reality of New Mexican Spanish is much more complex and quite different from a magical association with Spain ... The Spanish-heritage people of New Mexico and southern Colorado have no more direct bloodline links to Spain than do the inhabitants of Mexico or other regions of the Americas.
>
> (2008, p. 14)

Rather, early speakers of New Mexican Spanish were very much a part of their linguistic environment, borrowing words from the Pueblo-speaking people of the region, as well as English and French. New Mexican Spanish also shared with Mexican Spanish a tendency to borrow heavily from the language of the indigenous Nahuatl people, including such words as *chapulin* 'grasshopper,' *chile* 'chile pepper,' *cuates* 'twins,' *quelites* 'wild spinach,' and *tamal* 'tamale' (Bills & Vigil, 2008, p. 15). New Mexican Spanish also exhibits variation and has two major dialects: Traditional Spanish and Border Spanish. Despite the vitality of New Mexican Spanish for over four centuries, it is reportedly declining fast, due to its speakers shifting to English, as well as the influence that other Spanish varieties are imposing on the linguistic structure of the dialect (Bills & Vigil, 2008, p. 20).

10.8

Another variety of Spanish that has been used in North America a relatively long time is the dialect spoken by the **Isleños** of Louisiana. After France ceded the Louisiana Territory to Spain in 1764, the Spanish government recruited natives of the Canary Islands, or Isleños, to serve as soldiers and work as farmers in eastern Louisiana, beginning in 1778; however, Spain returned the territory to France in 1803, abandoning the Isleños in the process (Coles, 2011). Originating as a variety of Spanish used in rural areas in southern Spain and the Canary Islands, the Isleño dialect diverged from other

Spanish varieties even more sharply after the French returned to the area, due to the isolation of the Isleños from other Spanish-speaking communities in the US (Lipski, 1990), as well as their interaction with neighboring communities where Cajun French and Louisiana Creole were primarily spoken (see Chapters 11 and 13 for more on these varieties). In fact, the Isleños borrowed several words for the cultural artifacts they adopted from these communities, particularly from the Cajuns, from whom they borrowed *garsolé* 'sunbonnet' and *romana* 'dress,' as well as terms for local flora and fauna, such as *huancunú* 'hackberry tree' and *canar noir* 'black jack duck' (Coles, 2011). Isleño communities later attracted Caribbean and Central American immigrants, who, while largely adopting Isleño Spanish, also contributed lexical items to the dialect. Several factors have led to the obsolescence of the Isleño dialect in more recent years, including improved roads leading into the once-isolated communities where the variety was spoken, and the creation of schools in which English is the language of instruction and Spanish is forbidden (Craddock, 1981). In an effort to maintain Isleño, older people have learned English to teach the language and culture to younger members of the community; however, "[t]his well-intentioned use of English has inadvertently resulted in further language attrition" (Lestrade, 2002).

10.9

In addition to varieties of Spanish that have been spoken in the United States for centuries, new varieties of Spanish are emerging as speakers of the language begin to settle in areas that experienced relatively little Hispanic settlement in the past. In a study in one of these regions—the Mid-Atlantic South—Wolfram, Carter, and Moriello (2004) investigated the use of the diphthong /aɪ/ by Spanish-speaking adolescents learning English in North Carolina. Their objective in doing so was to determine whether these students accommodated to local speech norms by adopting the Southern characteristic of producing an unglided variant of /aɪ/, for example, by pronouncing *time* as *tahm* [ta:m]. The researchers found that adoption of the local variant was not pervasive and that speakers weakened the glide gradiently when they used /aɪ/, rather than accommodating wholly to the unglided variant. Furthermore, Wolfram et al. (2004) found that when speakers did accommodate linguistically, they had also adopted other cultural values of the community. In another study investigating a variety of Hispanic English developing in the same area, Wolfram, Kohn and Callahan-Price (2011, p. 10) found that the variety exhibited a "phonetic intermediacy between Spanish and English," that is, it presented phonetic features that were not wholly characteristic of either the Spanish or English varieties from which it had emerged.

Long-term contact between Spanish and English speakers in bilingual American communities has given rise to novel means of communication, with emergent language varieties often being used to identify speakers as members of these communities. These perfectly valid varieties have often been scorned by English and Spanish speakers alike as "Tex Mex" or "Spanglish," although such terms have often merely become fodder

> ### BOX 10.1 **Codeswitching**
>
> **Codeswitching** is an alternation between two or more languages during a conversation. It may be performed by alternating between the use of more than one language in a single sentence (intrasententially) or by using one language for one sentence and another language for the next (intersententially), as illustrated in these examples presented in Montes-Alcalá (2000, p. 219):
>
> 1. a. El lobo went to the old lady's house and la echó.
>   The wolf went to the old lady's house and threw her out.
>
>   b. She wanted to experiment. Quería ver qué había allá afuera del palacio.
>   She wanted to experiment. She wanted to see what was outside the palace.
>
> It is important to note that while codeswitching might appear to be random and chaotic to the casual observer, it follows rules and patterns like other language use. It is also not necessarily, nor even usually, the case that speakers who codeswitch are poor speakers of one or both of the languages they are switching between. Instead, speakers have a variety of reasons for codeswitching. One is that codeswitching serves as a way for speakers to show that they identify with two or more linguistic communities. Another is that speakers might be inclined to express a concept in the language of the culture that they perceive has a stronger link to the concept. It is important to keep in mind that "[c]odeswitching is a natural linguistic phenomenon commonly attested in bilingual communities in which two (or more) languages are in contact" (Montes-Alcalá, 2000, p. 218). As such, it is not merely speakers of English and Spanish who codeswitch, but any multilingual speaker can use codeswitching as a rhetorical strategy or an act of identity.

10.10

for reclamation by the speakers of these varieties. Please see the Companion Website for further discussion and debate about Spanglish.

In earlier chapters (namely, Chapters 4 and 5), we discussed the influence that Spanish has had on the lexicon of American English, particularly in the American Southwest. Here, we note that there were historical differences between the varieties of Spanish used in California and the varieties used in Texas and New Mexico that created lexical differences in the regional English vocabulary of these two areas. As Carver (1987, p. 223) reports, these variations were largely due to the different styles of ranching adopted in both regions. The foundations for Western ranching in both areas were established by the Spanish during the colonial years. However, as these areas, along with the rest of the West, began being integrated into the United States in the mid- to late 1800s, the ranching that was done in Texas became infused with English colonial cattle traditions that settlers from the South brought with them, while the ranching in California remained a largely Hispanic activity (Carver, 1987, p. 223). The divergent character of the activity in the two regions led to such lexical differences as the use of *buckaroo* 'cowboy, ranch hand' (from *vaquero*) in California and *wrangler* or *horse wrangler* (from *caballerango*) in Texas (Carver, 1987, p. 223). Other differences surface in the variation in the kinds of tools and work clothes used on ranches in both areas, as well as in the names for them, and the names used for different animals. (See Atwood, 1962; Bright, 1971; and Carver, 1987, for more.)

ATTITUDES ON SPANISH USE IN THE UNITED STATES

There is a wide range of attitudes concerning the use of Spanish in the United States. Bills and Vigil (2008, pp. 17–18) discuss the language myth that Spanish is in some way inferior to English. Based on linguistic grounds, this attitude has no merit, of course; both Spanish and English are perfectly good languages. Rather, the basis for this myth is apparently a social evaluation based on who speaks Spanish and that those who do often have a lower social status than those who do not. In addition to Anglos and other Americans who hold this myth to be true, "[m]any Hispanics, particularly the young and impressionable, buy into the power of [this] myth and perceive Spanish as loaded with all sorts of negative baggage" (Bills & Vigil, 2008, p. 18). This includes native speakers as they shift to English, which is often viewed as the language of the educated and more powerful in the United States.

A study of the attitudes of Los Angeles residents to Spanish and its use by Silva-Corvalán (2004) shows how complicated, and potentially conflicting, such views can be. In general, the study found a slight trend among younger Hispanics to hold more favorable views than their elders on the use of Spanish, reflecting perhaps recent societal changes in how bilingualism is viewed. These feelings manifest themselves in the freedom with which younger speakers use Spanish and defend their right to do so (Silva-Corvalán, 2004, p. 233). The study also found that many of those interviewed speakers were motivated less by the notion of maintaining Spanish than they were by the prospect of being bilingual (Silva-Corvalán, 2004, p. 225). In contrast to these positive trends in Spanish-speaking communities, the study revealed that members of other communities held less favorable attitudes concerning Spanish use, which were sometimes revealed through the use of Hispanic stereotypes (Silva-Corvalán, 2004, p. 226).

One manner in which English speakers express their attitudes concerning Spanish and Spanish speakers is through the use of **Mock Spanish,** a term coined by Hill (1998) to describe a phenomenon by which Spanish words and phrases are appropriated by non-Spanish speakers for humorous effect. In this way, it is common for speakers, who Hill describes as almost exclusively educated, middle- and upper-class whites, to intentionally distort certain aspects of Spanish, an example being the pronunciation of *buenos noches* 'good night' as *buenos nachos*. Additionally, common morphological rules from Spanish are overgeneralized so that a common Spanish ending such as *-o* will be suffixed to words in disregard of the rules of the language, such as *problemo*, rather than Spanish *problema* 'problem.' Hill (1998) calls this "incorporation," an act by which speakers of the dominant English language seize the desirable resources of the subordinate group of Spanish speakers and, in the case of Mock Spanish, use these for the purposes of ridiculing the group from which they've been taken. Adding insult to injury is that the Spanish speakers who are targeted by these acts are themselves expected to respect the linguistic rules of English and are even subjected to demands not only to speak English but to speak it correctly. Some scholars have pointed to an upward trend in the use of Mock Spanish in the media, an early example being Arnold Schwarzenegger's use of the catch phrase "Hasta la vista, baby," first in the movie *Terminator 2: Judgment Day* and then during his successful campaign for California governor (Romaine, 2010, p. 45).

10.11

There has also been some discussion of ideology that views Spanish as if it were a threat; Wolford and Carter report that

> the Spanish language has somehow become THE popular symbol of threat in recent years—a threat to English and, ipso facto, to US, to OUR WAY OF LIFE, and to that version of America constituted by and through the English language. That is, Spanish has come to function—rhetorically, politically, symbolically—as an unwanted cultural transformation.
>
> (2010, p. 111, emphasis in original)

Despite studies showing an uncertain future for the maintenance of Spanish as a heritage language in the United States (Wolford & Carter, 2010, p. 114), the Spanish-as-threat ideology is embedded in attitudes and even finds an audience in cultural productions, such as Huntington's *Who Are We? The Challenges to America's National Identity* (2004).

SPANISH MAINTENANCE AND LANGUAGE SHIFT IN THE UNITED STATES

Among heritage languages in the United States, Spanish has perhaps the greatest number of conditions favoring its survival. One of the most important of these is the large number of Spanish speakers already in the US. Perhaps just as significant, and not unrelated to that condition, is the close proximity that the US has to Spanish-speaking countries throughout the Americas, particularly Mexico, as well as the Spanish-speaking Caribbean islands. This bodes well for the maintenance of Spanish in the US in that it makes Spanish a significant tool for trade and diplomacy; more important, however, is that it makes travel and communications between the US and many countries in which Spanish is the dominant language relatively easy, which, in particular, enables Spanish speakers who are new to the US to remain in close contact with family, friends, and colleagues back in their home countries. Increases in the numbers of students enrolling in Spanish classes in American schools and the rise in popularity of Spanish mass media also support the maintenance of the language. Thus, Spanish appears on many fronts to be destined for a better fate in the US in terms of language maintenance than other languages that have come before.

While there are many signs pointing to the maintenance of Spanish in the US, however, some scholars depict Spanish as generally following the same path that other heritage languages have in terms of its speakers conforming to the linguistic demands of American culture (e.g., Potowski & Carreira, 2010, p. 76). Veltman (1988) claims that Spanish-speaking immigrants are assimilating to American language and culture even more quickly than earlier immigrant groups, reporting that these speakers are approaching a two-generation model of language shift to English rather than the three-generational model typical of immigrants of the 19th and early 20th centuries. With respect to Spanish in the southwestern United States, Bills and Vigil (2008, p. 19) contend that "[t]he rapidity with which Southwest Hispanics over the past half century are shifting to English and abandoning Spanish rivals the loss of the ethnic mother tongue by practically any ethnic group in documented history." Fishman (2004) argues that, given the fate of other prominent heritage languages in American history, and despite the large number of Spanish speakers in the US today, the future sustainability of the Spanish language on American soil is tenuous and therefore "must be viewed with concern and even alarm" (p. 117).

The key to the maintenance of Spanish in the United States, then, appears to be continued migration of Spanish speakers, no matter their countries of origin. Simply put, if speakers of Spanish continue migrating to the US and fill in the gaps left by speakers, or families or communities of speakers, who have shifted to English, then the language will survive in the US. If speakers stop migrating, then there is no reason to believe that the language will be able to avoid the fate of heritage languages that have come before, which have, for the most part, eventually shifted to English. In the next chapter, we investigate several heritage languages whose histories and current situations are both comparable to and very different from those of Spanish.

CONCLUSION

In this chapter, we examined the case of Spanish as a heritage language in the United States. Among heritage languages, Spanish is noteworthy in several regards, including the time span of its physical presence in the present-day US, and the large number of Spanish speakers currently residing in the nation, as well as the way in which many early Spanish speakers became Americans through annexation of their lands rather than through immigration. The size of the Spanish-speaking population in the US presents challenges in several areas, including business, education, and law, while at the same time presenting opportunities in these areas, particularly if the Spanish-speaking population in the US continues to grow at the present rate.

One aspect of Spanish use in the United States that commentators often seem to ignore is its great diversity, in terms of the different national varieties of Spanish that are spoken in the US, the changes that occur in these varieties once they arrive in the US and begin adopting local norms, and the varieties of Hispanic English that have emerged in different regions of the US. These varieties are often accompanied by attitudes that Spanish and English speakers hold about these varieties, and as Hispanic communities continue to evolve in the US, these different varieties and linguistic attitudes will also change over time. Due to limitations of space, we could only touch on some of the issues pertaining to Spanish diversity and language attitudes regarding Spanish; however, sources are provided on the Companion Website for learning more about these.

DISCUSSION AND RESEARCH QUESTIONS

1. Referring to Table 10.1, choose a country from Latin America to conduct research on and find answers to the following questions: Did anything specifically occur in the country to initiate immigration to the US during the late 1900s (e.g., civil war, natural disaster, economic woes)? Were immigrants representative of the population of the country as a whole or only of specific social groups (e.g., farmers, the poor, the wealthy, specific political, religious, or ethnic groups)? Did immigrants from the country move in large numbers to a specific place or places in the United States? If so, where did they go and what was the reason for the place(s) chosen? Is immigration from that country still taking place at the same rate it was between 1990 and 2000? Has the US government made any apparent efforts to encourage or discourage immigration from that particular country?
2. The attitudes concerning New Mexican Spanish discussed in this chapter have some parallels with attitudes regarding regional American English in the idea that dialects that retain archaic features are considered to have a stronger link to the colonial

power from which they originated. Consider the problems underlying such an idea in terms of language change and language attitudes. What are some of the myths embodied by such a notion?

3. What are your thoughts on Hill's discussion of Mock Spanish? Are there other languages that you have used or heard used in this way? Compare Mock Spanish with attitudes toward African American English or Yellow English, which is the stereotyped image of the speech of Asian Americans. What similarities and differences can you find?

10.12

11 Other Heritage Languages

GUIDING QUESTIONS

1. How have speakers of the different heritage languages presented in this chapter adhered to models of language shift and maintenance in the United States?

2. What kinds of media are available in the US for the heritage languages we present in this chapter?

3. What kinds of programs, if any, are there for the maintenance or revitalization of heritage languages in the US?

OVERVIEW

In this chapter, we describe several languages that have had a significant presence in the United States. For each, we begin by presenting the sociohistorical context of the language's speakers in the US, including their reasons for immigrating to the US, the primary areas they settled in, the size and diversity of their populations, the media presence of the language in the US, and educational opportunities for learning the language. For each language, we investigate the varieties of the language that are used in the US, and whether new varieties of the language have emerged in the US since its arrival. We also address the continued use or disuse of these languages by speakers within local communities in terms of language maintenance and language shift, as well as any efforts that have been made at revitalization in specific communities. Finally, we discuss whether these groups have contributed linguistically to regional varieties of American English and to the national variety as a whole.

COMMON MYTHS

> *Immigrants in the United Sates have always understood the need to leave their ancestral languages behind.*

> *There has been little or no effort historically to maintain heritage languages in the US.*

> *Historically, the use of heritage languages in the US has been limited to large cities.*

INTRODUCTION

In the previous chapter, we began our discussion of heritage languages by looking at Spanish, the most commonly used heritage language in the United States today. English and Spanish, however, are not the only languages with sizable populations in the modern US; thus, this chapter delves into several other languages that have or have historically had relatively large, and sometimes influential, populations in the US. Since limitations of space meant that only a small number of languages could be covered in this chapter, several factors were used to determine the languages to be presented, including the current and historical populations of speakers of the language, the linguistic family or region of the world that the language came from, and the ability of the language to illustrate important aspects of language maintenance and language shift. Using these criteria, French, German, Chinese, Tagalog, Arabic, and Yiddish were chosen for inclusion in this chapter.

There were also limitations on how much detail could be included for each of the languages that were selected. We present a brief history of each of these languages in the United States, provide demographics pertaining to the people who use them, and discuss the coverage these languages obtain in mass media and in education. As you read, you should be making connections between the history of groups of speakers and the contemporary use or disuse of each heritage language. It may be helpful to compare and contrast each group, not only with each other, but also with the histories of English and Spanish, which were presented in earlier chapters. We also discuss efforts to

11.1

maintain these languages in the face of historical and contemporary pressures to shift to English. Furthermore, we also describe programs that exist for each language, if any, in **language revitalization**, which is an attempt to reverse language shift, typically through the combined efforts of native speakers, linguists, community programs, and/or government agencies. On the Companion Website, we provide an extensive list of sources for readers who want to learn more about the languages described here.

FRENCH

French is a Romance language with a continued presence in North America longer than that of any other European language besides Spanish. French had a presence in northern New England, the Great Lake States, the Mississippi River Valley, Louisiana, and the Carolinas decades before British colonists and, later, Americans ventured into these areas. Like Spanish, the first large influxes of French speakers were not the result of voluntary immigration but came as the result of annexations, the largest of which was the Louisiana Purchase. A broad range of French varieties are used in the United States, including European French, Cajun French, and Colonial French. Furthermore, although immigration to the US from France is modest, the US draws many French speakers from post-colonial nations in which French is an official or a dominant language. These countries include Haiti and the former French colonies in Africa, such as Senegal, Gabon, and Chad.

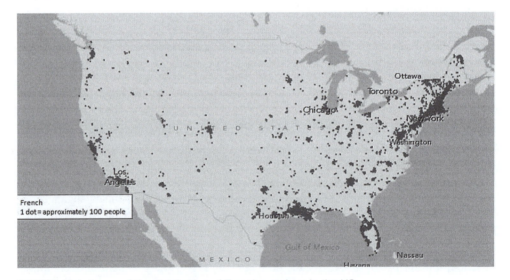

FIGURE 11.1 A map of the distribution of French speakers in the US.

Source: 2011 Language Mapper tool, US Census Bureau.

The 2011 ACS reports just over 1.3 million people using French at home in the United States, down from the numbers reported in the 2000 census (over 1.6 million) and the 1990 census (1.7 million) (US Census Bureau, 2010–2013). When combined with speakers of Cajun French and Louisiana Creole, the 2011 ACS reports just over two million people in the US using some variety of French at home. The states with the highest total number of French speakers are Florida, New York, Louisiana, California, and Massachusetts, and those with the highest percentages are Louisiana, Maine, Florida, and New Hampshire, reflecting the settlement history of French speakers in North America, which is discussed below. The metropolitan areas with the largest number of French speakers are New York City, Washington, Boston, and Miami. The areal distribution of French speakers in the US is shown in Figure 11.1.

A History of French in the United States

In spite of Pope Alexander VI limiting land claims in the New World to Portugal and Spain in 1493, the French were early explorers of the Americas. Giovanni de Verrazanno, a Florentine in the service of King Francis I, led the first French expedition to the present-day United States, exploring the waterways of New York before turning south and landing near present-day Wilmington, North Carolina, in 1524 (Pula, 1975). Other French explorers made several attempts at settlement off the coast of the Carolinas and at St. Augustine, Florida, but these attempts were foiled by famine, mutiny, inclement weather, and brutal attacks on the French by the Spanish.

The French enjoyed greater success in the northerly regions of the New World. During his expeditions in the 16th century, Jacques Cartier explored the vast territories around the St. Lawrence River, claiming the land in the name of France in 1534 and calling it "The Country of Canadas." Samuel de Champlain later founded and governed New France and Quebec City in 1608. The colony of Acadia that emerged from this period consisted of eastern Quebec, the Maritimes, and modern-day Maine north of the Kennebec River. New France was expanded as explorers, missionaries, and fur trappers and traders pushed into the North American interior by navigating the Great Lakes and Mississippi River. There was also northward expansion from the southern coast, as the French sailed into the Gulf of Mexico past Spanish forces in Florida and built settlements in Mobile and Biloxi, before establishing a city near the mouth of the Mississippi River in 1718 that they named La Nouvelle-Orléans, or New Orleans.

11.2

Thus, the French began amassing the foundation for a great colony ranging from Canada to the Gulf of Mexico, while at the same time confining the British to their holdings between the Atlantic Ocean and the Appalachian Mountains. However, the French found fortifying these holdings against English and Spanish encroachment impossible and began to concentrate their efforts on maintaining their claim to Quebec and the Louisiana Territory, a massive land holding west of the Mississippi River that would later be sold to the US. In 1713, some of France's claims to land in Canada were ceded to the British under the Treaty of Utrecht and, in 1755, after 40 years of marginalization by the British, Acadians—who were descendants of the 17th-century French colonists of Acadia—were officially exiled. Many were corralled into British ships from which they were to be set ashore in various American settlements along the eastern seaboard (Angers, 1989); however, the Acadians met with derision and were taken into servitude in some of the colonies and, in Virginia, they were not only refused entry but were sent to England as prisoners of war. Acadians often responded to these threats by taking flight and making their way to Quebec, to French colonies in the Caribbean, or to Louisiana, seeking aid from other people of French descent.

11.3

In 1803, the French ceded their holdings in America's Deep South and Great Plains to the United States for less than three cents per acre (the equivalent of about 50 cents today) in what is now commonly referred to as the Louisiana Purchase. When the region was annexed, it raised the concerns of some Americans over the dramatic increase in the number of French-speaking people in the United States. In 1812, Louisiana became the first and only state in which a non-English-speaking group commanded a popular majority at the time of its entry into the Union, and Congress required that the rights of English speakers be safeguarded in the state's first constitution. Louisiana's legislature operated bilingually as a practical necessity up until the Civil War, as numerous officials, including Jacques Villeré, who served as governor in the early 1800s, did not speak English (Crawford, 1997).

In addition to their presence in Louisiana and other areas of North America, some French speakers resided in the British colonies, particularly French Huguenots who arrived on the Atlantic seaboard after years of feuding with French Catholics in Europe. A steady influx of immigrants from France during the 17th and 18th centuries led to the creation of French settlements in the Mississippi Valley as well as New York, and the appearance of numerous French language newspapers on the East Coast during those years attests to the number of French speakers there. Between the mid-19th century and the early 20th century, French settlement thrived in the American West as a response to several events: (1) the California Gold Rush, which led the French, among many others, to boomtowns such as San Francisco; (2) the flight of Alsatian Jews to Los Angeles after Alsace and Lorraine became part of Germany; and (3) an economically motivated mass migration to the US in the late 19th and early 20th centuries. Despite the size of these migrations, permanent immigrants from France in most regions of the United States quickly blended into mainstream American society (Lindfield, 2000).

While earlier French speakers arriving as immigrants to the United States often came from France or Canada, there has been a greater increase in arrivals from former colonies of France in the Caribbean and Africa, as illustrated in Table 11.1. As shown, Haiti's contribution to the population of the United States was by far the greatest among countries in which French is the official language, and there was a significant increase in the Haitian population from 1990 to 2000. While the number of those in the US who were born in France also increased, proportionally the increases in the numbers

TABLE 11.1 US population born in French-speaking countries and regions

Country of birth	1990	2000
Haiti	225,393	419,317
France	119,233	151,154
Cameroon	3,161	11,765
Senegal	2,287	10,534
Ivory Coast (Côte d'Ivoire)	1,388	7,173
Guinea	1,032	5,062
Zaire (Democratic Republic of Congo)	3,387	4,989

Source: Adapted from US Census Bureau (2006).

of speakers from Cameroon, Senegal, the Ivory Coast, and Guinea were more impressive, with the US populations of each doubling during this time period.

French had an early media presence in the United States, as the first French newspaper in the country was printed in Boston in 1789. By the late 19th century, the number of French newspapers had boomed, and they were especially common in the New England states, particularly Massachusetts, where over 20 French newspapers were printed in the town of Lowell between 1874 and 1995. French newspapers were also published in New York City, New Orleans, and Philadelphia. Additionally, some newspapers, such as the *Detroit Gazette*, published in the Michigan Territory from 1817 to 1830, included articles in both English and French. Today, there are only a handful of newspapers written in French in the United States, as the French-speaking communities that the papers had relied on for readership have largely shifted to English. There are, however, several radio stations in the United States that feature spoken and/or music programming in French. Southern Louisiana has several stations that feature Cajun music, but there are also French-speaking stations in Miami, Florida, and central New Jersey. Furthermore, many French radio stations in Canada can be heard in American states sharing a border with Canada. Many of these stations are accessible online, including Radio Louisiane.

11.4

Often perceived as an important language of the arts, literature, and diplomacy, French has been a popular foreign language for American students in both secondary and post-secondary institutions. From 1976 to 1990, there was a 23% increase in the number of students in grades 9 through 12 taking French, for a total of just over a million students of the language; however, there was a slight decrease in that number from 1990 to 2000 (National Center for Education Statistics, 2012). Among those students graduating with a degree in a foreign language in 2011, French was the second most frequent for bachelor's, master's, and doctorate degrees (National Center for Education Statistics, 2012). There are also over 100 French immersion programs in K-12 schools throughout the United States.

11.5

Variation in French in the United States

Several varieties of French are spoken in the United States. Varieties of European French can be heard in the speech of tourists and some recent immigrants from France and other French-speaking countries in Europe. The French that developed in the northeastern United States is related to the variety of French spoken in Quebec, Canada, and, like Quebec French, it differs from European French in all aspects of the grammar. Due to their origins, Cajuns in Louisiana speak a variety of French related to that of the Acadians of the eastern Canadian provinces of Newfoundland and Nova Scotia; however, the variety has undergone changes due to **linguistic drift**. In fact, the word *Acadian* became the word *Cajun* through the common process of vowel deletion at the beginning of the word and the change of the middle consonant alveolar [d] to a sound that is similar in terms of articulation, the alveopalatal [ʤ]. In addition to its Acadian origins, Cajun has likely been influenced by its contact with a variety of French in Louisiana called Colonial French, as well as with the Louisiana Creole. In addition to different varieties of the French language, there are several creole languages spoken in the United States that had French as one of their source languages, including Louisiana Creole, Michif, and Haitian Creole, which are discussed in Chapter 13.

11.6

Current Status of French in the United States

Decreasing numbers of French speakers in the United States as well as declines in French language media outlets suggest that language shift from French to English is well underway. Even among those who identified themselves as French speakers in the 2011 ACS self-reported using English "very well" (79.6%) or "well" (13.9%), indicating that over 90% of French speakers in the United States are bi- or multilingual. Reports suggesting that the children of French speakers are adopting English as their native tongue do not bode well for maintenance of French in the US.

There is evidence, however, of the maintenance of French as a second language. French continues to remain popular among American students at the levels of college and high school for meeting foreign language requirements. In some areas of the country, as in several parishes in Louisiana, bilingual education and community programs are aimed at encouraging the use of French. Access to French radio programming and interest in French music forms such as Cajun and zydeco might also help to maintain varieties of French in the United States.

11.7

GERMAN

A West Germanic language closely related to English, German has had a presence in America dating all the way back to the Jamestown settlement. In the mid-19th century,

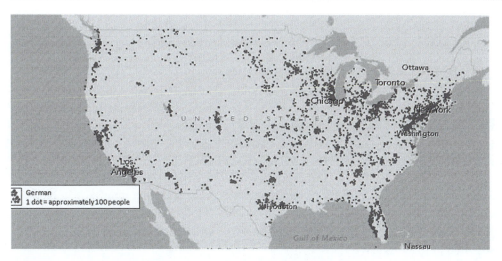

FIGURE 11.2 A map of the distribution of German speakers in the US.

Source: 2011 Language Mapper tool, US Census Bureau.

great waves of German-speaking immigrants to the United States had a strong influence on several regions of the country, particularly the Midwest. While there was apparently little extraordinary in the relations between Germans and other nationalities in the United States in the late 1800s and early 1900s, the opposition of American and German forces in World Wars I and II led to the German language being socially stigmatized and, in some cases, even legally banned, during the wars. These bans most likely resulted in the overall decline of German use in the United States, for example, in schools and government institutions.

The 2011 ACS reports just under 1.1 million people speaking German in American homes, a decrease of nearly 33% from the number in 1980 and constituting approximately 0.35% of the total American population. The states with the largest percentage of German speakers today are North and South Dakota, and the metropolitan areas with the greatest number of German speakers are New York, Chicago, Los Angeles, and Washington. The areal distribution of German speakers in the US is shown in Figure 11.2.

A History of German in the United States

The presence of the German language in America dates back to the early years of the British settlement at Jamestown (Rippley, 1976). However, it wasn't until the late 1600s that German speakers began moving into Pennsylvania as well as Upstate New York in large numbers, and still others moved into the tidewater region of Virginia and Maryland, where they made their living as craftsmen, vintners, and tobacco farmers.

The German states did not colonize in the New World during the Age of Discovery as did other Europeans, but German speakers lived in or near English and French colonies. For instance, migrants from the Rhineland of Germany, Switzerland, Alsace-Lorraine, and Belgium formed the "German Coast" in the New Orleans area beginning in 1721.

During the 19th century, German was spoken by more immigrants to the US than any other language besides English, as German speakers represented 23–37% of the total immigration for each decade between 1830 and 1890. At its peak in 1882, German immigration consisted of 250,630 new arrivals (Reichstein, 2001). By 1900, Germans made up large percentages of the population of several cities, especially in the Midwest, including Milwaukee (70%), Davenport (62%), Hoboken (58%), Cincinnati (54%), St. Louis (45%), Buffalo (43%), and Detroit (41%); in addition, approximately 40% of American farmland was owned by Germans (Fleckenstein,1998). Germans also forged their way into Texas from their point of entry at New Orleans and created communities established specifically for German immigrants, such as Fredericksburg and New Braunfels.

11.8

In the 19th century, state and local governments were impacted by the high number of German immigrants; for instance, there were both English and German (as well as Spanish) versions of the state constitution of Colorado, and the Wisconsin state constitution was also written in German (in addition to English and Norwegian). Some of the popularity of German during this period can be attributed not only to the high numbers of German immigrants, but also to immigrants from the Netherlands, Sweden, Norway, and Denmark, who knew German as a second language, or whose languages were closely enough related to German that they could understand it.

Among the Founding Fathers, there was some concern over the popular use of the German language in the United States. Benjamin Franklin was a particularly outspoken critic of the use of German in the US, and he questioned whether Germans were more interested in becoming Americanized or in Germanizing others (Read, 1937). Despite being the publisher of the first German language newspaper in America, Franklin (1751/1959) held some rather negative sentiments concerning the Germans:

> Why should the Palatine Boors be suffered to swarm into our Settlements, and by herding together establish their Language and Manners to the exclusion of ours? Why should Pennsylvania, founded by the English, become a Colony of Aliens, who will shortly be so numerous as to Germanize us instead of our Anglifying them, and will never adopt our Language or Customs, any more than they can acquire our Complexion?

11.10

> (As quoted in Baron, n.d.)

Conversely, other early leaders, such as Benjamin Rush, recognized that allowing immigrants to voluntarily assimilate to American ways over time rather than forcing linguistic unity on them would be the best policy, and thus advocated bilingual higher

---

BOX 11.1 Turnverein Movement

The concept of the Turnverein, which denotes a gymnastic or athletic club, was brought to the United States by a group of political refugees from the German states known as the Forty-Eighters. Turnvereins were established in Cincinnati and New York City in 1848; three years later, Turnvereins were built in Texas, and others were founded still later in other parts of the country. As part of this movement, the American Turnerbund (gymnastic league), now called the American Turners, was formed in 1850, and by 1923 over 30,000 members were enrolled in 22 districts and 172 societies (Metzner, 1924). The Turners were active in public education, and worked diligently to make education compulsory and to include physical training during the school day. They were also active politically and espoused such causes as abolition and the labor movement at different points in American history. German was regarded as the official language in Turnvereins; thus, they provided German speakers with opportunities to use their native tongue as they transitioned from their homelands to their adopted country.

As the number of German-speaking immigrants to the United States has declined, and as most German speakers in the US have shifted to English, some Turnvereins have closed their doors. Others, however, have responded by introducing cultural events and activities of interest to the greater public. The Denver Turnverein, for instance, held its final German Lodge meeting in July 2012. It now offers classes in a variety of dance styles, including swing, salsa, and tango.

11.9

---

education for Germans and other foreigners (Crawford, 1990). Although it was later said that Franklin regretted his harsh criticism of Germans, it is true that some German families in the states tended to retain and pass down several aspects of their culture, especially in rural areas of the Midwest and Texas (Hawgood, 1940). As part of this effort, German schools were constructed throughout the United States, with part of their mission being to preserve the German heritage. In 1900, there were 600,000 American elementary school children receiving at least part of their instruction through the German language (Kloss, 1977).

The opposition of American and German military forces during World War I resulted in bans on the use of German being implemented in states throughout the country and, during the war and its aftermath, an intolerance of all things German swept through the United States (Rodgers, 1958). During this period, streets with German names were replaced, and Americans with German surnames had them legally changed, often simply Anglicizing them, for example by changing Schmidt to Smith and Müller to Miller. In 1919, the town of Berlin, Michigan, changed its name to Marne, Michigan, to downplay its relationship with the German city and to pay homage to soldiers who fought in the Battle of the Marne in World War I. Foods with German-sounding names were even renamed; thus, for a short time, *sauerkraut* was referred to as *liberty* or *victory cabbage* and *hamburgers* were called *Salisbury steak*.

There were also legal restrictions placed on the German language due to the World Wars. In 1917, the legislature of Louisiana, for instance, passed an Act prohibiting all expressions of German culture and heritage in the state, including the German language in either its spoken or written form; the ban was lifted after the end of World War I but was reinstated during World War II (Merrill, 2005). Residents of German towns in the Texas Hill Country, where the language had largely been maintained, were forced to assimilate during and after World War I as the state required schools to adopt English-only instruction. In Nebraska, anti-German sentiment became so strong that at least one official made an inquiry to an Attorney General as to whether it would be possible to legally prohibit the use of a foreign language on the streets of a village or in any public place (Rodgers, 1958). Although the answer the official received discouraged further action in this regard, legislation was proposed in the aftermath of the war seeking to make English the only language of instruction in the state's schools. (See our detailed discussion of *Meyer v. Nebraska* (1923) in Chapter 15.)

11.11

The German newspaper business, which thrived throughout the US in the late 19th century, particularly in Midwestern cities (Romaine, 2001), was also adversely affected by anti-German sentiment. At the turn of the 20th century, German language publications in the United States numbered around 600. However, in the years immediately following World War I, these numbers decreased rapidly. By 1940, there were approximately 200 publications remaining, and today there are only about 40.

In terms of education, German has been a popular choice as a foreign language among college students, ranking third (after Spanish and French) among those graduating with degrees in a specific foreign language at the level of bachelor's, master's, and doctorate (National Center for Education Statistics, 2012) since World War II. Since that time, it has also ranked third among high school students taking a foreign language; however, while German has retained its ranking, the number of students taking the language has steadily decreased since the mid-1970s (National Center for Education Statistics, 2012).

Variation in German in the United States

11.12

In the United States, new varieties of German emerged in Pennsylvania, Texas, and Wisconsin. These varieties reflected the national and regional varieties of German that immigrants brought with them from Europe. But they were also products of their new communities, as the different varieties of German in these communities underwent leveling, in much the same way as Colonial American English had, and they adopted features from other languages in their immediate environment, particularly local varieties of English.

Of the different regional varieties of German in the US, Pennsylvania German, or, as it is often called, Pennsylvania Dutch, has the greatest number of speakers with approximately 118,000 (2010 Census). The dialect descended from the speech of people who migrated from present-day southern Germany, eastern France, and Switzerland and settled in Pennsylvania and neighboring colonies during the 17th and 18th centuries. Most speakers of this dialect are bilinguals who also speak English. The dialect is often associated with the Amish, although the Amish constitute only a small proportion of the total number of users. The geographic range of the dialect has expanded throughout North America; however, most of its speakers live in Pennsylvania, Ohio, Indiana, and Ontario. A biannual newspaper written in Pennsylvania German called *Hiwwe Wie Driwwe* has been in publication since 1997.

11.13

Current Status of German in the United States

The German language has had a long history in the United States, but its presence was especially influential in the 19th century, when immigration by people from German states in Europe peaked. Despite the stigmatization of German in the US during the World Wars of the 20th century, German has been a popular language for American students at all levels. Although it is still ranked third in popularity among students, the percentage of students taking German has declined as more students take Spanish or languages that are only recently becoming available to them, such as Chinese. Furthermore, unlike the case of Spanish and French, in which speakers of these languages are entering the US from post-colonial nations where these languages are used, there are no such nations from which German speakers are coming, so essentially the only German-speaking immigration is from Germany and Austria. Finally, the 2011 ACS reports that nearly all German speakers assessed themselves as speaking English "very well" (82.9%) or "well" (13.1%), suggesting that nearly all are bilingual (US Census Bureau, 2010–2013). Thus, there is not a positive outlook for the German language in the United States.

CHINESE

Spoken by about 20% of the world's population, Chinese has the largest number of speakers of any language in the world. A member of the Sino-Tibetan family of languages, Chinese also has the oldest writing system still in use, as texts using its original pictograph writing have been found on shells and stones tracing back to the

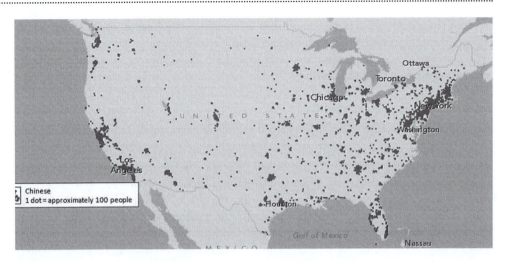

FIGURE 11.3 A map of the distribution of Chinese speakers in the US.

Source: 2011 Language Mapper tool, US Census Bureau.

11.14

Shang Dynasty (1600–1100 BCE) (Xiao, 2010). Chinese pictographs have since evolved into the ideographic form of writing used by the Chinese today.

In the United States, Chinese is the third-ranked language in number of speakers, after English and Spanish. The 2011 ACS reports over 2.8 million speakers of Chinese in the United States, with a 345.3% increase from 1980 to 2010 (US Census Bureau, 2010–2013). Three states account for a large majority of the total population of Chinese speakers in the United States: California, New York, and Hawaii. By World War I, the largest populations of Chinese speakers in the US resided in San Francisco, Oakland, Chicago, and New York (Tsai, 1986). Today, the top-ranking metropolitan areas for Chinese speakers in the US are New York, Los Angeles, San Francisco, and San Jose. The areal distribution of Chinese speakers in the US is shown in Figure 11.3.

A History of Chinese in the United States

The first major wave of Chinese immigration to the United States began with the California Gold Rush in 1848 and, by the 1850s, thousands of Chinese were entering North America to labor in mines or build the transcontinental railroad and, later, to work in agriculture and fishing. Many of the Chinese immigrants of this period had little education and financial means; marginalized by society, they often took up residence in the Chinatowns that arose in the West once the work they had been recruited for had been completed (Xiao, 2010). By 1860, the Chinese comprised the largest immigrant group in California; according to the 1870 Census, there was a total of 63,199 Chinese living in the United States, with 78% of them residing in California (Chang, 2003).

Beginning in the late 1800s, the Chinese were blatantly discriminated against in American immigration policy. The Chinese Exclusion Act was signed into law in 1882 to prohibit the immigration of Chinese; in 1888, it was expanded through the Scott Act to bar Chinese who had ever been in the US from returning once they had left. The Immigration Act of 1924 expanded the prohibition of the Chinese to other Asian groups as well. This prejudice was also evident in the field of education, as made clear in a unanimous resolution of the San Francisco School Board in 1886, which stated:

> No principal, teacher or employee of the Public Schools Department shall employ, patronize, aid or encourage the Chinese in any way, but shall do all in their power to legally promote their removal from this coast and to discourage further immigration.
>
> (As quoted in Baron, 1990, p. 133)

Additionally, labor unions also reacted negatively to the hiring of Chinese, and the Chinese were often subject to harsh treatment and poor conditions in the work they were able to obtain in the US.

In spite of this treatment, Chinese immigration continued throughout the 20th century; from 1910 to 1940, the Chinese were among the one million Asians who entered the United States via San Francisco's Angel Island Immigration Station (see discussion in Chapter 9). A second great wave of Chinese immigration began just after the Chinese Revolution in 1949 and consisted primarily of Chinese from Taiwan and Hong Kong, rather than from mainland China. The third wave was characterized by the rapid arrival of a large number of scholars and students in the last two decades of the millennium (Chang, 2003). Both the second and third waves of Chinese immigration to the US consisted of individuals with better education and financial means, and they were also received better, due to reformed immigration laws and improved relations with the Chinese government since the 1970s (Xiao, 2010).

11.15

With respect to mass media, Chinese newspapers have been printed in the United States since the days of the California Gold Rush, when *Golden Hills' News* began to circulate in San Francisco in 1854. The paper was printed for only a few months, reflecting a trend that would continue among Chinese newspapers in the US, due to the challenges these newspapers faced in printing with Chinese characters and in attracting readerships. Despite these obstacles, at least 26 Chinese newspapers were published in eight cities in the US during the 1800s, including the *Chinese Daily News*, which became the world's first Chinese daily newspaper when it was published in Sacramento in 1856 (Chiu, 2008). Today, there are many Chinese language radio stations and programs available on the AM and FM dial in the United States, most of them broadcast to audiences in the New York–New Jersey–Connecticut tri-state area, Philadelphia–Washington, or the major markets on the West Coast, particularly Los Angeles, San Francisco, and Seattle. There are also several Chinese-speaking television channels available by subscription, and several networks in New York City, Los Angeles, and San Francisco offer Chinese television programming.

Perhaps because of China's significance in the global marketplace, the popularity of Chinese as a second language taken for college credit has increased: in 1965, it was ranked 10th among the top 13 foreign languages taken at the college level, whereas, in 2009, it ranked sixth among the same 13 languages (National Center for Education Statistics, 2012). There has also been rapid growth in teaching Chinese as a foreign language at the level of middle school and high school in the last decade (Dillon, 2010). Due to their marginalization in American society and the belief among many Chinese people that they or their offspring would eventually return to China, there are many Chinese Heritage Language schools that were established in the US by earlier immigrants (Koehn & Yin, 2002). In 2004, there were about 600 of these schools, and about 160,000 students were enrolled in them (McGinnis, 2005, as reported in Xiao, 2010, p. 93).

Variation in Chinese in the United States

The first wave of Chinese immigrants to the United States mainly used the Cantonese variety of Chinese that is common to southern China and Hong Kong; however, the waves of Chinese immigration that followed comprised greater numbers of speakers of Mandarin, the variety of Chinese spoken in northern and southwestern China. But it was only recently that the number of Mandarin speakers in the United States surpassed the number of Cantonese speakers (Semple, 2009), and Mandarin has even become the variety of choice in Cantonese-speaking enclaves in the US (Sacchetti, 2009).

It should be noted that despite being called dialects of Chinese, varieties of Chinese are not necessarily mutually intelligible. While the two most common varieties of Chinese, Cantonese and Mandarin, share a great deal of vocabulary, they differ vastly in terms of phonology and syntax. In spite of these differences, however, the two linguistic systems are bound by both a common country of origin and the same orthography; therefore, they are referred to as dialects or varieties of Chinese, rather than as separate languages. Cantonese and Mandarin are the most widely used Chinese dialects in the US; two others that are used are Min and Wu.

Current Status of Chinese in the United States

As has traditionally been the case of heritage languages in the United States, Chinese is being lost as a native language by the children of Chinese immigrants, as they shift to English in mainstream schools (Xiao, 2010, p. 90). However, there are several factors that bode well for the maintenance of Chinese as a heritage language in the US. These include relatively high rates of Chinese immigration, the existence of communities with high concentrations of Chinese speakers, the expanding role of China in business and technology throughout the world, and the continuing popularity of Chinese Heritage Language schools. According to the 2011 ACS, of the Chinese speakers currently living in the United States, about 20% report speaking English "not well" and nearly 10% report not speaking English at all (US Census Bureau, 2010–2013).

TAGALOG

One of many languages indigenous to the Philippine Islands, Tagalog is an Austronesian language that serves as one of the two official languages of the Philippines, the other being English (Fonacier, 2010). The Tagalog language includes many words of Spanish and English origin, reflecting that the Philippines was a Spanish colony from 1521 to 1898 and then an American colony from 1898 to 1946. During the latter period, the educational system of the Philippines underwent significant reform, and English was implemented as the medium of instruction. Because of this, many, if not most, Tagalog speakers have had a working knowledge of English before entering the United States.

The 2011 ACS reports just under 1.6 million speakers of Tagalog in the United States, reflecting an almost 232% increase in the number of Tagalog speakers in the US from 1980 to 2010 and making Tagalog the fourth highest-ranked language used in American homes today. Of the total number of Tagalog speakers, 67% reported speaking English "very well," and 26% "well," numbers that are much higher than

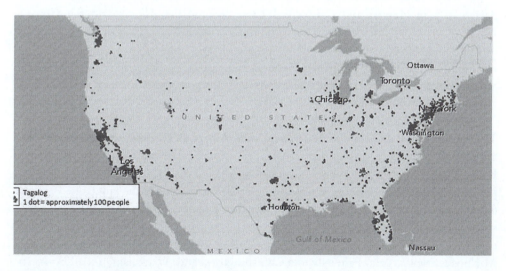

FIGURE 11.4 A map of the distribution of Tagalog speakers in the US.

Source: 2011 Language Mapper tool, US Census Bureau.

they are for speakers of other Asian languages residing in the United States (US Census Bureau, 2010–2013). In terms of geographic distribution, concentrations of Tagalog speakers tend to be in the West: California, Nevada, and Hawaii have the highest percentages of Tagalog speakers; the metropolitan areas with the largest numbers of Tagalog speakers are Los Angeles, San Francisco, New York, and San Diego. The areal distribution of Tagalog speakers in the US is shown in Figure 11.4.

A History of Tagalog in the United States

Although Tagalog was probably used among Filipino crew members on ships that visited American shores from the late 16th to the 19th century, the first major wave of immigration by Tagalog speakers to the United States occurred from 1898 to 1946, during which time the US had possession of the Philippine Islands. Many of those who immigrated to the US during this time worked as laborers, particularly on plantations in Hawaii and farms in California. After the former colony won its independence from the US, the American government limited the number of Filipinos who could immigrate to the US to 100 per year, which resulted in most Filipino immigrants being either the wives of American military personnel or Filipino Americans (Fonacier, 2010). Changes to US immigration policy during the second half of the 20th century allowed for greater numbers of Filipinos to enter the country, resulting in a rising number of Tagalog speakers as well. Many of the immigrants who have entered the US since restrictions were eased have been professionals in the healthcare industry (Fonacier, 2010).

11.16

Several newspapers written for a Filipino readership have been printed in the US, particularly in Hawaii and California. These include the *Abante* and the *Hawaii Filipino Chronicle*, both of which have an online presence today. KPHI, a radio station in Honolulu, Hawaii, launched in 2008, offers programming in Tagalog, aimed at Honolulu's large Filipino population. The station is also broadcast on cable throughout all of Hawaii. Cable television's *The Filipino Channel* was launched in 1994 and broadcasts from Redwood City, California.

11.17

Despite its ranking among the most common languages in the United States, Tagalog is offered as a course by relatively few American schools. Among the few K-12 schools that offer classes are the Bessie Carmichael Elementary School/Filipino Education Center in San Francisco, California, which has an English–Tagalog bilingual program; several high schools in California also offer courses in the language. Perhaps the greatest increase in opportunities for learning Tagalog has taken place at the post-secondary level: whereas only UCLA and the University of Hawaii offered Tagalog for college credit during the 1960s, the language is now taught at universities in Illinois, Michigan, New York, Pennsylvania, Washington, and Wisconsin, in addition to universities and community colleges in California and Hawaii. The Defense Language Institute in Monterey, California, also has a Tagalog program.

Variation in Tagalog in the United States

The use of both Tagalog and English among Filipinos has resulted in language varieties based on codeswitching between the two languages. According to Thompson (2003), Taglish was created by academics in the Philippine Islands who rejected the coining of new terms in Tagalog in favor of adopting existing English terminology for scientific concepts instead. Over time, Taglish won acceptance and was adopted for use by the media, and today it is used in Filipino communities in Australia, the United Kingdom, and the United States. In the US, advertisers in markets with high concentrations of Filipinos sometimes use Taglish to appeal to Filipino-Americans in the community. Taglish has also proven useful to Tagalog speakers for texting purposes. A related variety that places greater emphasis on English rather than Tagalog is called "Englog."

Current Status of Tagalog in the United States

Despite the high number of Tagalog speakers in the United States today, there are several signs that suggest that a shift to English is inevitable and that the maintenance of Tagalog in the US faces some serious challenges. First, the high percentage of Tagalog speakers who have a good command of English even before arriving in the US means that even continued immigration of Tagalog speakers might have little effect on its chances of survival in the US. This is borne out by data showing that only 6.7% and 0.5% of Tagalog speakers in the US report speaking English "not well" or "not at all," respectively (US Census Bureau, 2010–2013). Nevertheless, the growth of Tagalog programs and courses at the college level offers some hope for the maintenance of Tagalog, as does access via the Internet or cable to Tagalog language programming used in the media. Furthermore, despite that Filipinos are likely to shift to English when they reach the US, there is the possibility that they will use Tagalog or perhaps even Taglish as a means for projecting their identity as Filipinos.

11.18

ARABIC

Spoken by nearly 300 million people worldwide, Arabic is a Semitic language of the Afroasiatic family that has expanded globally in recent years; because of increased immigration to the United States, there has been a rapid increase in the total number of Arabic speakers in the country to nearly one million. Of these people, 63.3% self-report using English "very well" and 21.7% "well" (US Census Bureau, 2010–2013). The population of Arabic speakers in the United States is primarily concentrated in California, Michigan, and New York; the highest-ranking cities by total number of Arabic speakers are New York City, Detroit, Los Angeles, and Chicago (US Census Bureau, 2006–2008). Because many immigrants from the Middle East took jobs at the

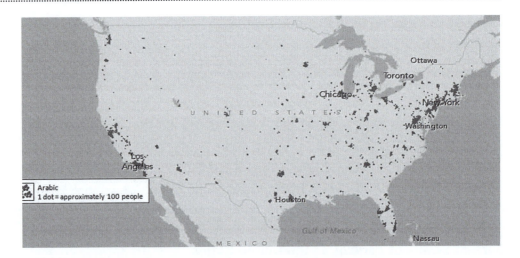

FIGURE 11.5 A map of the distribution of Arabic speakers in the US.

Source: 2011 Language Mapper tool, US Census Bureau

Ford River Rouge plant in the latter half of the 20th century, Dearborn, Michigan, is home to one of the most concentrated populations of Arabic speakers in the United States, comprising over 40% of the city's population (US Census Bureau, 2010–2013). The areal distribution of Arabic speakers in the US is shown in Figure 11.5.

A History of Arabic in the United States

Arabic-speaking sailors are believed to have reached the New World during the 16th century; furthermore, Arabic speakers were among the 18,000 Muslim Africans who were imported as part of the slave trade (Austin, 1984). However, it was not until the arrival of immigrants from the Ottoman province of Syria in the latter part of the 19th century that Arabic speakers were of sufficient numbers to form their own communities in the United States (Naff, 2000). This wave of Arabic-speaking immigrants consisted largely of farmers and artisans. Lebanese immigrants, in particular, became part of the pack-peddler tradition, selling their wares in every state and territory of the country in a network of peddling routes (Naff, 2000). After the decline of peddling as an occupation around 1910, many Lebanese began operating family businesses.

Another wave of Arabic immigration began in the aftermath of World War II and comprised immigrants of higher status who were motivated to leave their countries of origin because of political strife (Naff, 2000). During this wave, Arabic-speaking immigrants were attracted to the United States because of the status the nation enjoyed as the leading industrial, scientific, technological, and military power of the world. Unlike those who arrived in the preceding wave, men of this wave were generally

TABLE 11.2 Ancestry of Arab populations in the US

Ancestry	Percentage
Lebanese	26
Arab/Arabic	15
Egyptian	10
Syrian	8
Somalian	6
Iraqi	5
Assyrian/Chaldean	5
Palestinian	5
Moroccan	5
Jordanian	3
Sudanese	2
Other Arab	7

Source: Adapted from the Arab American Institute,
www.aaiusa.org/pages/demographics/.

employed as factory workers, while women, children, and older relatives operated family businesses to contribute to the family income.

11.19

Table 11.2 shows the ancestry of people from Arabic-speaking populations now living in the United States. As illustrated, Lebanese Americans constitute the majority of Arab Americans residing in the US, and for most individual states they are also the majority; however, the majority of Arab Americans in Georgia, New Jersey, and Tennessee are Egyptian Americans. In Arizona, the largest Arab American community is Moroccan; in Rhode Island, it is Syrian; and the Sudanese form the largest Arab American community in both Nebraska and South Dakota. Furthermore, there are relatively large Palestinian populations in California and Illinois, whereas Iraqis are largely associated with Michigan (Arab American Institute, 2014).

11.20

Arabic mass media has had a presence in the United States at least since the 1800s. Today, there are several newspapers, with either national or local distributions, including *The Arab American News*, which is a weekly bilingual newspaper based in Dearborn, Michigan, that began publishing in 1984. The weekly Arab American newspaper *Watan* was established in 1992 in Washington, DC, and has since expanded to locations in Los Angeles, San Francisco, and New York City. Radio stations that broadcast in Arabic are located in the New York City vicinity, Florida, and Michigan.

11.21

Enrollment in Arabic as a foreign language in colleges and universities has undergone a dramatic rise since the mid-1980s, with an increase in enrollment of just

11.22

over 600% over that time (National Center for Education Statistics, 2012). Furthermore, the conferring of bachelor degrees in Arabic has increased by nearly 500% from the 2004–2005 school year to 2009–2010 (National Center for Education Statistics, 2012). There has also been growth in the study of the Arabic language at the level of K-12 since the early 2000s, both in the number of students and in the number of schools offering classes in the language.

Variation in Arabic in the United States

With respect to variation in Arabic, it is first important to note that Arabic is a **diglossic language**, which means that it has distinct varieties, each being reserved for different social situations. The formal variety of the language is Modern Standard Arabic, and it is generally limited to the context of religion, education, and other formal situations, as well as writing. In everyday speech, however, speakers use their national variety of Arabic, which is usually associated with the capital city of that country. There is a broad range of variation in the national dialects, such that some are fairly similar to one another, and others so different that the speakers of one variety are unintelligible to the speakers of the other. In particular, countries that are geographically distant from one another, for example Morocco and Iraq, have very different varieties that reflect these great distances. Thus, there is some variation in the use of Arabic in the US based on patterns of settlement, that is, with regard to the tendency for people who are native to certain countries of the Middle East to move to specific regions of the US, as discussed above.

Dialectal differences are important in teaching Arabic in American schools. In college courses, Modern Standard Arabic is the written form that is taught; however, national dialects are used to teach spoken Arabic, and the variety that is taught depends on the teacher. Egyptian Arabic is among the dialects most commonly taught in American schools, due to the large body of native speakers of the dialect.

Current Status of Arabic in the United States

Like other heritage languages, Arabic is generally undergoing a shift to English in the United States. Although there has been a steady stream of immigration from the Middle East since the 1980s that might have maintained the use of Arabic in the US, many of these newcomers were already fluent speakers of English before arriving and, today, Arabic speakers who self-report speaking English "not well" or "not at all" comprise a relatively small percentage of the total number of Arabic speakers in the US, at 11.9% and 3.1%, respectively (Ryan, 2013). And although there have been increases in enrollment in Arabic courses and programs in American universities, especially since 9/11, many of the students in these classes are learning the language to obtain jobs in American government or the military, and not for more integrative reasons.

There are signs that Arabic speakers in the United States see some value in speaking Arabic and wish to retain their native tongue. During the last decade there has been a growing interest in Arabic culture, as evidenced by attendance at Arab film festivals and concerts (Shiri, 2010, p. 221). In addition to the courses in Arabic mentioned above, enrollment in courses on the history and culture of the Arabic world has increased (Shiri, 2010, p. 221). Programming on television and radio in the Arabic language has also expanded in recent years, particularly in metropolitan areas with large Arabic populations. This includes access to the Qatar-based *Al-Jazeera* channel, which is available via satellite or the web.

YIDDISH

Yiddish originated in the Rhineland as a language of the Ashkenazi Jews in the 10th century before expanding into Central and Eastern Europe and then, eventually, to other parts of the globe. It is classified as High German, a designation due to the origination of the language in the Alpine areas of German and Austria, as opposed to Low German, which refers to languages of the lowlands of the North German Plain. However, early in its history Yiddish incorporated elements of Hebrew, Aramaic, Slavic, and other languages with which it came into contact. Yiddish is the language of an ethnicity rather than a nationality; however, it was recognized as an official language of the Ukrainian People's Republic from 1917 to 1921. It is written in the Hebrew alphabet and, like Hebrew, is read from right to left.

Today, there are an estimated one million Yiddish speakers worldwide, mostly in Israel and the United States. The 2011 ACS reports 160,968 Yiddish speakers in the United States, reflecting a decrease of about 50% from 1980 to 2010, as speakers of Yiddish have effectively stopped immigrating to the US and new generations are typically not learning the language at home (Ryan, 2013). According to the 2007 ACS, all but about 12% of Yiddish speakers in America reside in New York City, Poughkeepsie, Miami, and Los Angeles, clearly indicating the urban orientation of Yiddish speakers in the US. New York City accounts for a large majority of the Yiddish speakers in the United States and, as such, dialects of English in New York City have adopted Yiddish features (Shin & Kominski, 2010).

A History of Yiddish in the United States

Although Jews began arriving in the New World perhaps as early as the 16th century, these were Sephardic Jews who spoke the Spanish-based Dzudezmo that developed on the Iberian Peninsula, rather than the Ashkenazi Jews who lived in Eastern Europe and modern-day Germany and spoke Yiddish. Use of Dzudezmo was effectively discontinued with the loss of older speakers and a decline in the immigration of native speakers of the language. The first East European Jewish congregation in America dates from 1819; however, until 1870 most Ashkenazi Jews migrated to the US from Germanic countries. Furthermore, it was not until the Jewish exodus from Russia in the 1880s that significant numbers of Yiddish speakers began arriving in America (Goldberg, 1981). By 1920, the Jewish population of New York City had "ballooned to a million and a half, making it the world's largest Jewish city" (Weinstein, 2001, p. 139). This increase not only meant a greater number of Yiddish speakers, but also more opportunities for its use. For instance, children growing up in Yiddish-speaking households at that time typically learned English in the public schools they attended, but beginning in 1910, began using and learning Yiddish in the new secular schools and summer camps that were being created by the Jewish community.

11.23

The growing population of Yiddish speakers in New York City in the 1920s led to a boom in Yiddish mass media there. At one time, there were as many as half a dozen Yiddish daily newspapers in New York, with a peak circulation of 400,000 and a readership perhaps three times that large (Goldberg, 1981). At the height of the Yiddish newspaper industry, the United States had at least 10 dailies written in Yiddish, with New York City-based newspapers also offering regional editions; in addition, New York City had 16 different Yiddish language radio stations in the 1920s (Weinstein, 2001). Yiddish theater was also a big draw in New York, particularly on the Lower East Side, and at its peak there were over a dozen Yiddish theater companies as well as Yiddish vaudeville acts performing nightly throughout the city.

Immigration reforms had a profound impact on Jewish immigration into the United States. As discussed in Chapter 9, the Immigration Act of 1924 limited annual immigration from a given country to only 2% of the total number of people from that country living in the US in 1890. This Act essentially eliminated immigration from Southern and Eastern Europe, one of the main sources of Yiddish speakers. Even more devastating was the loss of five to six million Jews in the Nazi concentration camps during World War II, endangering the language and ending European Jewish culture as it was then known. To escape persecution at the hands of the Third Reich, many Jews fled from Europe to other continents, including North America; eager to assimilate culturally in their new countries, many did not pass their language on to their children. Nevertheless, the size of the Yiddish-speaking population in New York City was large enough in the first few decades of the 20th century, and supplemented by enough Yiddish-speaking immigrants in the middle decades of the century, that it was maintained to some extent. Additionally, it was commonly used by Jewish comedians and other entertainers during the mid-20th century, which served as another way to maintain the language and also suggested that even among those who didn't speak the language, there were some who understood it.

11.24

BOX 11.2 YIVO

Yidisher Visnshaftlekher Institut (Yiddish Scientific Institite), or YIVO, was created as a center for the advancement of Yiddish language and culture by Max Weinreich in Vilna, Poland, in 1925. At the onset of World War II, with the German army advancing on Poland, YIVO moved to a new location in New York City, renaming itself the YIVO Institute for Jewish Research. One of YIVO's many publications is Weinreich's *History of the Yiddish Language* (2008). Weinreich's son, Uriel, also championed the cause of the Yiddish language and YIVO, and his work includes the *Modern English–Yiddish, Yiddish–English Dictionary* (1990) and *College Yiddish* (1999).

11.25

Variation in Yiddish in the United States

Due to the dwindling numbers of Yiddish speakers in the United States, we have little to say about variation in its use, regionally or socially. However, the contributions that Yiddish made to English, particularly as it is spoken in New York City, is worthy of mention here. Yiddish has served as the source of such words as *kibitzer* 'one who offers unsolicited advice'; *mishuggah* 'crazy'; *schlemiel* 'fool'; and *schlep* 'carry, drag.' Many of these words gained national currency in American English by way of the media, including comic strips, Broadway shows, Tin Pan Alley songs, and film and television set in New York City, where they were used to add color to situations or the speech of particular characters. Yiddish words used in American sitcoms and pop music, such as *schmooze*, *schmuck*, *schtick*, and *verklempt*, have gained exposure to global audiences that associate the words with American culture.

11.26

Due to their massive migrations to countries where English serves as the dominant language, including the US, Australia, and Great Britain, many Jews have shifted to English, which they have then infused with elements from other languages such as Modern or Classical Hebrew and Yiddish to facilitate communication within the Jewish community and to project a Jewish identity. The term "Jewish English" encompasses a broad range of variation: at one end, it is simply English with words from Yiddish and/or Hebrew occasionally surfacing and, at the other end, Yiddish and Hebrew features appear frequently and at every level of the grammar (Benor, 2009). The variety that a speaker uses along this spectrum depends on a number of socio-linguistic factors, including the speaker's devotion to Judaism, as the English of Orthodox Jews, for instance, is often more strongly influenced by Yiddish and Hebrew than that of secular Jews (Benor, 2009). Fishman (1985) contends that "English or some

11.27

Jewish variant thereof is probably the most widespread Jewish Language of our time" (p. 15). Time will tell how much American English will continue to absorb features from Jewish language and culture, as well as whether Jewish English will converge or diverge from other varieties of English.

Current Status of Yiddish in the United States

The sharp decline in the number of Yiddish speakers in the United States between the early 20th century and the present day provides evidence of the two- to three-generational shift at work, as younger Jewish Americans adopt English as their primary language. As has been the case for other heritage languages, the maintenance of Yiddish in the US has depended on an influx of speakers from elsewhere, which, in the case of Yiddish, was Europe. Once this flow stopped, many Yiddish speakers living in the US shifted to English. Additionally, in the aftermath of the Holocaust, many Jewish Americans and others supported Israel's choice of Hebrew as its official language, due in part to the reputation Yiddish had earned in the West as unsophisticated and to its association with lowbrow comedy (Katz, 2008).

11.28

The decline in the number of native Yiddish speakers notwithstanding, hope for the survival of Yiddish in the United States is not completely lost. A surge of interest in the Yiddish language began in the late 20th century, particularly among religious Jews, and this led to language revitalization on a number of fronts. As early as the 1980s, there was growth in Yiddish studies in post-secondary schools throughout the world, particularly in the US (Fishman, 1981). Such studies continue at American universities today and include online and summer programs. As part of this revitalization, a great number of books on the topic of the Yiddish language, aimed at both academic and non-academic audiences, have been published over the course of the last 50 years, and a newspaper, *The Forverts*, or *The Jewish Daily Forward*, has a Yiddish edition that runs several days a week and is available online. In addition, klezmer music, which is a genre of Jewish music that has existed for about 400 years, began gaining popularity in the US in the early 1980s (Weinstein, 2001). There is also a Yiddish radio program that is accessible online at www.yiddishvoice.com/.

11.29

11.30

CONCLUSION

In this chapter, we have described a small sample of heritage languages that are used in the United States today. The extensive histories of heritage languages such as French and German in the US show that languages besides English have long played a part in the daily lives of Americans and that this foundation of multilingualism has served the country well in many ways. These languages have played important roles both in rural areas of the country, as their speakers homesteaded, helped build railroads, and took part in the great gold and silver rushes of the 19th century, and in the cities, where speakers of heritage languages took work in the automotive plants, in the entertainment industry, and in the tech industry of the 20th century. In the 21st century, we continue to see an influx of heritage languages in the United States for many of the same general reasons we did earlier: for educational and economic opportunities that the US has to offer and for asylum from political turmoil in other parts of the world. At the same time, the specifics of these influxes continue to change in terms of the heritage languages that are spoken, the varieties that are used, and the ways in which they are used.

Historically, the maintenance of heritage languages in the US has not succeeded without the support of a continuous influx of new speakers, and these influxes remain important for their ability to energize these speech communities, as was discussed in Chapter 9. However, the small set of languages presented here illustrates that there is some variation in how languages are able to maintain themselves in the United States and that these languages continue to hold value for their speakers, who in turn find new ways to make linguistic contributions to American culture at the national, regional, and local levels. At the same time, these languages have been shaped by their experience in the United States to the extent that American varieties of these languages are distinct from their varieties anywhere else in the world.

Advancements in communication and travel, as well as recent research touting a range of benefits for multilingual speakers, may create changes in how Americans with heritage language backgrounds are able to maintain their native languages in the United States going forward. At any rate, these languages, and others as well, will be adding diversity to the linguistic landscape of the US for many years to come.

DISCUSSION AND RESEARCH QUESTIONS

1. Recall the comparison of the melting pot and mixed salad metaphors that was presented in Chapter 9. How do the histories and/or current statuses of the languages presented in this chapter support one of these metaphors over the other?
2. Given what you learned about the influence of non-English languages on American English in Chapter 4 and, even more so, in Chapter 5, in what areas of everyday life would you look for evidence of recent borrowings from heritage languages in regional or local American dialects? Can you find some specific examples of these kinds of borrowings—not already used in this book—that are used in American regions and/or communities? What are they, and what resources did you use to find them?
3. Consider your own family history and the language or languages that were spoken by your ancestors. What was the fate of these languages in terms of the models presented in this chapter? How has the language use of you or other members of

your family been affected by this process? Do your relatives or friends ever comment on the loss or maintenance of their ancestral languages? If so, what is said?

4. Create a chart or table in which you compare the key information presented for each language in this chapter, such as population numbers, timeline of initial and major waves of immigration, and levels of shift and maintenance. What do these comparisons reveal? What can you conclude about the effects of the maintenance of a language with regard to the history of its speakers? For any languages that you discussed in Question 1, how would they compare?

5. The US Census Bureau's new Language Mapper tool is an interesting way to visualize the usage of several of the languages spoken in the United States, and it provided the maps that were used in this chapter. First, compare the maps provided in this chapter. What do they tell us about differences in the distributions of speakers of these languages, at both the national and regional level? Next, go to the Language Mapper site (www.census.gov/hhes/socdemo/language/data/ language_ map.html) and examine maps for two different language groups. Now, investigate the regional distribution of the speakers of the different languages and discuss any similarities and differences you find. Second, for each language you choose, examine the differences in the regional distribution of all speakers versus those who report speaking English less than "very well." What do these figures tell you about the maintenance of these particular languages in the United States?

12 Native American Languages

GUIDING QUESTIONS

1. What is the status of Native American languages in the US today?

2. How has government policy affected Native American languages?

3. What can the study of Native American languages tell us about language in general?

OVERVIEW

This chapter introduces readers to Native Americans and their languages, with respect to their histories, variation among and within languages, and varieties of American Indian English. As part of this chapter, we discuss the relationships of Native American tribes with one another, as well as with European explorers and settlers, and examine how these relationships have affected individual languages. In addition, we examine how American policies concerning Native Americans have affected these languages, particularly in terms of abandonment, as many Native Americans have shifted to English, sometimes being forced to do so by American policies aimed at assimilation. Finally, we discuss current efforts to revitalize and maintain Native American languages for future generations.

COMMON MYTHS

> *Native American languages are simple languages, reflecting the simplicity of the people who speak them.*

> *Native American languages are all closely related.*

> *Native American languages have no value today.*

INTRODUCTION

12.1

In the previous two chapters, we examined several heritage languages in the United States. We further this discussion in the current chapter by looking at a group of heritage languages that were widespread in North America long before European exploration and settlement. Reflecting cultures with a presence in North America spanning thousands of years, Native American languages are a diverse and complex lot that hold significant value for their speakers, as well as linguists. The story of Native American languages since European exploration and colonization of the Americas has been one of loss, in numbers of speakers and entire languages, and of a shift to English—both as a natural development and as a mandatory policy enforced in federal boarding schools. These developments have made all Native American languages **endangered languages,** not only by virtue of having relatively few speakers, but also because most Native American children are being raised as monolingual speakers of English (McCarty, 2010, p. 47). Despite the bleak outlook for many of these languages, revitalization programs established for some of these languages by tribe members and linguists, as well as technological advances that can be used for the documentation and teaching of Native American languages, provide some hope that Native American languages will survive into the future.

A HISTORY OF NATIVE AMERICANS

For many years, scholars believed that the first indigenous peoples arrived in the Americas as recently as a few thousand years ago; however, more recent scholarship suggests that the first Native Americans crossed the Bering Strait from Asia into North America between 15,000 and 50,000 years ago, during or immediately following the last Ice Age glaciation (Fagan, 2011, p. 14). DNA evidence supports the idea that, during this period, Native Americans crossed into the Americas during one great and two lesser migrations (Reich et al., 2012). By the time the first Europeans crossed the Atlantic Ocean and reached the shores of North America, tribes of Native Americans pervaded the continent, tailoring their cultures—and languages—to the natural regions they inhabited.

Just as the timeline that Native Americans apparently followed in the shaping of precontact North America has changed with new archeological discoveries, estimates concerning the size of Native American populations before European contact have also been revised considerably since the earliest figures that were proposed. In 1910, the

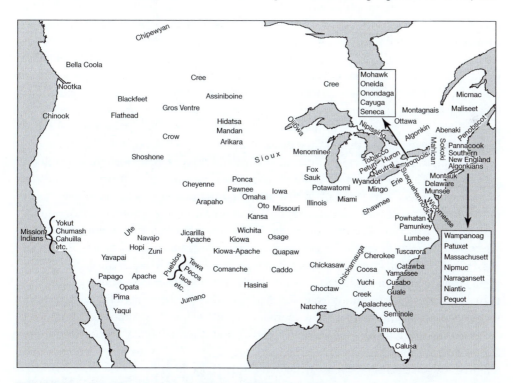

FIGURE 12.1 Map of precontact distribution of Native Americans

Source: Calloway, Colin G. *New Worlds for All: Indians, Europeans, and the Remaking of Early America*, p. xviii, Map 1. © 1997 The Johns Hopkins University Press. Reprinted with permission of Johns Hopkins University Press.

12.2

anthropologist James Mooney estimated the Native American population to have numbered approximately one million at the beginning of the 17th century; however, Koeber believed this estimate to be too high and, in 1939, offered a number closer to 900,000 (Snipp, 2007, p. 41). Later estimates increased dramatically in light of archeological findings, such as those at the Cahokia site in present-day St. Louis, Missouri, and a greater understanding of the devastating impact that Old World diseases had on New World populations. For example, Dobyns (1966) estimated that the number of precontact Native Americans was close to 10 million; as more data became available, he speculated that the true number was closer to 18 million (Dobyns, 1984). While some scholars have disputed these numbers, even by today's most conservative estimates the Native American population at the time of European colonization stood at about 5 million (Snipp, 2007, p. 43).

While some aspects of Native American history prior to European contact can only be inferred from archeological or other evidence, the history of Native Americans after the earliest Europeans landed on the Atlantic coast is relatively well documented. In summary, contact with early European explorers and settlers had debilitating effects on Native American populations. First, contact with Europeans exposed Native Americans to Old World diseases that their immune systems were defenseless against, such as smallpox and measles. These diseases proved to be so contagious that they even spread to communities that Europeans had yet to set foot in, as in the Southern Plains, where Native Americans may have experienced a measles epidemic as early as 1531 (Carlson, 1998, p. 8). The impact of Old World disease on Native American populations was devastating, sometimes wiping out entire communities, and the diseases were so painful that, upon realizing they had contracted a disease, some of those afflicted chose to commit suicide rather than let the disease run its course (Snipp, 2007, p, 42).

Ensuing warfare between Native Americans and Anglo settlers also took its toll on Native American populations. Although relations between Native Americans and the Jamestown settlers were generally peaceful in the early period of settlement, periods of peace alternated with petty skirmishes and brutal warfare being fought, often over land, between the settlers and Native Americans in the years that followed (Crawford, 1975, pp. 9–10). The withdrawal of the Spanish and French from the present-day American West during the 19th century set the United States on a course to reach the Pacific Ocean in an effort to attain its Manifest Destiny, leading to an increasing number of conflicts between Anglo-Americans and Native Americans after the War of 1812, with warfare reaching its peak in the middle of the century (Snipp, 2007, p. 45). Although it is difficult to ascertain the Native American death toll that resulted from war with Anglo-Americans, it is safe to say that thousands of Native American men, women, and children lost their lives on the battlefield and in attacks on villages.

Finally, there was a decline in the number of Native Americans during the 1800s due to forced relocations of various tribes for the purpose of clearing the way for Anglo-American settlement along the frontier. In 1830, the US Congress passed the Indian

Removal Act, which mandated that eastern tribes be relocated to "Indian Territory" west of the Mississippi River. The policy resulted in the "Trail of Tears" by which Native Americans were marched from the southeastern United States to present-day Oklahoma, beginning in 1831 and concluding with the removal of great numbers of Cherokee from Appalachia in 1839. Thousands of Native Americans died from exposure to disease, starvation, inclement weather, and violent acts committed against them by frontiersmen along the route. The harsh conditions of life on reservations took their toll as well, with the Native American population dropping to a low of 250,000 by 1890 (Brandon, 2003, p. 117). Figure 12.2 shows some of the Native American migrations that occurred as a result of European populations settling first on the coasts and then later moving inland, forcing Native Americans to relinquish their settlements and hunting grounds with the expansion of the frontier.

As Native American lives were lost with the growth of the European population in North America, there was also a decline in the number of Native American languages, from the 350 to 500 languages that existed at the end of the 15th century in the area now occupied by the United States (Romaine, 2001, pp. 154–155) to about

12.3

12.4

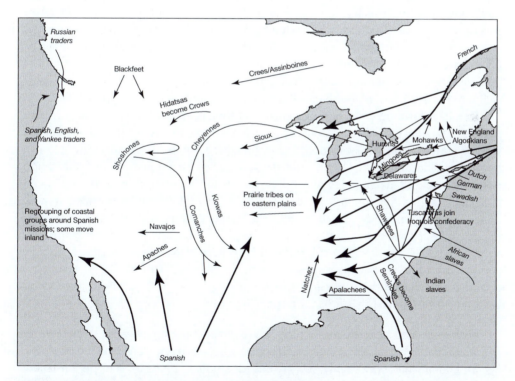

FIGURE 12.2 Post-contact movement in the New World.

Source: Calloway, Colin G. *New Worlds for All: Indians, Europeans, and the Remaking of Early America*, p. 148, Map 2. © 1997 The Johns Hopkins University Press. Reprinted with permission of Johns Hopkins University Press.

12.5

134 languages today (US Census Bureau, 2006–2008). While the loss of Native American languages is in great part due to the high mortality rates of their speakers, it also stems from an aggressive approach adopted by the federal government in the 19th century to facilitate the shift of Native Americans to Anglo-American culture through the prohibition of native language use. This approach focused especially on the education of Native American children. On this matter, Commissioner of Indian Affairs J.D.C. Atkins (1887) contended:

> The instruction of the Indians in [their] vernacular is not only of no use to them, but is detrimental to the cause of their education and civilization and no school will be permitted on the reservation in which the English language is not exclusively taught.

Policies supported by this philosophy were designed to exterminate Native American languages within one or two generations.

In 1879, the Carlisle boarding school opened in Pennsylvania and became the model for off-reservation boarding schools in their approach to forced assimilation, which included the separation of Native American children from their families and communities. Schools such as Carlisle had strict prohibitions against the use of Native American languages by students, and schoolchildren who insisted on using the languages regardless were subjected to physical and verbal abuse (McCarty, 2002; Reyhner & Eder, 2004). The Meriam Report (1928) roundly criticized the boarding schools for their poor conditions and questionable policies; however, many of these schools stayed open well into the 20th century, with enrollment in the schools peaking in the 1970s.

12.6

Despite reforms in education that included lifting prohibitions on the use of Native American languages, little was done to actively promote the use of these languages in schools until the 1960s. Legislation that included the Bilingual Education Act (1968), the Indian Education Act (1972), and the Indian Self-Determination and Education Assistance Act (1975) provided new opportunities for incorporating Native American languages in education and for tribes to make their own decisions with respect to how their children should be educated. In 1990, the US Congress passed the Native American Languages Act (NALA) to support the preservation of Native American languages, stating that "The status of the cultures and languages of Native Americans is unique, and the United States has the responsibility to act together with Native Americans to ensure the survival of these unique cultures and languages." In light of this, the federal government recognized that it had a responsibility to:

> encourage and support the use of Native American languages as a medium of instruction in order to encourage and support: a) Native American language survival, b) educational opportunity, c) increased student success and performance, d) increased student awareness and knowledge of their culture and history, and e) increased student and community pride.

(Atkins, 1887)

Additionally, the government enacted the legislation to "recognize the right of Indian tribes and other Native American governing bodies to use the Native American languages as a medium of instruction in all schools funded by the Secretary of the Interior."

12.7

In addition to a change in federal policy from one discouraging and even prohibiting Native American languages to one recognizing their significance, the views on Native American languages at the state level have also changed over time. For instance, when NALA was passed in 1990, only Hawaii, Minnesota, and Wisconsin had provisions concerning how Native American languages should be taught and by whom; however, an additional 13 states (Alaska, Arizona, Idaho, Montana, Nebraska, Nevada, New Mexico, North Dakota, Oklahoma, Oregon, South Dakota, Washington, and Wyoming) had added provisions related to Native American language curricula and teacher certification by 2003 (Warhol, 2011).

Despite losses of Native American languages, 134 are spoken in the United States today (although it is nearly certain that several of these languages will have died by the publication date of this book), by an estimated 372,095 speakers (Ryan, 2013). The diversity of these languages is an important part of the linguistic diversity of the United States, and the history of these languages is in some ways the history of the Americas. The remainder of this chapter will present various aspects of these languages and describe the efforts that have been made to document them, as well as current attempts to maintain and revitalize these languages for use by future generations.

12.8

NATIVE AMERICAN LINGUISTICS

While the term "Native American" can be useful as a term for a group of people who had a history in America prior to the landing of the first European explorers, it is important to highlight that this group comprises many individual tribes, with some having vast differences between them. These include differences in the physical characteristics of tribe members, occupations, the societal and familial organization within tribes, types of housing, and religious ceremonies. Among these cultural differences, the focus of our discussion, of course, centers on some of the vast differences between the languages of Native Americans.

Some of the first students of Native American languages were the French and Spanish missionaries who ventured to North America in the early 16th century. In New England, John Eliot translated the Bible into the Massachusett language in the mid-17th century, while Roger Williams became the first to write a book about a Native American language in English. Major work, however, did not begin until the early 20th century, when the German American anthropologist Franz Boas of Columbia University headed a research team that documented Native American culture throughout North America, with fieldwork conducted in a variety of locations by a number of linguists, including Edward Sapir, Leonard Bloomfield, Mary Haas, and Morris Swadesh. This work created and then relied on a general framework for the study of these languages that resulted in a plethora of volumes dedicated to the structure and use of specific Native American languages. Linguistic work on various facets of the structure and use of Native American languages continues today at SIL International (formerly, the Summer Institute of Linguistics) and at several American universities.

12.9   While linguists have continued to work on recording and preserving individual languages, some scholars have focused on how these languages are related to one another, many using the family tree model that was discussed in Chapter 1. The results of this work suggest the difficulty of creating generalizations concerning the Native American experience, socially as well as linguistically. The geographical boundaries of tribes in precontact North America were fuzzy at best and, even before colonial expansion pushed them westward, some Native American tribes migrated frequently. Such migrations sometimes forced other tribes to migrate as well or, at other times, led to strong alliances among distinct tribes, such as the Cheyenne and Arapaho. Under these circumstances, there was a great deal of cultural mixture and, in the process, tribes often borrowed the linguistic features of languages spoken by other tribes with which they came into contact to use in their own languages.

Highlighting the complexity of the relationships between these languages, numerous genetic classifications of Native American languages have been proposed over the years. John Wesley Powell of the Bureau of American Ethnology (1891) offered a classification of 58 language stocks. Sapir (1929) relied on word and grammatical structure to propose a classification comprising six major phyla: (1) Eskimo-Aleut; (2) Algonquian-Wakashan; (3) Na-Dene, which included Tlingit and Athabaskan; (4) Penutian, which included Yokuts, Takelma, Chinook, and Sahaptin; (5) Hokan-Siouan, which included Pomo, Salinan, Iroquoian, Caddoan, and Muskogean; and (6) Azteco-Tanoan, which includes Nahuatl and Zuni. In subsequent years, many scholars have used the classifications of Powell and Sapir as foundations for their own work, often showing relationships between languages that cut across groupings in these classifications (e.g., Shipley, 1957; Newman, 1964). Greenberg (1987) concurred with Sapir's classification in general; however, he merged several of Sapir's language phyla into a single one (namely, Algonquian-Wakashan, Penutian, Hokan-Siouan, and Azteco-Tanoan into Amerind) to arrive at three major phyla, a classification he had previously proposed (Greenberg, 1960) and that was similar to an independent finding by Lamb (1959). Greenberg's classification, however, received much criticism from both inside and outside the field of linguistics for "lumping" languages together (see, e.g., Campbell, 1997; Fagan, 2011). The debate surrounding such work suggests the diversity and complexity of Native American languages and cultures.

BOX 12.1 Native American Lingua Francas

Throughout this book, we have described the outcome of contact between languages in terms of borrowing and language shift. Another outcome consists of situations in which speakers of different languages adopt a common language for the purposes of communication. A language that is used in such a way is called a **lingua franca**. In some conversations, a native language of some of the speakers and a second language of others is chosen as the lingua franca, for example when native English speakers and native French speakers converse in English. In others, a language that is native to none of the speakers, but is known as a second language to all, is adopted as the lingua franca; this would be the case, for instance, if native speakers of Swahili and English used French as a medium of communication.

Because some Native American tribes migrated often and needed to communicate with other tribes they encountered, lingua francas were an important part of the linguistic repertoires of Native Americans. The Algonquian language Ojibwa (or Chippewa) was used as a lingua franca by several tribes in the Great Lakes region, including the Menominee, Potawatomi, and Fox; it may have become the regional lingua franca due to the primary location of the Ojibwa at the strategic outlets of Lake Michigan and Lake Superior. The language was eventually learned by Europeans so that they could conduct trade with the tribes of the region, and French missionaries learned how to represent the language in writing (Keesing, 1971). After treaties with the American government segregated the region's tribes, the use of Ojibwa as a lingua franca was discontinued, and its use reverted to that of a tribal language.

Plains Indian Sign Language (PISL) emerged as one of several sign languages that Native Americans used for communication over long distances. It also developed as a lingua franca used by the large number of diverse languages with a presence on the Great Plains, including languages from the Algonquian, Athabaskan, Siouan, Caddoan, Kiowan, and Uto-Aztecan families, before expanding into a universal sign language for intertribal use (Carlson, 1998). PISL became an aid in storytelling—a use it still has today—and was also adopted as a means of communication by the deaf in Native American communities. Although the number of current users of PISL is unknown, the language is used by both hearing and deaf in Native American communities today.

COMPANION @ WEBSITE

12.10

> **BOX 12.2 Tribal Names**
>
> Only in some cases did tribes use the same names for themselves that Anglo-Americans used for them; rather, it was common for early English-speaking explorers to learn the names for tribes from neighboring tribes or trading partners (Bakker, 1997). For example, the tribal name *Comanche* comes from a Ute word meaning 'they fight with us,' but members of the tribe actually call themselves *Numinu* 'the people.' Additionally, English speakers adopted the French names for several tribes, including the *Gros Ventre* 'big belly,' a people of the Pacific Northwest who call themselves *A'aninin* 'white clay people.' These differences in nomenclature can present issues when conducting historical research on tribes and may have also factored into language classification problems.
>
> The story of how the Salish became known as the Flatheads provides an interesting lesson on tribal naming and language use in general. At the time of European contact, the Salish tribe lived in an area comprising parts of Montana, Idaho, Wyoming, and British Columbia, where many tribes practiced a procedure in which members had their heads compressed by artificial means to change the shape of them. However, it was not because the Salish practiced headshaping that they were called *Flatheads*; rather, it was because they did not engage in the practice. Tribes that practiced headshaping considered their own heads to have a pointed shape after undergoing the procedure and, in contrast, considered the heads of the Salish tribe to be relatively flat; thus, they named them *Flatheads*. When the first Europeans arrived in the region, they simply called the Salish what their neighbors called them, learning only later that members of the tribe referred to themselves as *Salish* 'the people.'

VARIATION AMONG LANGUAGES

Given the number and diversity of Native American languages, it is difficult to make generalizations concerning their structure and use in an exhaustive manner. However, in an effort to show the extent to which these languages differ from each other and from other languages commonly used in the United States, particularly English, we offer examples from several Native American languages in the sections below. The structural diversity of Native American languages provides an opportunity for us to introduce some linguistic concepts that are not commonly used with English, among others, so there is a good deal of linguistic terminology in the section that follows.

Phonology

In terms of their sound systems, many Native American languages have a relatively small number of vowels compared to English and other Indo-European languages, but consonant inventories vary greatly (Yamamoto & Zepeda, 2004). Choctaw, a language originally spoken in the southern Mississippi Valley, for instance, makes do with three basic vowel sounds /i, a, o/ that can each be articulated as either long or short, a quantitative distinction in vowel length that affects meaning. Navajo, however, uses four vowels /a, e, i, o/, each of which can be either short or long, and nasalized or non-nasalized. With respect to consonants, Cree, an Algonquian language used in Canada and in some Northern states of the US west of Lake Superior, has eight in its inventory, whereas Eastern Pomo, a language of Northern California, has 38 (McClendon, 1996).

While English recognizes voicing, that is, the activation of the vocal folds as a feature distinguishing voiced consonants /b, d, g/ from their voiceless counterparts /p, t, k/, there are several Native American languages that do not recognize the presence or absence of voicing as distinct sounds and, thus, as making a difference in meaning. Cree and Nez Perce, a Sahaptian language of the Pacific Northwest, are two Native American languages that do not make a distinction between a voiced sound or its voiceless counterpart. In these languages, voiced sounds occur only in specific contexts in which surrounding sounds are voiced, such as between vowels. This example is illustrative of a common phonological process called **assimilation**, whereby a speaker modifies a sound by adopting one or more features of the sounds in its environment.

Aspiration is another feature that proceeds differently in English than it does in some Native American languages. In earlier chapters, we mentioned that aspiration in English amounts to a puff of air after stop consonants that is rarely noticed by native speakers and does not in itself contribute to meaning. However, aspiration is meaningful in Cree (Ellis, 2000). For example, the following Cree utterances have different meanings, despite the only phonetic distinction between the two being the presence of aspiration (represented by a superscript 'h') in one and not the other:

[wiːcihik] 'help me!'
[wiːcihihk] 'help him!' (Wolfart & Carroll, 1973, p. 9)

Thus, aspiration is used to make an important distinction in who should be the recipient of an action in Cree. In addition to differences in how speakers of Cree and English perceive aspiration, there is also a significant difference in how they produce it: in English, aspiration is articulated as a puff of air following certain consonants, that is, it is post-aspiration, whereas in Cree it is a puff of air preceding consonants, that is, it is pre-aspiration. This is illustrated in the previous example, as well as the following, which shows how the presence or absence of aspiration with /t/ makes a difference in meaning:

[e:wa:bamit] 'when he sees me'
[e:wa:bami^ht] 'when he is seen' (Wolfart & Carroll, 1973, p. 9)

Thus, even seemingly minor differences in languages can have important effects at the level of meaning.

Morphology

BOX 12.3 Morphological Classifications of Languages

Languages are sometimes classified based on how many morphemes a word can comprise. Languages that allow for only a small number of morphemes per word are called **isolating** or **analytic** languages. In some languages of this type, root words are invariable, that is, they allow neither affixes nor word-internal changes; rather, grammatical relationships are shown through word order and the use of distinct words that serve as grammatical markers. Chinese is the best example of a language of this type. At the other end of the spectrum are **synthetic** languages, which allow their root words to take affixes freely; thus, these languages exhibit a high morpheme-to-word ratio. Spanish, French, Russian, and German are all considered synthetic languages. **Poly-synthetic** languages are a special type of synthetic language that allow for many morphemes per word, sometimes resulting in a word having a meaning that other languages might need an entire sentence to express. Several languages spoken in Papua New Guinea and Siberia are considered polysynthetic.

Many Native American languages are classified as polysynthetic languages (see Box 12.3). The following example from Paiute, a language spoken in southwestern Utah, illustrates how morphemes are joined together in polysynthetic languages to form words with complex meanings:

wii-to-kuchum-punky-rugani-yugwi-va-ntu-m
knife-black-buffalo-pet-cut-up-sit-future participle-animate plural
'they who are going to sit and cut up a black cow'

(Sapir, 1929, p. 30)

The following paradigm in Cree provides additional evidence of how polysynthetic languages allow morphemes to be added to root morphemes to add greater detail to simple concepts:

> *no:tin* 'fight someone'
> *no:tinike:* 'fight with people'
> *no:tinike:stamaw* 'fight with people on someone's behalf'
> *no:tinike:stama:so* 'fight with people on one's own behalf'

Because this linguistic phenomenon is characteristic of many Native American languages, and because the linguistic outcome of adding morphemes in such a way is salient to speakers whose languages do not allow for this, the characteristic is sometimes depicted in stereotypes of Native American speech. However, it must be reiterated that not all Native American languages are polysynthetic; while none is analytic, some are only "mildly synthetic" (Mithun, 1999, p. 38).

In addition to prefixing and suffixing, some Native American languages use a type of affixation called **infixing**, a process by which a morpheme is inserted into a previously self-contained morpheme or word. In English, infixing is used to add emphasis in words such as *fan-friggin-tastic*, where the infix *-friggin-* is used to separate the root morpheme *fantastic*. Because this process is rather limited in the numbers and the types of words it can be used to create, infixing is not considered to be productive in English. In Lakota, a Siouan language of the Upper Midwest, however, infixing is used to mark person in some verb forms, as in the following:

> *máni* 'he walks'   *ma-wá-ni* 'I walk'
> *aphé* 'he hits'   *a-wá-phe* 'I hit'
> *hoxpé* 'he coughs'   *ho-wá-xpe* 'I cough'

> (Albright, 2000, p. 2)

Other Native American languages that use infixation productively are Saanich, a variety of North Straits Salish spoken in the Pacific Northwest (Montler, 1989), and Yurok (Garrett, 2001), a language spoken in northwestern California.

Pronoun paradigms also exhibit significant differences between Native American languages and English. In our earlier discussion of regional American English, we mentioned that the lack of a distinction between singular and plural *you* has resulted in the adoption of several different regional variants for the plural form, such as *y'all*, *you guys*, or *you'uns*. In Cree, the distinction between singular and plural *you* is made through the use of a suffix that is added to the singular form to indicate plurality: *ki:la* 'you' (sg.) → *ki:lawa:w* 'you all.' Additionally, the English first-person plural *we* does not change form depending on whether it includes the person being spoken to (inclusive *we*) or it does not include the person being spoken to (exclusive *we*); rather, this clarification is typically left to context. However, in Cree, *ki:lana:naw* is used to show

BOX 12.4 **Reduplication**

Unlike other morphological processes, **reduplication** does not involve the addition of a fixed morpheme; rather, it adds a morpheme that varies according to the phonological shape of the word to which it is being attached (Wilbur, 1973), as it is a copy of at least part of the root. When the entire root is copied and affixed, as in *putt-putt*, the process is called **total reduplication**; when only a part of the root is used, as in *chit-chat*, the process is called **partial reduplication**. Reduplication is often considered iconic in that it employs repetition as a linguistic device to indicate repetition, plurality, frequency, and volume; it is also used onomatopoetically to express a variety of sounds, particularly repetitive ones. In general, reduplication is not used productively in Indo-European languages; in English, it is often used in baby talk or, perhaps even more often, to describe baby talk, as in *mama* and *dada*. However, it is found in some words and expressions, often evoking a playful or light-hearted mood when these words are used (e.g., *teeny-tiny*, *flip-flop*, *choo-choo*).

Several Native American languages make productive use of reduplication. In Koasati, a Muskogean language of Louisiana, reduplication is used to show repetition. In Yaqui, a Uto-Aztecan language of Arizona, reduplicated forms, such as **mi-mi**ik-sime 'continued giving,' **ko-ko**che 'sleep' (plural subject), and **kok-ko**che 'very sleepy,' are used to show repetition, subject–verb concord, and intensity, respectively (Harley & Amarillas, 2003, pp. 2–3). The Interior Salish languages of the Pacific Northwest employ reduplication to mark first person singular referents, to form special counting forms for people and animals, and to refer to the concept of being "out of control" (Anderson, 1996, p. 11). Reduplication is used with Yaqui verb forms to indicate habitual aspect, as in these examples:

Aapo bwiika	*Aapo **bwi-bwi**ka*
'He is singing'	'He sings'
Aapo yena	*Aapo **ye-ye**na*
'He is smoking'	'He smokes'
Aapo vahume	*Aapo **va-va**hume*
'He is swimming'	'He swims'

(Harley & Amarillas, 2003, p. 4)

Reduplication is also used productively in African languages and in American creoles, the latter of which is addressed to some extent in the next chapter.

inclusion, and *ni:lana:n* exclusion, with respect to 'we.' The Cherokee language uses pronominal prefixes to create three distinct second-person pronouns for singular, plural, and dual 'you two.' It also includes a first-person dual inclusive 'you and me' and a dual exclusive 'me and someone other than you.' Such paradigms illustrate that the structures of Native American languages are neither uniform with respect to each other nor simple in comparison to English and other Indo-European languages.

Syntax

Languages can also be classified by their syntax. More specifically, these classifications are decided by the typical order of the syntactic elements of Subject, Verb, and Object in sentences of the language. English, for instance, is considered a Subject Verb Object (SVO) language, because in a basic English sentence it is most common for the subject to appear first, followed by the verb, and then, optionally, an object, as in "I like Mary," which comprises the subject *I*, the verb *like*, and the object *Mary*. English shares its classification as an SVO language with 42% of the world's languages (Tomlin, 1986), including Chinese. SOV languages are even more common than SVO and include Japanese and Turkish. Together, SVO and SOV account for nearly 90% of the world's languages. Some languages (Arabic and Welsh) are VSO; however, VOS and OVS are relatively rare. OSV is particularly rare among the world's languages; however, it is the canonical word order in the idiolect of at least one character in a major American film franchise of the last 40 years, as well as the order of topicalized English sentences, such as "Ice cream, I like; ice storms, I don't."

12.11

In terms of syntax, there are examples of Native American languages with canonical word orders falling into five of the six word order types that are logically possible: SVO, SOV, VOS, VSO, and OVS (Finegan & Rickford, 2004). Many Native American languages exhibit SOV order, including Northern Paiute, as shown in the following example:

> *Nɨ puku punni*
> I   horse see.
> 'I see the horse.'
>
> (Snapp, Anderson, & Anderson, 1982, p. 10)

Several Native American languages are known to exhibit relatively free word order; for instance, Cree allows all six possible configurations of word order (Dahlstrom, 1991). However, in such cases, word order variation often makes a difference in the emphasis of sentences, as shown in the following Cree example:

> *kakwecimew   kiseyiniwa*
> he asked   old man
> 'He asked the old man.'

> *kiseyiniwa   kakwecimew*
> old man   he asked
> 'It was the old man he asked.'

(Wolfart & Carroll, 1981, p. 83)

Additionally, Kickapoo is an SVO language that exhibits free order, including the relatively rare VOS order (Yamamoto & Zepeda, 2004, p. 162).

Lexicon/Semantics

Cultural differences are often reflected in the organization of the lexicon. One domain in particular in which Native American languages exhibit variation is **kinship terminology**, a domain that can hold valuable information concerning the societal organization of groups of people, while also raising interesting and important questions on how such lexical categories affect the worldviews of the speakers who use them. For example, in Yaqui, a Uto-Aztecan language spoken in Arizona and Mexico, the genders and relative ages of individual speakers play a role in their use of kinship terms, as shown in Table 12.1. According to the paradigm, both female and male speakers use the same terms for all female referents, even making the same lexical distinction between older and younger sisters. However, females and males apply different sets of terms to male referents: whereas male speakers derive *saila* (younger brother) from the word for *sai* 'older brother' through the addition of the diminutive suffix *–la*, females use the same word, *wai*, to refer to both their younger sisters and younger brothers. Thus, in the speech of Yaqui females, *wai* denotes a general category of younger siblings. Such an example illustrates that languages hold many possibilities for viewing and grouping objects together in the world, and Native American languages present many of these possibilities. The Companion Website provides other examples of Native America kinship systems and other semantic domains that suggest differences in the worldviews held by speakers of different Native American languages.

12.12

TABLE 12.1 Kinship terms in Yaqui

Referents	Terms used by females	Terms used by males
mother	*ae*	*ae*
older sister	*ako*	*ako*
younger sister	*wai*	*wai*
father	*hapchi*	*achai*
older brother	*avachi*	*sai*
younger brother	*wai*	*saila*

VARIATION WITHIN INDIVIDUAL LANGUAGES

In addition to variation among different Native American languages, individual Native American languages present a wide range of regional and social variation as well. The broad geographical territory that speakers of a single Native American language covered often resulted in the development of regional varieties of a language. The Cherokee language at one time, for example, comprised at least three regional dialects: (1) the Lower; (2) the Middle, or Kituhwa; and (3) the Overhill, or Western, with each differing phonologically and lexically from the others. Regional varieties of Cree include Plains Cree, Woodlands Cree, Swampy Cree, Moose Cree, Eastern Cree, and Naskapi. The Blackfoot language is generally considered to consist of four regional varieties: Siksiká (Blackfoot), Aapátohsipikani (Northern Piegan), Kainai (Blood), and Aamsskáápipikani (Southern Piegan), the first three of which are spoken in Canada and the fourth in northwestern Montana.

Some Native American languages exhibit variation that is based on the gender of the speaker and/or hearer. Haas (1944) found gender-related differences in the suffixes that men and women used on verb forms in the Koasati language, with women using the more archaic forms. For instance, Haas found a linguistic rule that when women use certain verb forms that end in a short vowel followed by /n/, the same verbs used by men have a lengthened vowel followed by /s/; thus, *lakawčín* 'Don't lift it!' is pronounced *lakawčí:s* by men, and *tačilwân* 'don't sing!' as *tačilwâ:s*. The frequency with which gender-related differences play a role in variation in some Native American languages and the complexity of these variable rules have dissuaded some Native Americans from using these languages, particularly in front of older generations. For instance, in reporting on the Gros Ventre language of northern Montana, Leap (1981) notes the reluctance of younger speakers to speak the language in front of elders for fear of misusing linguistic features typically reserved for use by the opposite sex, and being ridiculed for doing so.

12.13

AMERICAN INDIAN ENGLISH

According to Leap (1993), the prohibition of native languages in boarding schools and the mingling of young Native Americans within these schools led to the creation of American Indian English. This ethnic dialect refers to varieties of English spoken by Native Americans in communities throughout North America. Some researchers have proposed that the features of American Indian English originated from nonstandard varieties of English, whereas others contend that varieties of American Indian English reflect language interference from the native language of speakers during the acquisition process. All agree that American Indian English is systematic and that it is often used as an act of identity by Native Americans.

American Indian English presents several general features. Leap (1993) found that "on the whole, sound systems of Indian English rearrange sound contrasts found in standard English usage, but contain very few sound segments that are completely alien to standard English phonology" (p. 45). Several researchers have pointed to the self-application of the word *Indian*, pronounced as "Ind'n" (Lincoln, 1993; Seifert, 2013) by different tribes as a marker of the pride that Native Americans take in their cultural history. Leap (1993) argues that despite the stigmatization associated with it, Native American English is a variety in its own right that allows people to participate in the activities of their communities. As such, with respect to Native American students, he argues against the use of classroom activities requiring them to renounce their native English-related proficiency before developing standard English skills, advising teachers to "recognize that Indian English is not a marker of language deficiency and that being fluent in these codes does not prevent speakers from acquiring fluency in other varieties of English" (Leap, 1993, p. 284).

While American Indian English can be marked by general features, the idea of a monolithic "Indian" has been criticized by some scholars (e.g., Deloria, 2004; Meek, 2006), and varieties spoken by specific tribes often integrate features from the heritage languages of their speakers. Leap (1982) states: "[T]here are many Indian English-es," each with its own unique linguistic properties at the levels of phonology, syntax, semantics, and others, and he estimates that there are over 200 Indian Englishes in the United States (Leap, 1993). In a study of the English used by young people in a Blackfeet community in Montana, Seifert (2013) reports on the use of the expression *hoa*, an interjection retained from the Blackfoot language employed as a marker of cultural identity (pp. 161, 176), often in contexts where it adds an element of lightheartedness to teasing by simultaneously indexing and promoting in-group identity (p. 13). The same speakers also frequently use the Blackfoot word *sah* 'no' to express disbelief in conversations that are otherwise conducted in English (Seifert, 2013, p. 166).

Another variety of American Indian English that has attracted much attention is that of the Lumbee Indians of North Carolina. The linguistic roots of Lumbee are enigmatic and lacking in clear-cut native characteristics; however, research suggests that the Lumbee may have descended from a multitribal situation and that the language probably derives from Iroquoian, Siouan, and Algonquian languages (Dannenberg & Wolfram, 1998, p. 140). While Lumbee English shares many features with more mainstream varieties of American English, two ways in which the variety distinguishes itself are in the distribution of *be* in its grammar (Dannenberg & Wolfram, 1998) and in its reduction of consonant clusters (Torbert, 2001).

MAINTENANCE AND REVITALIZATION OF NATIVE AMERICAN LANGUAGES

As noted by Weatherford (1991, p. 197), "The common use of English by North American Indians leads some people to the conclusion that Indian languages have died." While estimates of the number of Native American languages that existed prior to European colonization clearly indicate that many Native American languages have indeed been lost, many still have a presence in the United States today, as the latest numbers from the US Census show (Table 12.2). Of these languages, the highest-ranking by number of speakers is Navajo, an Athabaskan language of the southwestern United States; ranking second and third, respectively, are Yupik, a language spoken in Siberia and Alaska, and Dakota, a Siouan language spoken in the Upper Midwest, especially in North and South Dakota. The category "Other Native American languages" highlights the large proportion of Native American languages with small numbers of speakers, comprising as it does nearly 50,000 speakers of more than 100 languages, with no individual language having more than 2,000 speakers.

Such numbers suggest the immediacy with which work must be done if Native American languages are to be documented and revitalized. Locating and interviewing

TABLE 12.2 Most common Native North American languages and numbers of speakers, 2006–2010

Language	Estimated number of speakers
Navajo	169,471
Yupik	18,950
Dakota	18,616
Apache	13,063
Keres	12,945
Cherokee	11,610
Choctaw	10,343
Zuni	9,686
Ojibwa	8,371
Pima	7,270
American Indian language (not specified)	8,298
Other Native North American languages	47,238

Source: Adapted from US Census Bureau (2011).

12.14

last living speakers of languages is important to this goal, and such work, done with a speaker of the Chemehueyi language in Arizona, was highlighted in the film *The Linguists* (Kramer, Miller, & Newberger, 2008). Even in those cases in which languages have been learned as a second language by tribe members or by linguists, as in the case of Chickasaw, the loss of monolingual speakers of that language can have a devastating impact on the documentation of the language.

12.15

That many Native American languages are at the edge of extinction is apparent; however, one might ask why this should matter. The primary issue is one of identity and the loss of identity that results from language loss. Generally speaking, separate tribes speak separate languages, with each language defining its speakers as a people. Leap reports a Cherokee educator explaining to him:

> For most Indian tribes, the most symbolic thing to them is their language. The Cherokee talk their language and by this they are able to define the tribe . . . There was a time when we lost most of our people over sixty. If we did not have our rituals written down, we would not have them today. Young people in urban areas do not know how to speak their native language and I think it is critical they learn. If they don't, they will be in a bind because you cannot be an Indian and go home and not know how to speak your language.
>
> (1981, p. 134)

For Native Americans, their languages thus serve as integral parts of their identities— as individuals, as members of tribes, and as Native Americans. In *Coming to Light: The Edward S. Curtis Story* (Makepeace & Makepeace, 2001), a documentary that focuses on an early photographer of Native American life, an interviewee from the Kwakiutl tribe, Stanley Hunt, says:

12.16

> I lost my language. Once you lose the language, you lose pretty much everything with it, because all our stories and everything, all our rules and regulations about life are in our language and if you don't speak our language, then you're kind of, you're lost.

Thus, Native American languages, like all heritage languages, play an important role in establishing and maintaining the identities of those who use them as a language or whose ancestors used them as a native language. Use of these languages has other rewards as well; for instance, educational research has found that including heritage language instruction as part of curricula can instill a sense of pride among Native American students and improve academic performance (McCarty, 2002).

The preservation of Native American languages is also important to linguists, for a variety of reasons. Every language provides insight into what is possible in language as a whole, and so any language that dies before it is at least documented represents a loss of valuable information concerning what is possible in human languages (Nettle & Romaine, 2000, p. 69). Native American languages hold a special place in this endeavor because of their diversity and their importance in conveying the history of America and the American people, and recognition of this usefulness and that these languages were being lost was part of the motivation for anthropologists and linguists to begin documenting Native American languages over a hundred years ago. Nettle and Romaine argue:

> Linguistic diversity, then, is a benchmark of cultural diversity. Language death is symptomatic of cultural death: a way of life disappears with the death of a language. The fortunes of languages are bound up with those of its speakers.
>
> (2000, p. 7)

Languages, however, are not only important to academics for the information they impart with respect to language structure and use, but languages add to the breadth of general human knowledge, much of it local, in different parts of the world. Along these lines, scholars point to what the loss of native cultures means in terms of the loss of scientific and medical wisdom. Such losses include detailed and valuable information on medicinal plants, wind patterns, moon phases, fish, and rice (Harrison, 2007, p. 15). As Nettle and Romaine claim:

> language is part of a complex ecology that must be supported if biodiversity is to be maintained. Despite the existence of a vast amount of largely undocumented scientific knowledge in the world's indigenous languages, what goes by the name of modern science is still based largely on the worldview of Europeans and their languages, especially English.
>
> (2000, p. 77)

Finally, languages provide insights necessary for the understanding of how the human mind operates. When we investigate and catalog different possibilities in language structure and use, we are also looking at the possibilities of human cognition:

> The entire world needs a diversity of ethnolinguistic entities for its own salvation, for its greater creativity, for the more certain solution of human problems, for the constant rehumanization of humanity in the face of materialism, for fostering greater esthetic, intellectual, and emotional capacities for humanity as a whole, indeed, for arriving at a higher state of human functioning.
>
> (Fishman, 1982, p. 7)

In light of the past losses with regard to Native American languages, and the imminent threat to the remaining languages, tribes have begun working, many times

BOX 12.5 Code Talkers

In the World Wars of the 20th century, the US armed services required codes by which messages could be used to coordinate battlefield operations. Due to the possibility of such messages being intercepted by the enemy, the military required codes that would be difficult, if not impossible, to decipher. As the basis for these codes, the US armed services recognized the potential of Native American languages, as there was little danger of the enemy recognizing these languages or being able to decipher them even if they did. Thus, native speakers of these languages were recruited to serve as **code talkers** and, in this capacity, the Choctaw language served as the basis for a code during World War I that the Germans were never able to crack.

Based on the success of the Choctaw code, several Native American languages were used as the basis for codes during World War II. In Europe, these languages included Cherokee, Lakota, Meskwaki, and Comanche. Meanwhile, in the Pacific Theater of Operations, where the United States and Japan were engaged in war, Navajo was called upon for the task. In many ways, Navajo was perfectly suited for this use: it had a grammatical complexity shared by few other languages, few people outside the Navajo tribe knew how to speak the language, and few books on the grammar of the language existed at the time. Thus, the enemy would not only have difficulty recognizing the language and understanding it, but unless enemy forces had access to native Navajo speakers, they would be unable to transmit authentic-sounding messages in codes based on the language.

In creating the Navajo code, English words that were used frequently in military communications were replaced wholly by Navajo words with similar meanings, or with metaphorical readings, as illustrated in Table 12.3. The words were then compiled in codebooks and memorized by the code talkers so that the codebooks themselves were never used in battle. When the code required modification, the code talkers convened in Hawaii to modify it in person and later trained those who were unable to attend.

The Navajo code was uncomplicated by cryptographic standards; however, it was never cracked and remained in use until the Vietnam War. The operation was declassified in 1968, paving the way for code talkers to be recognized for their service, for which each of the original Navajo code talkers received a US Congress Gold Medal in 2000. Several books have been written by or about code talkers; the movie *Windtalkers* (2002) presents a fictional account of Navajo men who served as code talkers in the US Marine Corps.

12.17

12.18

12.19

BOX 12.5 *(continued)*

TABLE 12.3 Excerpt from *Navajo Code Talkers' Dictionary*

English words for ship types	Navajo word	Literal translation
ships	toh-dineh-ih	sea force
battleship	lo-tso	whale
aircraft	tsidi-moffa-ye-hi	bird carrier
submarine	besh-lo	iron fish
mine sweeper	cha	beaver
destroyer	ca-lo	shark
transport	dineh-nay-ye-hi	man carrier
cruiser	lo-tso-yazzie	small whale
mosquito boat	tse-e	mosquito

Source: Department of Defense (1945).

in conjunction with linguists, on ways to preserve and revitalize Native American languages. Besides changes in policy at the federal and state level regarding education and the importance of tribal languages in terms of identity, research on language acquisition and bilingualism of the past several decades has also influenced the language policies adopted by individual tribes, as exposing children to the language is considered of paramount importance. As Nettle and Romaine (2000, p. 8) contend: "The pulse of a language clearly lies in the youngest generation. Languages are at risk when they are no longer transmitted naturally to children in the home by parents or other caretakers." Thus, several revitalization programs have focused specifically on teaching children the native languages of their tribes. For instance, families with children from birth to five years old in the village of Sipaulovi, Arizona, are being recruited to participate in the Hopi Lavayi Nest Model Program, a pilot revitalization program designed to encourage Hopi to raise their children to speak the language so they can keep it alive and pass it on to future generations. In another project, a linguist and a Blackfoot speaker worked together to elicit lullabies that could then be used for pedagogical purposes (Miyashita & Shoe, 2009).

12.20

Some individual languages are developing multi-faceted approaches to ensure survival of the tribal language. In addition to teaching their children to use the language of their ancestors at an early age, the Hopi have created a group called the Hopi Literacy Project to focus attention on promoting the language. As part of this work, the tribe has worked on several publications, including a comprehensive Hopi–English dictionary (Hopi Dictionary Project, 1998).

12.21

BOX 12.6 Sequoyah

Sequoyah was a Cherokee born in what is now eastern Tennessee around 1770. Although by trade Sequoyah was a silversmith, he had also become enamored with the ability of English speakers to represent their language in written form and, in 1809, began experimenting with approaches to writing Cherokee. His analyses led him to believe that the best system for writing Cherokee was a **syllabary**—a set of written symbols used to represent syllables (rather than individual sounds)—and, in 1821, he completed a syllabary for Cherokee that comprised 85 symbols, some of which were borrowed from Latin and others that resembled symbols from the Greek alphabet. Despite the complexity of the Cherokee language, Sequoyah's syllabary proved to be learned by speakers of the language relatively easily and quickly, and the Cherokee Nation adopted it as its official writing system in 1825 (Brandon, 2003). Later, Sequoyah studied other Native American languages to determine whether it was feasible for his system to be adapted for them. Although Sequoyah's system remains the most famous among them, writing systems for other Native American languages have since been devised (Walker, 1981).

12.22

Technology is playing an important role in preserving and potentially revitalizing some Native American languages. As illustrated by the links embedded throughout this chapter and on the Companion Website, the Internet provides access to a plethora of Native American language materials, including corpora, lessons, and audio recordings of native speakers of a variety of languages. It has been speculated that the passage of the Community Radio Act by Congress in 2011 could be a boon to tribes looking for ways to keep their languages alive (Hauk, 2012) as they use radio airwaves to broadcast the sounds of Cherokee, Hopi, and Creek. In 2010, Apple teamed up with iPhone to make the Cherokee language available to those interested in using the syllabary of Sequoyah to communicate via text messaging. A project at Yale University uses recent technology to translate letters and other materials written in Cherokee for use in linguistic analysis and language teaching.

12.23

CONCLUSION

In this chapter, we examined Native American languages, which existed in North America for thousands of years before the arrival of Europeans. In addition to their historical value, Native American languages are noteworthy for their diversity, with respect to the linguistic differences between them as well as their differences from languages of Europe and elsewhere around the world. These differences make Native American languages a valuable resource for gaining insight into human language and for obtaining knowledge about the world in which we live.

Unfortunately, Native American languages have been dying since the first Europeans landed in North America and, for many of these languages, we have little or no record of their existence today. Those that do remain are an integral part of the identity and culture of the people who speak them, but many of these languages are endangered, some of them being kept alive by only a handful of speakers. As is the case with other heritage languages in the United States, there is, and has been for some time, a great deal of pressure for speakers of Native American languages to shift to English, especially young speakers, many of whom are now being raised with no knowledge of their ancestral language. Thus, as the elders of Native American communities die, they often take their native languages with them, and with the death of these languages an entire way of life vanishes, since so much of the history and so many of the traditions of groups are bound together by their language.

Although the outlook for all Native American languages is grim, tribe members and linguists, sometimes with the help of government agencies, have undertaken projects designed to maintain and revitalize some of these languages. Such efforts have incorporated traditional linguistic methods such as dictionary making and language teaching, but they have also begun to take advantage of computing for the collection, storage, and distribution of recorded speech data that can be used for linguistic analysis and teaching. Finally, revitalization projects have also employed the latest in technology designed for communications via the Internet, social media, and cell phone applications to pique interest in these fascinating languages.

12.24

DISCUSSION AND RESEARCH QUESTIONS

1. Given some of the great differences between North American tribes, as illustrated by their languages, is it justifiable to group them under the umbrella term "Native Americans"? Why or why not? What are the advantages or disadvantages of doing so? Is "Native Americans" the best name for this group? Or is there a better alternative among the other names that have been used?

2. Figure 12.1 in this chapter provides an overview of the distribution of Native American tribes before contact with European explorers and settlers. Choose several neighboring tribes from the figure and chart their movement to their later locations as shown in the map in Companion Website link 12.8. Using concepts

that were presented in this chapter, as well as in earlier chapters, discuss linguistic changes that might have occurred in the languages you selected due to this movement.

3. News stories discussing the death of individual languages often have quotes from the last speaker lamenting that he/she regrets not taking steps earlier to teach the language to younger generations. Who has the right to make decisions about whether or not an endangered language should be revitalized? Is it solely up to the speakers or the community in which it is used? What if they don't realize until too late? What role, if any, should governments, linguists, and institutions of higher learning play in these decisions and in the implementation of language revitalization programs?

4. Download a Native American language learning app (either the Cherokee or Ojibway app that we provided links to earlier in the chapter or one that you find through your own online search) and examine its use. What kinds of features does it have? Is it easy to use? Is the app useful to someone who knows nothing about the language or does the user need to have some prior skills in the language? How well do you think someone could get to know the language through the app? How could the app be improved?

13 Pidgins and Creoles in the United States

GUIDING QUESTIONS

1. What are pidgins and creoles?

2. What are the pidgins and creoles that are spoken in the United States? Where and by whom are they spoken?

3. What kinds of linguistic features are associated with pidgins and creoles?

4. How do American pidgins and creoles relate to English as well as to other heritage languages of the United States?

OVERVIEW

In this chapter, we focus on the use of pidgins and creole languages in the United States. The discussion of pidgins is a return to a phenomenon that was introduced briefly in the previous chapter, as a pidgin is a unique kind of *lingua franca*—one that is created on-the-fly to meet the communicative needs of speakers who don't share a common language. We also discuss languages called creoles that emerge in multilingual situations and that differ from pidgins in that they have native speakers and, consequently, are linguistically more complex than pidgins. Although they have often been denigrated as corruptions of "real" languages, pidgins and creoles are their own unique linguistic systems that, as a group, share a number of common features. For linguists, pidgins and creoles are also significant for the insight they possibly offer into language creation and evolution. More importantly, these linguistic varieties serve as important forms of communication, as well as markers of identity, for the speakers who use them. As part of this discussion, we focus on several pidgins and creoles that have developed on American soil. We also address creole languages that originated in other areas of the world but have significant populations in the United States today.

COMMON MYTHS

Creoles are defective versions of real languages.

Creole speakers are lazy and unwilling or unable to speak standard languages correctly and thus resort to speaking creoles.

Pidgins and creoles acquire linguistic features solely from the language of the dominant group in multilingual situations.

INTRODUCTION

What options are available to people who need to communicate but do not share a common language? If the contact situation is very brief, such as someone trying to order a meal or asking for directions when traveling, speakers may default to gesturing and using a few basic words from the languages they do know. In the case of immigration, where there is long-term, if not permanent, contact, speakers might choose to learn the language of their new homeland and shift to that language over time. In other contact situations, speakers may not share the same native language but instead discover that they share a third language, or a lingua franca, that can be used. Another type of language contact situation that arises, however, is one in which none of these conditions apply and, by necessity, a completely new linguistic system is created to meet the needs of the speakers who are involved in the contact. If the new linguistic system that emerges from these different languages has no native speakers of its own, we call it a **pidgin**; if it has native speakers, we call it a **creole**. Together, we refer to these as **contact languages**.

In this chapter, we describe the use of pidgins and creoles as heritage languages in the United States. Wrongly considered to be bastardized versions of their source languages, pidgins and creoles have often been stigmatized; yet, these languages have been used to fulfill important needs for their speakers in the situations in which they are required and, at least in the case of creoles, are vital to the identities of those who speak them. For linguists, pidgins and creoles are of interest because of the light they are able to shed on language genesis and evolution. American pidgins and creoles are also noteworthy in that they further highlight the close connection between the development of a linguistic system and the experiences and needs of a set of speakers, as we have seen earlier in the development of regional and social dialects in American English and in the use of heritage languages throughout the United States.

PIDGINS

A pidgin is a simplified linguistic system created in multilingual situations where people share no common language but have a need to communicate, typically, for the purpose of trade. Pidgins are created by using features from the different languages of the participants involved in the contact situation to facilitate only the communicative task at hand. For instance, let's say that two or more groups of speakers have come together as part of the fish trade. What communicative features would they need to haggle over prices in this situation? A small vocabulary that includes words for fish, money, and a way to quantify both. Beyond that the linguistic system would require only a simplified grammar, without the tenses or complex structures that might be required by other, more abstract communicative acts. In the context of trading fish, speakers wouldn't need to talk about love or existentialism, nor would it be necessary to use the subjunctive or even the past tense, let alone the past perfect. Their only concern is to buy and sell fish. The pidgin suffices for this task.

As time goes on, the pidgin can develop to meet the additional needs of its speakers. If, for instance, a buyer and seller wish to arrange a meeting in six months, then they must enter a way of referring to time into the linguistic system. If they need to talk about current issues, such as an oil spill that is affecting fish prices or a new government policy that is changing the way these speakers conduct their business, then new words must be admitted into the system; if communicative acts require more complex syntax, then processes for creating those sentences will have to be added as well. Through this development, pidgins become more like other languages.

In general, the linguistic features that make up a new pidgin are those that it incorporates from the languages used by speakers in the contact situation. If the people who are creating the pidgin are speakers of English, Russian, and Tlingit, for example, the new system takes those languages as its **source languages** and reflects these contributions. If the participants are speakers of French, Mohawk, and Ojibwa, then the pidgin that is created is a reflection of those sources instead. The contact situations that pidgins are created in are not typically static, but are dynamic, and thus the languages that are represented in a given language contact situation can change over time. For example, if, after the pidgin is created, the English and Russian speakers stop showing up to trade fish with the Tlingit people, and Korean and Tagalog speakers take their place, then elements from the latter languages can be added to the pidgin as well. Thus, the multilingual settings that pidgins are formed in are dynamic situations where different languages are often added to or subtracted from the mix over time. (An interactive *Atlas of Pidgin and Creole Language Structures* can be found online at: http://apics-online.info/contributions#2/30.4/10.2.)

13.1

An important aspect of the formation of pidgins is that one of their source languages is classified as a **superstrate**, which is the language of the socially dominant speakers in the language contact situation, and one or more source languages are classified as the pidgin's **substrates**, which are the languages of the socially dominated speakers. Pidgins typically have only a single superstrate language and, because this language also typically provides most of the vocabulary to a pidgin, a superstrate is also often referred to as a **lexifier**. However, pidgins typically have more than one substrate language in their formation and, in fact, some linguists believe there must be more than one substrate in the contact situation for a pidgin to form (e.g., Whinnom, 1971). While superstrates contribute most of the vocabulary, substrates appear to be more influential with regard to the phonology, morphology, and syntax, that is, the grammar. Some of the differences between superstrates and substrates are summarized in Table 13.1.

TABLE 13.1 Differences between superstrates and substrates

Source type	Social status	Number	Major contributions
Superstrate	Dominant	Usually one	Lexicon
Substrate	Dominated	Typically more than one	Syntax, morphology, phonology

Furthermore, because of their apparent similarity to other languages via their lexicon, pidgins (as well as creoles) are often referred to as being "based" on their lexifiers; for example, Nigerian Pidgin is an *English-based* lingua franca spoken in Africa. This convention is occasionally used in the text below.

Structurally, pidgins are simplified systems that lack the complexity of the superstrate and substrate languages that are used to create them. First, the phonology of pidgins is highly variable to allow for differences exhibited by different speakers of different languages; because pidgin languages are rarely standardized but are instead focused on meeting the communicative needs of their speakers, such variation is generally overlooked in conversation. At the same time, it is typical for sounds that are difficult to articulate—whether they be from the superstrate or the substrates—to be replaced with simpler sounds that all the speakers can articulate. For instance, due to their difficulty, the sounds [ð] and [θ], the first sounds in *that* and *thank*, respectively, might be replaced by the sounds [d] and [t], which are sounds that are more common in the world's languages, and thus are more likely to be shared by everyone participating in the conversation. Consonant clusters are often simplified, either through the deletion of one or more sounds (e.g., *strong* pronounced as [trɔŋ]; *dust* as [dʌs]; *wasp* as [was]) or through the insertion of one or more vowels between consonants (e.g., *please* as [pəliz], *film* as [fɪləm]).

Pidgins are also much simpler in terms of morphology than their source languages. For instance, even when their source languages use morphology to show plurality, pidgins often leave plural nouns bare and show plurality in other ways; for example, by use of a numeral adjective, as in *two house*. There is also a tendency to eliminate or overlook morphological irregularities that occur in the source languages. For instance, in most varieties of English there is an irregularity in that verbs in the indicative mood take the suffix *-s* to show agreement with third-person singular nouns, as illustrated in Table 13.2. However, such distinctions are often leveled in pidgins so that the third-person form in Table 13.2 would assume the same form as others, that is, *he/she/it talk*.

TABLE 13.2 Subject–verb concord in English

I talk		we talk
	you talk	
he/she/it talk<u>s</u>		they talk

At the level of syntax, pidgins sparingly use **function words**, which are words with little meaning used to meet the demands of grammar. In English, function words include prepositions, determiners, and conjunctions. The following sentence from Ghanaian Pidgin English shows the minimal use of function words that is characteristic of pidgins.

1. nobɔdi gò ask jù paspɔt.
   'Nobody will ask you for a passport.'

(Huber, 2013)

Rather than utilizing function words, pidgins place greater emphasis on **content words**, typically nouns, verbs, and adjectives, which refer to objects, actions, and characteristics. Pidgins also rely greatly on context to convey the intended meaning of an utterance.

Finally, the lexicons of pidgins tend to be relatively small and generally consist only of words that are necessary for the immediate contact situation. These small lexicons often result in **polysemy**—when a word conveys more than a single meaning; **multifunctionality**—when a word has more than one syntactic function; and **circumlocution**—when lexical items consist of phrases rather than single words (Holm, 2000). For instance, in the Eskimo Trade Jargon, a pidgin used by late 19th-century Inuit and European whalers in Canada and Alaska, the verb *kaukau* 'eat' meant 'bite' when used in regard to the actions of a sled dog (polysemy); the adjective *kaktuña* 'hungry' could be used as a noun meaning 'hunger' (multifunctionality); and *kaktuña* followed by *múkki* 'dead' meant 'starvation' (circumlocution) (Holm, 2000, p. 599).

Because pidgins are often only used for relatively short periods of time and are limited in the functions they can be used to perform, there has been little documentation of pidgins that might have emerged in North America, such as in trade situations between Native Americans and the early Europeans. However, Mobilian Jargon was a pidgin that was reported by early missionaries on the Mississippi River. Named after the Mobilian Indians, Mobilian Jargon was a pidgin spoken by various tribes and European settlers as a lingua franca along the Gulf Coast and in the Mississippi Valley until the 20th century. There has been debate among scholars as to when Mobilian Jargon originated: whereas some researchers contend that it was used by tribes before Europeans arrived, Crawford (1978, p. 21) claims that Mobilian Jargon originated after the arrival of French missionaries to the area in the 17th century, citing the lack of reference to the language in the writings of the earliest European explorers.

Another pidgin that was used in the present-day United States is Chinook Jargon, which originated as a trade language first used among the speakers of the diverse Native American languages of the Pacific Northwest. It is unclear when Chinook Jargon originated; however, its popularity appears to have peaked in the mid-1800s, when Chinook Jargon dictionaries were compiled and published (see, e.g., Gibbs, 1863). Although its lexicon primarily consisted of vocabulary from the Native American languages Chinook and Nuuchahnulth, Chinook Jargon had a variety of sources, including French, as evidenced by its inclusion of such words as *la tete* 'head' and *le mah* 'hand,' and English, from which it borrowed *man* and *nose*. A testament to the pervading influence of Chinook Jargon in the region is in the adoption of several of its words by speakers of English, including *high mucky-muck*, *potluck*, *skookum*, and, possibly, *moolah*. A creolized form of Chinook Jargon (that is often referred to as Chinuk Wawa) is used by several hundred speakers in Oregon today.

13.2

CREOLES

While pidgins have no native speakers, creoles do, a distinction that has significant linguistic effects. Because they have native speakers, creoles are no longer limited to the immediate language contact situation that pidgins are; rather, these languages are used by families, by playmates, and in some situations by entire communities, which means that they are no longer restricted in the same way that pidgins are, in terms of how and where their speakers use them. Furthermore, unlike pidgin speakers, creole speakers can be monolingual. Thus, creoles are required to accommodate all the linguistic needs of their speakers, allowing them, for example, to deal with the abstract as well as the concrete, to discuss the past and the future, and to express their hopes, their dreams, and their fears. In other words, they do all the things that other languages do.

Although the specific details of creole genesis are subject to debate, a widely held view is that creole languages develop in relatively stable contact situations where a pidgin serves as the common linguistic system; as children are raised in these situations, they acquire the pidgin used by their families and employ it in interactions with other children outside the home. According to this view, language contact situations that become permanent, as, for example, happened through colonization and slavery, are instrumental in the development of creoles, as they require people to interact on a daily basis with each other, and children are born and raised in these situations. Under such conditions, a pidgin would then undergo **creolization**, a process whereby the linguistic system moves toward full grammatical complexity, as its range of uses, as well as the needs of its speakers, expand. As part of this expansion, the lexicon of a creole would

---

BOX 13.1 Reduplication in Creoles

Many creoles use reduplication productively for a variety of purposes, many of them iconic in nature. For example, reduplication is used to indicate plurality and iterativity, as in the following examples from Jamaican Creole: *wass* 'wasp' → *wass-wass* 'wasps'; *wiss* 'vine' → *wiss-wiss* 'vines'; *batta* 'to beat' → *batta-batta* 'to beat repeatedly' (Cassidy, 1961). Intensity is another characteristic shown through the use of reduplication in Jamaican Creole, as in *preachy-preachy* 'preaching too much'; *wee-wee* 'very small'; *flat-flat* 'very flatly'; and *plenty-plenty* 'plentifully' (Cassidy, 1961), and in Ndjuka, a creole of Suriname whose superstrate is English, as in *tuu* 'true' → *tuutuu* 'very true'; and *nyun* 'new' → *nyunyun* 'brand new' (Huttar & Huttar, 1994). Reduplication is also used productively for attenuation, as in Ndjuka: *baaka* 'black' → *baakabaaka* 'blackish'; *weti* 'white' → *wetiweti* 'whitish'; *lebi* 'red' → *lebilebi* 'reddish'; *guun* 'green' → *guunguun* 'greenish'; and *lontu* 'round' → *lontulontu* 'roundish' (Huttar & Huttar, 1994). Reduplication is used by many creoles even when it is not productively used by their superstrates; its use as a productive word-formation process in many African languages suggests that creoles incorporate reduplication via those languages rather than through their lexifiers.

incorporate new means of expression to fulfill its new role, which now extends far beyond the simple linguistic demands of, say, the temporary fish trade.

In light of this relationship, pidgins and creoles share some of the same linguistic characteristics. There is relatively little affixation used in creoles, particularly with respect to inflectional morphology. For instance, creoles do not typically mark subject–verb agreement, just as pidgins do not, as illustrated in Table 13.2. Rather than through affixation, creoles often show plurality through the use of a number or a demonstrative pronoun before the noun, as reported for Gullah, an American creole of the southeastern United States: *five dog* 'five dogs' and *them boy* 'those boys' (Turner, 1949/1973, p. 223). Turner points out that many West African languages use this pluralization strategy, and thus this strategy could be evidence of African substrates at work in Gullah.

However, creoles present important grammatical differences from pidgins. The syntax of creoles, for instance, is generally much more developed than pidgin syntax. As one example, creoles incorporate markers of tense, mood, and aspect, otherwise known (collectively) as **TMA markers**. These examples from Gullah show several temporal distinctions that TMA markers allow speakers to make (Cunningham, 1992):

2. a.   We **been see** that man thief that man car. [simple past]
         'We **saw** that man steal that man's car.' (p. 48)

    b.   My head **də hurt** me. [present progressive]
         'My head **is hurting** me.' (p. 50)

    c.   I **beenə see** that boy a long time. [past progressive]
         'I **have been seeing** that boy for a long time.' (p. 50)

    d.   He **be try** to sing. [habitual *be*]
         'He **[often] tries** to sing.' (p. 53)

Thus, TMA markers allow for speakers of creoles to convey more nuanced expressions of time than speakers of pidgins can. Along with serial verb constructions, reduplication, and lack of inflectional morphology, TMA markers are one of several features that appear in many creoles around the world, regardless of their source languages.

Another linguistic feature commonly associated with creoles is the **serial verb construction** (SVC), in which multiple verbs appear in a clause in which they share the same grammatical subject, are not joined by conjunctions, and express simultaneous or immediately consecutive actions. For example, an SVC appears in the following sentence from Hawaiian Creole (Bickerton, 1977):

3.   dei don hæv no kaz, dei **wawk** fit **go** skul
     they do-not have no cars they **walk** feet **go** school
     'They didn't have any cars, they **went** to school on foot.'

As suggested in the gloss of this example, English has a variety of other syntactic structures that it can rely on rather than using SVCs. Although English does provide some examples, as in the sentence "**Go tell** your sister," they are considered to be marginal by some linguists. Aikhenvald (2006), for instance, contends that such examples cannot be considered the same as SVCs, given, among other things, a number of restrictions on their use (p. 45). At any rate, it is generally accepted that SVCs appear more frequently and have greater functionality in pidgins and creoles than in their superstrate languages (Todd, 1974).

As is the case for other languages, creoles are not static but exhibit a great deal of variation in their usage. One of the ways in which varieties of creoles are classified is by their position on a **creole continuum,** which recognizes that creoles comprise several varieties that range from their most creolized forms to forms that are very similar to those of their superstrates. This occurs in situations in which creoles remain in contact with their lexifiers, and there are social motivations for their speakers to acquire the dominant form. For example, Haitian Creole is the language commonly spoken in homes in Haiti, but French, the superstrate language of the creole, is taught and used as the medium of instruction in the school system. The resulting varieties are then seen as forming a continuum between the **acrolect** (the variety closest to the superstrate) and the **basilect** (the variety farthest from the superstrate), with intervening varieties called **mesolects.** When a creole develops to become more similar to its acrolect through the loss of creole features, the process is called decreolization.

TABLE 13.3 Creole continuum

Variety	Description
Acrolect (top)	Standard variety of lexifier
Mesolects (middle)	Varieties lying in between acrolect and basilect
Basilect (lowest)	Emergent creole

While creoles could technically form anywhere that pidgins were spoken, they tended to develop, and are still used, in certain parts of the world, particularly in areas in which plantations were a vital part of the economy. Furthermore, the origins of many of these languages, as well as the plantations that supported their growth, were linked to the Atlantic slave trade and are thus distributed throughout the Americas, particularly on islands and in coastal regions with access to the Atlantic Ocean.

AMERICAN CREOLES

In this section, we introduce the reader to several creole languages with strong associations with the present-day United States, namely, Gullah, Louisiana Creole, and Hawaiian Creole. Like many of the world's contemporary creoles, American creoles had their beginnings in the slave trade and the plantation society of past centuries. While these languages have similarities in their social histories and linguistic structures that link them together, they also present some very real differences that mark them as unique American languages. Figure 13.1 provides an overview of the areal distributions of the major pidgins and creoles that developed in the area that is now the United States. It is important to note that the shaded areas are meant to indicate the general distribution of these languages either now or at some point in the past. The map is not meant to suggest that everyone in the shaded areas spoke these languages, nor that the languages were necessarily confined to these areas. Finally, the map does not indicate all the

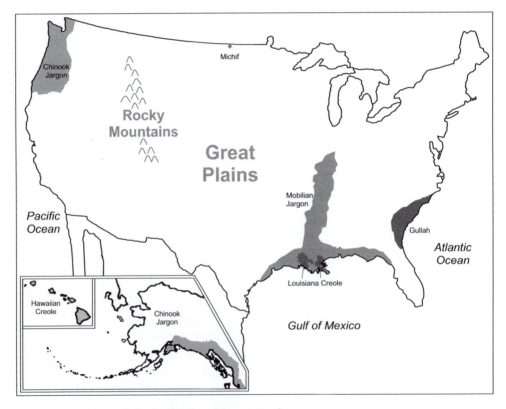

FIGURE 13.1 Distribution of major American contact languages.

Source: Courtesy of Dana Gorman.

contact languages that have developed in North America, but only those that are discussed in some detail in this chapter.

Gullah

Gullah (also called Geechee or Sea Island Creole) is a creole language spoken by descendants of slaves primarily in the southeastern United States. Gullah's superstrate is English, and its substrates are a variety of West and Central African languages. The language is commonly associated with the rice plantations that were established in the 1700s between Georgetown and Beaufort on the South Carolina coast (Nichols, 1981, p. 73); later, the language expanded from Jacksonville, North Carolina, to Jacksonville, Florida, and extended about 35 miles inland from the Sea Islands. Estimates of the number of Gullah speakers vary widely: Hancock (1977) estimated there to be 125,000 speakers of Gullah, including 7,000 to 10,000 monolinguals, while Nichols (1981) reported on estimates as high as 300,000 speakers. According to the 2010 Census, there are only 350 Gullah speakers; however, Ethnologue (n.d.) reports the ethnic population as being much larger (~250,000). Most Gullah speakers also speak English, and thus it is not surprising that the use of Gullah is underreported, particularly in the Census (see discussion in Chapter 9). In addition to the majority of Gullah who remain on the Sea Islands or in coastal communities in South Carolina and Georgia, small clusters of Gullah speakers have been reported living in New York City and Detroit (Ethnologue, n.d.).

13.3

Gullah's origins are uncertain. Hancock (1980), for instance, contends that the Gullah language came directly from an English creole that was spoken on the Guinea Coast and that intervening stages between Africa and North America made little difference to the creole. On the other hand, Cassidy (1994) argues that while a West African pidgin or trade language might have played a part in the history of Gullah, the lion's share of its creolization was probably done on the island of Barbados. One of the reasons for this uncertainty is that little is known about the early years of Gullah in North America, due to the geographic isolation of Gullah speakers on the Sea Islands, which remained essentially inaccessible until well after World War II. During this time, mosquito-borne diseases that were pervasive on the islands deterred white plantation owners and overseers from playing an active role in the management of plantations, and thus Gullah speakers were largely left to their own devices and had little interaction with others (Nichols, 2004). Even after the emancipation of the slaves, little was known about Gullah due to the isolation of their communities, other than that the language was spoken by ex-slaves on the Sea Islands and that it was largely unintelligible to English speakers from other regions of the US (see Mencken, 1921). Early scholars who knew of Gullah (e.g., Krapp, 1924; Johnson, 1930) generally assessed it as almost wholly English and, as such, often dismissed it as "broken English" and even "baby talk."

However, research that began with the work of Lorenzo Dow Turner in the mid-20th century (see Box 13.2) revealed that the lexicon of Gullah consists of thousands of Africanisms that could be traced back to West and Central African languages, including Wolof, Yoruba, Bambara, Fula, Mende, and many other languages from the African continent. Furthermore, despite earlier claims to the contrary, Turner and other researchers found the structure of Gullah to differ from that of English in several ways and to pattern more closely with African languages or with other creoles. For instance, Gullah's phonological inventory includes consonants called **ejectives** that are created when the glottis and mouth closure are released nearly simultaneously to create the sounds [p', t', k', ʃ'], which are sounds that are also found in many African languages (Turner, 1949/1973, pp. 240–241). (For audio examples of these sounds, see the chart titled "Consonants [Non-Pulmonic]" at http://web.uvic.ca/ling/resources/ipa/charts/IPAlab/IPAlab.htm.) Gullah also combines its sounds in ways that English does not; for instance, a nasal consonant at the beginning of a word can precede a non-nasal consonant to create such combinations as [mb, mp, mw, nd, ŋg], which occur with some frequency in words and personal names in Gullah. While such consonant clusters are

---

13.4

BOX 13.2 **Lorenzo Dow Turner**

Lorenzo Dow Turner was born in Elizabeth City, North Carolina, in 1890. After earning his Ph.D. from the University of Chicago in 1926 by writing a dissertation entitled *Anti-Slavery Sentiment in American Literature Prior to 1865*, Dr. Turner taught in several English departments, including his alma mater, Howard University, as well as Fisk University and Roosevelt College. Soon after becoming a professor, his research interests turned to linguistics, and he was the first black member accepted by the Linguistic Society of America, joining the organization in 1931. In the 1930s, he conducted fieldwork for the American Linguistic Atlas Projects, specifically interviewing speakers on and around the Sea Islands of Georgia and South Carolina, and he also studied African languages in England. His research was guided by the hypothesis that the history of Gullah could not be established without taking African languages into account—an idea that had largely been ignored by scholars before his time—and the culmination of his work was published as *Africanisms in the Gullah Dialect* (1949) to high praise in the linguistic community. DeCamp (1973) called Turner's work the touchstone, in that it "convince[d] his academic peers that at least in Gullah, and perhaps also in black English generally, the black American has a genuine and continuous linguistic history leading back to Africa" (p. xi).

not found in English, they do occur in several African languages, including Kongo, Ewe, and Twi (Turner, 1949/1973, p. 241). Finally, Gullah also includes a set of sounds called labiovelar plosives, [gb] and [kp], each of which is produced as a single sound in such words as *gbaŋ* 'tightly' and *'kpaɲa* 'the remains after some destructive force' (Turner, 1949/1973, p. 241).

At the level of morphology, Gullah exhibits several characteristics that it shares with other creoles. As mentioned earlier, Gullah nouns are often marked for plurality by a separate numeral adjective or demonstrative pronoun preceding the noun, rather than by suffixation. Gender is marked not by the affixes that some languages often take, but by placing a modifier such as *woman* or *man* before the noun it modifies to produce, for example, *man chicken* 'rooster,' a strategy also used in many West African languages (Turner, 1949/1973). Finally, Gullah uses reduplication productively to intensify several different parts of speech, as in *ŋam* 'to eat' → *ŋamŋam* 'to eat or devour'; *dɛ* 'there' → *dɛdɛ* 'exactly there'; and *tru* 'true' → *trutru* 'very true'; it is also used in animal names and onomatopoetic expressions, as in *bidibidi* 'a small bird'; *huhu* 'an owl'; and *pakpakpak* 'to knock' (Turner, 1949/1973).

Gullah has several syntactic features that identify it as a creole. For instance, Gullah speakers use *for* or *fuh* to introduce some verbal complements rather than *to*, as in the following examples:

4. a. He də try **for** sing a song.
        'He is trying **to** sing a song.'   (Cunningham, 1992)

    b. . . . I had gone to my aunt house **fuh** see my baby sister.
        '. . . I had gone to my aunt's house **to** see my baby sister.'(Nichols, 2004)

Gullah also allows serial verb constructions, a feature that is often associated with creole languages, as described above:

5. a. i **tɛk** (s)tɪk **kɪl** əm
        he **take** stick **kill** him
        'He **killed** him with a stick.'   (Turner, 1949/1973)

    b. Uh **ran go** home
        I **ran go** home
        'I **ran** home.'   (Mufwene, 2008)

    c. [I] just take a day **go walk** this place walk that place.
        'I just take a day to **walk** here and there.'   (Cunningham, 1992)

At the same time, Gullah shares many features with varieties of English, particularly African American English, including the following examples (from Nichols, 1981):

6. a. he ugly [null copula]
   b. ... when my daddy **be** working, they always have lot of peaches [habitual *be*]
   c. I **done** know [perfective *done*].

The presence of these features in Gullah suggests a relationship between it and African American English, which we discuss on pp. 266–267.

Although its imminent demise was predicted over a century ago (Williams, 1895), Gullah continues to survive due to such factors as group identity, loyalty, residential patterns, and the ability of Gullah speakers to switch codes (Mufwene, 1997), and the language and culture of the Geechee people are recognized as important links between North American culture and certain African cultures (Twining & Baird, 1991). The Gullah/Geechee people, long considered "a nation within a nation," united on July 2, 2000 to declare themselves as a nation. However, despite this recent recognition of the social, and particularly sociohistorical, importance of Gullah/Geechee language and culture, the people and their way of life are facing serious challenges. As Mufwene concludes in his article "The Ecology of Gullah's Survival":

13.5

even if Gullah's death may not be predicted with certainty, Gullah may be endangered. Economic, rather than traditional sociolinguistic factors, seem to bear most critically on this condition. They will largely determine how much longer Gullah will be spoken, if it is moribund at all.

(1997, p. 78)

Louisiana Creole

A creole with French as its superstrate and several West African languages as its substrates, Louisiana Creole developed on the plantations of southern Louisiana after the arrival of the French in the early 1700s and the subsequent importation of 5,500 West African slaves to the region between 1719 and 1743 (Klingler, 2003). Speakers of the language are mainly concentrated in several parishes in south and southwest Louisiana; however, there are also speakers of the creole residing in metropolitan Chicago, in and around Beaumont, Texas, and in communities throughout California. Due to difficulties in obtaining accurate numbers for creole speakers, either because of how census questions are worded or by how speakers identify themselves linguistically, estimates for speakers of Louisiana Creole are uncertain. Klingler and Neumann-Holzschuh (2013), however, report fewer than 10,000 speakers today. Furthermore, there are few fluent speakers of Louisiana Creole below the age of 60, which suggests that the language is not being passed on to future generations.

13.8

Like Gullah, the exact origins of Louisiana Creole are uncertain; however, it is likely that two French varieties exerted an influence on the emerging creole: (1) a maritime

BOX 13.3 **Gullah in the Media**

Literary representations of Gullah have appeared in print since the late 1800s in works by Joel Chandler Harris in his depiction of Daddy Jack in the Uncle Remus stories (1883) and by Ambrose Gonzales in *The Black Border* (1922). Despite questions concerning the motivations and objectivity of these authors, research has suggested that both writers, particularly Gonzales, provide important data for those interested in the use of Gullah at a certain time and place (e.g., Haskell, 1964; Mille, 1997). A native of the South Carolina Low Country and winner of the Pulitzer Prize, Julia Peterkin also used Gullah in many of her novels and short stories.

The Gullah/Geechee culture was featured in the independent film *Daughters of the Dust* (1991—see Dash & Dash, 1991), which was filmed on St. Helena Island, South Carolina. The film critic Roger Ebert wrote of the movie's use of the Gullah language: "The fact that some of the dialogue is deliberately difficult is not frustrating, but comforting; we relax like children at a family picnic, not understanding everything, but feeling at home with the expression of it" (Ebert, 1992). The film's director, Julie Dash, also wrote two books related to that experience that placed Gullah in the spotlight: *Daughters of the Dust: The Making of an African-American Woman's Film* (1992) and *Daughters of the Dust: A Novel* (1997). The movie was added to the National Film Registry of the Library of Congress in 2004.

The language and culture of Gullah have been alluded to on television, notably in the family television show *Gullah Gullah Island*, which ran from 1994 to 1998. The title of the show has been useful as a cultural reference linking the name of the show to real-world problems in Gullah communities (Suhay, 2013). The language and the culture of Gullah also received media coverage when Candice Glover, a native of St. Helena Island and a speaker of Gullah, won Season 12 of *American Idol* in 2013.

13.6

13.7

French spoken by the sailors of slave ships; and (2) a colonial variety of French spoken in Louisiana by both well-educated elite as well as French people with little or no education, including a subculture of criminals (Marshall, 1997). Scholars have noted that the difficulty of acquiring slaves in Louisiana made it more common for slaves who spoke the same or related languages to work the same fields there, which may have resulted in slaves retaining their languages longer and in there being a delay in the development of Louisiana Creole (Marshall, 1997).

Louisiana Creole has several of the structural features associated with creoles in general, and with French-based creoles in particular, that differentiate it from other varieties of French spoken in the region:

> It is in its verbal system that Louisiana Creole bears its greatest affinity to other French-based lexifier creoles and, at the same time, is most clearly distinguishable from Cajun French. For while Cajun displays a fairly rich inflectional morphology, in Louisiana Creole, as in other creoles, there is relatively little inflectional morphology and notions of tense, mood, and aspect are expressed primarily by means of a series of free morphemes placed before the verb.
>
> (Klingler, 2003, p. 234)

The language uses the morphological process of reduplication productively, as in *cap-cap* (a type of heron), *cigale zi-zi* 'cicada'; *zozo* 'bird'; *tata* 'thank you'; *tac-tac* 'popcorn'; and *être en toc toc* 'to be drunk' (Klingler, Picone, & Valdman, 1997, pp. 171–172). However, the serial verb constructions generally associated with creoles are relatively rare in Louisiana Creole (Valdman & Klingler, 1997; Squint, 2005). Louisiana Creole retains the determiners used before nouns in French, such as *la* and *le*; however, in basilectal forms of the creole, these follow the nouns they modify rather than precede them as they do in Standard French (Klingler, 2003). This distinction is not maintained in varieties that are closer to the superstrate.

Louisiana Creole is in a state of attrition due to several factors. The first is that it has undergone decreolization just as other creoles have done since the breakdown of the plantation system in North America. The second is that many speakers in communities that once used Louisiana Creole have since shifted to either English or French, and this shift to these languages has been exacerbated by the creole's association with slavery, which has motivated young people to distance themselves from it. Third, the areas in which the creole was once frequently used are no longer geographically isolated.

Because many feel that the loss of the language will contribute, if not directly lead, to a loss of culture, there have been some efforts to revitalize Louisiana Creole. Poetry and fiction written in the language have appeared in print since the 1980s, and a series of lessons on the language were published in *Creole Magazine* in the early 1990s (Squint, 2005). Furthermore, zydeco has become a popular type of music associated with the culture. However, as in all cases of language endangerment, if Louisiana Creole is to be maintained, then younger speakers must acquire the language before its remaining speakers are lost. To this end, tools of technology must be harnessed to aid in the documentation and teaching of the language, using some of the work that has been done documenting endangered Native American languages (which was presented in the previous chapter) as a model. Unfortunately, recent efforts to revitalize French in parts of Louisiana have benefited Cajun and Colonial French at the expense of Louisiana Creole, due to its stigmatization in some social circles.

13.9

13.10

Hawaiian Creole

Hawaiian Creole is the native language of a large number of people born or raised in Hawaii, regardless of ethnic origin, and the second language of many more residents of the islands. According to Ethnologue (n.d.), as of 2012, there are approximately 600,000 speakers of Hawaiian Creole on the Hawaiian Islands, with vigorous use by 100,000 to 200,000, and 400,000 who use it as a second language. Another 100,000 speakers of the language live in the continental United States, particularly on the West Coast, in Las Vegas, Nevada, and in Orlando, Florida.

13.11

Of the three creoles highlighted in this section, Hawaiian Creole was the last to form, emerging from a pidgin used on plantations in the 1800s by the English speakers who managed the plantations and the immigrants from East Asia, the South Pacific, and southern Europe who worked them. Thus, English is the superstrate of Hawaiian Creole, and its major substrates are the Hawaiian language, Cantonese, and Portuguese, in contrast to the African languages that served as the substrates of Gullah and Louisiana Creole. As the Hawaiian pidgin creolized, more workers were introduced to the population from other parts of the world, and elements of Japanese, Korean, Tagalog, and Spanish were subsequently added to the language.

13.12

Hawaiian Creole has several linguistic features that show similarities with other creoles. In terms of phonology, many Hawaiian Creole speakers pronounce the sounds /θ/ and /ð/ as /t/ and /d/, respectively, so that the words *thin* and *then*, for example, are articulated as *tin* and *den*. With respect to syntax, Hawaiian Creole uses *fo* rather than the English *to* for introducing some verbal complements, as in the following:

7. a.   Ai chrai **fo** kaech om.
         I try **fo** catch em.
         'I tried **to** catch it.'

    b.   Eribadi kam **fo** si daet haus.
         Everybody come **fo** see dat house.
         'Everybody comes **to** see that house.'

Hawaiian Creole has serial verb constructions; however, some scholars have pointed out their limited functions in the language (see, e.g., Sebba, 1987, p. 214; Adone, 2012, p. 55).

One feature of Hawaiian Creole that is apparent to speakers of English when they hear it is its intonation patterns, particularly in yes-no questions. In most varieties of American English, the common intonation pattern in this regard is one in which pitch rises so that the question ends with the highest pitch of the utterance. In Hawaiian Creole, the pattern commonly used for yes-no questions is falling pitch so that the lowest pitch occurs on the final syllable of the utterance.

Despite that many Hawaiians consider the language that they simply call "Pidgin" to be an important part of their identity, there is a wide range of attitudes concerning Hawaiian Creole. Some of these feelings were instilled in the English Standard Schools that were built in the 1920s with English as their medium of instruction. However, a rebirth of Hawaiian culture in the 1970s also instilled a sense of pride among speakers of Hawaiian Creole, which has been reflected in several ways. These consist of a growing body of Hawaiian Creole literature on the islands that includes a translation of the Bible called *Da Jesus Book*, as well as best-selling books that incorporate Hawaiian Creole in various ways, and courses and programs in the language at the University of Hawaii.

The Status of American Creoles in the United States

The American creoles presented here hold a unique place among languages because of the extent to which they have developed on American soil and serve as important reminders of the nation's history. Because of the similarities they have with their superstrates, as well as their linguistic differences and the low social status of their speakers, American creoles have often been stigmatized by society and considered

---

BOX 13.4 Michif

The United States and Canada are also home to a **mixed language**, which is a language formed through the fusion of two contributing languages. Called Michif, this language is spoken by up to a thousand residents of communities in North Dakota and in the Canadian provinces of Saskatchewan and Manitoba. The language emerged in the early 19th century as a combination of the Cree and French languages, the result of marriage between Cree women and French trappers and fur traders. Thus, while these couples and their offspring had access to well-formed languages, they still created a new language with elements of both languages (Bakker, 1997). As a general rule, the grammar of Michif combines nouns from French and verbs from Cree, and the language is unique in that it retains much of the complexity of its source languages; for instance, its nouns adhere to French rules of gender and agreement, while its Cree verbs are polysynthetic. Thus, Michif differs from creoles in that its features can be clearly traced back to the language that contributed them, whether that source was French or Cree, and this important difference applies to other mixed languages as well. In addition to French and Cree, the lexicon of Michif also includes words borrowed from English and from neighboring Native American languages, such as Ojibwe and Assiniboine.

13.13

linguistically inferior by speakers of other languages. However, as we have shown in this chapter, there is much more to the structures of creoles than that which they have incorporated from superstrate languages; rather, the structural properties of creoles suggest that they have adopted much from their substrate languages as well.

The relationship of Gullah and African American English is especially mis-understood in this context because of the linguistic features, as well as the similar histories and language contact situations, that the two share. Although the Creolist Hypothesis (Stewart 1967, 1968; Dillard 1972) does postulate that AAE emerged from a creole, many scholars assume that this source was a widespread plantation creole that no longer exists as opposed to the geographically isolated Gullah. Thus, while the origin of AAE is still unknown, it is clear that it and Gullah are not considered to be, or to be derived from, the same language.

As is the case for all Native American languages, American creoles are generally considered endangered, as older speakers are not passing on their linguistic legacy to younger speakers. Instead, these younger speakers primarily acquire English or French (in the case of some Louisiana Creole speakers) as their first language, or they learn them in schools. As we have argued throughout this book, and will reiterate in the conclusion below, there are many reasons why these heritage languages should be maintained.

OTHER CREOLES IN THE UNITED STATES

In addition to those creoles that developed on American soil, there are also creole languages spoken in the United States that are from other areas of the world, including Haiti, Jamaica, and the Cape Verde Islands. Haitian Creole is a language comprising French and various West African languages with just under 7 million speakers in Haiti and approximately 7.7 million speakers worldwide (Ethnologue, n.d.). Speakers of Haitian Creole in the United States largely reside in New York City, Boston, and Florida, especially in the cities of Miami, Fort Lauderdale, and Palm Beach. According to Ethnologue (n.d.), the English-based Jamaican Creole is spoken by over 2.5 million speakers in Jamaica and 3.2 million worldwide, with significant Jamaican-speaking communities existing in New York City, Washington, DC, Miami, and Puerto Rico. Finally, Cape Verdean Creole (CVC), which is a Portuguese-based creole that incorporates many words from various West African languages, has nearly 400,000 speakers in the Cape Verde Islands and nearly a million total worldwide, with a large population in New England (Halter, 2005). Cape Verdeans have had a presence in the United States since the 18th century, when young men from the islands were recruited by New England whaling expeditions and moved to ports in Massachusetts and Rhode Island to be near their work, and remained in the US after the decline of the whaling industry.

13.14

Immigrants to the United States who speak creoles that were developed in other parts of the world add an interesting dimension to the linguistic diversity of the US. In addition to their native creoles, some bring knowledge of other languages as well. For instance, some Cape Verdeans learn Portuguese as students in Cape Verde, where it is the language of government, literature, and mass media; thus, first-generation Cape Verdeans in the US often speak both CVC and Portuguese, whereas subsequent generations shift from Portuguese to English, reserving the creole for home use (Carvalho, 2010, p. 228). Thus, some creole speakers might shift from one of their languages to English more quickly than other heritage language speakers, without necessarily abandoning their first language.

CONCLUSION

In this chapter, we have introduced readers to several linguistic systems that emerge from language contact situations. For a variety of reasons, such as the relatively small numbers of speakers of these languages and, in some cases, their geographic isolation, many Americans know little about pidgins and creoles, an issue this chapter has sought to rectify. In support of this introduction, we have provided links on the Companion Website to many sources where readers can learn more about pidgins and creoles.

Like other heritage languages, there are many reasons why creoles should be maintained. First and foremost is that creoles are important symbols of identity for their speakers. Second, they are based in cultures that are rich in history, and the loss of these languages would mean an irretrievable loss of culture once they are gone. Contact languages are also of great value to linguists, as they give insight into how languages are created and develop, and they provide interesting sets of data that help to reveal the diversity of linguistic structures. In relative terms, creoles were formed only recently; thus, they may offer insights into language creation and evolution that other kinds of languages cannot. Pidgins offer a view of humans at their most creative and pragmatic, as they create languages on-the-fly in dynamic situations.

In terms of the American linguistic diversity that this book pays homage to, pidgins and creoles provide some of the best examples there are to offer. Unlike the European languages that arrived with more than a thousand years of history under their belts, many of the contact languages that were the focus of this chapter originated in the Americas and developed in contact situations in the Western Hemisphere. They are the linguistic products of people who have faced some of the greatest adversity in the American experience and, as such, their languages offer a unique view into the American past. At the same time, they provide glimpses into the nature of multilingualism and multi-culturalism that should be important to all Americans, given that these are apparently a mainstay of American life and could ultimately be among our greatest resources.

DISCUSSION AND RESEARCH QUESTIONS

1. There has been a common practice to name pidgins and creoles with reference to their superstrate languages, such as Haitian French Creole or Nigerian Pidgin English. However, some argue that this places an unnecessary, and even inappropriate, emphasis on the superstrate. Discuss why this practice is problematic, linguistically and socially, and give recommendations for better naming practices.
2. How does the stigma attached to pidgins and creoles reflect a standard language ideology?
3. Should Gullah, Louisiana Creole, and Hawaiian Creole be considered and categorized as indigenous languages in the United States? If so, should they receive the same support that Native American languages, such as Cherokee, Navajo, and Cree, do? Why or why not?

14 American Sign Language

GUIDING QUESTIONS

1. Where and how did American Sign Language (ASL) begin?

2. What is the structure of American Sign Language?

3. Who uses American Sign Language?

4. What is the relationship between ASL and American Deaf culture?

5. What is the connection between ASL and English?

OVERVIEW

This chapter examines the creation and development of a sign language for America's Deaf community. It discusses and details the structure of the language, including dialectal variation, and looks at the history of its use (or disuse) within the American educational system. It also presents social issues and controversies within the Deaf community, such as the debate over the use of cochlear implants.

COMMON MYTHS

> *There is one universal sign language used by all deaf people.*

> *ASL is a signed version of English.*

> *ASL is not a language but simply a series of gestures.*

> *ASL signs mimic the shape or action of the noun or verb.*

> *Sign language is simply fingerspelling.*

INTRODUCTION

In Chapter 1, we defined *language* as "an open, arbitrary, conventional system of sounds used for communication within a linguistic community," but this definition overlooks the fact that while most languages are spoken, some are articulated through nonverbal signs. Except for the mode of transmission—spoken languages utilize auditory processes, whereas sign languages comprise complex visual-spatial structures (National Association of the Deaf, 2008)—all other aspects of our definition of *language* apply to signing. All sign languages are individual, complex systems in their own right, with their own grammars, their own lexicons, and their own pragmatic rules. They change and vary, and they are generally not mutually intelligible with other sign (or spoken) languages. Crucially, they are not simply gestured versions of spoken languages. And significantly, like spoken languages, they are intimately related to the identities of the communities that use them. In other words, languages transmitted through signs are in every way equal to spoken languages and, as such, we must expand our definition of *language* to read: An open, arbitrary conventional system of sounds—and signs—used for communication within a linguistic community.

According to Ethnologue (n.d.), there are over 135 sign languages worldwide (out of approximately 7,100 total living languages listed). However, as with spoken languages, it is difficult to determine the exact number of sign languages due to:

14.1

questions of genetic classification (which systems are separate languages and which are dialects of the same language); the number of people using the language ("**village signs**" are often shared by smaller communities and thus are not widely known or counted); and the relatively recent establishment of standardized deaf education in many countries. Furthermore, as pointed out in McCaskill, Lucas, Bayley, and Hill (2011), language— whether signed or spoken—is intrinsically connected to community, culture, and identity; thus, "[t]here are basically as many sign languages as there are viable Deaf communities" (p. 1).

Before we begin our discussion of American Sign Language (ASL), we need to make one note about terminology. In the ASL literature, it is common practice to distinguish between the terms **deaf** and **Deaf**. The first term is used in reference to those with profound hearing loss, whereas the second is applied to those who identify with a larger Deaf culture, regardless of their ability to hear. While most people who are associated with a Deaf community are either partially or fully lacking in the sense of hearing, many are not, and Deaf communities include family members of those who are deaf, those who work with deaf populations, such as interpreters, and others who align themselves with Deaf culture. Furthermore, not everyone who is deaf identifies with the Deaf community. As such, *Deaf* and *deaf* index significantly different populations as well as language use. Additionally, the term *d/Deaf* is also used as a reference to both groups. All of these terms will be used throughout this chapter.

ASL AND THE AMERICAN DEAF COMMUNITY

The principal linguistic system for the American Deaf community is American Sign Language, or ASL (National Association of the Deaf, n.d.). The exact number of people who use ASL in the United States is unknown; different sources report anywhere from 100,000 to 15 million users of the language. However, after analyzing these various sources, Mitchell, Young, Bachleda, and Karchmer (2006) conclude that the correct number falls between 250,000 and 500,000. Even by this relatively low estimate, ASL is still one of the most commonly used languages in the United States, as fewer than 7% of the languages spoken in the US consist of more than 250,000 speakers. (Several publications, academic as well as popular, claim that ASL is the fourth most used language in the US; however, the statistic used to support this claim is from an erroneous misreading of a study on language and courtroom interpretation (for more, see Mitchell et al., 2006, p. 22).)

One of the reasons for this wide range of estimates stems from the use of ASL by people who are hearing as well as people who are hard of hearing; moreover, not all who are deaf use ASL. Therefore, the number of people who are hard of hearing is not the sole population accounted for when calculating the number of ASL users in the United States. Traditional sources of language demographics are not useful for determining the number of users of ASL in the US, either. The US Census Bureau, for example, does not collect information regarding ASL in either their decennial survey or the American Community Survey. According to the US Census Bureau FAQ page:

> The three questions used to capture languages spoken and English-speaking ability are not designed to identify those who use ASL. The design of the question is to gather the number of people speaking languages other than English at home, identify which languages are being spoken, and to get the number of people who have difficulty with English . . . With that in mind, those who use ASL are presumed to know English. Those who report using American Sign Languages, ASL, or some variation of those words are coded as being English speakers.
>
> (US Census Bureau, n.d.)

Not only does the Census specifically fail to ask about the use of ASL, it actually ignores details concerning ASL and merges the language with English. The assumption that most ASL users know English is not entirely erroneous—as Lucas and Valli (2004) state, "almost all Deaf users of ASL [in the US] are bilingual" (p. 241); however, in approaching ASL this way, pertinent information concerning its speakers is lost. Furthermore, even if ASL were to be coded in the Census, the current wording of the language question might confuse survey participants so as to make their answers unreliable. To the question "Does this person *speak* a language other than English at home?" an ASL user may answer "No," since ASL is not a spoken language.

Despite the challenges encountered in calculating the precise number of ASL users in the US, it appears that the total number of users has been growing in recent decades. Not only do more deaf children and adults have access to ASL education, there has also been a significant increase in teaching ASL as a second language to those who are not hard of hearing. In fact, due to the increase of ASL courses in both US and Canadian school systems, Padden argues that the number of second-language users of ASL "surely exceeds the number of primary users" (2011, p. 26).

THE STRUCTURE OF AMERICAN SIGN LANGUAGE

Like any other language, spoken or signed, ASL is a fully formed, rule-governed linguistic system. Many people erroneously believe that ASL is simply a signed version of English. On the contrary, it is an independent, complex system, as different from English as English is from Arabic, Swahili, or Portuguese.

Today, ASL is acknowledged as a complex language, but it was not always so. Recognition of ASL as a complete linguistic system began with the publication of William Stokoe's *Sign Language Structure* in 1960. Since then, a flourishing body of research on ASL has developed, with numerous projects focusing on many diverse

14.2

aspects of the language (see Lucas, 2001; McCaskill et al., 2011; Napoli, Mai, & Gaw, 2011). Thus, ASL can be—and is—examined, analyzed, described, and discussed like any other linguistic system. Research on ASL can also be used to help answer the larger questions that exist about what language is and how it works. A full description of the structure of ASL would take volumes; in the interest of time and space, this chapter provides an overview of some of the basics of its syntax, morphology, phonology, and lexicon. Additionally, we describe some of the idiolectal and dialectal variation that exists in ASL.

Whereas spoken languages are articulated by the manipulation of air as it passes through the vocal tract, ASL is primarily constructed through manual signs. However, signs are not created solely by manipulating the shape of the hands; ASL also utilizes the head, face, and body. Crucially, position of the sign and movement are significant factors in generating and distinguishing meaning. Additionally, some signs are one-handed, while others are two-handed, and two-handed signs can be either symmetrical or asymmetrical. Just as the slight difference of vibration in an English speaker's vocal folds distinguishes between a /p/ and a /b/, relatively small distinctions in position, shape, or movement are linguistically meaningful and productive. In linguistic terms, handshape, movement, location, palm orientation, and facial expression are the phonology and morphology of ASL.

Figure 14.1 shows the signs for MOM and THANK YOU. (Note that the convention for writing ASL in English is to place the sign in all caps.) Here, we see the signer using his dominant hand, in this case the right, to form the signs. For MOM (MOTHER uses the same sign), the hand is open, and all five fingers are spread wide apart. The sign for THANK YOU has a similar handshape with the palm open and all five fingers extended; however, the fingers are held together. Additionally, the position of the hand is somewhat similar in that, for both signs, the hand is placed near the lower part of the face; however, and significantly, the first sign is articulated with the thumb at the chin, while the second places the fingers at the mouth. In terms of orientation, the sign for MOM has the palm perpendicular to the face, and for THANK YOU the palm is placed toward the signer. Finally, the structure of a sign may contain movement. While the picture does not show any movement for MOM, alternate variations of the word include signers wiggling their fingers or quickly tapping their chins twice with their thumb. In signing THANK YOU, movement is always included, and the signer moves the hand away from his mouth and down toward the direction of the person being thanked.

Words that are semantically related can also have similar constructions. For example, the words MOM and DAD (Figure 14.2) use the same handshape, orientation, and movement; however, the position of each is different. In fact, this difference in position indexes another, larger semantic pattern: many male-related signs are produced close to the forehead, whereas female-related signs are made near the cheek or chin (Butterworth & Flodin, 1995). These semantic connections can be seen by comparing the signs MOM, DAD, GRANDMA, and GRANDPA in Figures 14.2 and 14.3.

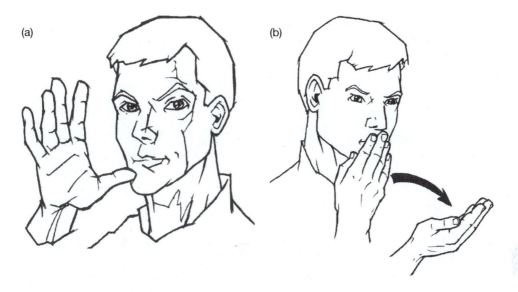

FIGURE 14.1 ASL signs for (a) MOM and (b) THANK YOU.

Source: lifeprint.com. Reprinted with permission.

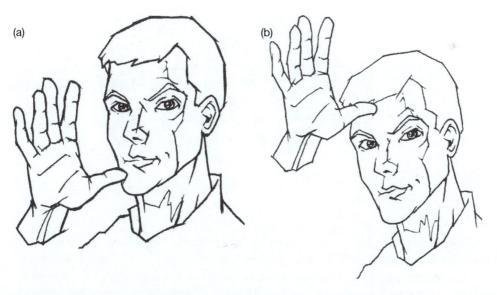

FIGURE 14.2 ASL signs for (a) MOM and (b) DAD.

Source: lifeprint.com. Reprinted with permission.

(a)

(b)

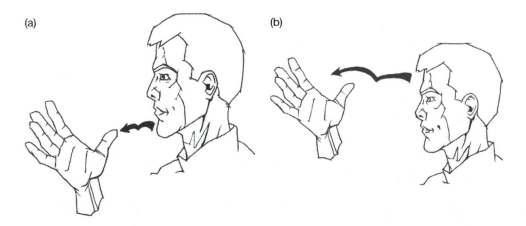

FIGURE 14.3 ASL signs for (a) GRANDMA and (b) GRANDPA.

Source: lifeprint.com. Reprinted with permission.

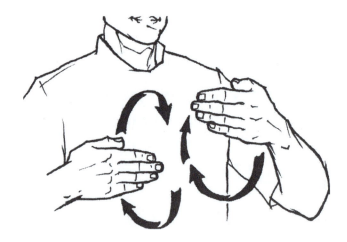

FIGURE 14.4 ASL sign for HAPPY.

Source: lifeprint.com. Reprinted with permission.

While thus far we have been focusing on signs formed around the face, the physical area where signs are made actually ranges from the head to the waist and from shoulder to shoulder. The majority of signs are formed at the head, face, or neck; however, as Figure 14.4 shows, the sign HAPPY is made at the chest. Since facial expressions also have a role in ASL, placing signs closer to the face allows for conversational partners to observe all aspects of the discussion more easily (Butterworth & Flodin, 1995).

HAPPY is also a good example of a sign that is two-handed. Both hands move up, against the chest, and outward in a circular motion. Whereas simultaneous movement of both hands is required to produce this sign, in some two-handed signs only the dominant hand moves. Notably, the production of a sign as one- or two-handed or the inclusion of movement can, for certain signs, be dialectal. (Variation in ASL is discussed further below.)

Just as there is no one-to-one correlation between the sound and meaning of a word in spoken language, the formation (shape, position, movement) of a sign with regard to its meaning in ASL is also arbitrary. For example, there is no more reason for the sign MOM to be made by placing the thumb lower on the face than it is for DAD or, for that matter, to be represented by touching the face at all, than there is for the same concept to be connected to the English phones [d], [æ], and [d]. Similarly, lexical items in sign languages are not simple imitations of the concepts they represent.

That said, there are signs in ASL that are considered iconic in that they do represent the shapes or structures of their referents. Figure 14.5 shows the sign CAT, in which the thumb and forefinger, placed together, start under the nose and move outwards, representing a cat's whiskers. While the sign does not imitate the entire shape of a cat, it is not completely arbitrary either; it uses the visual imagery of one of the animal's prototypical features. Other examples of iconic signs include ELEPHANT and TREE; please refer to the companion site for pictures of these and other signs.

14.3

Fingerspelling is another productive component of ASL. As opposed to lexical signs, in which each sign represents a concept, fingerspelling provides individual signs for each

FIGURE 14.5 ASL sign for CAT.

Source: lifeprint.com. Reprinted with permission.

14.4

letter of the English alphabet. (Please see the Companion Website for a chart of the fingerspelling alphabet.) Signers commonly use this alphabet to spell out words for which there are no specific signs in ASL, including personal and place names. Additionally, "beginning signers can freely use fingerspelling to spell a word when they are not familiar with the basic sign" (Butterworth & Flodin, 1995, p. 20). Many people who are otherwise unfamiliar with ASL as a discrete language have been introduced to the concept of fingerspelling, but because they do not recognize fingerspelling as only a minor part of a larger linguistic system, they often misconstrue ASL as a signed version of written English.

As a fully formed language, ASL also has a set grammar that governs phrase and sentence structure. Sentences in ASL generally follow a subject + predicate word order; however, ASL syntax is variable, allowing for **topicalization**—moving highlighted information to the front of the sentence. For example, statements about time may be fronted, such as in the sentence, "Tomorrow, I'll do the dishes." In addition, the process of transforming a statement into a question occurs through a deliberate change in the user's facial expression and body positioning. For example, yes/no questions are asked with raised eyebrows and a slight forward tilting of the head and shoulders.

14.5
14.6

The verbal system of ASL also includes complex structures, and sign placement and movement provide additional syntactic information concerning verb tense. For example, to express present tense, signs are made immediately in front of the body, whereas future tense is conveyed by a forward movement away from the body; statements about the past move backward (Tennant & Brown, 2010). (The sign for WILL, indicating future tense, is shown in Figure 14.6.) Similarly, while starting with the sign WILL, a signer

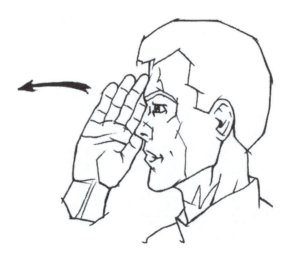

FIGURE 14.6 ASL sign for WILL.

Source: lifeprint.com. Reprinted with permission.

may use "a double arching movement to mean 'someday' or 'the distant future'" or "a single large strong movement [to] mean 'a long time from now'" (lifeprint.com).

Due to the difference between oral/auditory and manual/visual production and processing, the discourse structure of ASL can differ from that of spoken languages. For example, in some instances, ASL syntax allows the user to present two lexical items simultaneously by forming a separate sign with each hand. This simultaneous signing generally gives additional pragmatic meaning to the utterance (Crystal, 1995, p. 435). Furthermore, the speed of forming the sign and the size of the signing space are other ways to add pragmatic meaning or to show intensity. There is a rich body of ASL poetry that shows the depth of innovation and range of flexibility that is available to creative signers. There are even ASL users who specialize in interpretation at musical concerts.

14.7
14.8

There are also differences between the Deaf and hearing communities in the pragmatic rules that govern socially appropriate communication. Sustained eye contact is a crucial facet of ASL conversation, and there is a strong preference for directness over indirectness by its users:

BOX 14.1 ASL Interpretation as Internet Sensation

American Sign Language and the US Deaf community received national attention after a 2012 press conference given by New York Mayor Michael Bloomberg. The press conference, which was an update on New York's readiness and reaction to Hurricane Sandy, was discussed in many national media outlets, as well as on blog posts, Twitter, and Facebook feeds, not because of Mayor Bloomberg's own words, but for the way his ASL interpreter, Lydia Callis, portrayed them.

14.9

    Callis's body movements, gestures, and facial expressions—significant and meaningful elements of ASL—were seen by those outside of the Deaf community as parts of an extravagant performance rather than aspects of linguistically appropriate discourse. An NPR report even claimed that "her expressive style . . . fascinated many and provided a bit of a bright light amid all the dark news about Superstorm Sandy" (Memmott, 2012). Callis's linguistic energy was especially notable in contrast to Bloomberg's own delivery, which was considered to be relatively monotone. However, that which many Americans saw as a flashy performance was recognized in the Deaf community simply as the work of an ASL interpreter who was good at her job.

14.10

Because of its highly visible nature, ASL is a very public language. There is no way to "whisper" in sign language—anyone present who knows ASL will understand what is being said. Thus, ideas about privacy are different in the Deaf community. Deaf individuals may tend to ask personal questions and share personal information readily. Very few topics are considered inappropriate for discussion.

(Humphrey & Alcorn, 2001, as cited in Hemberger & Morrow, n.d.)

For example, money is not considered a taboo subject and asking directly about personal matters, which in other communities might be perceived as nosy or gossipy, is acceptable. Moreover, instead of introducing someone (or oneself) by occupation, one is introduced in terms of whom they know. Finally, because the use of ASL is dependent on face-to-face interactions, time spent together is valued in the Deaf community and, as such, more time is devoted to greeting and leave-taking practices than it is in hearing communities (Hemberger & Morrow, n.d.).

VARIATION IN AMERICAN SIGN LANGUAGE

Like all languages, ASL comprises many linguistic varieties or dialects that have formed over time due to regular linguistic change. Variation is also present in every facet of the ASL linguistic system. There are lexical differences, that is, different signs for a single concept, similar to the *coke–soda–pop* distinction in American English. As discussed by Lucas, Bayley, and Valli (2003), examples of lexical variation in ASL include the different signs used for PIZZA, HALLOWEEN, and BIRTHDAY. There are also phonological and morphological differences, such as variation in the size of signing space, the horizontal position of the sign, the production of a sign as one- or two-handed, the use of mouth movements, the use of repetition, and other aspects of linguistic structure (McCaskill et al., 2011, p. 9). Furthermore, these linguistic differences often reflect the regional, social, and cultural identities of the signers. As stated by McCaskill et al.:

> [S]ign languages are . . . differentiated internally according to social criteria in the same way that spoken languages are. That is, varieties of sign languages exist, and the social factors that help define them include both those that play a role in spoken-language variation—region, age, gender, socioeconomic status, race—and others that are unique to language use in Deaf communities. The latter include the language policies implemented in deaf education, the home environment (e.g., Deaf parents in an ASL-signing home vs. hearing parents in a nonsigning home) and the sightedness (or not) of the signer, as in Tactile ASL, the variety used by deaf-blind individuals.
>
> (2011, p. 1)

In the following sections, we present three varieties of ASL that are associated with different sets of signers: Black ASL, Tactile ASL, and Baby Sign. The first is a dialect that developed organically through language change, while the latter two were developed to meet the needs of particular populations.

Black ASL

One dialect that has received recent attention in public as well as academic discussions is Black ASL. At first, discussions of this variety of ASL were anecdotal; however, newer empirical research has not only confirmed its existence but has also given significant treatment to the description of its structure and history, as well as its social context and position (see McCaskill et al., 2011). In short, Black ASL developed from two distinct yet overlapping influences: the history of racial segregation in America and contact with African American English.

14.11

Like their nondeaf counterparts, black deaf students were relegated to racially segregated schools or classrooms early in the nation's history, and this segregation continued in some schools for over a decade after the ruling of *Brown v. Board of Education* in 1954, in which the Supreme Court declared segregation in American public schools unconstitutional. Additionally, some states, including Tennessee, had laws stating that black deaf students could only be taught by black teachers, thus further limiting the interaction of black and white signers (McCaskill et al., 2011, p. 15). It was this geographical and social isolation that led directly to the development of Black ASL. "Attendance by Black deaf children at segregated schools or departments was clearly a matter of discrimination and racism and never a matter of choice, but the result was a strong sense of group membership and personal identity" (McCaskill et al., 2011, p. 9). Thus, Black ASL is not only a remnant of racial segregation, but, crucially, it is a unifying linguistic system that indexes cultural solidarity in the face of institutionalized discrimination. As such, the development of Black ASL parallels the development of African American English.

There are many differences between mainstream ASL and Black ASL. For example, some signs are associated almost exclusively with white or black varieties (see Figures 14.7 and 14.8). Users of Black ASL produce more two-handed signs and use more repetition than users of mainstream ASL do. Furthermore, while all signers, white and black, may lower signs that are typically positioned at the forehead, dialectal differences govern this to a greater or lesser degree (McCaskill et al., 2011, p. 10). Additionally, users of Black ASL incorporate words and phrases into ASL from African American English. Finally, researchers have found that Black ASL is actually more conservative in terms of language change than other forms of ASL, due to the fact that black signers at one time did not have regular access to the novel signs and linguistic changes that occurred within white signing communities.

14.12

FIGURE 14.7 Signs for STUCK in Black ASL and PREGNANT in Mainstream ASL.

Source: Courtesy of *The Washington Post*/Getty Images.

FIGURE 14.8 Signs for (a) WELL DRESSED in Mainstream ASL and (b) TIGHT in Black ASL.

Source: Courtesy of *The Washington Post*/Getty Images.

Tactile ASL

Tactile ASL is a variety of ASL that is used by people who are both deaf and blind. In most cases, Tactile ASL is used by individuals who were born deaf (or became deaf early in life), became fluent in ASL, and then lost their sight later in life. In particular, it is used by those with the genetic condition Usher syndrome Type I, in which deafness occurs at birth, but loss of vision is delayed until the teenage years (McCaskill et al., 2011, p. 7). In Tactile ASL, nonmanual markers, such as facial expressions, are changed to be signed manually, and all signs are formed in the hands of the conversation partner.

14.13

Baby Sign

While not technically a dialect of ASL, Baby Sign has received a significant amount of attention over the last decade. Baby Sign (which became well known through the movie *Meet the Fockers*) is best described as a subset of ASL that is used by and for hearing infants and toddlers who have yet to begin using spoken language. Baby Sign is usually abandoned by the family after the child learns to speak and, as such, most users are exposed to only a limited vocabulary consisting of those concepts that parents and babies would need to communicate most, such as MORE, POTTY, and UP. (Figure 14.9 shows the sign MORE, one of the earliest signs taught to babies.) The concept of Baby Sign is based on research showing that babies are able to communicate manually at an earlier age than they are verbally and that the babies of signing parents begin using language earlier than those of nonsigning parents. In fact, Dr. Joseph Garcia, one of

14.14

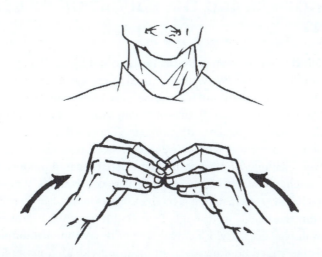

FIGURE 14.9 ASL sign for MORE, generally one of the first signs taught in Baby Sign.

Source: lifeprint.com. Reprinted with permission.

14.15

the founders of Baby Sign, "noticed that the children of his deaf friends were communicating with their parents as early as six months old using sign language and had substantial vocabularies as early as nine months old," whereas most hearing children in hearing families do not speak their first words until they are approximately twelve months old (www.babysignlanguage.com/basics/history/).

BOX 14.2 Hawaii Sign Language

While ASL is considered to be the language of the American Deaf community, it is not the only signed system that is found in the United States. Hawaii Sign Language, or HSL, is a language that developed within and for the Deaf community in Hawaii. Ethnologue (n.d.) currently marks this language as "nearly extinct," noting that the Deaf community in Hawaii has moved more toward the use of ASL. In fact, "there are only about a hundred Hawaiians left who know the language, most of them over sixty years old" (Wiecha, 2013). However, steps are currently being taken to preserve the language, including the development of a dictionary and course materials.

14.16

A HISTORY OF ASL AND THE EDUCATION OF DEAF AMERICANS

There was no unified linguistic system for deaf people in the United States until the early 19th century. Until then, those who were deaf used **home signs,** manual systems created for communication among family and friends. Because home signs were often developed only to the extent needed for basic communication, most "systems" comprised only a limited vocabulary and no structured grammar. There are, however, examples of larger, more complex systems of home signs that have been used within individual communities. One example of this is the sign system that developed on Martha's Vineyard in Massachusetts. Among the early settlers of Martha's Vineyard were two English families who were carriers of a recessive condition for deafness (Padden, 2011, p. 24). Thus, from the late 17th through 19th centuries, a significant portion of the island's population was deaf, and a manual system of communication developed that was shared by the wider community, not just individual households. However, established Deaf communities in which hearing and nonhearing folk both signed were quite rare.

Because most communities did not have a shared sign system, many deaf people were socially isolated, and most deaf children were unable to attend school. However, one New England minister, Thomas Hopkins Gallaudet (1787–1851), concerned that his neighbor's deaf child was being denied access to an education, began to search for a way to help all deaf children in the United States. While there were no schools for the deaf at that time in the US, several had already been established in France, Spain, England, and Germany. Therefore, Gallaudet left for Europe in 1815 in search of a way to educate deaf Americans.

Gallaudet first traveled to England and Scotland to learn about the oral method of deaf education being used there, but the directors of the British schools were unwilling to share their pedagogical strategies with him (Lucas & Valli, 2004, p. 238). However, while in England, Gallaudet met the Abbé Roch-Ambroise Cucurron Sicard, the director of the Royal Institution for the Deaf in Paris. Not only was the Abbé Sicard willing to share information about the educational model used at his institution, which included the use of French Sign Language (Langue des signes française, or LSF), he also invited Gallaudet to stay at the Institution to observe the school and learn the language (Lucas & Valli, 2004, p. 238). After several months in Paris, Gallaudet traveled back to the United States, accompanied by one of Sicard's students, Laurent Clerc, and in 1817 Gallaudet and Clerc opened the Connecticut Asylum for the Education and Instruction of Deaf and Dumb Persons, later renamed the American School for the Deaf. (According to McCaskill et al., 2011, the American School for the Deaf admitted black students in 1852, thus becoming the first integrated school in Connecticut.)

Therefore, it was French Sign Language—not spoken English or even British Sign Language—that served as the model for and became the linguistic base for ASL. LSF was created by the Abbé Charles Michel de L'Epée, who founded the Royal Institution for the Deaf in 1755. Having observed the home signs that were used within deaf families, the Abbé de L'Epée sought to create a standardized, manual system that could be shared by hearing as well as nonhearing people, and through his work French Sign Language was created.

While the development of ASL was initiated by Gallaudet and Clerc, it was also influenced by the home signs the students brought with them to the school, including the system used in Martha's Vineyard. As more people learned ASL, it expanded to incorporate a full lexicon and grammatical system, and it spread to wider and wider populations as it was adopted by other deaf schools that were beginning to open across the country (Padden, 2011). Although it has developed as its own language for almost 200 years, ASL is still closely connected to LSF, and today the two continue to share a significant portion of their vocabularies.

By 1863, there were 22 schools for the deaf throughout the United States, including schools in New York (founded in 1818) and Pennsylvania (1820) (Butterworth & Flodin, 1995, pp. 11–12). Additionally, in 1864, one school, the Columbia Institution for the Instruction of the Deaf and Dumb and Blind, in Washington, DC, was authorized by Congress to confer college degrees, and thus the first college for the hard of hearing was founded:

> [Thomas's son, Edward Miner] Gallaudet was made president of the institution, including the college, which that year had eight students enrolled. He presided over the first commencement in June 1869 when three young men received diplomas. Their diplomas were signed by President Ulysses S. Grant, and to this day the diplomas of all Gallaudet graduates are signed by the presiding U.S. president . . . Through an act of Congress in 1954, the name of the institution was changed to Gallaudet College in honor of Thomas Hopkins Gallaudet.
>
> (History of Gallaudet University, n.d.)

14.17

Now a university, Gallaudet granted degrees to 216 undergraduate and 178 graduate students in 2013 (www.gallaudet.edu/news/gallaudet_144th_commencement.html).

While ASL was adopted by deaf schools in the early to mid-1800s, there was a shift in pedagogical thought by the end of the century, and oral education became the primary method of instruction by 1880 (Lucas & Valli, 2004). This method taught deaf students to speak and to read lips, and in most schools that used the oral method, neither teachers nor students were allowed to use signs in the classroom. Proponents of oralism, such as Alexander Graham Bell, argued that speaking and lip-reading would allow for the integration of deaf children into mainstream society. Furthermore, several proponents even used Darwin's *The Origin of Species* (1859) to argue that speaking was a more "evolved" manner of communication. As such, one consequence of the promotion of oralism was the subsequent demotion of ASL from a valid language, as many began to perceive it as an ungrammatical code rather than a complex linguistic system. As McCaskill et al. define it: "Oralism [is] the belief that spoken language is inherently superior to sign language" (2011, p. 26). Students in schools where oralism was promoted and ASL forbidden have reported feeling that this method "drastically hampered their learning and affected their academic achievement" (McCaskill et al., 2011, p. 27).

The educational policy forbidding ASL was not applied equally across all deaf schools, and while white students were transitioned to oral education, the pedagogy in black deaf classrooms was not changed. Therefore, many black students were allowed to continue using ASL as their primary mode of communication:

> Because of the continued use of sign language in the classroom . . . the ironic result of this policy of discrimination may have been that southern deaf African Americans, in spite of the chronic underfunding of their schools, received a better education than most deaf White students.
>
> (Baynton, 1996, p. 46, as cited in
> McCaskill et al., 2011, p. 26)

Furthermore, even though ASL was not permitted in most schools, deaf students commonly used signs to communicate outside of the classroom and, therefore, ASL continued to be passed down to subsequent generations.

As researchers began taking an academic interest in ASL and recognizing it as a complex, grammatical language, deaf schools again employed ASL as the language of instruction. Noting that ASL was a more natural way to communicate for those who were hard of hearing, and in the wake of the Civil Rights movement, which challenged the treatment of many minorities, including linguistic minorities and disabled Americans, many schools did switch back to ASL in the 1970s. Today, different schools take different approaches; some schools favor orality, others use ASL, and some focus on bilingualism in both ASL and oral English.

SOCIAL ISSUES AND CONTROVERSIES IN THE DEAF COMMUNITY

As discussed above, one's partial or complete lack of hearing does not automatically guarantee identification with or involvement in a larger Deaf culture in the United States. The distinction between a mainstream hearing culture and a Deaf culture is not trivial, and the question of whether or not an individual associates with Deaf culture is a very personal choice that has social, psychological, and even linguistic outcomes. Is identifying with a Deaf community a point of social pride and cultural independence? Or is it an unnecessary (perhaps even problematic) push against mainstream integration?

Many of the significant differences between Deaf and hearing communities stem from fundamentally different views of deafness. Is deafness a disability or a difference, a condition or a culture? Particularly for those who are hearing, it can be difficult to conceive of deafness as anything but an unfortunate condition that one must overcome. However, those who align with the Deaf community do not see deafness as something that needs to be cured. They do not view themselves as individuals who are disabled, but instead as members of a minority culture (Sparrow, 2005). By this view, deaf people are able to lead full and happy lives, not in spite of their deafness, but because of it.

The decision to identify with Deaf or mainstream American culture is one of the core themes modeled within the television show *Switched at Birth* (ABC Family). While the show is primarily a teen drama about two girls who were switched in the hospital and sent home with the wrong families, one of the girls is deaf (having lost her ability to hear due to an illness as a toddler), and several other characters, adults and teens, are also deaf. Some of them speak aloud and read lips, while others use ASL as their primary form of communication. Against a background of teen angst in which all of the characters are searching for their own identities, the d/Deaf characters also explore

14.18

and express their beliefs about the use of sign and being included in (and excluded from) Deaf culture. The presentation of the narrative is influenced by Deaf culture as well; rather than portray every line of the script through spoken English and simultaneous translation, several scenes include dialogue that is only signed (but which is presented in subtitles for audience members who do not know ASL) (Nussbaum, 2012).

While the issue of Deaf culture may not be taken altogether seriously in the context of a televised teen drama, the struggle for identity by d/Deaf individuals is a truly serious matter that affects every deaf person. There have been—and will continue to be—larger debates that revolve around d/Deafness in America. In the following sections, we introduce readers to three discussions or debates that have occurred in the last few decades concerning deafness and a Deaf community: the development of a town for the Deaf; cochlear implants for children; and the fight for a Deaf president at Gallaudet.

Signing Town: Laurent, South Dakota

Questions of Deaf culture and mainstream assimilation appeared in the national spotlight in the early 2000s when a man named Marvin Miller presented his concept for an American town specifically for the Deaf community. Hard of hearing himself, Miller proposed a community where the entire town would be built around the social, political, and practical needs of those who are deaf and their families. He envisioned a place where his four deaf children would be able to see deaf role models at every level of society, from shop owners to firefighters, from politicians to physicians. Miller planned to name the town Laurent after Laurent Clerc, and he even found available space for the development of the project in South Dakota. Every aspect of the town would be structured for deaf residents:

> homes and businesses . . . would incorporate glass and open space for easy visibility across wide distances. Fire and police services would be designed with more lights and fewer sirens. High-speed Internet connections would be available all over town, since the Internet and Video Relay Service have become vital modes of communication for deaf people. And any shops, businesses or restaurants would be required to be sign-language friendly.
>
> (Davey, 2005)

However, while many people showed great interest in Miller's proposal, there were also those who argued that such a town would be isolating and would keep families from integrating into more mainstream communities. Finally, even though funding had been found and over 100 families expressed interest in buying a home in Laurent, the idea never materialized.

BOX 14.3 **"Our Signing Town: A journey towards building the world's first fully integrated town"**

(Blog post from www.laurentsd.com, November 20, 2006.)

Why are we so committed to this?

The answer: This small town will change everything.

The playing field will be leveled in:

- Politics
- Education
- Religion
- Recreation
- Social dynamics
- Health and mental health

In America, democracy and votes are almost everything. With them, you have power to change or shape your community to reflect the local values and needs. With education, we will have the ability to decide what happens to our children—deaf, hearing and hard of hearing—ourselves. Not somebody else. Us. We get to decide what standards our children will aspire to. We get to decide how they are taught about English, ASL, oralism, deaf culture, our history, and more. With religion, we can work to ensure that places of worship is [*sic*] totally accessible so not one will be left out. Socially, our community will evolve even more towards interdependence . . . as well as better understanding of who we are, why we do what we do and where we are going as a community. In health and mental health care, we will see breakthroughs in treatment because members of our community will finally understand why they are suffering and how to help themselves to a better life.

This is why we can not and will not give up.

Cochlear Implants

One of the most contested debates concerning deafness is the use of cochlear implants for children. A cochlear implant is a medical device that allows those who are profoundly deaf or hard of hearing to receive and process sound. The implant transmits auditory input as electric impulses through the auditory nerve to the brain, bypassing the ear and any of its damaged areas. The brain then processes these signals as sound. As the National Institute on Deafness and Other Communication Disorders (NIDCD) states, "An implant does not restore normal hearing. Instead, it can give a deaf person a useful representation of sounds in the environment and help him or her to understand speech" (2011). Both children and adults can be fitted with cochlear implants, and some models can work in children as young as 12 months old (NIDCD, 2011). (Please visit the Companion Website for illustrations and more information on the mechanics of a cochlear implant.)

14.19

Because children most often receive cochlear implants between the ages of two and six, they are able to adjust to processing sound and gain access to the hearing world at the earliest stages of their lives. Furthermore, the earlier a child learns a language, the easier it is for him/her to become a fluent and, perhaps, native speaker; this applies to any person, regardless of hearing capacity, and with any language, spoken or signed. Therefore, proponents of cochlear implants argue that if children are able to hear through the use of this technology, then why not give them the opportunity to hear for the majority of their lives and to process spoken language when it is easiest for them to do so? Additionally, 90% of deaf children are born to hearing households, and most parents want their children to have the same experiences in the hearing world that they did, experiences that the parents themselves can relate to and understand.

14.20

However, cochlear implantation is not only a medical issue but is a social, psychological, and cultural issue as well, and thus the debate is much more complex. The argument from the Deaf community is that the younger the children are when they receive cochlear implants, the less of an opportunity they have to recognize, understand, and embrace their deafness. Proponents of this view want deaf children to understand that their difference is not a deficiency, and they believe that deaf children should be able to choose for themselves whether or not they want to identify with mainstream society or with a cohesive Deaf culture. Thus, in this view, cochlear implants are not seen as a cure for deafness, because deafness is not seen as a condition that needs to be cured. Furthermore, the connection of age and language learning applies to ASL as well. If children are taught ASL at the earliest age possible, then they are more likely to be fluent in the language. Many who are against cochlear implants for children are not arguing that no one should obtain this technology; they understand there are benefits. However, they also stress that deaf children should be raised to understand their deafness and that these children should be given the opportunity to choose cochlear implants for themselves later in life. There are also those in the Deaf community who view the increased use of cochlear implants as an attack on Deaf culture itself. As more people are disassociated from the Deaf community, not only would this minority culture be eliminated, but the use of ASL would also die out.

14.21

Deaf President Now

In March 1988, protests broke out at Gallaudet University after the Board of Trustees announced Dr. Elisabeth Zinser, who is hearing, as the school's seventh president. Arguing that it was time for a deaf president at Gallaudet, students locked and barricaded gates, forcing the university to close. The protesters made several demands, including the resignation of both the president and the chair of the board of trustees. After several days of continued protests—and significant media attention—their demands were met. Dr. Zinser stepped down, and the board named Dr. I. King Jordan as the first deaf president of the university. Dr. Jordan, who continued to serve as Gallaudet's president until 2006, stepped into the position with one clear message: "A deaf person can do anything a hearing person can, except hear" (*Deaf Mosaic*, 1988). Since then, the slogan "Deaf President Now" (DPN) has become synonymous with self-determination and empowerment for deaf and hard of hearing people everywhere (Deaf President Now, 2013).

14.22

CONCLUSION

In this chapter, we have presented the history, structure, and social context of American Sign Language, a language created specifically for Deaf communities within the United States that has become an important marker of Deaf culture and unity. ASL is used by a wide range of people, both hearing and deaf, and interest in ASL has grown significantly over the last few decades. According to the Modern Language Association's report on languages taught in higher education, the number of students studying ASL in colleges and universities has increased dramatically—from 1,602 in 1990 to 91,763 in 2009—making it the fourth most studied language, after Spanish, French, and German (MLA, 2010).

As more people study ASL, more people will be able to recognize it for the complex language that it is. This is especially important in that ASL is often misunderstood to be a signed version of English or a simple use of hands and body to mimic individual concepts. Additionally, as researchers learn more about the grammatical structure of ASL and sociolinguistic variation within it, they are able not only to better understand ASL itself, but also to arrive at a broader knowledge of all linguistic systems. A comprehensive theory of language must take into account the structure, cognition, and usage of ASL and other signed systems.

Finally, the linguistic study of the language has helped those who use it to recognize the power of their own communication. As Garretson (1980) says: "To know, once and for all, that our 'primitive' and 'ideographic gestures' are really a formal language on par with all other languages of the world is a step towards pride and liberation" (as quoted in McCaskill et al., 2011, p. 3). And as Mathur and Napoli (2011, p. 6) state, "acquiring language is a human right that most people enjoy without struggle." For those who cannot hear spoken language, the use of an independent, authoritative signed language is invaluable.

DISCUSSION AND RESEARCH QUESTIONS

1. Using the examples presented in this chapter, or by finding others in another source, explain how the term *accent* can be applied to ASL.
2. Analyze the connection between language and identity by comparing and contrasting the use of American Sign Language and African American English.
3. Choose one of the issues surrounding ASL and Deaf America for a class debate. Possible choices include cochlear implants, oralism versus sign language education, or the Deaf President Now movement. While you can start with the information presented in this chapter, there is a great deal of information on both sides of these issues presented in a variety of academic and popular sources.
4. What does the discussion on cochlear implants say about a critical period for language acquisition?
5. There is a significant amount of research on other sign languages from around the world. Choose one of these languages and investigate either its structure or its sociohistorical development. (We recommend looking into Nicaraguan Sign Language.) A full list of sign languages can be found at www.ethnologue. com/subgroups/deaf-sign-language.

15 Official English

1. Does the United States need an official language?

2. Why should the US make English its official language?

3. How many states have declared English as their official language?

4. Does one need to know English to become a US citizen?

5. What is the connection between an official language and national identity?

6. What is the connection between English and an American identity?

OVERVIEW

In this chapter, we explore the question of whether English should be made the official language of the United States, and we examine the complex set of concepts that are incorporated into the varied responses to this question. First, we discuss the idea that language is a reflection of national identity and the belief of some that a country must be linguistically homogeneous in order to be politically unified. Second, we present a history of key Official English legislation in the United States, at both the state and federal levels, and we investigate the history of legislative support for minority languages. Third, we examine both sides of this, often heated, debate by presenting several of its key arguments, both pro and con. Overall, this investigation reveals that facts about language and language use quickly become intertwined with nonlinguistic issues such as national identity, immigration history, American politics, and economic policies; as such, this chapter exposes the ways in which language becomes politicized.

COMMON MYTHS

> *English is the official language of the United States.*

> *All countries have official languages.*

> *English will quickly lose prominence in the United States unless it is supported through Official English legislation.*

> *When one language is declared as official, it automatically becomes illegal to use any other language.*

> *A country can have only one official language.*

INTRODUCTION

15.1

The aim of this chapter is to outline the core issues of the Official English debate as well as to provide readers with enough information to think critically about both the issue and the conversations surrounding it. We provide facts about the English language, US history, and nationalism and contextualize the debate historically as well as contemporarily. We hope that this discussion, combined with the level of knowledge about linguistic diversity in the United States that has been attained by reading this book, will help readers to make their own informed decisions about whether English should be the official language of the United States. That said, this is a highly complex issue and, as such, we will not be able to cover every aspect of the debate in this short chapter; however, there are many excellent sources available for any reader who wants to research this issue further. (Please see the Companion Website for a list of recommended readings.) At the same time, it is important for readers to bear in mind that there are also countless sources available to the public that present information that is, at best, misleading and, at worst, blatantly wrong. Therefore, we also strive to give readers enough information from both sides of the debate so that they are able to assess and critique the public discourse on the subject.

LANGUAGE AS A REFLECTION OF NATIONAL IDENTITY

English is not now, nor has it ever been, the official language of the United States. Early in the Colonial period, English emerged as the most dominant language in North America and maintained this position throughout the American Revolution and the development of a new nation. This prominence persists today and is evidenced by the vast majority of Americans who not only speak English but do so fluently and mono-lingually, as well as by the language's uncontested role in government and education. Despite this clear dominance, many Americans believe it is important, if not imperative, that the US government and its citizens take steps to support and maintain the prominence of English through official legislation.

For many, language is a marker of national identity and, as such, the use of one language by a population promotes unity and even assimilation. This view is clearly expressed by the linguist Jacob Grimm (of fairytale fame), who actually defined a country by its linguistic practices, claiming that "a nation is the totality of people who speak the same language" (1846; as cited in Townson, 1992, p. 92). For those who immigrate to a new land, the acquisition and use of the dominant language serve as a strong symbol of allegiance to their new home. In fact, the shift to a national language and the surrender of the familial language can even be seen as payment for the opportunity to immigrate (Wiley, 2004, p. 323).

Many countries around the world have chosen to make an official connection between language and nation. The United States, along with the United Kingdom and Australia, is in the minority in terms of countries that have not declared an official language. Interestingly, even without this official status, English is considered the dominant national language in each of these three countries. According to the CIA *World Factbook* (2013), not only have the majority of the world's recognized nation-states named official languages, but 50 countries have actually declared English as their official language. However, Crawford notes:

> So far, no country has designated English as its *sole* official language, with legal restrictions on the use of other languages by government. Most nations where English is *an* official language—such as Canada, India, the Philippines, and South Africa—are officially bilingual or multilingual. That is, they grant legal protections for speakers of languages in addition to English.
>
> (2008, p. 1; emphasis in original)

The connection between language and national identity has been at the foreground of the debate on Official English in the US since the founding of the country. As we saw in Chapter 8, John Adams and Noah Webster made direct connections between language and national identity, particularly with regard to a standard English ideology. While prolific in their writing on this issue, Adams and Webster were not of the majority opinion and, thus, no declaration of official language was made during the creation of early American policy. As is true in other post-colonial nations, declaring the language of a former colonial master as official would have been ideologically difficult for early Americans. If language represents national unity, then an early declaration of Official English would have been viewed as evidence of a continued positive relationship with England, and its acceptance would have presented a true conundrum for many American patriots. Accordingly, the Founding Fathers made only one official statement about language, although it is a highly significant one: "Congress shall make no law . . . abridging the freedom of speech . . ." (US Constitution, Amendment 1). It must be noted, however, that the Bill of Rights does not explicitly limit this right to any specific language.

While the Founding Fathers chose to not legislate an official connection between language and an American identity, a direct link between language and nationality is fostered through the requirements for US citizenship. In what can be framed as either a pointed statement of American identity or a gatekeeping function to deny entry to certain types of immigrants, the 1906 Naturalization Act set the first language requirement. Dated June 29, 1906, c. 3592, sec. 8 of the Naturalization Act states the following as conditions of citizenship:

15.2

> That no alien shall hereafter be naturalized or admitted as a citizen of the United States who can not speak the English language: Provided, That this requirement shall not apply to aliens who are physically unable to comply therewith, if they are otherwise qualified to become citizens of the United States: And provided further, That the requirements of this section shall not apply to any alien who has prior to the passage of this Act declared his intention to become a citizen of the United States in conformity with the law in force at the date of making such declaration: Provided further, That the requirements of section eight shall not apply to aliens who shall hereafter declare their intention to become citizens and who shall make homestead entries upon the public lands of the United States and comply in all respects with the laws providing for homestead entries on such lands.
>
> (Mallory, 1914, p. 1778)

Here, not only does the Naturalization Act officially promote the use of English, but it implies that knowledge of English is a fundamental requirement for American citizenship—that is, unless one is willing to homestead.

English language skills continue to be a part of the standard requirements to become a US citizen today. On the path to citizenship, applicants must pass two tests: a civics test and an English language test. According to the US Citizenship and Immigration Services Policy Manual:

A naturalization applicant must only demonstrate an ability to read, write, speak, and understand words in ordinary usage. Ordinary usage means comprehensible and pertinent communication through simple vocabulary and grammar, which may include noticeable errors in pronouncing, constructing, spelling, and understanding completely certain words, phrases, and sentences.

An applicant may ask for words to be repeated or rephrased and may make some errors in pronunciation, spelling, and grammar and still meet the English requirement for naturalization. An officer should repeat and rephrase questions until the officer is satisfied that the applicant either fully understands the question or is unable to understand English.

(USCIS Policy Manual, n.d.)

15.3

Therefore, while some proficiency in English must be demonstrated, fluency or even high-level proficiency is not required. Furthermore, the English requirement can be waived for those who meet certain age or medical criteria (USCIS, n.d., "Exemptions & Accommodations"). Fewer than 100 words are listed as requirements for the US Naturalization Test; Table 15.1 presents a selection of these vocabulary items. In other words, even though English is supported by the path to US citizenship, complete knowledge of English is not required. Thus, we should ask: To what extent does the citizenship test support or promote the connection between language and an American

15.4

TABLE 15.1 Selected vocabulary required for the US Naturalization Test

Civics	People	Holidays
American Indians	John Adams	Memorial Day
Bill of Rights	Abraham Lincoln	Independence Day
Capital	George Washington	Labor Day
Citizen/Citizens		Columbus Day
Civil War	**Places**	Thanksgiving
Congress	Alaska	
Father of Our Country	America	**Other**
Flag	California	Pay
Freedom of speech	Canada	Dollar bill
Government	Mexico	Vote
President	New York City	Elects
Right	United States	Red
Senators	US	White
State/States	Washington, DC	Blue

Source: Adapted from US Citizenship & Immigration Services, "Study Materials for the English Test."

identity? Does the vocabulary that is included suggest that knowledge of these English terms is necessary to understand and/or participate in American democracy? Does it suggest that one must know English to understand what it is to be American?

Regardless of the level of language proficiency tested, *any* requirement of English is interpreted by some as a strong statement of support for all immigrants to learn English. The requirement is also seen as an overt symbol of the link between linguistic, cultural, and political assimilation. As immigrants take steps to learn English, they take steps toward becoming "true" Americans. As stated by Teddy Roosevelt: "No man can be a good citizen if he is not at least in the process of learning to speak the language of his fellow citizens" (as quoted in Miller, 2011, p. 34).

15.5

15.6

15.7

BOX 15.1 **Nuestro Himno: "Our Anthem"**

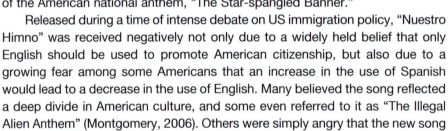

In 2006, there was a brief, yet intense, controversy surrounding the release of "Nuestro Himno," a Spanish language rendition of the American national anthem, "The Star-spangled Banner."

Released during a time of intense debate on US immigration policy, "Nuestro Himno" was received negatively not only due to a widely held belief that only English should be used to promote American citizenship, but also due to a growing fear among some Americans that an increase in the use of Spanish would lead to a decrease in the use of English. Many believed the song reflected a deep divide in American culture, and some even referred to it as "The Illegal Alien Anthem" (Montgomery, 2006). Others were simply angry that the new song was not an exact translation of the English version of the song.

Proponents of "Nuestro Himno" claimed that the new version would allow for Spanish-speaking Americans not yet fluent in English to better understand the message behind the song. They argued that instead of reflecting two disparate identities, the two versions unified both English and Spanish speakers under a singular message of American patriotism. Furthermore, as Miller (2011) points out, Spanish translations of the anthem have been around since 1919: "Official and unofficial translations of 'The Star-spangled Banner' circulated in the late nineteenth and early twentieth centuries in German, Latin, Yiddish, French, and Spanish" (p. 4).

Incidentally, "The Star-spangled Banner" was written in 1814 when Francis Scott Key crafted new lyrics to the melody of an old English drinking song called "To Anacreon in Heaven." His work became the national anthem of the United States in 1931.

Henry Ford was another well-known supporter of the idea that English is a crucial part of an American identity, and the school that was set up for his immigrant factory workers made an assimilated citizenry one of its primary goals. Along with lectures on morality and hygiene, employees were given free (albeit mandatory) English and citizenship classes. In fact, "Ford's English School provided basic citizenship and language training for so many immigrants, that the US Naturalization Service counted graduation from the Ford English School as meeting most of the requirements needed to take the citizenship exam" (The Henry Ford). Even the graduation ceremony itself was unabashedly symbolic of American cultural and linguistic assimilation:

> Graduates of Ford's English School wearing their "native dress" descend into a large pot labeled "The American Melting Pot." After going through a virtual smelting process, the immigrant's identity was boiled away, leaving a new citizen to emerge from the pot wearing American clothes and waving American flags.
>
> (The Henry Ford, http://collections.thehenryford.org/ Collection.aspx?objectKey=254569)

THE "MELTING POT" OF THE ENGLISH SCHOOL OF THE FORD MOTOR COMPANY AT DETROIT

FIGURE 15.1 The Melting Pot Ceremony at Ford English School, July 4, 1917.

Source: From the collections of The Henry Ford: P.O.7227/THF 106-481. Reprinted with permission.

As we have seen, the connection between language and national identity is not only a belief strongly held by many, but is also a notion fostered in various ways throughout US history. Even with such support, however, English has never been declared the official language of the United States. Of course, this does not mean the issue has been ignored altogether. In the following section, we discuss several pieces of legislation presented at the federal and state levels with the aim of making English the official language.

HISTORY OF OFFICIAL ENGLISH LEGISLATION

Federal Legislation

The first federal proposal to make English the official language of the United States was introduced in 1982 when Senator S.I. Hayakawa (R-CA) added an amendment to a piece of immigration legislation (S. 2222). The amendment stated:

It is the sense of the Congress that-

(1) the English language is the official language of the United States, and

(2) no language other than the English language is recognized as the official language of the United States.

(As cited in U.S. English, www.us-english.org)

15.8

(A link to the complete piece of legislation as well as Senator Hayakawa's full speech to the Senate can be found on the Companion Website.) Despite significant support for the amendment, the legislation stalled as the immigration bill was never voted into law. Throughout his career, Senator Hayakawa continued to fight for Official English legislation, and in 1983 he founded the group "U.S. English," which describes itself as "the nation's oldest and largest non-partisan citizens' action group dedicated to preserving the unifying role of the English language in the United States" (www.us-english.org/).

15.9

Since then, official language legislation has been presented several times to Congress. (Please see the Companion Website for a full list of federal proposals.) The first congressional vote on Official English was held in 1996. Called the "English Language Empowerment Act," this law would have made English the "sole language of most federal documents, communications, and services" (Crawford, 2008, p. 2). It passed by a vote of 259 to 169 in the House of Representatives but failed to garner support in the Senate.

The most recent legislative proposal for Official English was the "English Language Unity Act." Originally written in 2007, this Act has been presented to the House and/or the Senate every two years, but it has never been passed into law. The most current version of the Act was presented concurrently before the House (H.R. 997) and the Senate (S. 464) in March 2013. The legislation reads:

> To declare English as the official language of the United States, to establish a uniform English language rule for naturalization, and to avoid misconstructions of the English language texts of the laws of the United States, pursuant to Congress' powers to provide for the general welfare of the United States and to establish a uniform rule of naturalization under article I, section 8, of the Constitution.
>
> (S. 464)

15.10

As written, the English Language Unity Act would "preserve and enhance" the role of English as the primary language of the United States as well as legislate that all official functions of the government are to be conducted in English. However, as stated in Section 163c of the bill, several "official functions of the government" are not included:

1. teaching of languages;
2. requirements under the Individuals with Disabilities Education Act;
3. actions, documents, or policies necessary for national security, international relations, trade, tourism, or commerce;
4. actions or documents that protect the public health and safety;
5. actions or documents that facilitate the activities of the Bureau of the Census in compiling any census of population;
6. actions that protect the rights of victims of crimes or criminal defendants; or
7. using terms of art or phrases from languages other than English.

> (http://beta.congress.gov/bill/113th-congress/
> senate-bill/464/text)

The House bill was referred to the House Judiciary Subcommittee on Immigration and Border Security in April 2013, and the Senate bill was referred to the Committee on Homeland Security and Governmental Affairs. Neither bill was ever presented for a vote.

State Legislation

English has never been declared an official language of the United States at the federal level, but 30 states have passed their own independent language legislation (see Figure 15.2). Two of these states—Alaska and Hawaii—actually have multiple official languages. Alaska recognizes not only English but also 20 indigenous languages as official. In Hawaii, English is co-official with Hawaiian. (Note that Hawaiian is different from Hawaiian Creole, which was discussed in Chapter 13.) Furthermore, there are three additional states—New Mexico, Oregon, and Washington—that do not have

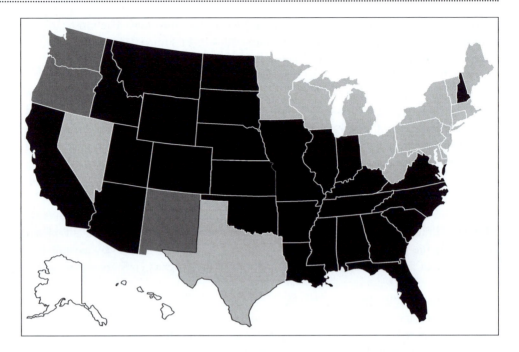

FIGURE 15.2 Official English legislation, by state (black = Official English; light gray = No language legislation; dark gray = English plus; white = Multiple official languages).

15.11

Official English laws but have passed "English Plus" resolutions that officially endorse multilingualism. (Please see the Companion Website for links to passed or pending legislation for each state.)

As discussed in Chapters 10 and 11, non-English languages have played significant roles in the early political and legislative histories of several states. Some of the earliest state language legislation was not concerned with the promotion of English only but was actually implemented in order to support the rights of other languages. For example, the first constitution of California (1849) required that all statutes be translated into Spanish. Additionally, for many years after it achieved statehood, Louisiana functioned bilingually; in fact, several of the state's officials, including one of its early governors, spoke only French (Crawford, 2008). Of course, even in the early history of the US most official language laws were implemented specifically for the purpose of supporting and encouraging the prominence of English only. The US "generally withheld statehood from territories until they contained English-speaking majorities," as it did in the cases of Michigan and New Mexico (Baron, 1990, p. xv). Additionally, the boundaries for Colorado, Arizona, and Nevada were drawn to ensure that their populations were primarily English-speaking (Baron, 1990, p. xv).

Of the states with current legislation in place, Nebraska has the oldest Official English legislation, having passed it in 1920. Another early adopter of this kind of legislation, Illinois made "American" instead of English the official language in 1923. In 1969, this law was "quietly amended" to read Official *English* (Baron, 1990, p. 130).

Of course, not every state that has voted on the issue has passed Official English legislation. In 2008, Ohio passed an Official English bill in the House by a simple majority, but it was never voted on in the Senate. Moreover, some states, such as New Jersey, have introduced legislation that never reached a vote. For other states, the passage of such legislation required multiple attempts. For example:

> a 1988 ballot initiative in Arizona mandated: "This state shall act in English and no other language." The measure was so extreme that it even applied to state legislators, who were forbidden to communicate with constituents in any language but English. It passed narrowly but was later ruled unconstitutional and never took effect. Arizona voters adopted a less restrictive version of Official English in 2006.
>
> (Crawford, 2008, p. 9)

Certain cities and counties have also felt the need to legislate language locally, even in states that have already passed Official English legislation. In 2009, the city of Nashville, Tennessee, rejected a ballot to make English official. In contrast, Cherokee County, Georgia, unanimously passed the Cherokee County English Language Ordinance to preserve and enhance the role of English as the common language. English was already the official language at the state level when each of these local-level bills was presented.

15.12

Although many states (or local governments) have adopted Official English legislation, the scope and application of these laws differ from state to state. A study conducted by U.S. English (2006) reports that in 2005, 45 states offered driver's license exams in languages other than English. There is a wide range in the number of languages in which these exams are offered, from two (in Colorado, Nebraska, and Texas, among others) to 32 (in California) (U.S. English, www.usenglish.org/view/305). In fact, the question of whether to offer driver's license tests in multiple languages is itself a contentious issue, and debates on the issue are heated. While some see these tests as a positive step toward minority language support, others view them as a disincentive for immigrants to learn English and integrate fully into American society. The Chairman of U.S. English, Mauro E. Mujica, even called the number of languages in which states offer driver's license exams "a barometer of multilingual government at the state level" (U.S. English, 2006). (Refer to the Companion Website for information on one former gubernatorial candidate in Alabama who made the elimination of multilingual driver's license exams a core part of his campaign platform.) Alternatively, some argue that offering such accommodations as drivers' tests in the native language of people applying for them actually helps immigrants assimilate

15.13

15.14

more quickly into American society and allows "the government to communicate with those who do not speak English to promote compliance with laws" (Wiley, 2010, p. 264).

Meyer v. State of Nebraska

Often referenced in discussions of English as the official language as well as discussions of foreign language education, the US Supreme Court case *Meyer v. State of Nebraska* (1923) is an example of language legislation at both the state and federal levels. The case drew serious attention in 1920, when a parochial school instructor was convicted of teaching a collection of Bible stories in German at a time when Nebraska law stated: "No person, individually or as a teacher, shall, in any private, denominational, parochial or public school, teach any subject to any person in any language other than the English language" (as cited in *Meyer v. State of Nebraska*, 1923). The law also dictated that the instruction of non-English languages could be offered only to children who had passed the eighth grade. The law did not apply to ancient or dead languages, such as classical Greek, Hebrew, or Latin, but did apply to modern languages, and as the law was written at the end of World War I, it most likely targeted the use of German specifically.

The Nebraska State Supreme Court upheld the original 1920 ruling, which focused on the connection between language and a national ideology. The Court stated:

> It is said the purpose of the legislation was to promote civic development by inhibiting training and education of the immature in foreign tongues and ideals before they could learn English and acquire American ideals, and "that the English language should be and become the mother tongue of all children reared in this State."
>
> (107 Neb. 657, as cited in *Meyer v. State of Nebraska*, 1923)

Thus, the Court not only upheld the principles of Official English legislation but also reaffirmed the position that foreign languages could interfere with American ideals.

Ultimately, the ruling was overturned in 1923 when the US Supreme Court held that the law was in conflict with the Fourteenth Amendment because it did not apply equally to all people and thus unfairly targeted language minorities. (Please see the Companion Website for the text of the Fourteenth Amendment.) As the Court stated: "The protection of the Constitution extends to all, to those who speak other languages as well as to those born with English on the tongue" (*Meyer v. State of Nebraska*, 1923). Furthermore, while noting the communicative benefits of a shared language, the Court also recognized the problems with this type of control over language use and language learning:

15.15

Perhaps it would be highly advantageous if all had ready understanding of our ordinary speech, but this cannot be coerced by methods which conflict with the Constitution—a desirable end cannot be promoted by prohibited means.

(Meyer v. State of Nebraska, 1923)

As such, *Meyer v. Nebraska* is often cited in discussions challenging the constitutionality of Official English legislation.

15.16

Having reviewed some of the Official English legislation that has been proposed at the federal and state levels, we recognize that the actual wording of individual bills and laws varies significantly, thus affecting what is actually covered by these measures. As such, it is crucial to read the exact phrasing of the documents in order to understand the scope and reach of any legislation. Furthermore, we also recognize that there is no unified view of Official English within the United States, and this division points to the myriad arguments both for and against that underlie discussions of Official English legislation.

ARGUMENTS FOR AND AGAINST

This section presents several of the key arguments for and against the passage of English as the official language of the United States. There are numerous practical, political, and ideological arguments on both sides of the Official English debate, many of which are quite compelling. Please note that we have attempted to present each side objectively, and thus we do not problematize any of the arguments within each subsection. Furthermore, many of these arguments, like those pertaining to the economy, may represent either side, depending on how they are framed. Therefore, we ask readers to think through all of the arguments, weighing their strengths and weaknesses, and judging their soundness.

Pro Arguments

The most common and perhaps strongest argument for making English the official national language concerns the relationship between language and national identity. A unified citizenry is a core ideal of any nation, and a shared language is a strong symbol of a unified community. A unified nation does not necessarily index a homogeneous population—not everyone has to look or act alike—but, as history shows, a country that is fundamentally divided cannot function, and a population that does not speak the same language is divided. The United States is a country of immigrants who have come together to become a part of an American identity and, in the American melting pot, linguistic and cultural diversity are shed to create a unified whole. As Teddy Roosevelt (1919) said:

> We have room for but one language here and that is the English language, for we intend to see that the crucible turns our people out as Americans, of one American nationality, and not as dwellers in a pollyglot [*sic*] boardinghouse.

Many Americans recognize that their own families once went to great lengths to assimilate linguistically and culturally, but they fail to see current generations of immigrants taking similar steps. Thus, they believe that making English the official language of the United States would prompt immigrants to learn the language of their new country. Even though some English is required to obtain citizenship, there is still no language requirement for entering the country, and immigrants may be in the United States for several years before they have to demonstrate any kind of proficiency in English. This type of legislation would encourage immigrants to learn English as early as possible, and thus, having acquired the language, they could then serve as models for other immigrants to do the same. Additionally, support for the use of other languages allows immigrants to remain isolated from the rest of the country. Not only

---

BOX 15.2 Language Disunity in Quebec

An example of multilingualism and national disunity often referenced in Official English debates is the language situation in the Canadian province of Quebec. The majority of the population of Quebec is French speaking and is culturally as well as linguistically distanced from the rest of English-speaking Canada. In fact, the citizens of Quebec voted on a referendum in 1995 that, if passed, would have counted as the province's first step toward becoming an independent state. The referendum failed, but barely, as the vote was 49.4% for and 50.6% against, showing a strong division within the population (CNN, 1995). While no similar referenda have been voted on since 1995, an increase in overt animosity toward English has become apparent in recent years: "Quebec's ruling Parti Quebecois is pushing a new law through the provincial parliament that would further reduce the use of English in schools, hospitals and shops" (Mallinder, 2013). However, citizens of the province continue to be divided on the issue:

> a number of elite institutions on both sides of the linguistic divide, including the Quebec Bar Association, the Human Rights Commission and the province's 48 post-secondary colleges, have come out against the proposed law, warning the changes will trample on individual rights.
>
> (Mallinder, 2013)

would Official English send a message that everyone in the United States should share a single language, but such legislation would also explicitly support English as the principal language.

Another core argument in support of declaring Official English pertains to the economy; specifically, the US government would be able to save extraordinary amounts of money if it no longer had to pay for services and documents in multiple languages. For example, translators, particularly good translators, cost money. A 2009 report found that the United States had spent $4.5 billion "on outsourced language services since 1990" (Kelly et al., 2009, as cited in Common Sense Advisory, 2010). Instead of spending billions of dollars on translation services, the US could use the money saved by reducing these costs to fund English courses for those who need them. Similarly, governmental paperwork would be streamlined, and greater efficiency in government is always a worthy goal. Furthermore, an increase in the number of proficient English speakers in the US would reduce the need for translators for emergency services, for health care, and in the judicial system, areas in which inaccurate translation can actually mean life or death.

An additional economic argument in favor of Official English is that immigrants who know English have greater economic opportunities than those who do not. Simply stated, immigrants with English proficiency are able to get better jobs. According to Educational Testing Services, in 1999 "the average employed immigrant who spoke English very well earned $40,741, more than double the $16,345 earned by immigrants who did not speak English at all" (as cited by U.S. English, www.us-english.org/userdata/file/FactsandFigures.pdf). Even when jobs are scarce, having English skills increases the employment opportunities available to an individual. A good, steady job allows one to integrate more fully into society.

As a primarily linguistic argument, English should be the official language in order to promote ease of communication. If everyone spoke English, then citizens would be able to understand one another, as day-to-day communication is easier if everyone

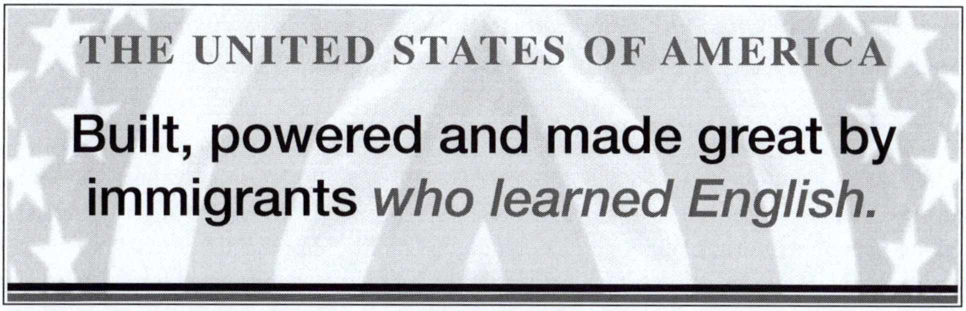

THE UNITED STATES OF AMERICA
Built, powered and made great by immigrants *who learned English.*

FIGURE 15.3 Bumper sticker distributed by U.S. English.

Source: www.us-english.org/bumpersticker. Reprinted with permission.

speaks the same language. Additionally, while translation services can be helpful, they are not always accurate. A shared language eliminates the need for translators and the problems that arise with poor translation. Inability to communicate with the rest of the population is not only frustrating for those who do not know English; it also keeps them from being able to say what they mean or from stating what they truly believe, issues of fundamental importance for a functioning democracy. Moreover, the ability to communicate in English does not eliminate the possibility of communicating in other languages as well.

The action groups U.S. English and Pro English both stress that "Official English" is not the same as "English Only." As stated by Pro English:

15.17

> Having English as our official language simply means that for the government to act officially, or legally, it must communicate in English. It means the language of record is the English language, and that no one has a right to demand government services in any other language.

(www.proenglish.org/official-english/english-only.html)

Passing Official English legislation would not end the use of non-English languages: Other languages would continue to be taught in schools, people would be able to use whatever language they wanted to at home, and Official English would apply only to government and not to private businesses. In fact, Official English legislation generally has exceptions in place for public safety, national security, foreign language teaching, Native American languages, and ASL interpretation.

15.18

A final argument for making English the official language of the United States is that such legislation would not dramatically change life in America. From this perspective, the main goal of Official English is to maintain the status quo and to give primacy and support to that which is already dominant. Thus, it simply sends a message of encouragement to those who want to learn English rather than forcing severe changes. It would be like naming apple pie the official food of the United States: It would not mean that everyone had to eat apple pie or that apple pie was the only food that could be eaten but would simply recognize that apple pie held a special emblematic role in American culture. Thus, from this perspective, Official English legislation is primarily symbolic.

Con Arguments

While many see monolingualism as a representation of national unity, others view the act of officially giving one language primacy over others as inherently discriminatory against speakers of other languages. Those against making English the official language of the United States fail to see such legislation as a positive step toward national unity or a balanced economy. To them, it is instead a negative, reactionary response that indicates fear or resentment toward a new immigrant population. In fact, many debates about Official English closely follow other political discussions about immigration,

15.19

particularly in locations that are seeing or have recently seen large increases in new immigrant populations. Thus, many view official language policies as inherently xenophobic messages that say, "Conform or get out."

While the argument for national unity is strong, monolingualism does not necessarily equate to social and political unity. Moreover, multilingualism does not necessarily lead to national discord. In fact, in an analysis of 170 different nation-states, Fishman (1991) concluded that "linguistic heterogeneity could not predict either civil strife or gross national product." He found, instead, that "[c]ivil strife was related to long- and short-term deprivation and coercive power relationships" (as cited in Potowski, 2010, p. 12).

Even though the United States has seen an increase in immigration in recent decades, the two- to three-generational shift to English (discussed in Chapter 9) is still the dominant pattern; immigrants are learning English on their own, without a push from Official English legislation. Additionally, according to Potowski:

> Fears about immigrants not learning English are often accompanied by what we might call the "my grandparent" myth. It goes something like this: "When my grandparents immigrated from [name of country], they did not need bilingual education or special services in their language. They simply worked hard and learned the language. Today's immigrants want everything handed to them." What this sentiment ignores, however, is that life in the 1800s and early 1900s required very little knowledge of English to make a decent wage in the areas of manufacturing where many immigrants worked. High levels of literacy, or even a high school diploma, were not necessary as they are today. It is very likely that this person's grandparents would be at a much greater disadvantage in the twenty-first century as immigrants to the USA without English abilities.

> (2010, p. 5)

Therefore, contemporary fears of current immigrants not assimilating in the same way or within the same time frame as previous generations are generally unfounded. What appears to be greater use of English among immigrants of previous generations was more likely the outcome of the standard generational shift to English at a time of light immigration rather than a refusal to learn English by present-day immigrants.

Another argument against Official English claims that because there is no inherent link between language use and citizenship, English proficiency is not a requirement for American patriotism. While it is true that some knowledge of English is required to become a naturalized citizen in the United States, as was shown above, the citizenship exam assesses only minimal proficiency. Therefore, naturalized citizens are not required to function solely in English in all aspects of life, such as in the legal system, the health care system, basic tax forms, or even driver's license tests, that is, areas that are generally affected by Official English laws. Furthermore, even if the citizenship test did require a high level of English proficiency, or even fluency, would Official English laws be applicable to those who have not yet become naturalized citizens? This question is not insignificant; in 2012 alone, over one million people (1,031,631) were given Legal Permanent Resident status, that is, their "green card" (Monger & Yankay, 2013), and 757,434 people became naturalized citizens (Lee, 2013). Requiring English proficiency for every one of these individuals would be impossible, unless English tests were distributed at all border crossings, which is, at the very least, impractical.

As stated in the previous section, the Official English debate also includes linguistic arguments based on the practical needs of communication. Opponents of Official English do indeed recognize that communication would be easier if everyone in a community shared the same language; however, they also recognize that this type of legislation would reduce support for those who are still learning English. As mentioned in Chapter 2, the acquisition of a second language is difficult; it takes time, perhaps many years, for anyone—but particularly for adults—to become proficient in a second language. Translators, bilingual documents, and state-sponsored English as a Second Language (ESL) courses help all citizens, regardless of their language skills, to function together in a singular society. Stripping non-English languages from any governmentally run system keeps patriotic Americans who are not fully proficient in English out of the democratic process. Not only does it hinder limited-English speakers in their ability to read necessary documents, it also sends the message that unless you speak English, your voice and ideas are unwanted.

Some argue that official language legislation gives individuals a legal coatrack on which to hang their own linguistic (or ethnic) prejudices. Although supporters of Official English legislation are adamant that speakers will continue to possess the right to use any language they choose and that any restrictions on language use will apply only to governmental administration, their assertions may be more abstract than real. According to linguist Dennis Baron (n.d.), "[f]or the past two centuries, proponents of official-English have sounded two separate themes, one rational and patriotic, the other emotional and racist." Negative stereotypes of immigrants and disapproving statements about minority languages are already prominent; if English were to be given official status, such legislation could easily be interpreted as a referendum of support for these negative reactions. While many may try to argue that this is simply a hypothetical concern, the following story, which was recently told to one of this book's authors, shows the reality of the situation:

> While walking down the street in Georgia, where English is the official language, two speakers of American English were having a conversation in French and were met with the following proclamation from a fellow pedestrian: "You need to learn to speak [expletive] English. This is America," and this was immediately followed by advice for the speakers to "learn the language" or "leave the country."
>
> (Kris Knisely, personal communication)

Of course, one cannot claim that Official English legislation is solely responsible for such comments, as they occur even in places where official language legislation does not exist; however, opponents argue that this type of legislation has the potential of being interpreted as supporting, if only implicitly, the public expression of these views and, in some cases, may even encourage discrimination against those who do not speak American English natively.

In such cases, the use of a language other than English is viewed as a shibboleth—a catalyst or justification for categorizations of "us" versus "them." Consequently, speakers are profiled based on their use of non-English languages, or even on their use of non-native accented English. For example, because language is often entwined in discussions of US immigration and citizenship, language use is sometimes used to index presumed immigration status. (For an example of such linguistic profiling by police in Arizona, please see the Companion Website.) While xenophobic reactions to languages and their users may not be the direct intention of Official English legislation, opponents argue that they are often an indirect result. As stated in Crawford (2008), "Language-restrictionist laws are never just about language. Inevitably they reflect attitudes toward—and authorize discrimination against—the speakers of certain languages" (p. 5).

15.20

From an economic perspective, proponents of Official English claim such legislation will save taxpayers money; however, opponents claim that such legislation will do more economic harm than good. For example, even though money might be saved on interpretation and translation services, this does not take into consideration the loss of jobs and wages to those who provide those services. According to the Bureau of Labor Statistics (2013), there were 58,400 interpreters and translators employed in the United States in 2010, with a projected increase of 24,600 by 2020. When jobs are lost, unemployment benefits increase and both consumer spending and tax revenue decrease, negatively affecting the economy for the entire country. Thus, with regard to economic arguments about Official English legislation, opponents of these laws argue that the range of significant economic outcomes, based in a complex, integrated economy, must be taken into consideration.

As a cost-saving measure, Official English legislation often includes cuts to ESL programs, but some laws do include provisions for their support. However, these provisions can create further economic burdens. The Migration Policy Institute estimates that there are 5.8 million legal residents who need English language instruction in order to pass the US naturalization exam and participate in civic life:

> Based on an average of 110 hours of instruction to rise one level of English ability, it will require about 277 million hours of English language instruction a year, for six years, to bring all current adult LPRs [Lawful Permanent Residents] to a level of English proficiency needed to pass the naturalization test (for those age 25 and older) or to begin post-secondary education (for youths ages 17 to 24).
>
> (McHugh, Gelatt, & Fix, 2007, p. 6)

Even if only 50% of those who need English language instruction participated, such a program would cost $1.2 billion dollars per year for six years. Moreover, if the US were to extend such services to the estimated 6.4 million undocumented residents through legalization programs, an additional 319 million hours of language instruction and $2.9 billion a year for six years would also be necessary (McHugh et al., 2007, p. 9).

While the economic costs of Official English legislation are clearly substantial, the social costs are also significant. Loss of heritage languages can lead to linguistic insecurity and/or a loss of cultural identity. Instead of the intended outcome of assimilation into a new, solely American identity, such legislation may lead immigrants to feel displaced, as if they belong to neither their new nor old communities. With no linguistic support, social isolation could become unbearable, as immigrants are forced to remain on the periphery of American life. Conversely, many non-native English speakers, faced with feelings of displacement and isolation, might find even the smallest amount of linguistic support to be a compassionate gesture from their adopted country. One cannot forget that official language policy is both political and personal. The people it affects are just that—people. They are individuals with hopes, dreams, and feelings, rather than a set of statistics void of all emotion.

For some, the isolation of individuals from the rest of America is reason enough to oppose Official English, but official language legislation may also isolate the entire United States from the greater global community. It is imperative for Americans to demonstrate proficiency in languages other than English for a variety of reasons, not the least of which include issues of international business and national security. Multilingualism is a precious natural resource to be nurtured and grown, not an affliction to be treated or eradicated. Although English is spoken throughout the world, the majority of its speakers learn English as a second language (ESL). Furthermore, not many ESL speakers are fluent in (American) English. In order to ensure proper levels of communication with foreign nations, US citizens must learn to function in more than one language and to meet other speakers halfway. Rather than pushing its citizens toward English monolingualism, the United States should actually support American multilingualism.

If the US were to support the maintenance of non-English languages, it would have significant resources of bilingual speakers in, perhaps, hundreds of languages. However, instead of supporting the maintenance of non-English languages that are already spoken, the United States spends significant money, first, on educational programs that transition students to monolingual English in their younger years and, second, on teaching non-English ("foreign") languages to monolingual English speakers in later years. On this issue, Fishman argues that it is inconsistent and hypocritical for a country to support financially and politically native English speakers' acquisition and use of non-English languages while simultaneously discouraging native heritage speakers' own language maintenance (2004). Native speakers not only know their languages fluently, they also understand and recognize the cultural nuances of communicating with someone from a different background. The most appropriate candidates for positions that require intercultural communication are the same individuals who are most pressured to stop speaking their native languages. Thus, discouraging the maintenance of native languages does a disservice not only to the individuals who lose their native languages but also to the United States as a whole, economically, politically, socially, and linguistically.

Support of multilingualism in the United States—that is, encouraging the population to become fluent in English as well as to maintain their heritage languages—is also of great benefit to our national security. After 9/11, the US scrambled to find fluent Arabic speakers and, over the course of the next decade, spent significant monies and resources on language training. As a result, the US government has started to acknowledge the necessity of American multilingualism. In 2005, the Department of Defense presented their "Defense Language Transformation Roadmap" in which they officially recognized:

> the reality that the Department of Defense needs a significantly improved organic capability in emerging languages and dialects, a greater competence and regional area skills in those languages and dialects, and a surge capability to rapidly expand its language capabilities on short notice.
>
> (p. 1)

In 2006, the US State Department created the National Security Language Initiative (NSLI) to "dramatically increase the number of Americans learning critical need foreign languages such as Arabic, Chinese, Russian, Hindi, Farsi, and others through new and expanded programs from kindergarten through university and into the workforce" (Powell & Lowenkron, 2006).

15.21

One final argument presented by opponents of Official English is the futility of such legislation, as they contend that Official English legislation will do nothing more than maintain the status quo. While proponents argue that Official English legislation promotes the shift to monolingual English, contemporary research shows that this linguistic shift is already underway, even without a push from linguistic legislation. For example, the vast majority of people in the US who report speaking another language at home also report that they speak English "well" or "very well." In other words, even without specific legislation, English currently functions as the official language, just as it has throughout US history. As Miller notes:

15.22

> No language (or form of a language) has ever been designated an official national speech or "standard" in the United States, but even a cursory glance at the best-selling [literature] anthologies and literary histories seems to imply that only one language has been used to convey Americans' ambitions and to tell their stories.
>
> (2011, p. 18)

Therefore, why spend significant economic, political, and social resources to pass legislation that really won't do much, particularly when negative social outcomes are such a strong possibility?

Even Teddy Roosevelt, who was stringently against maintaining multilingualism and non-assimilation, acknowledged that "it would be a duty to see that they [immigrants who were not already proficient in English] were given ample opportunity to learn to read and write" (Miller, 2011, p. 48). Of course, Roosevelt also said that immigrants should be deported if they did not learn English within a certain amount of time.

15.23

LEGISLATIVE SUPPORT FOR MINORITY LANGUAGE SPEAKERS

A central concern within the Official English debate is the type of support granted—or not granted—to those with limited English proficiency (LEP). Some individuals on both sides of the debate believe the government shoulders zero obligation to provide language services to those who are not English proficient. Others argue that if the government were to require (or even recommend) English language skills, then it follows that the government should bear the responsibility for encouraging ESL and offering English acquisition courses as well as translation and interpretation services.

The following are examples of US legislative measures developed to offer language support to those with limited English proficiency:

15.24

- *Improving Access to Services for Persons with Limited English Proficiency*: Executive Order 13166 was signed into law by President Clinton in 2000. This order, which was reaffirmed by President Bush in 2001, required all federal agencies "to make their programs accessible to limited-English proficient persons" (Crawford, 2008, p. 10) and "to improve access to federally conducted and federally assisted programs and activities for persons who, as a result of national origin, are limited in their English proficiency" (Executive Order 13166, www.justice.gov/crt/about/cor/Pubs/eolep.php).
- *Language Access Act (LAA)*: Signed into law by DC Mayor Anthony Williams in 2004, the primary purpose of the LAA is "to provide equal access and participation to public services, programs and activities for residents of the District of Columbia who are Limited or Non-English proficient." Through this law, the Office on Latino Affairs (OLA) "has advocated to ensure that culturally and linguistically competent city services are delivered to the Spanish-speaking residents of the District" (http://ola.dc.gov/page/language-access-and-advocacy-program).

15.25
15.26

- *Language Access Executive Order*: NYC Executive Order 120 was signed by New York Mayor Michael Bloomberg in 2008. In this order, all city agencies must take "reasonable steps to develop and implement agency-specific language assistance plans regarding LEP persons" and "provide services in languages based on at least the top six LEP languages spoken by the population of New York City." It also allows for the translation of essential public documents and for interpretation services (Executive Order 120, www.nyc.gov/html/om/pdf/2008/pr282-08_eo_120. pdf). As stated by Bloomberg:

> The fundamental basis of government is its interaction with its citizens. If people don't know what we do, don't know what they should do, what the law requires them to do, don't know how to get services, all the money that we're spending providing those services, providing those laws, is meaningless.
>
> (As cited in Potowski, 2010, p. 8)

CONCLUSION

In this chapter, we examined several issues surrounding Official English legislation: language as a reflection of national identity, the history of Official English legislation in the United States, arguments for and against Official English, and legislation to support those with limited English proficiency. While the Official English movement has garnered increased prominence since the 1980s, it is by no means a new issue in the US. In fact, many of the same kinds of discussions that we consider contemporary were being held more than a century ago. As stated by Baron:

> the conditions producing today's official English movement have been present in the United States since before the country's founding two centuries ago, and the arguments both for and against official English have been repeated with slight variations and little concrete effect, since that time.
>
> (1990, p. xiii)

Even though the primary focus of this debate appears to be language, the question of Official English is not a solely linguistic matter. Rather, it centers on the connections between language, society, and nationalism. The discourse of Official English often conflates language and immigration (often illegal immigration), and highlights those aspects of society that language can represent, such as unity, diversity, and assimilation. It is a blend of many different, often contradictory, concerns. In fact, according to Baron (n.d.), "Official-English is an emotional issue for many people, involving questions of patriotism as well as racism, language loyalty as well as assimilation." Overall, Official English is a complex issue in which language continues to politicize and be politicized.

Some argue that the Official English debate reveals that language is not only politicized but also racialized, and they question the motivation behind such legislation.

Are these proposed laws really statements for American unity, are they proclamations that uphold xenophobic reactions, or do they reveal a yearning for an assimilated, nonchanging populace? Are we afraid we might not understand—and thus might not relate to—those around us? Or by arguing against a national language are some simply stirring up the melting pot?

Not only should we examine the motivations behind such laws, but once a piece of legislation is presented, it is imperative that we pay attention to how it is written. What aspects of government or society will Official English legislation affect? Are supports in place for citizens or residents with limited English proficiency? Are exemptions in place for the elderly or the illiterate, for Native American languages or ASL, for language instruction or national security? Does the legislation slash budgets or increase them? Are heritage languages dismissed or celebrated?

Finally, we ask our readers: Is it possible to create a law that both upholds English as a unifying language and supports the use of other languages? James Crawford, the president of the Institute for Language and Education Policy, argues:

> America needs English Plus—well developed skills in many languages to enhance international competitiveness and national security . . . Rather than attempting to stamp out language diversity with English Only laws, we should conserve and develop multiple language skills to encourage community harmony, foster cultural expression, and meet the nation's needs.

(2008, p. 11)

15.27

There are many strong and valid points on both sides of this debate, and we encourage you to think through the various, complex issues and linguistic facts when deciding which arguments best align with your own views of language and linguistic diversity in the United States. We also encourage you to remember the complexities of the issue should you be presented with the opportunity to vote on Official English.

DISCUSSION AND RESEARCH QUESTIONS

1. Ask 10 people why they believe English should or should not be the official language of the United States and analyze the responses they give. Are there any patterns in the types of arguments they make? Are particular concepts, such as unity, economy, or immigration introduced, and, if so, are they addressed by those on both sides of the debate or are they discussed only by one particular side?
2. Conduct research on the history of Official English legislation for your own state or local government. Make sure to look for legislation that did not pass or was not presented for a vote, as well as for bills that were made into law. You might also

want to see which other political, social, and economic debates or discussions coincided with the introduction of official language legislation.

3. Choose three pieces of Official English legislation, and compare and contrast the areas that are specifically affected (e.g., education, bilingual ballots, private business) as well as those that are excluded (e.g., emergency services, indigenous languages).

4. Look at the ads presented by U.S. English (www.us-english.org/view/29) and categorize the types of arguments they make. Are they primarily based on immigration, nationalism, or even on issues of language itself? Are they ideological, social, political, or economic?

5. Review the mission statement given by Pro English (proEnglish.org). Do you agree with their guiding principles? Does their agenda match their stated principles?

References

Adams, C. (1971). *Boontling: An American lingo*. Austin, TX: University of Texas Press.

Adams, J. (1780). *The revolutionary diplomatic correspondence of the United States, vol. 4, J. Adams to President of Congress*. Retrieved from www.pbs.org/speak/seatosea/official american/johnadams/#national.

Adams, M. (1999). Slayer slang (part 2). *Verbatim, The Language Quarterly* 24(4): 1–7.

Adamson, R. (2007). *The defence of French: A language in crisis?* Clevedon, UK and Buffalo, NY: Multilingual Matters.

Adone, D. (2012). *The acquisition of creole languages: How children surpass their input*. Cambridge: Cambridge University Press.

Aikhenvald, A. (2006). *Serial verb constructions in typological perspective*. In A.Y. Aikhenvald, & R.M.W. Dixon (Eds.) *Serial verb constructions: A cross-linguistic typology* (pp. 1–68). Oxford: Oxford University Press.

Albarran, A.B., & Hutton, B. (2009). *A history of Spanish language radio in the United States*. Denton, TX: The Center for Spanish Language Media, University of North Texas.

Albright, A. (2000). The productivity of infixation in Lakhota. In P. Munro (Ed.) *U.C.L.A. working papers in linguistics: Papers in Lakhota*.

Algeo, J. (2001). External history. In J. Algeo (Ed.) *The Cambridge history of the English language, vol. VI: English in North America* (pp. 1–58). Cambridge: Cambridge University Press.

Alim, H.S., & Baugh, J. (Eds.) (2007). *Talkin black talk: Language, education and social change*. New York: Teachers College Press, Columbia University.

Alim, H.S., & Smitherman, G. (2012). Obama's English. *The New York Times*, September 8.

Allen, H.B. (1973–1976). *Linguistic atlas of the Upper Midwest, vols. 1–3*. Minneapolis, MN: University of Minnesota Press.

American Heritage (2011). *American heritage dictionary of the English language* (5th ed.). Boston, MA: Houghton Mifflin Harcourt.

American Sign Language University (ASLU). Retrieved from lifeprint.com.

Anderson, B. (2003). *An acoustic study of southeastern Michigan Appalachian and African American Southern migrant vowel systems.* (Unpublished doctoral dissertation), University of Michigan, Ann Arbor.

Anderson, G.D.S. (1996). Interior Salish reduplication in a diachronic perspective. In *Proceedings of the twenty-second annual meeting of the Berkeley Linguistics Society: Special session on historical issues in Native American languages* (pp. 11–24), Berkeley, CA, February 16–19.

Anderton, D.L., Barrett, R.E., & Bogue, D.J. (1997). *The population of the United States* (3rd ed.). New York: The Free Press.

Angers, T. (1989). *The truth about the Cajuns.* Lafayette, LA: Acadian House Publishing.

Antieau, L.D. (2004). Language. In Rick Newby (Ed.) *The Greenwood encyclopedia of American regional cultures: The Rocky Mountain region* (pp. 255–285). Westport, CT: Greenwood Publishing.

Antieau, L.D. (2006). A distributional analysis of rural Colorado English. (Unpublished doctoral dissertation), University of Georgia, Athens.

Antieau, L.D. (2012). *Seeing double: Syntactic doubling phenomena in the Linguistic Atlas of the Middle Rockies.* Invited talk at the University of Mississippi Modern Languages Dept., Oxford, MS, February.

Antieau, L., & Darwin, C. (2013). Fatback and gunnysacks: Lexical variation in the Southeast and the middle Rockies. *Southern Journal of Linguistics* 37(2): 39–56.

Arab American Institute (2014). *Demographics.* Retrieved from www.aaiusa.org/pages/demographics/.

Atkins, J.D. (1887). *Annual report of the Commissioner of Indian Affairs to the Secretary of Interior for the year 1887.* Washington, DC: Government Printing Office.

Atwood, E.B. (1953). *A survey of verb forms in the eastern United States.* Ann Arbor, MI: University of Michigan Press.

Atwood, E.B. (1962). *The regional vocabulary of Texas.* Austin, TX: University of Texas Press.

Austin, A.D. (1984). *African Muslims in antebellum America: A sourcebook.* New York: Garland.

Bailey, G., & Tillery, J. (1996). The persistence of Southern American English. *Journal of English Linguistics* 24: 308–321.

Bakker, P. (1997). *A language of our own: The genesis of Michif, the mixed Cree–French language of the Canadian Metis.* New York: Oxford University Press.

Baldwin, J. (1979). If Black English isn't a language, then tell me, what is? *The New York Times,* July 29. Retrieved from www.nytimes.com/books/98/03/29/specials/baldwin-english.html.

Barck, O.T., & Lefler, H.T. (1958). *Colonial America.* New York: Macmillan.

Baron, D. (1990). *The English-only question: An official language for Americans?* New Haven, CT and London: Yale University Press.

Baron, N. (2000). *Alphabet to email: How written English evolved and where it's heading.* London: Routledge.

Baron, D. (n.d.). English only. *Do you speak American?* PBS. Retrieved from www.pbs.org/speak/seatosea/officialamerican/englishonly/.

Bauer, L. (1988). *Introducing linguistic morphology.* Edinburgh: Edinburgh University Press.

Baugh, J. (2006). Bridging the great divide (African American English). In W. Wolfram, & B. Ward (Eds.) *American voices: How dialects differ from coast to coast* (pp. 217–224). Malden, MA: Blackwell.

Benor, S.B. (2009). Jewish English: Description. *Jewish Language Research*. Retrieved from www.jewish-languages.org/jewish-english.html.

Bickerton, D. (1977). *Change and variation in Hawaiian English, vol. 2*. Honolulu, HI: Social Sciences and Linguistics Institute, University of Hawaii.

Bills, G.D. (1997). New Mexican Spanish: Demise of the earliest European variety in the United States. *American Speech* 72: 154–171.

Bills, G.D., & Vigil, N.A. (2008). *The Spanish language of New Mexico and southern Colorado: A linguistic atlas*. Albuquerque, NM: University of New Mexico Press.

Blake, N.M. (1972). *History of American life and thought*. New York: McGraw-Hill.

Boas, H.C. (2009). *The life and death of Texas German*. Durham, NC: Duke University Press.

Boorstin, D.J. (1958). *The Americans: The colonial experience*. New York: Random House.

Bowie, D. (2003). Early development of the card-cord merger in Utah. *American Speech* 78: 31–51.

Brandon, W. (2003). *The rise and fall of North American Indians: From prehistory through Geronimo*. Lanham, MD: Taylor Trade.

Bright, E. (1971). *A word geography of California and Nevada*. Berkeley, CA: University of California Press.

Bright, W. (1976). *Variation and change in language*. Stanford, CA: Stanford University Press.

Brown, V. (1991). Evolution of the merger of /ɪ/ and /ɛ/ before nasals in Tennessee. *American Speech* 66: 303–315.

Brown v. Board of Education, 347 U.S. 483 (1954).

Bucholtz, M. (2004). Language, gender, and sexuality. In E. Finegan, & J.R. Rickford (Eds.) *Language in the U.S.A.: Themes for the twenty-first century* (pp. 410–429). Cambridge: Cambridge University Press.

Bucholtz, M. (2011). "It's different for guys": Gendered narratives of racial conflict among white California youth. *Discourse and Society* 22(4): 385–402.

Buchstaller, I. (2001). *He goes* and *I'm like*: The new quotatives re-visited. Paper presented at the 30th annual conference on *New Ways of Analyzing Variation* (NWAV 30), Raleigh, NC, October 11–14. Retrieved from www.ling.ed.ac.uk/~pgc/archive/2002/proc02/buchstaller02.pdf.

Bureau of Labor Statistics, US Department of Labor (2013). *Occupational outlook handbook, 2012–13: Interpreters and translators*. Retrieved from www.bls.gov/ooh/media-and-communication/interpreters-and-translators.htm.

Burkette, A., & Antieau, L.D. (2012). Introduction: Variation, pattern, change, and choice—Targets of Linguistic Atlas query. *American Speech* 87: 373–377.

Butters, R.R. (2001). Grammatical structures. In J. Algeo (Ed.) *The Cambridge history of the English language, vol. VI: English in North America* (pp. 325–449). Cambridge: Cambridge University Press.

Butterworth, R.R., & Flodin, M. (1995). *The Perigee visual dictionary of signing* (3rd ed.). New York: Perigee.

Calloway, C.G. (1997). *New worlds for all: Indians, Europeans, and the remaking of Early America*. Baltimore, MD: The Johns Hopkins University Press.

Campbell, L. (1997). *American Indian languages: The historical linguistics of Native America*. Oxford: Oxford University Press.

Campbell, L. (1998). *Historical linguistics: An introduction* (2nd ed.). Cambridge, MA: MIT Press/Edinburgh University Press.

Carlson, P.H. (1998). *The Plains Indians.* College Station, TX: Texas A&M University Press.

Carranza, M.A., & Ryan, E.B. (1975). Evaluative reactions of bilingual Anglo and Mexican American adolescents toward speakers of English and Spanish. *International Journal of the Sociology of Language* 6: 83–104.

Carroll, L. (1871). *Through the looking-glass.* London: Macmillan.

Carter, P.M., Lynch, A., & Neal, D. (2013). Sociolinguistic and social psychological motivation for loss: Mapping the perception of Spanish and English among Miami Latinos. Paper presented at the LSA Annual Meeting, Boston, MA, January 5.

Carvalho, A.M. (2010). Portuguese in the U.S.A. In K. Potowski (Ed.) *Language diversity in the U.S.A.* (pp. 223–237). Cambridge: Cambridge University Press.

Carver, C.M. (1987). *American regional dialects: A word geography.* Ann Arbor, MI: University of Michigan Press.

Cassidy, F.G. (1961). *Jamaica talk: Three hundred years of the English language in Jamaica.* London: Macmillan.

Cassidy, F.G. (1993). Area lexicon: The making of DARE. In D.R. Preston (Ed.) *American dialect research* (pp. 94–105). Amsterdam: John Benjamins.

Cassidy, F.G. (1994). Gullah and the Caribbean connection. In M. Montgomery (Ed.) *The crucible of Carolina: Essays in the development of Gullah language and culture* (pp. 16–22). Athens, GA: University of Georgia Press.

Cassidy, F.G., & Hall, J.H. (1985). *Dictionary of American regional English.* Cambridge, MA: Belknap Press at Harvard University Press.

Central Intelligence Agency (CIA) (2013). *The world factbook.* Washington, DC: Central Intelligence Agency. Retrieved from www.cia.gov/library/publications/the-world-factbook/fields/2098.html.

Chambers, J. (1995). *Sociolinguistic theory.* Oxford: Blackwell.

Chang, I. (2003). *The Chinese in America: A narrative history.* New York: Penguin.

Charity Hudley, A.H., & Mallinson, C. (2011). *Understanding English language variation in U.S. schools.* New York: Teachers College Press.

Ching, M. (1982). The question intonation in assertions. *American Speech* 57: 95–107.

Chiu, K. (2008). Asian language newspapers in the United States: History revisited. CALA e-journal 9. Retrieved from http://cala-web.org/node/648.

Christian, D. (1991). The personal dative in Appalachian speech. In P. Trudgill, & J.K. Chambers (Eds.) *Dialects of English: Studies in grammatical variation* (pp. 11–19). London: Longman.

Chwat, S. (1994). *Speak up! American regional accent elimination: Learn to speak standard American English.* New York: Crown Publishers.

CNN (1995). Quebec vote is "a wake up call." CNN World News, October 31. Retrieved from www.cnn.com/WORLD/9510/canada/10-31/.

Coates, J. (1993). No gap, lots of overlap: Turn-taking patterns in the talk of women friends. In D. Graddol, J. Maybin, & B. Stierer (Eds.) *Research language and literacy in social context* (pp. 177–192). Cleveland, OH: Multilingual Matters.

Coates, J. (1996). *Women talk: Conversation between women friends.* Oxford: Blackwell.

Coles, F. (2011). Selectively, reluctantly global: The Isleños of Louisiana. *Globality Studies Journal*, 27 (October 29). Retrieved from http://globality.cc.stonybrook.edu/?p=227.

Common Sense Advisory. (2010). U.S. federal government spends US$4.5 billion on outsourced translation and interpreting services. January 7. Retrieved from www.commonsenseadvisory.com/Default.aspx?Contenttype=ArticleDet&tabID=64&moduleId=392&Aid=1076&PR=PR.

Craddock, J. (1981). New World Spanish. In C.A. Ferguson, & S.B. Heath (Eds.) *Language in the U.S.A.* (pp. 196–211). Cambridge: Cambridge University Press.

Crawford, J. (1990). Language freedom and restriction: A historical approach to the official language controversy language. In J. Reyhner (Ed.) *Effective language education practices and native language survival* (pp. 9–22). Choctaw, OK: Native American Language Issues.

Crawford, J. (1997). Language legislation in Louisiana. *Canards*. Retrieved from www.languagepolicy.net/archives/can-la.htm.

Crawford, J. (2008). Frequently asked questions about official English. Institute for Language and Education Policy, November. Retrieved from www.elladvocates.org/documents/englishonly/OfficialEnglishFAQ.pdf.

Crawford, J.M. (1975). Southeastern Indian languages. In J.M. Crawford (Ed.) *Studies in southeastern Indian languages* (pp. 1–120). Athens, GA: University of Georgia Press.

Crawford, J.M. (1978). *The Mobilian trade language.* Knoxville, TN: University of Tennessee Press.

Crystal, D. (1995). *The Cambridge encyclopedia of the English language.* Cambridge: Cambridge University Press.

Crystal, D. (2004). *The stories of English.* New York: Overlook Press.

Crystal, D. (2008). 2b or not 2b? *The Guardian*, July 4.

Cunningham, I.A.E. (1992). A syntactic analysis of Sea Island Creole. *Publication of the American Dialect Society* 75. Tuscaloosa, AL: University of Alabama Press.

Curzan, A., & Adams, M. (2006). *How English works: A linguistic introduction.* New York: Pearson Longman.

D'Arcy, A.F. (2005). Like: Syntax and development. (Unpublished doctoral dissertation), University of Toronto.

Dahlstrom, A. (1991). *Plains Cree morphosyntax.* New York: Garland Publishing.

Dailey-O'Cain, J. (1999). The perception of post-unification German regional speech. In D.R. Preston (Ed.) *Handbook of perceptual dialectology, vol. 1* (pp. 239–259). Amsterdam: John Benjamins.

d'Anglejan, A., and Tucker, R. (1973). Sociolinguistic correlates of speech style in Quebec. In R. Shuy, & R. Fasold (Eds.) *Language attitudes: Current trends and prospects* (pp. 29–52). Washington, DC: Georgetown University Press.

Dannenberg, C., & Wolfram, W. (1998). Ethnic identity and grammatical restructuring: Be(s) in Lumbee English. *American Speech* 73: 139–159.

Dash, J. (1992). *Daughters of the dust: The making of an African-American woman's film.* New York: The New Press.

Dash, J. (1997). *Daughters of the dust: A novel.* New York: Dutton.

Dash, J. (Producer), & Dash, J. (Director) (1991). *Daughters of the dust* (motion picture), Kino International.

Davey, M. (2005). As town for deaf takes shape, debate on isolation re-emerges. *The New York Times*, March 21. Retrieved from www.nytimes.com/2005/03/21/national/21deaf.html.

de Crevecoeur, J. (1782/1904). *Letters from an American farmer, vol. 6.* Carlisle, MA: Applewood Books.

Deaf Mosaic, episode 402. March 1988. Retrieved from www.youtube.com/watch?v=OtsYVeRuBuw.

Deaf President Now. (2013). Gallaudet University website. Retrieved from www.gallaudet.edu/dpn_home.html.

DeCamp, D. (1973). Foreword. In L.D. Turner, *Africanisms in the Gullah dialect* (pp. v–xv). Ann Arbor, MI: University of Michigan Press.

Deloria, P.J. (2004). *Indians in unexpected places.* Lawrence, KS: University Press of Kansas.

Demirci, M., & Kleiner, B. (1999). The perception of Turkish dialects. In D.R. Preston (Ed.) *Handbook of perceptual dialectology, vol. 1* (pp. 263–281). Philadelphia, PA: John Benjamins.

Denning, K., & Leben, W.R. (1995). *English vocabulary elements.* New York: Oxford University Press.

Department of Defense. (1945). *Navajo code talkers' dictionary.* Retrieved from www.defense.gov/specials/americanindian/dictionary.html.

Department of Defense. (2005). *Defense language transformation roadmap.* Retrieved from www.defense.gov/news/mar2005/d20050330roadmap.pdf.

Dillard, J.L. (1972). Black English: Its history and usage in the United States. New York: Random House.

Dillon, S. (2010). Foreign languages fade in class—except Chinese. *The New York Times*, January 21. Retrieved from www.nytimes.com/2010/01/21/education/21chinese.html?_r=0.

Di Paolo, M. (1993). Propredicate *do* in the English of the intermountain West. *American Speech* 68: 339–356.

Dobyns, H. (1966). Estimating aboriginal American population: An appraisal of techniques with a new hemispheric estimate. *Current Anthropology* 7: 395–416.

Dobyns, H. (1984). Native American population collapse and recovery. In W.R. Swagerty (Ed.) *Scholars and the Indian experience* (pp. 17–35). Bloomington, IN: Indiana University Press.

Doyle, J.A. (1907). *The English in America: The colonies under the House of Hanover.* London: Longmans, Green.

Dumas, B.K. (2000). U.S. pattern jury instructions: Problems and proposals. *Forensic Linguistics* 7: 49–71.

Dyer, G.W., Moore, J.T., Elliott, C.M., & Moxley, L.A. (1985). *The Tennessee Civil War veterans questionnaires.* Easley, SC: Southern Historical Press.

Ebert, R. (1992). Review of the film *Daughters of the Dust*, directed by J. Dash, 1991. *Chicago Sun-Time*, March 13.

Eble, C. (2004). Slang. In E. Finegan, & J. Rickford (Eds.) *Language in the U.S.A.* (pp. 375–386). New York: Cambridge University Press.

Eckert, P. (1989). *Jocks and burnouts: Social categories and identity in the high school.* New York: Teachers College Press, Columbia University.

Eckert, P. (1998). Age as a sociolinguistic variable. In F. Coulmas (Ed.) *The handbook of sociolinguistics* (pp. 151–167). Oxford: Blackwell.

Eckert, P. (2004). Adolescent language. In E. Finegan, & J. Rickford (Eds.) *Language in the U.S.A.* (pp. 361–374). New York: Cambridge University Press.

Edwards, W. (1992). Sociolinguistic behavior in a Detroit inner-city black neighborhood. *Language in Society* 21: 93–115.

Ellis, A.J. (1869–1889). *On early English pronunciation, with especial reference to Shakspere and Chaucer, vols. 1–5*. London: Asher.

Ellis, C.D. (2000). *Spoken Cree, vol. 1*. Edmonton, Alberta: University of Alberta Press.

Ellis Island Timeline (n.d.). Retrieved from www.ellisisland.org/genealogy/ellis_island_timeline.asp.

Endangered Language Alliance (n.d.). Retrieved from http://endangeredlanguagealliance.org/main/about.

Erard, M. (2012). Are we really monolingual? *The New York Times*, January 14. Retrieved from www.nytimes.com/2012/01/15/opinion/sunday/are-we-really-monolingual.html?_r=0.

Ethnologue (n.d.). *Ethnologue: Languages of the world*. Retrieved from www.ethnologue.com.

Executive Order 120 (2008). *Citywide policy on language access to ensure the effective delivery of city services*. Retrieved from www.nyc.gov/html/om/pdf/2008/pr282-08_eo_120.pdf.

Executive Order 13166 (2000). *Improving access to services for persons with limited English proficiency*. Retrieved from www.justice/gov.crt/about/cor/Pubs/eolep.php.

Evans, B. (2004). The role of social network in the acquisition of local dialect norms by Appalachian migrants in Ypsilanti, Michigan. *Language Variation and Change* 16: 153–167.

Evans, B. (2012). "Seattletonian" to "Faux Hick": Perceptions of English in Washington state. *American Speech* 86(4): 383–414.

Fagan, B. (2011). *The first North Americans: An archeological journey*. New York: Thames & Hudson.

Fennell, B., & Bennett, J. (1991). Sociolinguistic concepts and literary analysis. *American Speech* 66: 371–379.

Finegan, E., & Rickford, J.R. (Eds.) (2004). *Language in the U.S.A.: Themes for the twenty-first century*. Cambridge: Cambridge University Press.

Fischer, D.H. (1989). *Albion's seed: Four British folkways in America*. New York: Oxford University Press.

Fischer, J. (1958). Social influences on the choice of a linguistic variant. *Word* 14: 47–56.

Fisher, J.H. (2001). British and American, continuity and divergence. In J. Algeo (Ed.) *The Cambridge history of the English language, vol. 6* (pp. 59–85). Cambridge: Cambridge University Press.

Fisher, J.H., & Bornstein, D.D. (1984). *In forme of speche is chaunge: Readings in the history of the English language*. Lanham, MD: University Press of America.

Fishman, J.A. (1981). *Never say die: A thousand years of Yiddish in Jewish life and letters*. The Hague: Mouton.

Fishman, J.A. (1982). Whorfianism of the third kind: Ethnolinguistic diversity as a worldwide societal asset. *Language in Society* 11: 1–14.

Fishman, J.A. (1985). The sociology of Jewish languages from a general sociolinguistic point of view. In J.A. Fishman (Ed.) *Readings in the sociology of Jewish languages* (pp. 3–21). Leiden: Brill.

Fishman, J.A. (2004). Multilingualism and non-English mother tongues. In E. Finegan, & J.R. Rickford (Eds.) *Language in the U.S.A.: Themes for the twenty-first century* (pp. 115–132). Cambridge: Cambridge University Press.

Fleckenstein, E.A. (1998). The distinguished German ethnic population of America—(XVI). *Der Volksfreund/People's Friend* (Buffalo), May/June 1998.

Fonacier, E.C. (2010). Tagalog in the U.S.A. In K. Potowski (Ed.) *Language diversity in the U.S.A.* (pp. 96–109). Cambridge: Cambridge University Press.

Forgue, G.J. (1986). American English at the time of the Revolution. In H.B. Allen, & M.D. Linn (Eds.) *Dialect and language variation* (pp. 511–523). Orlando, FL: Academic Press.

Fought, C. (2001). Facts and myths about Chicano English. *Language Magazine* 1(3).

Fought, C. (2003). *Chicano English in context*. New York: Palgrave Macmillan.

Fought, C. (2006). *Language and ethnicity*. Cambridge: Cambridge University Press.

Franklin, B. (1751/1959). *Observations concerning the increase of mankind, peopling of countries, etc.* In L.W. Labaree (Ed.) *The papers of Benjamin Franklin, vol. 4* (p. 234). New Haven, CT: Yale University Press.

Fridland, V. (2003). Network strength and the realization of the Southern Vowel Shift among African Americans in Memphis, Tennessee. *American Speech* 78: 3–30.

Frost, W.G. (1899). Our contemporary ancestors. *Atlantic Monthly* 83: 311–319.

Gardner, R.C., & Clément, R. (1990). Social psychological perspectives on second language acquisition. In H. Giles, & W.P. Robinson (Eds.) *Handbook of language and social psychology* (pp. 495–517). Chichester, UK: John Wiley & Sons.

Garrett, A. (2001). Reduplication and infixation in Yurok: Morphology, semantics, and diachrony. *International Journal of American Linguistics* 67(3): 264–312.

Gastil, J. (1990). Generic pronouns and sexist language: The oxymoronic character of masculine generics. *Sex Roles* 23: 629–643.

Gaudio, R. (1994). Sounding gay: Pitch properties in the speech of gay and straight men. *American Speech* 69: 30–57.

Gibbs, G. (1863). *Dictionary of the Chinook Jargon, or, Trade Language of Oregon (abridged)*. New York: Cramoisy Press.

Gibson, C.J., & Jung, K. (2006). Historical census statistics on the foreign-born population of the United States: 1850–2000. Population division working paper no. 81. Washington, DC: US Census Bureau.

Gibson, C.J., & Lennon, E. (1999). Historical census statistics on the foreign-born population of the United States: 1850–1990. Population division working paper no. 29. Washington, DC: US Census Bureau. Retrieved from www.census.gov/population/www/documentation/twps0029/twps0029.html.

Gilliéron, J., & Edmont, E. (1902–1910). *Atlas linguistique de la France*. Paris: Champion.

Gledhill, C. (2000). *The grammar of Esperanto. A corpus-based description*. München: Lincom Europa.

Goldberg, B.Z. (1981). The American Yiddish press at its centennial. In J. Fishman (Ed.) *Never say die: A thousand years of Yiddish in Jewish life and letters* (pp. 513–522). The Hague: Mouton.

Gonzalez, A. (1922). *The black border*. Columbia, SC: The State Company.

Gonzalez-Barrera, A., & Lopez, M.H. (2013). Spanish is the most spoken non-English language in U.S. homes, even among non-Hispanics. *FACTANK: News in the numbers*, August 13. Retrieved from www.pewresearch.org/fact-tank/2013/08/13/spanish-is-the-most-spoken-non-english-language-in-u-s-homes-even-among-non-hispanics/.

Görlach, M. (1987). Colonial lag? The alleged conservative character of American English and other "colonial" varieties. *English World-Wide* 8: 41–60.

Gottliebson, R.O., Lee, L., Weinrich, B., & Sanders, J. (2007). Voice problems of future speech-language pathologists. *Journal of Voice* 21: 699–704.

Gould, P., & White, R. (1986). *Mental maps* (2nd ed.). Boston, MA: Allen & Unwin.

Green, L.J. (2002). *African American English: A linguistic introduction*. Cambridge: Cambridge University Press.

Green, L.J. (2011). *Language and the African American child*. Cambridge: Cambridge University Press.

Greenberg, J.H. (1960). The general classification of Central and South American languages. In A. Wallace (Ed.) *Men and cultures: Selected papers of the 5th International Congress of Anthropological and Ethnological Sciences, 1956* (pp. 791–794). Philadelphia, PA: University of Pennsylvania Press.

Greenberg, J.H. (1987). *Language in the Americas*. Stanford, CA: Stanford University Press.

Gumperz, J. (1964). Linguistic and social interaction in two communities. In B. Blount (Ed.) *Language, Culture and Society* 14: 283–299.

Haas, M.R. (1944). Men's and women's speech in Koasati. *Language* 20: 142–149.

Hall, J.H. (1997). *LAGS* and *DARE*: A case of mutualism. In C. Bernstein, T. Nunnally, & R. Sabino (Eds.) *Language variety in the South revisited* (pp. 297–308). Tuscaloosa, AL: University of Alabama Press.

Hall, J.H. (2004). The Dictionary of American Regional English. In E. Finegan, & J.R. Rickford (Eds.) *Language in the U.S.A.: Themes for the twenty-first century* (pp. 92–112). Cambridge: Cambridge University Press.

Halter, M. (2005). Cape Verdeans in the United States. In I. Skoggard, & C.R. Ember (Eds.) *Encyclopedia of diasporas: Immigrant and refugee cultures around the world* (pp. 615–623). New York: Springer.

Hancock, I. (1977). A typological survey of the world's pidgins and creoles. In A. Valdman (Ed.) *Pidgin and creole linguistics* (pp. 277–294). Bloomington, IN: Indiana University Press.

Hancock, I. (1980). Texan Gullah: The creole English of the Bracketville Afro-Seminoles. In J.L. Dillard (Ed.) *Perspectives on American English* (pp. 305–332). The Hague: Mouton.

Harley, H., & Amarillas, M. (2003). Reduplication multiplication in Yaqui: Meaning x form. In L. Barragan, & J. Haugen (Eds.) *Studies in Uto-Aztecan, papers on endangered and less familiar languages, vol. 5* (pp. 101–140). Cambridge, MA: MITWPL.

Harris, J.C. (1883). *Nights with Uncle Remus*. New York: Century.

Harrison, J.A. (1884). Negro English. *Anglia* 7: 232–279.

Harrison, K.D. (2007). *When languages die: The extinction of the world's languages and the erosion of human knowledge*. Oxford: Oxford University Press.

Hartley, L.C. (1999). A view from the West: Perceptions of U.S. dialects by Oregon residents. In D.R. Preston (Ed.) *Handbook of perceptual dialectology, vol. 1* (pp. 315–333). Amsterdam: John Benjamins.

Haskell, A.S. (1964). The representation of Gullah-influenced dialect in 20th century South Carolina prose, 1922–30. (Unpublished doctoral dissertation), University of Pennsylvania, Philadelphia.

Haugen, E. (1972). Dialect, language, nation. In J.B. Pride, & J. Holmes (Eds.) *Sociolinguistics* (pp. 97–111). Harmondsworth: Penguin.

Hauk, A. (2012). Radio free Cherokee: Endangered languages take to the airwaves. *The Atlantic.* Retrieved from www.theatlantic.com/entertainment/archive/2012/08/radio-free-cherokee-endangered-languages-take-to-the-airwaves/261165/.

Hawgood, J.A. (1940). *The tragedy of German-America.* New York City: G.P. Putnam's Sons.

Heine, B., & Nurse, D. (2000). Introduction. In B. Heine, & D. Nurse (Eds.) *African languages: An introduction* (pp. 1–10). Cambridge: Cambridge University Press.

Hemberger, L., & Morrow, K. (n.d.). Improving classroom behaviors and social interactions: Respecting the Deaf community. *Teaching Students with Sensory Impairments.* Retrieved from www.trinity.edu/org/sensoryimpairments/HI/SS/HI%20-%20Chap%206%20-%20III.pdf.

Hill, J.H. (1998). Language, race, and white public space. *American Anthropologist* 100: 680–689.

History of Baby Sign Language (n.d.). Retrieved from www.babysignlanguage.com/basics/history.

History of Gallaudet University (n.d.). Retrieved from www.gallaudet.edu/gallaudet_university/about_gallaudet/history.html.

Holm, J. (2000). *An introduction to pidgins and creoles.* Cambridge: Cambridge University Press.

Holmes, J. (1990). Hedges and boosters in women's and men's speech. *Language & Communication* 10(3): 185–205.

Holmes, J. (1995). *Women, men and politeness.* London and New York: Longman.

Hopi Dictionary Project. (1998). *Hopìikwa Lavàytutuveni: A Hopi dictionary of the Third Mesa dialect with an English–Hopi finder list and a sketch of Hopi grammar.* Tucson, AZ: University of Arizona Press.

Hubbell, A.F. (1950). *The pronunciation of English in New York City. Consonants and vowels.* New York: King's Crown Press, Columbia University.

Huber, M. (2013). Ghanaian Pidgin English. In S. Michaelis, P. Maurer, M. Haspelmath, & M. Huber (Eds.) *Survey of pidgin and creole languages, vol. 1* (pp. 167–175). Oxford: Oxford University Press.

Hundt, M. (2009). Colonial lag, colonial innovation, or simply language change? In G. Rohdenburg, & J. Schlüter (Eds.) *One language, two grammars: Morphosyntactic differences between British and American English* (pp. 13–37). Cambridge: Cambridge University Press.

Huntington, S. (2004). *Who are we? The challenges to America's national identity.* New York: Simon & Schuster.

Huttar, G.L., & Huttar, M.L. (1994). *Ndyuka.* London: Routledge.

Jackson, E.H. (1956). An analysis of certain Colorado Atlas field records with regards to settlement history and other factors. (Unpublished doctoral dissertation), University of Colorado, Boulder.

Jespersen, O. (1922). *Language: Its nature, development and origin.* London: George Allen & Unwin.

Johnson, E. (1996). *Lexical change and variation in the southeastern United States, 1930–1990.* Tuscaloosa, AL: University of Alabama Press.

Johnson, G.B. (1930). St. Helena songs and stories. In T.J. Woofter, Jr. (Ed.) *Black yeomanry: Life on St. Helena Island* (pp. 49, 53). New York: Holt.

Johnson, R.I., Hooper, L., Goodykoontz, B., & Dearborn, F.R. (1942). *English for you and me.* Boston, MA: Ginn and Company.

Johnson, S. (1755). *Dictionary of the English language.* London: W. Strahan.

Johnstone, B. (2011). Place, language, and semiotic order. Paper presented at Urban Symbolic Landscapes conference, Helsinki, Finland, May.

Johnstone, B. (2013). *Speaking Pittsburghese: The story of a dialect.* Oxford: Oxford University Press.

Johnstone, B., Bhasin, N., & Wittkofski, D. (2002). Dahntahn Pittsburgh: Monophthongal /aw/ and representations of localness in southwestern Pennsylvania. *American Speech* 79: 115–145.

Jones, G.M., Schieffelin, B.B., & Smith, R.E. (2011). When friends who talk together stalk together: Online gossip communication. In C. Thurlow, & K. Mroczek (Eds.) *Digital discourse: Language in the new media* (pp. 26–47). Oxford: Oxford University Press.

Joreen (1970). The bitch manifesto. In S. Firestone and A. Koedt (Eds.) *Notes from the second year: Women's liberation: Major writings of the radical feminists.* Pamphlet.

Justice, E. (2012). African origins website launches vast expansion. Retrieved from http://news.emory.edu/stories/2012/08/upress_origins_launches_expansion/campus.html.

Katz, D. (2008). Language: Yiddish. In *YIVO encyclopedia of Jews in Eastern Europe.* Retrieved from www.yivoencyclopedia.org/article.aspx/Language/Yiddish.

Keesing, F.M. (1971). *The Menomini Indians of Wisconsin: A study of three centuries of cultural contact and change.* New York: Johnson Reprint Company.

Kelleher, A. (2010). What is a heritage language program? *Heritage Briefs.* Washington, DC: Center for Applied Linguistics. Retrieved from www.cal.org/heritage/pdfs/briefs/What-is-a-heritage-language-program.pdf.

Kelley, R.D.G., & Lewis, E. (Eds.) (2005). *A history of African Americans to 1880, vol. 1.* Oxford: Oxford University Press.

Kennetz, K. (2008). German and German disunity. (Unpublished doctoral dissertation), University of Georgia, Athens.

Kiesling, S.F. (1998). Men's identities and sociolinguistic variation: The case of fraternity men. *Journal of Sociolinguistics* 2/1: 69–99.

Kiesling, S.F. (2009). Fraternity men: Variation and discourses of masculinity. In N. Coupland, & A. Jaworski (Eds.) *The new sociolinguistics reader* (pp. 187–200). Basingstoke: Palgrave Macmillan.

Klingler, T.A. (2003). *If I could turn my tongue like that: The creole language of Pointe Coupee Parish, Louisiana.* Baton Rouge, LA: Louisiana State University Press.

Klingler, T.A., & Neumann-Holzschuh, I. (2013). Louisiana Creole. In S.M. Michaelis, P. Maurer, M. Haspelmath, & M. Huber (Eds.) *The survey of pidgin and creole languages, vol. II: Portuguese-based, Spanish-based and French-based languages* (pp. 229–240). Oxford: Oxford University Press.

Klingler, T.A., Picone, M., & Valdman, A. (1997). The lexicon of Louisiana French. In A. Valdman (Ed.) *French and Creole in Louisiana* (pp. 145–182). New York: Plenum Press.

Kloss, H. (1977). *The American bilingual tradition*. New York: Newbury House.

Koehn, P.H., & Yin, X.H. (2002). Chinese American transnationalism and U.S.–Chinese relations: Presence and promise for the trans-Pacific century. In P.H. Koehn, & X.H. Yin (Eds.) *The expanding roles of Chinese Americans in U.S.–China relations: Transnational networks and trans-Pacific interactions* (pp. xi–xxxx). Armonk, NY: M.E. Sharpe.

Kontra, M. (2002). Where is the "most beautiful" and the "ugliest" Hungarian spoken? In D. Long, & D.R. Preston (Eds.) *Handbook of perceptual dialectology, vol. 2* (pp. 207–220). Amsterdam: John Benjamins.

Kramarae, C. (1982). Gender: How she speaks. In E.B. Ryan & H. Giles (Eds.) *Attitudes toward language variation: Social and applied contexts* (pp. 84–98). London: Edward Arnold.

Kramer, S., Miller, D.A., & Newberger, J. (Producers/Directors) (2008). *The linguists* (motion picture), Ironbound Films.

Krapp, G.P. (1924). The English of the Negro. *American Mercury*, pp. 190–195.

Krapp, G.P. (1925). *The English language in America* (2 vols.). New York: Century.

Krapp, G.P., & Dobbie, E.V.K. (1936). *The Exeter book*. Columbia, NY: Columbia University Press.

Kretzschmar, W.A., Jr. (2000). Postmodern dialectology. *American Speech* 75: 235–237.

Kretzschmar, W.A., Jr. (2009). *The linguistics of speech*. Cambridge: Cambridge University Press.

Kretzschmar, W.A., Jr. (2010). Language variations and complex systems. *American Speech* 85: 263–286.

Kretzschmar, W.A., Jr. (2012). Variation in the traditional vowels of the eastern states. *American Speech* 87: 378–390.

Kretzschmar, W.A., Jr., & Tamasi, S. (2003). Distributional foundations for a theory of language change. *World Englishes* 22: 377–401.

Kurath, H. (1928). The origin of dialectal differences in spoken American English. *Modern Philology* 25: 285–295.

Kurath, H. (1949). *A word geography of the eastern United States*. Ann Arbor, MI: University of Michigan Press.

Kurath, H. (1972). *Studies in area linguistics*. Bloomington, IN: Indiana University Press.

Kurath, H., & McDavid, R.I. Jr. (1961). *The pronunciation of English in the Atlantic states*. Ann Arbor, MI: University of Michigan Press.

Kurath, H., Hanely, M.L., Lowman, G.S., Jr., & Bloch, B. (Eds.) (1939–1943). *Linguistic Atlas of New England* (3 vols. in 6). Providence, RI: Brown University, for ACLS (2nd rev. ed., New York: AMS Press, 1973).

Labov, W. (1963). The social motivation of a sound change. *Word* 19: 273–309.

Labov, W. (1966/2006). *The social stratification of English in New York City*. Washington, DC: Center for Applied Linguistics.

Labov, W. (1969). The logic of nonstandard English. *Georgetown Monographs on Language and Linguistics* 22: 1–22, 26–31.

Labov, W. (1970). The study of language in its social context. *Studium Generale* 23: 30–87.

Labov, W. (1972). Academic ignorance and Black intelligence. *The Atlantic Monthly*, June. Retrieved from www.theatlantic.com/past/docs/issues/95sep/ets/labo.htm.

Labov, W. (1990). The intersection of sex and social class in the course of linguistic change. *Language Variation and Change* 2: 205–254.

Labov, W. (1991). The three dialects of English. In P. Eckert (Ed.) *New ways of analyzing sound change* (pp. 1–44). New York: Academic Press.

Labov, W. (1996). The organization of dialect diversity in North America. Retrieved from www.ling.upenn.edu/phono_atlas/ICSLP4.html.

Labov, W., & Ash, S. (1997). Understanding Birmingham. In C. Bernstein, T. Nunnally, & R. Sabino (Eds.) *Language variety in the South revisited* (pp. 508–573). Tuscaloosa, AL: University of Alabama Press.

Labov, W., Ash, S., & Boberg, C. (1997). A national map of the regional dialects of American English. Retrieved from www.ling.upenn.edu/phono_atlas/NationalMap/NationalMap.html.

Labov, W., Ash, S., & Boberg, C. (2006). *The atlas of North American English: Phonetics, phonology, and sound change*. The Hague: Walter de Gruyter.

Lakoff, R. (1975). *Language and women's place*. New York: Harper & Row.

Lamb, S.M. (1959). Some proposals for linguistic taxonomy. *Anthropological Linguistics* 1(2): 3–49.

Lambert, W.E. (1967). The social psychology of bilingualism. *Journal of Social Issues* 23: 91–109.

Lance, D.M. (1999). Regional variation in subjective dialect divisions in the United States. In D.R. Preston (Ed.) *Handbook of perceptual dialectology, vol. 1* (pp. 283–314). Amsterdam: John Benjamins.

Lanehart, S.L. (Ed.) (2009). *African American women's language: Discourse, education, and identity*. Newcastle: Cambridge Scholars Publishing.

Langford, I. (2000). Forensic semantics: The meaning of murder, manslaughter and homicide. *Forensic Linguistics* 7: 72–94.

Larmouth, D., & Remsing, M. (1993). "Kentuck" English in Wisconsin's Cutover Region. In T. Frazer (Ed.) *"Heartand" English: Variation and transition in the American Midwest* (pp. 215–228). Tuscaloosa, AL: University of Alabama Press.

Launspach, S.A. (2012). The journey to Idaho: The use of oral history tapes and census data to trace the history of regional dialect features. *Idaho Yesterdays* 53(1 & 2). Retrieved from http://134.50.3.223/idahoyesterdays/index.php/IY/article/view/55/83.

Leap, W.L. (1981). American Indian languages. In C.A. Ferguson, & S.B. Heath (Eds.) *Language in the U.S.A.* (pp. 116–144). Cambridge: Cambridge University Press.

Leap, W.L. (1982). The study of American Indian English: Status and direction of inquiry. In H.G. Bartelt, S. Penfield-Jasper, & B.L. Hoffer (Eds.) *Essays in Native American English* (pp. 1–22). San Antonio, TX: Trinity University Press.

Leap, W.L. (1993). *American Indian English*. Salt Lake City, UT: University of Utah Press.

Lee, J. (2013). *U.S. naturalizations: 2012*. Department of Homeland Security Annual Flow Report, March. Retrieved from www.dhs.gov/sites/default/files/publications/ois_natz_fr_2012.pdf.

Lestrade, P.M. (2002). The continuing decline of Isleno Spanish in Louisiana. *Southwest Journal of Linguistics* 21: 99–118.

Liberman, M. (2005). Uptalk uptick? *Language Log*, December 15. Retrieved from http://itre.cis.upenn.edu/~myl/languagelog/archives/002708.html.

Liberman, M. (2011). Vocal fry: "Creeping in" or "still here"? *Language Log*, December 12. Retrieved from http://languagelog.ldc.upenn.edu/nll/?p=3626.

Lincoln, K. (1993). *Indi'n humor: Bicultural play in Native America*. New York: Oxford University Press.

Lindfield, J. (2000). *The French in the United States: An ethnographic study*. Westport, CT: Bergin and Garvey.

Linneman, T.J. (2013). Gender in Jeopardy! Intonation variation on a television game show. *Gender & Society* 27: 82–105.

Lippi-Green, R. (2004). Language ideology and language prejudice. In E. Finegan, & J. Rickford (Eds.) *Language in the U.S.A.* (pp. 289–304). New York: Cambridge University Press.

Lippi-Green, R. (2012). *English with an accent: Language, ideology, and discrimination in the United States* (2nd ed.). London and New York: Routledge.

Lipski, J.M. (1990). *The language of the Isleños: Vestigial Spanish in Louisiana*. Baton Rouge, LA: Louisiana State University Press.

Lipski, J.M. (2008). *Varieties of Spanish in the United States*. Washington, DC: Georgetown University Press.

Liu, F., Antieau, L., & Yu, H. (2011). Toward automated consumer question answering: Automatically separating consumer questions from professional questions in the healthcare domain. *Journal of Biomedical Informatics* 44: 1032–1038.

Long, D. (1999). Mapping non-linguists' evaluations of Japanese language variation. In D.R. Preston (Ed.) *Handbook of perceptual dialectology, vol. 1* (pp. 199–226). Amsterdam: John Benjamins.

Long, D., & Yim, Y.-C. (2002). Regional differences in the perception of Korean dialects. In D. Long, & D.R. Preston (Eds.) *Handbook of perceptual dialectology, vol. 2* (pp. 249–275). Amsterdam: John Benjamins.

Lowth, R. (1762). *A short introduction to English grammar*. Basle: Tourneisin.

Lucas, C. (Ed.) (2001). *The sociolinguistics of sign languages*. Cambridge: Cambridge University Press.

Lucas, C., & Valli, C. (2004). American Sign Language. In E. Finegan & J.R. Rickford (Eds.) *Language in the U.S.A.: Themes for the twenty-first century* (pp. 230–244). Cambridge: Cambridge University Press.

Lucas, C., Bayley, R., & Valli, C. (2003). *What's your sign for PIZZA? An introduction to variation in ASL*. Washington, DC: Gallaudet University Press.

McCarty, T.L. (2002). *A place to be Navajo—Rough Rock and the struggle for self-determination in indigenous schooling*. Mahwah, NJ: Lawrence Erlbaum.

McCarty, T.L. (2010). Native American languages in the U.S.A. In K. Potowski (Ed.) *Language diversity in the U.S.A.* (pp. 47–65). Cambridge: Cambridge University Press.

McCaskill, C., Lucas, C., Bayley, R., & Hill, J. (2011). *The hidden treasure of Black ASL: Its history and structure*. Washington, DC: Gallaudet University Press.

McClendon, S. (1996). Sketches of Eastern Pomo, a Pamoan language. In I. Goddard (Ed.) *Handbook of American Indians, vol. 17* (pp. 507–550). Washington, DC: Smithsonian Institute.

McDavid, R.I., Jr. (1958). American English dialects. In W.N. Francis (Ed.) *The structure of American English* (pp. 480–543). New York: The Ronald Press Co.

McDavid, R.I. (1972). Field procedures: Instructions for investigators, Linguistic Atlas of the Gulf States. In L. Pederson, R.I. McDavid, Jr., C.W. Foster, & C.E. Billiard (Eds.) *A manual for dialect research in the southern states* (pp. 35–60). Tuscaloosa, AL: University of Alabama Press.

McDavid, R.I., & McDavid, V.G. (1951). The relationship of the speech of American Negroes to the speech of whites. *American Speech* 26: 3–17.

McDavid, R.I., Jr., & O'Cain, R.K. (1973). Sociolinguistics and linguistic geography. *Kansas Journal of Sociology* 9: 137–156.

McHugh, M., Gelatt, J., & Fix, M. (2007). Adult English language instruction in the United States: Determining need and investing wisely. *Migration Policy Institute*, July. Retrieved from www.migrationpolicy.org/pubs/nciip_english_instruction073107.pdf.

McIntyre, J.E. (2008). Splittists. *The Baltimore Sun*, May. Retrieved from http://weblogs.baltimoresun.com/news/mcintyre/blog/2008/05/splittists.html.

McLemore, C. (1991). *The pragmatic interpretation of English intonation*. Austin, TX: University of Texas.

Madison, J. (2011). Is the Southern accent dying? How new research shows upper and middle classes are losing their drawl. *Daily Mail Online*, May 20. Retrieved from www.dailymail.co.uk/news/article-1389264/Is-Southern-accent-dying-How-new-research-shows-upper-middle-classes-losing-drawl.html#ixzz32RgGrWum.

Madrigal v. Quilligan, No. 75-2057 (C.D. Cal. *1975*).

Makepeace, A. (Producer), & Makepeace, A. (Director) (2001). *Coming to light: The Edward S. Curtis story* (documentary), Seventh Art Releasing.

Mallory, J.A. (1914). *Compiled statutes of the United States 1913, vol. 2*. St. Paul, MN: West Publishing.

Mallinder, L. (2013). Rebelling against Quebec's 'language police.' *BBC News Magazine*, May 6. Retrieved from www.bbc.co.uk/news/magazine-22408248.

Mann, S.L. (2011). Gay American English: Language attitudes, language perceptions, and gay men's discourses of connectedness to family, LGBTQ networks, and the American South. (Unpublished doctoral dissertation), University of South Carolina, Columbia.

Mann, S.L. (2012). Speaker attitude as a predictive factor in listener perception of gay men's speech. *Journal of Language and Sexuality* 1: 206–230.

Marckwardt, A. (1958). *American English*. Ann Arbor, MI: University of Michigan Press.

Marshall, M. (1997). The origin and development of Louisiana Creole French. In A. Valdman (Ed.) *French and Creole in Louisiana* (pp. 333–349). New York: Plenum Press.

Martyna, W. (1978). What does "he" mean? Use of the generic masculine. *Journal of Communication* 28: 131–138.

Mathur, G., & Napoli, D.J. (2011). *Deaf around the world: The impact of language*. Oxford: Oxford University Press.

Maynard, J. (2008). First Spanish-language newspaper founded 200 years ago. *Newseum*, September 15. Retrieved from www.newseum.org/news/2008/09/first-spanish-language-newspaper-founded-200-years-ago.html.

Maynor, N. (1994). The language of electronic mail: Written speech. In G.D. Little, & M. Montgomery (Eds.) *Centennial usage studies* (pp. 48–45). Tuscaloosa, AL: University of Alabama Press.

Meek, B.A. (2006). And the Injun goes how! Representations of American Indian English in (white) public space. *Language in Society* 35(1): 93–128.

Meinig, D.W. (1965). The Mormon culture region: Strategies and patterns in the geography of the American West, 1847–1964. *ANNALS, Association of American Geographers* 55: 191–221.

Mellinkoff, D. (1963). *The language of the law*. Boston, MA: Little, Brown.

Memmott, M. (2012). A bright light during dark days: Bloomberg's sign language star. *The Two-Way: Breaking News from NPR*, October 30. Retrieved from www.npr.org/blogs/thetwo-way/2012/10/30/163940098/a-bright-light-during-dark-news-bloombergs-sign-language-star.

Mencken, H.L. (1921). *The American language: An inquiry into the development of English in the United States* (2nd ed.). New York: A.A. Knopf.

Mendez v. Westminster School District et al., 64 F. Supp. 544 (S.D. Cal. 1946).

Mendoza-Denton, N. (2008). *Homegirls: Language and cultural practice among Latina youth gangs*. Malden, MA: Blackwell.

Mendoza-Denton, N. (2011). The semiotic hitchhiker's guide to creaky voice: Circulation and gendered hardcore in a Chicana/o gang persona. *Journal of Linguistic Anthropology* 21(2): 261–280.

Meriam, L. (1928). *The problem of Indian administration: Report of a survey made at the request of Honorable Hubert Work, Secretary of the Interior, and submitted to him, February 21, 1928/Survey Staff: Lewis Meriam . . . [et al.].* Baltimore, MD: Johns Hopkins Press.

Merriam-Webster (1994). *Merriam-Webster's dictionary of English usage*. Springfield, MA: Merriam-Webster.

Merriam-Webster Online (n.d.). Noah Webster's spelling reform. Retrieved from www.merriam-webster.com/info/spelling-reform.htm.

Merrill, E.C. (2005). *Germans of Louisiana*. New York: Penguin Books.

Metcalf, A. (2000). *How we talk: American regional English today*. Boston, MA: Houghton Mifflin.

Metzner, H. (1924). *A brief history of the American Turnerbund* (T. Stempfel, Jr., trans.). Pittsburgh, PA: National Executive Committee of the American Turnerbund.

Meyer, R. (2014). The *New York Times*' most popular story of 2013 was not an article: It was that dialect quiz. *The Atlantic*, January 17. Retrieved from www.theatlantic.com/technology/archive/2014/01/-em-the-new-york-times-em-most-popular-story-of-2013-was-not-an-article/283167/.

Meyer v. State of Nebraska, 262 U.S. 390 (1923). Retrieved from www.law.cornell.edu/supct/html/historics/USSC_CR_0262_0390_ZO.html.

Mille, K.W. (1997). Ambrose Gonzalez's Gullah: What it may tell us about variation. In C. Bernstein, T. Nunnally, & R. Sabino (Eds.) *Language variety in the South* (pp. 98–112). Tuscaloosa, AL: University of Alabama Press.

Miller, J.L. (2011). *Accented America: The cultural politics of multilingual modernism.* Oxford: Oxford University Press.

Milroy, J., & Milroy, L. (1985). Linguistic change, social network and speaker innovation. *Language in Society* 21: 339–384.

Milroy, L. (1980). *Language and social networks.* London: Basil Blackwell.

Milroy, L. (1987). *Language and social networks* (2nd ed.). Oxford: Basil Blackwell.

Minnick, L.C. (2004). *Dialect and dichotomy: Literary representations of African American speech.* Tuscaloosa, AL: University of Alabama Press.

Minnick, L.C. (2010). Dialect literature and English in the U.S.A. In R. Hickey (Ed.) *Varieties of English in writing: The written word as linguistic evidence* (pp. 163–196). Amsterdam: John Benjamins.

Mitchell, R.E., Young, T.A., Bachleda, B., & Karchmer, M.A. (2006). How many people use ASL in the United States? Why estimates need updating. *Sign Language Studies* 6(3): 306–335.

Mithun, M. (1999). *The languages of native North America.* Cambridge: Cambridge University Press.

Miyashita, M., & Shoe, S.C. (2009). Blackfoot lullabies and language revitalization. In J. Reyhner, & L. Lockard (Eds.) *Indigenous language revitalization: Encouragement, guidance and lessons learned* (pp. 183–190). Flagstaff, AZ: Northern Arizona University.

Modern Language Association (MLA) (2010). *Enrollments in languages other than English in United States institutions of higher education, Fall 2009.* New York: MLA.

Monger, R., & Yankay, J. (2013). U.S. permanent legal residents, 2012. *Department of Homeland Security annual flow report*, March 2013. Retrieved from www.dhs.gov/sites/default/files/publications/ois_lpr_fr_2012_2.pdf.

Montes-Alcalá, C. (2000). Attitudes towards oral and written codeswitching in Spanish–English bilingual youths. In A. Roca (Ed.) *Research on Spanish in the U.S.* (pp. 218–227). Somerville, MA: Cascadilla Press.

Montgomery, D. (2006). An anthem's discordant notes. *The Washington Post*, April 28. Retrieved from www.washingtonpost.com/wp-dyn/content/article/2006/04/27/AR2006042702505.htmlv.

Montgomery, M. (1997). The Scotch-Irish element in Appalachian English: How broad? How deep? In H.B.C. Wood, Jr. (Ed.) *Ulster and North America: Transatlantic perspectives on the Scotch-Irish* (pp. 189–212). Tuscaloosa, AL: University of Alabama Press.

Montgomery, M. (1999). In the Appalachians they speak like Shakespeare. In L. Bauer, & P. Trudgill (Eds.) *Language myths* (pp. 66–76). New York: Penguin.

Montgomery, M. (2001). British and Irish antecedents. In J. Algeo (Ed.) *The Cambridge history of the English language, vol. VI: English in North America* (pp. 86–153). Cambridge: Cambridge University Press.

Montler, T.R. (1989). Infixation, reduplication, and metathesis in the Saanich actual aspect. *Southwest Journal of Linguistics* 9(1): 92–107.

Mufwene, S. (1997). The ecology of Gullah's survival. *American Speech* 72: 69–83.

Mufwene, S. (2001). African-American English. In J. Algeo (Ed.) *The Cambridge history of the English language, vol. VI: English in North America* (pp. 291–324). Cambridge: Cambridge University Press.

Mufwene, S. (2008). Gullah: Morphology and syntax. In E.W. Schneider (Ed.) *Varieties of English vol. 2: The Americas and the Caribbean* (pp. 551–571). Berlin: Mouton de Gruyter.

Mufwene, S., Rickford, J.R., Bailey, G., & Baugh, J. (Eds.) (1998). *African-American English: Structure, history and use*. New York: Routledge.

Munson, B., & Babel, M. (2007). Loose lips and silver tongues, or projecting sexual orientation through speech. *Language and Linguistics Compass* 1(5): 416–449.

Munson, B., McDonald, E.C., DeBoe, N.L., & White, A.R. (2006). Acoustic and perceptual bases of judgments of women and men's sexual orientation from read speech. *Journal of Phonetics* 34: 202–240.

Murray, T.E. (1993). Positive anymore in the Midwest. In T.C. Frazer (Ed.) *Heartland English: Variation and transition in the American Midwest* (pp. 125–136). Tuscaloosa, AL: University of Alabama Press.

Murray, T.E. (2004). Positive 'anymore' in the West. Paper presented at the American Dialect Society session, Rocky Mountain Modern Language Association annual meeting, Boulder, CO, October.

Murray, T.E., & Simon, B.L. (1999). *Want* + past participle in American English. *American Speech* 74: 140–164.

Murray, T.E., & Simon, B.L. (2002). At the intersection of regional and social dialects: The case of *like* + past participle in American English. *American Speech* 77: 32–69.

Naff, A. (2000). Growing up in Detroit: An immigrant grocer's daughter. In N. Abraham, & A. Shryock (Eds.) *Arab Detroit: From margin to mainstream* (pp. 107–148). Detroit, MI: Wayne State University Press.

Napoli, D.J., Mai, M., & Gaw, N. (2011). *Primary movement in sign languages: A study of six languages*. Washington, DC: Gallaudet University Press.

National Association of the Deaf (2008). *Position statement on American Sign Language*. Silver Spring, MD: National Association of the Deaf.

National Association of the Deaf (n.d.). *American Sign Language*. Retrieved from www.nad.org/issues/american-sign-language.

National Center for Education Statistics (2012). *Digest of education statistics, 2011*, NCES 2012-001. Washington, DC: National Center for Education Statistics.

National Institute on Deafness and Other Communication Disorders (NIDCD) (2011). *Cochlear implants*. Retrieved from www.nidcd.nih.gov/health/hearing/pages/coch.aspx.

Nettle, D., & Romaine, S. (2000). *Vanishing voices: The extinction of the world's voices*. Oxford: Oxford University Press.

Newman, S.S. (1964). Comparison of Zuni and California Penutian. *UAL* 30: 1–13.

Nichols, P. (1981). Creoles of the U.S.A. In C.A. Ferguson, & S.B. Heath (Eds.) *Language in the U.S.A.* (pp. 69–91). Cambridge: Cambridge University Press.

Nichols, P. (2004). Creole languages: Forging new identities. In E. Finegan, & J.R. Rickford (Eds.) *Language in the U.S.A.: Themes for the twenty-first century* (pp. 133–152). Cambridge: Cambridge University Press.

Nichols, S.P. (1989). The Official English movement in the United States with special reference to New Mexico and Arizona. (Unpublished master's thesis), University of New Mexico, Albuquerque.

Niedzielski, N.A., & Preston, D.R. (2000). *Folk linguistics*. Berlin: Mouton de Gruyter.

Nussbaum, E. (2012). Seen but not heard: The revelatory silence of "Switched at Birth." *The New Yorker*, September 24.

Office on Latino Affairs (n.d.). *Language access and advocacy program*. Retrieved from http://ola.dc.gov/page/language-access-and-advocacy-program.

Padden, C.A. (2011). Sign language geography. In G. Mathur, & D.J. Napoli (Eds.) *Deaf around the world: The impact of language* (pp. 19–53). Oxford: Oxford University Press.

Pederson, L. (1983). *East Tennessee folk speech: A synopsis*. Bamberger Beitrage, 12. Frankfurt: Lang.

Pederson, L. (1996). LAMR/LAWS and the main chance. *Journal of English Linguistics* 24: 239–249.

Pederson, L. (2001). Dialects. In J. Algeo (Ed.) *The Cambridge history of the English language, vol. VI: English in North America* (pp. 253–290). Cambridge: Cambridge University Press.

Pederson, L., & Madsen, M.W. (1989). Linguistic geography in Wyoming. *Journal of English Linguistics* 2: 17–24.

Pederson, L., McDaniel, S., & Adams, C. (1986–1992). *Linguistic Atlas of the Gulf States* (7 vols.). Athens, GA: University of Georgia Press.

Pei, M. (1967). *The story of the English language*. Philadelphia, PA: Lippincott.

Pew Research Center (2012). *Latino voters in the 2012 election*. Retrieved from www.pew hispanic.org/files/2012/11/2012_Latino_vote_exit_poll_analysis_final_11-07-12.pdf.

Pickering, J. (1816). *Collection of words and phrases which have been supposed to be peculiar to the United States of America*. Boston, MA: Cummings and Hilliard.

Picone, M. (1997). Enclave dialect contraction: An external overview of Louisiana French. *American Speech* 72: 117–153.

Pierrehumbert, J.B., Bent, T., Munson, B., Bradlow, A.R., & Bailey, J.M. (2004). The influence of sexual orientation on vowel production. *Journal of the Acoustical Society of America* 116: 1905–1908.

Pinker, S. (1994). *The language instinct*. New York: Harper Perennial Modern Classics.

Podesva, R.J. (2004). On constructing social meaning with stop release bursts. Paper presented at Sociolinguistics Symposium 15, Newcastle upon Tyne, UK, April.

Podesva, R.J. (2006). Phonetic detail in sociolinguistic variation: Its linguistic significance and role in the construction of meaning. (Unpublished doctoral dissertation), Stanford University, Stanford, CA.

Potowski, K. (2008). "I was raised talking like my mom": The influence of mothers in the development of MexiRicans' phonological and lexical features. In J. Rothman, & M. Niño-Murcia (Eds.) *Linguistic identity and bilingualism in different Hispanic contexts* (pp. 201–220). New York: John Benjamins.

Potowski, K. (Ed.) (2010). *Language diversity in the U.S.A.* Cambridge: Cambridge University Press.

Potowski, K., & Carreira, M. (2010). Spanish in the U.S.A. In K. Potowski (Ed.) *Language diversity in the U.S.A.* (pp. 66–80). Cambridge: Cambridge University Press.

Powell, D., & Lowenkron, B. (2006). National security language initiative. *Fact Sheet, U.S. Department of State*, January 5. Retrieved from http://2001-2009.state.gov/r/pa/prs/ps/2006/58733.htm.

Powell, J.W. (1891). *Indian linguistic families of America, north of Mexico*, vol. 7. Washington, DC: US Government Printing Office.

Preston, D.R. (1985). Mental maps of language distribution in Rio Grande do Sul (Brazil). *The Geographical Bulletin* 27: 46–64.

Preston, D.R. (1989). *Perceptual dialectology*. Dordrecht: Foris.

Preston, D.R. (1996). Where the worst English is spoken. In E. Schneider (Ed.) *Focus on the U.S.A.* (pp. 297–360). Amsterdam: John Benjamins.

Preston, D.R. (1997). The South: The touchstone. In C. Bernstein, T. Nunnally, & R. Sabino (Eds.) *Language variety in the South revisited* (pp. 311–351). Tuscaloosa, AL: University of Alabama Press.

Preston, D.R. (1999). A language attitude approach to the perception of regional variety. In D.R. Preston (Ed.) *Handbook of perceptual dialectology, vol. 1* (pp. 359–374). Philadelphia, PA: John Benjamins.

Prichard, H.E. (2009). Linguistic variation and change in Atlanta, Georgia. (Unpublished undergraduate honors thesis), Emory University, Atlanta, GA.

Pro English (n.d.). *What is Official English?* Retrieved from www.proenglish.org/official-english/english-only.html.

Pula, J. (1975). *The French in America, 1488–1974: A chronology and factbook*. Dobbs Ferry, NY: Oceana Publications.

Purnell, T., Idsardi, W., & Baugh, J. (1999). Perceptual and phonetic experiments on American English dialect identification. *Journal of Language and Social Psychology* 18: 10.

Pyles, T. (1971). *The origins and development of the English language*. New York: Harcourt Brace Jovanovich.

Pyles, T., & Algeo, J. (1993). *The origins and development of the English language* (4th ed.). Fort Worth, TX: Harcourt Brace Jovanovich.

Quirk, R., & Wrenn, C.L. (1957). *An Old English grammar*. New York: Henry Holt.

Read, A.W. (1937). Bilingualism in the middle Colonies, 1725–1775. *American Speech* 12: 93–99.

Reaser, J. (2010). Developing sociolinguistic curricula that help teachers meet standards. In K. Denham, & A. Lobeck (Eds.) *Linguistics at school: Language awareness in primary and secondary education* (pp. 91–105). Cambridge: Cambridge University Press.

Reich, D., Patterson, N., Campbell, D., Tandon, A., Mazieres, S., Ray, N., et al. (2012). Reconstructing Native American population history. *Nature* 488: 370–374.

Reichstein, A.V. (2001). *German pioneers on the American frontier: The Wagners in Texas and Illinois*. Denton, TX: University of North Texas Press.

Reyhner, J., & Eder, J. (2004). *American Indian education: A history*. Norman, OK: University of Oklahoma Press.

Rickford, J. (1999). *African American Vernacular English: Features, evolution, educational implications*. Oxford: Blackwell.

Rickford, J., & Rickford, R. (2000). *Spoken soul*. New York: John Wiley & Sons.

Rickford, J., Wasow, T., Zwicky, A., & Buchstaller, I. (2007). Intensive and quotative *all*: Something old, something new. *American Speech* 82(1): 3–31.

Rippley, L.J. (1976). *The German-Americans*. Boston, MA: Twayne Publishers.

Roach, J. (2006). Young Americans geographically illiterate, survey suggests. *National Geographic News*, May 2. Retrieved from http://news.nationalgeographic.com/news/2006/05/0502_060502_geography.html.

Rodgers, J.W. (1958). The foreign language issue in Nebraska, 1918–1923. *Nebraska History* 39: 1–22.

Romaine, S. (2001). Contact with other languages. In J. Algeo (Ed.) *The Cambridge history of the English language, vol. VI: English in North America* (pp. 154–183). Cambridge: Cambridge University Press.

Romaine, S. (2010). Language contact in the U.S.A. In K. Potowski (Ed.) *Language diversity in the U.S.A.* (pp. 25–46). Cambridge: Cambridge University Press.

Romaine, S., & Lange, D. (1991). The use of like as a marker of reported speech and thought: A case of grammaticalization in progress. *American Speech* 66(3): 227–279.

Roosevelt, T. (1919). Letter to Mr. Richard K. Hurd, January 3, 1919. (Held at the Library of Congress.)

Rothschild, N. (2013). Sweden's new gender-neutral pronoun: Hen. *Slate*, April 12. Retrieved from www.slate.com/articles/double_x/doublex/2012/04/hen_sweden_s_new_gender_neutral_pronoun_causes_controversy_.html.

Ryan, C. (2013). Language use in the United States: 2011. *American Community Survey Reports*.

Sacchetti, M. (2009). A new accent in Chinatown. *The Boston Globe*, February 26. Retrieved from http://boston.com/news/local/massachusetts/articles/2009/02/26/a_new_accent_in_chinatown/.

Sangster, C. (n.d.). *Received Pronunciation and BBC English*. Retrieved from www.bbc.co.uk/voices/yourvoice/rpandbbc.shtml.

Salinger, J.D. (1951). *The catcher in the rye*. Boston, MA: Little, Brown.

Sapir, E. (1929). Central and North American languages. *Encyclopedia Brittanica, vol. 5*. (pp. 138–41). Chicago, IL: Encyclopedia Brittanica.

Sebba, M. (1987). *The syntax of serial verbs: An investigation into Sranan and other languages*. Amsterdam: John Benjamins.

Seifert, N.R. (2013). The cross-cultural classroom in the context of radical language shift: Humor, teasing, and the ethnolinguistic repertoire in the Blackfeet Nation. (Unpublished doctoral dissertation), University of Texas, Austin.

Semple, K. (2009). In Chinatown, sound of the future is Mandarin. *The New York Times*, October 22, p. A1.

Shay, S. (2008). *The history of English: A linguistic introduction*. San Francisco, CA and Washington, DC: Wardja Press.

Shin, H.B., & Bruno, R. (2003). *Language use and English-speaking ability: 2000*. Census 2000 Brief, October. Retrieved from www.census.gov/prod/2003pubs/c2kbr-29.pdf.

Shipley, W. (1957). Some Yukian-Penutian lexical resemblances. *IJAL* 23: 269–274.

Shiri, S. (2010). Arabic in the U.S.A. In K. Potowski (Ed.) *Language diversity in the U.S.A.* (pp. 206–222). Cambridge: Cambridge University Press.

Silva-Corvalán, C. (2004). Spanish in the Southwest. In E. Finegan, & J.R. Rickford (Eds.) *Language in the U.S.A.: Themes for the twenty-first century* (pp. 205–229). Cambridge: Cambridge University Press.

Smith, J. (1624). *Generall historie of Virginia, New England and the Summer Isles.* London: I. Dawson & I. Haviland.

Smith, P.M. (1985). *Language, the sexes and society.* New York: Blackwell.

Smith, S. (1820). Review of A. Seybert, Statistical Annals of the United States. *The Edinburgh Review* 33: 69–80.

Smitherman, G. (1977). *Talkin and testifyin: The language of black America.* Detroit, MI: Wayne State University Press.

Smitherman, G. (1994). *Black talk: Words and phrases from the hood to the amen corner.* New York: Houghton Mifflin.

Smitherman, G. (1995). If I'm lyin, I'm flyin: An introduction to the art of the snap. In J. Percelay, S. Dweck, & M. Ivey (Eds.) *Double snaps* (pp. 14–33). New York: William Morrow.

Smitherman, G. (2006). *Word from the mother: Language and African Americans.* New York: Routledge.

Smyth, R., Jacobs, G., & Rogers, H. (2003). Male voices and perceived sexual orientation: An experimental and theoretical approach. *Language in Society* 32(3): 329–350.

Snapp, A., Anderson, J.L., & Anderson, J. (1982). Northern Paiute. In R.W. Langacker (Ed.) *Sketches in Uto-Aztecan grammar, III: Uto-Aztecan grammatical sketches.* Dallas, TX: Summer Institute of Linguistics and the University of Texas at Arlington. *Summer Institute of Linguistics Publications in Linguistics* 57(3): 1–92.

Snipp, C.M. (2007). An overview of American Indian populations. In G.H. Capture, D. Champagne, & C. Jackson (Eds.) *American Indian nations: Yesterday, today and tomorrow* (pp. 38–48). Walnut Creek, CA: Altamira Press.

Sparrow, R. (2005). Defending Deaf culture: The case of cochlear implants. *The Journal of Political Philosophy* 13(2): 135–152.

Squint, K. (2005). A linguistic and cultural comparison of Haitian Creole and Louisiana Creole. *Postcolonial Text* 1(2). Retrieved from http://postcolonial.org/index.php/pct/article/view Article/375/813.

Steinway, S. (2014). The American Heritage Dictionary usage panel. Posted on the blog: "An archivist mines the usage ballots," January 28. Retrieved from http://ahdictionary.tumblr.com/post/74834243179/an-archivist-mines-the-usage-ballots.

Stewart, W. (1967). Sociolinguistic factors in the history of American Negro dialects. *The Florida FL Reporter* 5(2): 11, 22, 24, 26, 28.

Stewart, W. (1968). Continuity and change in American Negro dialects. *The Florida FL Reporter* 6(1): 3–4, 14–16, 18.

Stokoe, W.C., Jr. (1960). *Sign language structure: An outline of visual communication systems of the American Deaf.* Studies in linguistics: Occasional paper 8. Buffalo, NY: University of Buffalo Linguistics Department.

Strunk, W., & White, E.B. (1979). *The elements of style.* New York: Macmillan.

Strunk, W., & White, E.B. (2000). *The elements of style* (4th ed.). New York: Longman.

Subtirelu, N. (2014). Who is articulate?: Biased perceptions of language. *Linguistic Pulse*, May 8. Retrieved from http://linguisticpulse.com/2014/05/08/who-is-articulate-biased-perceptions-of-language/.

Suhay, L. (2013). Real-life "Gullah Gullah Island" in danger. *Christian Science Monitor*, October 2. Retrieved from www.csmonitor.com/The-Culture/Family/Modern-Parenthood/2013/1002/Real-life-Gullah-Gullah-Island-in-danger.

Sweet, H. (1877). *A handbook of phonetics, vol. 2*. London: Clarendon.

Tagliamonte, S. (2012). *Variationist sociolinguistics: Change, observation, interpretation*. Chichester: Wiley-Blackwell.

Tagliamonte, S., & Denis, D. (2008). Linguistic ruin? LOL! Instant messaging and teen language. *American Speech* 83: 3–33.

Tamasi, S.L. (2000). Linguistic perceptions of southern folk. Paper presented at the annual meeting of the American Dialect Society, Chicago, IL.

Tamasi, S.L. (2003). Cognitive patterns of linguistic perceptions. (Unpublished doctoral dissertation), University of Georgia, Athens.

Tamasi, S.L. (2008). Linguistic accommodation in medical communication. Paper presented at Sociolinguistic Symposium 17, Amsterdam, The Netherlands, April.

Tannen, D. (1990). *You just don't understand: Women and men in conversation*. New York: Ballantine Books.

Tennant, R.A., & Brown, M.G. (2010). *The American Sign Language handshape starter* (2nd ed.). Washington, DC: Gallaudet University Press.

The Henry Ford (n.d.). Retrieved from http://collections.thehenryford.org/Collection.aspx?objectKey=254569.

Thompson, R.M. (2003). *Filipino English and Taglish: Language switching from multiple perspectives*. Amsterdam: John Benjamins.

Todd, L. (1974). *Pidgins and creoles*. Boston, MA: Routledge & Kegan Paul.

Tomlin, R.S. (1986). *Basic word order: Functional principles*. London: Croom Helm.

Toole, J.K. (1980). *A confederacy of dunces*. Baton Rouge, LA: Louisiana State University Press.

Torbert, B. (2001). Tracing Native American language history through consonant cluster reduction: The case of Lumbee English. *American Speech* 76: 361–387.

Townson, M. (1992). *Mother-tongue and fatherland: Language and politics in German*. Manchester: Manchester University Press.

Trudgill, P. (1972). Sex, covert prestige and linguistic change in the urban British English of Norwich. *Language in Society* 1: 179–195.

Truss, L. (2003). *Eats, shoots & leaves: The zero tolerance approach to punctuation*. New York: Penguin.

Tsai, S.H. (1986). *The Chinese experience in America*. Bloomington, IN: Indiana University Press.

Tucker, R.G., & Lambert, W.E. (1969). White and Negro listeners' reactions to various American-English dialects. *Social Forces* 47(4): 463–468.

Turner, L.D. (1949/1973). *Africanisms in the Gullah dialect*. Chicago, IL: University of Chicago Press.

Twain, M. (1885). *The adventures of Huckleberry Finn*. New York: Charles L. Webster.

Twining, M., & Baird, K. (1991). *Sea Island roots: The African presence in the Carolinas and Georgia*. Trenton, NJ: Africa World Press.

Upward, C. (1997). American spellings for British schools? *Journal of the Simplified Spelling Society* 21: 30–32.

US Census Bureau (2006–2008). *Detailed languages spoken at home and ability to speak English for the population 5 years and over: 2006–2008 (ACS).* Retrieved from www.census.gov/hhes/socdemo/language/index.html.

US Census Bureau (2010–2013). *American Community Survey.* Retrieved from www.census.gov/acs/www.

US Census Bureau (2012). *The foreign-born population in the United States: 2010.* Retrieved from www.census.gov/prod/2012pubs/acs-19.pdf.

US Census Bureau (n.d.). *Language use: Frequently asked questions.* Retrieved from www.census.gov/hhes/socdemo/language/about/faqs.html.

USCIS (n.d.). Exemptions & accommodations. Retrieved from www.uscis.gov/us-citizenship/citizenship-through-naturalization/exceptions-accommodations.

USCIS Policy Manual (n.d.). Chapter 2: English and civics testing. Retrieved from www.uscis.gov/policymanual/HTML/PolicyManual-Volume12-PartE-Chapter2.html#S-D.

U.S. English (n.d.). Facts and Figures. Retrieved from www.us-english.org/userdata/file/FactsandFigures.pdf.

U.S. English (2006). New U.S. English study finds 45 states offer foreign language driver's license exams. U.S. English, February 28. Retrieved from www.usenglish.org/view/186.

Valdés, G. (2005). Bilingualism, heritage learners, and SLA research: Opportunities lost or seized? *Modern Language Journal* 89(3): 410–426.

Valdman, A., & Klingler, T.A. (1997). The structure of Louisiana Creole. In A. Valdman (Ed.) *French and Creole in Louisiana* (pp. 109–144). New York: Plenum Press.

Van Cott, J.W. (1990). *Utah place names: A comprehensive guide to the origins of geographic names: A compilation.* Salt Lake City, UT: University of Utah.

van Gelderen, E. (2006). *A history of the English language.* Amsterdam and Philadelphia, PA: John Benjamins.

Veltman, C. (1988). *The future of the Spanish language in the United States.* New York and Washington, DC: Hispanic Policy Development Project.

Venezky, R.L. (2001). Spelling. In J. Algeo (Ed.) *The Cambridge history of the English language, vol. VI: English in North America* (pp. 340–357). Cambridge: Cambridge University Press.

von Schneidemesser, L. (1996). Soda or pop? *Journal of English Linguistics* 24: 270–287.

vos Savant, M. (2004). Ask Marilyn. *Parade Magazine*, April 11.

Walker, W. (1981). Native American writing systems. In C.A. Ferguson & S.B. Heath (Eds.) *Language in the U.S.A.* (pp. 145–174). Cambridge: Cambridge University Press.

Warhol, L. (2011). *Native American language policy in the United States.* Heritage Briefs Collection. Washington, DC: Center for Applied Linguistics.

Weatherford, J. (1991). *Native roots: How the Native Americans enriched America.* New York: Fawcett Columbine.

Webelhuth, G., & Dannenberg, C. (2006). Southern American English personal datives: The theoretical significance of dialectal variation. *American Speech* 81: 31–55.

Webster, N. (1789). *Dissertations on the English language: With notes, historical and critical.* Boston, MA: Isaiah Thomas and Company.

Webster, N. (1828). *American dictionary of the English language.* New York: S. Converse.

Webster, N. (1908). *The elementary spelling book.* New York: American Book Company.

Weinreich, M. (2008). *History of the Yiddish language* (2 vols.). New Haven, CT: Yale University Press.

Weinreich, U. (1990). *Modern English–Yiddish, Yiddish–English dictionary*. New York: YIVO.

Weinreich, U. (1999). *College Yiddish*. New York: Yiddish Scientific Institute.

Weinstein, M. (2001). *Yiddish: A nation of words*. South Royalton, VT: Steerforth Press.

Weldon, T. (2004). African American English in the middle classes: Exploring the other end of the continuum. Paper presented at NWAV 33: New Ways of Analyzing Language Variation, Ann Arbor, MI, October.

West, C. (1984). *Routine complications, troubles with talk between doctors and patients*. Bloomington, IN: Indiana University Press.

Whedon, J. (Producer) (1997–2003). *Buffy the vampire slayer*, 20th Century Fox Television.

Whinnom, K. (1971). Linguistic hybridization and the "special case" of pidgins and creoles. In D. Hymes (Ed.) *Pidginization and creolization of languages* (pp. 91–115). London: Cambridge University Press.

Whisler, K. (2007). Hispanic print continues to show significant growth. Retrieved from www.latinoprintnetwork.com/assets/StateofHispanicPrint.pdf.

Whisler, K. (2008). Hispanic print media continues its climb. *El Reportero* 18(3).

Wiecha, K. (2013). Linguists discover existence of distinct Hawaiian Sign Language. *The Rosetta Blog*, March 8. Retrieved from http://rosettaproject.org/blog/02013/mar/8/linguists-discover-existence-distinct-hawaiian-sig/.

Wilbur, R.B. (1973). *The phonology of reduplication*. Bloomington, IN: Indiana University Linguistics Club.

Wiley, T.G. (2004). Language planning, language policy, and the English-Only movement. In E. Finegan, & J.R. Rickford (Eds.) *Language in the U.S.A.: Themes for the twenty-first century* (pp. 319–338). Cambridge: Cambridge University Press.

Wiley, T.G. (2010). Language policy in the U.S.A. In K. Potowski (Ed.) *Language diversity in the U.S.A.* (pp. 255–271). Cambridge: Cambridge University Press.

Williams, J.G. (1895). A study in Gullah English. *The Charleston (SC) Sunday News*, February 10.

Williams, R. (1643). *A key into the language of America*. London: Dexter.

Witherspoon, J. (1815). *The works of John Witherspoon, vol. 9*. Edinburgh: J. Ogle.

Wolfart, H.C., & Carroll, J.F. (1973). *Meet Cree: A guide to the language*. Lincoln, NB: University of Nebraska Press.

Wolfart, H.C., & Carroll, J.F. (1981). *Meet Cree* (2nd ed.). Edmonton, Alberta: University of Alberta Press.

Wolford, T., & Carter, P.M. (2010). The "Spanish as threat" ideology and cultural aspects of Spanish attrition. In S. Rivera-Mills, & D. Villa (Eds.) *Spanish in the U.S. Southwest: A language in transition* (pp. 111–131). Madrid: Iberoamericana/Vervuert.

Wolfram, W. (1969). *A sociolinguistic description of Detroit Negro speech*. Washington, DC: Center for Applied Linguistics.

Wolfram, W. (2004). The grammar of urban African American Vernacular English. In B. Kortmann, & E.W. Schneider (Eds.) *Handbook of varieties of English* (pp. 111–132). Berlin: Mouton de Gruyter.

Wolfram, W. (2007). Sociolinguistic folklore in the study of African American English. *Linguistic and Language Compass* 1: 292–313.

Wolfram, W., & Christian, D. (1976). *Appalachian speech*. Washington, DC: Center for Applied Linguistics.

Wolfram, W., & Reaser, J. (2014). *Talkin' Tar Heel: How our voices tell the story of North Carolina*. Chapel Hill, NC: University of North Carolina Press.

Wolfram, W., & Schilling-Estes, N. (1998). *American English: Dialects and variation*. Malden, MA: Blackwell.

Wolfram, W., & Torbert, B. (2006). When linguistic worlds collide (African American English). In W. Wolfram, & B. Ward (Eds.) *American voices: How dialects differ from coast to coast* (pp. 225–232). Malden, MA: Blackwell.

Wolfram, W., Carter, P., & Moriello, B. (2004). Emerging Hispanic English: New dialect formation in the American South. *Journal of Sociolinguistics* 8/3: 339–358.

Wolfram, W., Kohn, M.E., & Callahan-Price, E. (2011). Southern-bred Hispanic English: An emerging socioethnic variety. In J. Michnowicz, & R. Dodsworth (Eds.) *Selected proceedings of the 5th workshop on Spanish sociolinguistics* (pp. 1–13). Somerville, MA: Cascadilla Proceedings Project.

Wolk, L., Abdelli-Beruh, N.B., & Slavin, D. (2012). Habitual use of vocal fry in young adult female speakers. *Journal of Voice* 26(3): e111–e116.

Wright, L. (2001). Third-person singular present-tense *-s*, *-th*, and zero, 1575–1648. *American Speech* 76(3): 236–258.

Wurtzel, E. (1999). *Bitch: In praise of difficult women*. New York: Anchor.

Xiao, Y. (2010). Chinese in the U.S.A. In K. Potowski (Ed.) *Language diversity in the U.S.A.* (pp. 81–95). Cambridge: Cambridge University Press.

Yamamoto, A.Y., & Zepeda, O. (2004). Native American languages. In E. Finegan, & J.R. Rickford (Eds.) *Language in the U.S.A.: Themes for the twenty-first century* (pp. 153–181). Cambridge: Cambridge University Press.

Zelinsky, W. (1973). *The cultural geography of the United States*. Englewood Cliffs, NJ: Prentice Hall.

Zentella, A.C. (2004). Spanish in the Northeast. In E. Finegan, & J.R. Rickford (Eds.) *Language in the U.S.A.: Themes for the twenty-first century* (pp. 182–204). Cambridge: Cambridge University Press.

Zimmer, B. (2009). The language of social media: "Unlike" any other. *Thinking map visual thesaurus*, May 7. Retrieved from www.visualthesaurus.com/cm/wordroutes/the-language-of-social-media-unlike-any-other/.

Zwicky, A.M. (1997). Two lavender issues for linguists. In A. Livia, & K. Hall (Eds.) *Queerly phrased: Language, gender, and sexuality* (pp. 21–34). New York: Oxford University Press.

Index